C000157729

Generals of the Bulge

Copyright © 2015 by Jerry D. Morelock

Published by
STACKPOLE BOOKS
5067 Ritter Road
Mechanicsburg, PA 17055
www.stackpolebooks.com

All rights reserved, including the right to reproduce this book or portions thereof in any form or by any means, electronic or mechanical, including recording or by any information storage and retrieval system, without permission in writing from the publisher. All inquiries should be addressed to Stackpole Books, 5067 Ritter Road, Mechanicsburg, PA 17055.

Printed in the United States of America

10 9 8 7 6 5 4 3 2 1

Library of Congress Cataloging-in-Publication Data

Morelock, J. D., 1946–
  Generals of the Bulge : leadership in the U.S. Army's greatest battle / Jerry D. Morelock. — First edition.
     pages cm
  Includes bibliographical references.
  ISBN 978-0-8117-1199-9
1. Ardennes, Battle of the, 1944–1945. 2. Generals—United States. 3. Command of troops. I. Title.
  D756.5.A7M67 2015
  940.54'219348—dc23
                                2014038386

Generals of the Bulge
Leadership in the
U.S. Army's Greatest Battle

Jerry D. Morelock

STACKPOLE
BOOKS

This book is respectfully dedicated to four heroes of the Battle of the Bulge and to their comrades in arms:

Gen. Bruce C. Clarke
And the men of
Combat Command B, 7th Armored Division
St.-Vith, Belgium
17–23 December 1944
The thundering line of battle stands.
—Julien Grenfell, *Into Battle*

Col. Roy U. Clay
And the men of the
275th Armored Field Artillery Battalion
St.-Vith, Belgium
16–23 December 1944
Then shells and bullets swept the icy woods.
—Louis Simpson, *The Battle*

Eugene H. Garrett
And the men of
B Battery, 285th FA Observation Battalion
Baugnez Crossroads, Malmedy, Belgium
17 December 1944
Down in a row the brave tin soldiers fall . . .
—Robert Graves, *Recalling War*

Lt. L. Martin Jones
And the men of the
106th Infantry Division
Schnee Eifel Plateau
16–19 December 1944
In a circle of fire and bayonets.
—F. S. Flint, *Lament*

CONTENTS

FOREWORD

In mid-December 1944, the Allied armies of Gen. Dwight D. Eisenhower appeared to be on the verge of victoriously ending the war with Nazi Germany when, in a last-ditch, all-out gamble to compel the Allies to sue for peace, Hitler ordered the only major German counteroffensive of the war in northwest Europe. What ensued was called the Battle of the Bulge, but that hardly began to describe what took place over the next six weeks in the Ardennes Forest in the bloodiest and costliest campaign fought during World War II by the U.S. Army. The Battle of the Bulge, historian Charles B. MacDonald later wrote, was the "greatest pitched battle ever fought by American arms." The 600,000 Americans who participated constituted "more than three times the number that fought on both sides at Gettysburg."

Although the battle was fought and eventually won by ordinary GIs, the actions and decisions of the generals in command of the campaign were crucial, and in several instances decisive. It is the story of those generals and their leadership that is the focus of Jerry D. Morelock's *Generals of the Bulge*, a substantially revised and updated edition of his *Generals of the Ardennes: American Leadership in the Battle of the Bulge*.

When the National Defense University Press first published it in 1994, Morelock's *Generals of the Ardennes* was not widely disseminated and thus did not have the extensive reading audience that this book fully merits. The earlier edition was highly praised by Patton's official biographer, Martin Blumenson, who called it, "a fascinating read in military history . . . it is good to be reminded, as Morelock has done, of their exploits and failures." But, as Blumenson aptly noted, Morelock's book is "more than a guided tour of the past; it is, by extension and inference, a practical exercise in personnel selection. Morelock has illustrated a basic question for all military institutions: how can an army in peacetime select and prepare the leaders for the next war?"

This fundamental question, and the challenge it poses, has not changed in the seventy years since the end of World War II. To the contrary, in this complicated and ever-changing age of smaller wars and terrorist conflict, the need to identify and train our future leaders is now more important than ever.

What the generals who commanded in the Battle of the Bulge faced was one of the greatest challenges any commander could possibly confront in combat, exacerbated by the most appallingly cold winter weather in more than a half-century.

As an historian, I am pleased to re-introduce this book to a new generation of readers. *Generals of the Bulge* not only adds an important chapter to the history of this incredible battle, but also is a remarkably readable and superbly researched story of how generalship wins—and sometimes can nearly lose—wars.

—*Carlo D'Este*
Author of *Patton: A Genius For War* and
Eisenhower: A Soldier's Life

INTRODUCTION

Jerry D. Morelock has used the Battle of the Bulge in World War II to assess the professional military skills and personal leadership characteristics of selected American officers operating on the six top echelons of command: Dwight D. Eisenhower at the supreme Allied command level; Omar N. Bradley at army group; William H. Simpson at army; Troy H. Middleton at corps; Alan W. Jones at division; and Bruce C. Clarke at combat command. How they performed during the reaction to the powerful German Ardennes counteroffensive of December 1944, probably the greatest pitched battle fought in the European Theater of Operations by United States forces, is the subject of Morelock's investigation and analysis.

The general officers Morelock has chosen to look at are instructive. Coming from different backgrounds, they display a remarkable range of activity. Each one illustrates the system for selection and advancement of leaders during the interwar period—or lack of a system—that brought him to the top of the profession of arms in the United States Army of the Second World War.

Morelock's procedure is the same in each of the several case studies. After narrating and discussing each commander's career up to the time of the German attack, he describes the actions in the ensuing combat and weighs the decisions each made. He then summarizes the effectiveness of their leadership.

The result is a fascinating read in military history. Most of the commanders of World War II have fled from our memories. The mere passage of time since that global conflict and also the emergence of newer heroes in more recent wars have pushed these commanders from our minds. All too soon, any recollection of the battlefield performance of our Second World War commanders—the good along with the bad—will be gone. It is good to be reminded, as Morelock has done, of their exploits and failures.

But Morelock's work is more than a guided tour of the past; it is, by extension and inference, a practical exercise in personnel selection.

Morelock has illustrated a basic question for all military institutions: How can an army in peacetime select and prepare the leaders for the next war? Those whose task it is to determine and groom the top warriors of the succeeding generations will find much of value in Colonel Morelock's study.

—*Martin Blumenson*

Professor Martin Blumenson (1918–2005) held the King Chair at the Naval War College, the Johnson Chair at the Army War College, and the Mark Clark Chair at The Citadel. He authored numerous books, including *The United States Army in World War II: European Theater of Operations: Breakout and Pursuit*, a volume in the official history of the war; *The Patton Papers*; *Patton: The Man Behind the Legend*; *Mark Clark*; *Masters of the Art of Command*; *Heroes Never Die*; *The Duel for France, 1944*; and *The Battle of the Generals*.

PREFACE

BAUGNEZ CROSSROADS, BELGIUM: 17 DECEMBER 1944

Pvt. Eugene Garrett and his fellow American soldiers of Battery B, 285th Field Artillery Observation Battalion—an outfit whose combat mission was locating enemy artillery using "sound and flash" techniques—had been riding in the cold, cramped cargo beds in the backs of Army 2¹/₂-ton trucks for hours when shortly after midday on 17 December 1944, their convoy stopped at a crossroads on the top of a hill a few miles south of Malmedy, Belgium. The trucks carrying Garrett's Battery B were part of a longer convoy of 7th Armored Division Artillery units, one of several convoys comprising Brig. Gen. Robert W. Hasbrouck's 7th Armored Division. Assigned to Lt. Gen. William H. Simpson's Ninth U.S. Army, the 7th Armored was moving south over icy roads from the Aachen, Germany, area to Belgium's Ardennes region, thinly held by Lt. Gen. Courtney B. Hodges's First U.S. Army. The previous afternoon, an urgent order dispatched directly from Allied Supreme Commander, General Dwight D. "Ike" Eisenhower, had set Hasbrouck's division in motion toward a rapidly developing westward "bulge" being forced in the American front line by a powerful, surprise German attack. Within hours of the predawn December 16 start of the German onslaught, Ike had astutely recognized the danger presented by its rapidly expanding scope and the serious threat it posed to the integrity of his forces' brittle front line in the undermanned Ardennes.

"We had been stopping frequently for short breaks throughout our drive south," Garrett recalled over four decades later, "so when our trucks stopped not long after passing through Malmedy, we assumed it was another short break—we didn't even bother to take our weapons with us when we dismounted from the trucks." Garrett soon discovered, however, that this was no ordinary rest break—through the vagaries of chance and an unfortunate accident in timing, he and his fellow Battery B soldiers had run smack into the panzer-tipped spearhead of the German Ardennes Offensive, *Waffen-SS* lieutenant colonel Joachim Peiper's powerful *Kampfgruppe* ("battle group" comprised of 4,800 soldiers and 600 vehicles) of 1st SS Panzer Division. Garrett related that the Americans—including some U.S. military policemen who had been at Baugnez Crossroads directing convoy traffic—were quickly rounded up by Peiper's heavily armed troops who began swiftly and systematically stealing all of the GIs' watches and other valuables. "We knew they were SS," Garrett said. "We had heard all the terrible stories about Hitler's SS and we had great fear of them." A cocky eighteen year old, however, Garrett unwisely "called the German who stole my watch a son-of-a-bitch. The German responded by hitting me in the mouth with the butt of his rifle and then told me in English 'That will teach you to cross the Siegfried Line!'" While Garrett lamented the loss of his watch and nursed his bloody mouth, he suddenly witnessed a horrifying preview of the fate awaiting the American POWs: "One of our officers, a Captain I think, protested that the Germans were stealing our soldiers' watches. A German calmly put a pistol to the Captain's forehead and pulled the trigger, shooting him dead right between the eyes."

Around 1:00 P.M. or shortly thereafter, Garrett and the approximately 120 American POWs were marched into a nearby open field and lined up in several ranks facing the crossroad intersection. Not long afterward, a German half-track vehicle stopped on the road in front of the Americans. "A German officer stood up in the open back of the half-track," Garrett related, "pulled out his pistol and shot a GI in the front rank—the GI was a medic with a red cross painted on his helmet, but the German shot him dead." Understandably, some of the American POWs started nervously milling about as if to break ranks and flee; but U.S. officers shouted for them to stand fast lest it provoke more German firing. They might have saved their breath—the Germans soon began firing anyway, and a heavy fusillade of machine-gun and small-arms fire tore through the ranks of the American POWs, cutting down scores of the helpless, unarmed GIs. Garrett reacted instinctively: "I was not hit by the German shooting, but I immediately dropped to the ground. My only wound was my bleeding mouth where the German I had called a son-of-a-bitch had 'butt-stroked' me earlier. I laid on the ground as quiet as I could and pretended to be dead."

Not daring to move or even to raise his head slightly to see what was happening, Garrett did not witness—as some of his fellow survivors later affirmed happened—German officers walking among the GI bodies methodically finishing off any Americans they found to be still alive. Garrett was, however, able to observe a steady flow of German armored vehicles passing through the crossroads—he counted over 100 driving by during the remainder of the afternoon. He recalled, "As the German tanks and half-tracks passed by us on the road for the rest of the day, they fired their machine guns and rifles into the bodies of the GIs lying in the field." Finally, just after 4:00 P.M. as the short winter day turned to a long dark night, Garrett reached his breaking point: "I got to the point where I just couldn't take it any longer. I knew that I was either going to freeze to death lying there on the frozen ground or go out of my mind. I jumped up and ran for the woods." At the same time, other GIs who were still alive also spontaneously sprang up and started to run. Many, like Garrett sprinted for the woods, while a few others ran to hide in the Café Bodarwé, one of the few buildings at the crossroads—the latter GIs had unwisely chosen their escape route, and their intended refuge soon turned into a death trap. Germans set fire to the café and shot dead any GIs who tried to flee the flames.

"I hid in a woodpile," Garrett explained, "and during the night I was able to make my way back down the hill to Malmedy. But the GIs at Malmedy were so jumpy after hearing all the rumors flying around about English-speaking German soldiers wearing American uniforms that they treated me like a POW! Can you believe it? Our own guys kept me under armed guard for a day and a half." Despite his harsh treatment after his narrow escape from death, Garrett was incredibly lucky—when U.S. forces later recaptured the area on 14 January 1945, they found at least eighty frozen American bodies lying dead under the snow at Baugnez Crossroads.[1]

Eisenhower's quick-thinking decision 16 December 1944 to send the 7th Armored Division to reinforce the hard-pressed First Army resulted in one of the epic defensive stands that ultimately allowed American commanders to regain control of the battle and turn the tide of the German offensive—the magnificent week-long defense of the vital road network at St.-Vith by Brig. Gen. Bruce C. Clarke's Combat

Command B, 7th Armored Division. Yet, as so often is the case with the decisions that senior leaders must make in the heat of desperate combat, Ike's command decision also had a more tragic consequence—it sent Garrett and his Battery B comrades to their fateful, deadly encounter at Baugnez Crossroads. This illustrates the stark reality with which wartime commanders at all levels must live—the sobering knowledge that their combat decisions, whether they ultimately result in success or failure for their forces, will always mean sending men to their deaths.

AMERICA'S "GENERALS OF THE BULGE"

In the seventy years since the Ardennes offensive pushed an enormous westward bulge in the American line and threatened to split the Allied armies in two,[2] the characterization of the battle leadership demonstrated by the senior American commanders who stopped and then turned back this German thrust has swung like a pendulum between hero worship and scorn. During the heady days immediately following the Allied victory over Nazi Germany and imperial Japan, the victorious American commanders were fêted and honored as genuine military geniuses who had out-generaled the best the enemy had to offer. Memoirs thrown together from the daily diaries kept by wartime aides-de-camp were quickly published and became bestsellers.[3] Gen. George S. Patton Jr., who died suddenly and at the pinnacle of his fame and glory, achieved the status of military icon, with his often eccentric leadership style (but seldom his genius for war) imitated by later generations of "Old Blood & Guts" wannabes.

Yet in ensuing years, the sharpened pens of some revisionist historians have rewritten the earlier accounts and reinterpreted the leadership performance of the senior Americans. The impetus for this later trend came from America's former British Allies who, stung by the seeming unfairness of standing alone against Hitler in 1940–1941 only to be rewarded ultimately by seeing their empire crumble and their country reduced to second-rate status, lashed out in frustration and envy at senior Americans.[4] They resented the men they viewed as military amateurs who bumbled through a global war principally on the strength of the world's greatest economy but who nonetheless received credit for masterminding the defeat of German military professionals.

These views eventually spread across the Atlantic and were picked up by historians in this country. Even such respected military writers and historians as Martin van Creveld and Martin Blumenson joined in. Van Creveld's conclusions that "the American officer corps of World War II was less than mediocre . . . [and was] often guilty of bad leadership" are typical.[5] Blumenson, Patton scholar and author of two volumes of the U.S. Army's official history of the war, has questioned the overall quality of American senior leaders, calling them "bland and plodding" and damning their leadership as "workmanlike rather than bold, prudent rather than daring," satisfied with the safe rather than the imaginative way.[6] Our World War II leaders, Blumenson wrote, "displayed serious flaws in conception and execution," and were "unable to adapt and adjust to the new requirements of leadership."[7]

Given this wide spread of opinions of senior American leaders over the years, what judgment can be made today about their actual performance? Would a study of their conduct of one of the supreme leadership challenges of the war in Europe—the Battle of the Bulge—reveal the senior American commanders to be exceptional men of military legend? Or do their Ardennes actions merit Blumenson's and van Creveld's stinging criticisms?

The reality, it seems, lies between these two conflicting opinions. Like most military operations throughout the history of warfare, the Ardennes battle was characterized by failures in leadership as well as successes, and the leadership demonstrated by the Americans is not an exception. The facts are more complex and bear scrutiny, even after seventy years. Eisenhower and Patton weren't the only heroes, and even they made mistakes. Battle analysis is always a learning experience, as is any close review of leadership and command.

Much has been assumed about American leadership during World War II and the Battle of the Bulge, and many of these assumptions are either wrong, gross oversimplifications, or misinterpretations of what actually occurred. In the postwar glow of victory, the facts were often lost in the general feeling of superiority held by the victorious Allies. British military historian and theorist Sir Basil Liddell Hart recognized this tendency when he warned: "Everything in war looks different at the time from what it looks in the clearer light that comes after the war. Nothing looks so different as the form of the leaders. The public picture of them at the time is not only an unreal one, but changes with the tide of success."[8]

During the nearly three-quarters of a century since the Ardennes struggle ended, much of the leadership demonstrated by American commanders at crucial points in the fighting has become lost in the legends created from this greatest of U.S. battles. Patton did not win the battle singlehandedly, however important was his army's dramatic change of direction to relieve the defenders of beleaguered Bastogne. If our collective memories of the Battle of the Bulge contain only "Patton" and "Bastogne," we cheat future generations out of a rich heritage of combat leadership history. In addition to examining the leadership of America's more famous Battle of the Bulge commanders such as Patton, Eisenhower, and Gen. Omar Bradley, the case studies in this book also aim to bring out the critical role played by several important and outstanding but little-known commanders whose leadership significantly affected the battle's outcome. Men such as Gen. William Simpson, Maj. Gen. Troy H. Middleton, and Brig. Gen. Bruce C. Clarke should have their names burned into our collective memory along with Patton, Eisenhower, and Bradley. Historians Blumenson and James L. Stokesbury have provided an apt comment as well as a fitting tribute to these lesser-known commanders when they judged:

> The highly developed art of generalship that emerged in World War II spawned many great commanders, but the struggle was so immense in scope that all but a very few have been virtually forgotten. Some soldiers who receive a footnote in the history of World War II would have been the subjects of legends in the days before men could write.[9]

History is a great teacher, but only if we choose to study its implications with honesty. In this book, five case studies focus on how selected senior U.S. commanders influenced the conduct of the Ardennes offensive—the Battle of the Bulge—in December 1944.

Each case study illuminates the demonstrated leadership of the senior leaders by answering two central questions:

- What *characteristics* of leadership and character were displayed?
- How did they *affect* the overall battle?

The principal purpose of the case studies is not to retell the story of the battle in exhaustive detail. That has already been done in many excellent histories, and new books on the Battle of the Bulge appear with regularity. Rather, the leadership studies in this book seek to use the battle as a framework within which to describe, study, and evaluate the command decisions, actions, and leadership impact of several American commanders who led the desperate struggle in the Ardennes. This book analyzes the American brand of battle leadership in World War II and how it affected this battle and the war.

Since these case studies examine the leadership and character of each principal general in light of a common historical scenario—the Battle of the Bulge—during which these leaders interacted and many of their actions overlapped, some redundancy in the individual chapters is unavoidable. However, every effort has been made to keep this to the minimum necessary to ensure that the examination and analysis of each commander's battle leadership is as thorough and comprehensive as possible.

CHAPTER 1

The American Army in the Ardennes, 1944–45

The powerful German Ardennes offensive, launched in the early morning hours of 16 December 1944, precipitated the greatest single battle ever fought by the American Army.[1] At the Battle of the Bulge's end a month later, it had become, in the words of historian Charles B. MacDonald who had fought in it as an infantry company commander, "the greatest single victory in U.S. history."[2]

Born of desperation, Hitler's last gamble struck a thinly held sector of the Allied line with a strength and fury that no one on the Allied side thought possible at this stage of the war. Expecting the battle-wise enemy commanders to husband their remaining mobile forces and dwindling stocks of war materiel for defense against the upcoming Allied invasion of Germany itself, Allied leaders either failed to realize or refused to admit that Hitler had taken absolute control of the war's prosecution.[3] In October, the Nazi dictator presented his plan for an Ardennes counterstroke to Field Marshal Gerd von Rundstedt, commander of Germany's western armies. Hoping to achieve the same success as the brilliant Ardennes attack against the French in May 1940, Hitler used "the same basic pattern as the 1940 master-piece."[4] Devised to split the Allied line in two at its weakest point, the offensive's aim was to isolate the British-Canadian armies in the north from the American armies in the south. Hitler optimistically hoped this would allow his forces to annihilate the British and Canadian

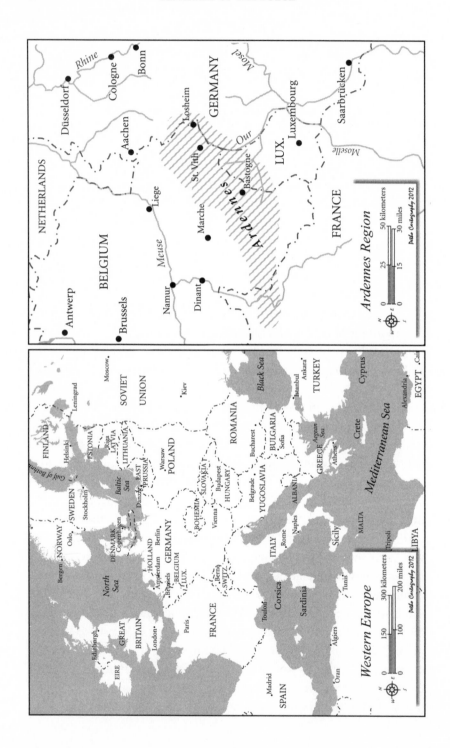

armies or, failing that, at least put Germany in a favorable position to negotiate a separate peace agreement with the western Allies, avoiding a disastrous and humiliating unconditional surrender.[5]

The two principal German commanders charged with the responsibility of carrying out this massive counteroffensive were Sepp Dietrich (SS General and Hitler's crony from the Nazi Party's early Munich days)[6] and Hasso von Manteuffel (called "the Panzer General" for his successes with armored formations). Manteuffel outlined the offensive's purpose and overall scheme of maneuver in a postwar interview:

> The object defined [by Hitler's plan] was to achieve a decisive victory in the West by throwing in two panzer armies—the 6th under Dietrich, and the 5th under me. The 6th was to strike north-west, cross the Meuse beyond Liége and Huy, and drive for Antwerp. It had the main role, and main strength. My army was to advance along a more curving line, cross the Meuse between Namur and Dinant, and push toward Brussels—to cover the flank.[7]

Anchoring the offensive's left flank were the infantry forces of Gen. Erich Brandenberger's Seventh Army.[8] None of these German commanders cared much for the plan or had any serious conviction that Hitler's goal of capturing Antwerp would succeed. However, they were sworn by Hitler to attempt to carry out the plan to the best of their abilities, and they had long ago fully committed their considerable military skills to carrying out the Nazi dictator's schemes.[9] Since it was also starkly evident that it would be the last time in the war that the German Army would have the wherewithal to launch a major offensive, commanders and soldiers alike desperately wanted to make the most of this final opportunity.

The brunt of this surprise offensive was borne by Maj. Gen. Troy H. Middleton's understrength, overextended U.S. VIII Corps. Comprising slightly more than three divisions, the VIII Corps held a frontage more than three times wider than that normally assigned to a corps. Each U.S. division was expected to defend a sector of about 26 miles, which made maintaining a continuous, unbroken front line impossible.[10] Moreover, the length of the line and thinness of his defenses forced Middleton to forego any thought of holding back a strong mobile reserve to plug gaps in an emergency. If attacked by a major enemy force, Middleton's beleaguered troops would have to rely on help from outside the Ardennes. And that outside help arriving on time and with sufficient force to aid Middleton would rely totally on the skill, competence, and timely decisions of the American Army's senior leadership—Allied Supreme Commander Gen. Dwight Eisenhower, Lt. Gen. Omar Bradley at 12th Army Group, and First Army commander Lt. Gen. Courtney Hodges.

Complicating Middleton's task was the condition of his troops. Two of his three infantry divisions were still recovering from their devastation in the bloody Huertgen Forest fighting of the previous three months, and the third had no combat experience at all.[11] (A fourth unit, the 9th Armored Division, was assigned to VIII Corps, but one of its three combat commands was attached to the neighboring V Corps and another was plugging a yawning gap in Middleton's overextended front line.) The 68,822 troops of VIII Corps were supported by 242 tanks and 394 pieces of corps and divisional artillery.[12]

At 0530 hours on 16 December 1944, nearly 200,000 German assault troops attacked Middleton's sector all along his 80-mile front. Supported by 1,900 pieces of artillery and almost 1,000 tanks, the German forces, with surprise on their side and heavily outnumbering the American defenders, made dramatic gains.[13] Allied leadership reacted quickly, however, to regain control of the battle, and in the first few hours after the attack began, reinforcements were rushing to the threatened sector. By the end of January 1945, over 600,000 U.S. troops, backed by 1,300 tanks and nearly 2,000 artillery pieces, were involved in stopping, then reversing, the German tide.[14]

The price paid to achieve this "greatest single victory" was terribly high, with casualty figures massive on both sides in this bitter, confused fighting in appalling conditions of weather and terrain. Allied forces lost nearly 80,000 men to all causes—all but 1,400 were Americans. Bradley's 12th Army Group believed it suffered over 50,000 casualties (40,000 infantrymen) in just the first week of the battle. German records are incomplete; estimates of German casualties range

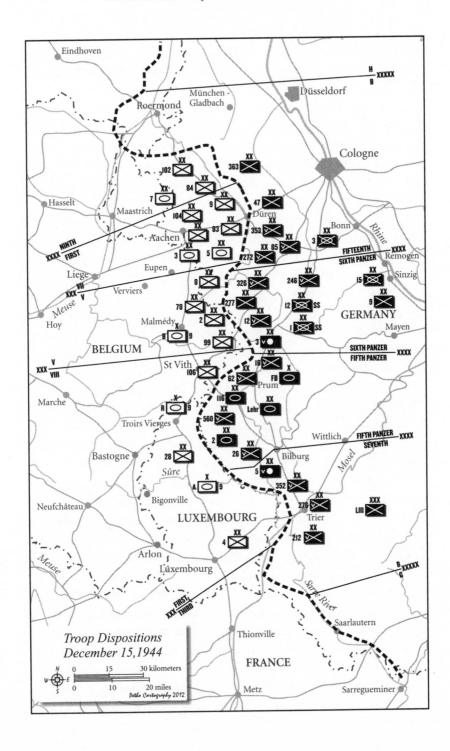

*Troop Dispositions
December 15, 1944*

Petho Cartography 2012

from 90,000 to 120,000. The higher figure seems closer to the truth, because German railroad records indicate that, in December alone, they evacuated nearly 70,000 wounded from the Ardennes area.[15] When killed in action, captured, and missing are added, German loss figures must be staggering. Tragically, Battle of the Bulge casualties were not limited to the fighting men of both sides—at least 3,000 civilians living in the battle zone in Belgium and Luxembourg died, including several hundred who were ruthlessly murdered by German *Waffen-SS* combat units.[16]

The Allied concentration of forces in the Ardennes region at the conclusion of the battle helped shape the nature of the Allies' final assault on Germany. American and British Armies would continue to advance on multiple axes into the heart of the Reich—and Montgomery's hopes of leading a "single thrust" to Berlin were ended for good.[17]

Hitler's Ardennes offensive consumed Germany's last remaining reserves of mobile forces in the west, leaving the devastated Reich without the means to effectively resist the Allies' final attacks. Once the Rhineland was overrun and the Rhine River barrier was pierced in March 1945, Allied armies surged forward and roamed freely through Germany against only crumbling resistance. Begun as Hitler's last attempt to salvage part of his collapsing empire, the Battle of the Bulge sped up Germany's final collapse.[18]

To these immediate effects on the outcome of the war must be added the long-term effects the Ardennes fighting has had over the psyche of the American Army. This battle produced some of the greatest and longest enduring myths and legends in U.S. Army history. Despite the appearance of myth-dispelling works by noted historians, including Russell Weigley, Charles B. MacDonald, Forrest Pogue, Hugh Cole, Stephen Ambrose, Carlo D'Este, Rick Atkinson, and John and David Eisenhower, the legends persist.[19] Many people, including senior Army leaders, still equate the entire battle with the siege of Bastogne and believe Patton won the battle singlehandedly.[20] More than one generation of Army leaders has grown up on "lessons learned" from a battle never fully understood by those preaching the lessons. Understanding the real "lessons" from the U.S. Army's greatest battle requires moving beyond the myths and closely examining the battle leadership demonstrated by American senior commanders during the Ardennes offensive. Yet, the appropriate starting place for that effort is to examine the nature of the instrument these senior commanders wielded—the American Army in the Ardennes.

SETTING THE STAGE: THE U.S. ARMY IN EUROPE

By 1944 the U.S. Army had evolved into a superbly equipped, highly mobile force of 89 divisions, formed from 1,292 battalions of infantry, armor, artillery, and other combat arms. Ground combat soldiers aggregated 2,300,000 out of the Army's total strength of 7,004,000.[21] Although both the Germans and Russians mobilized more manpower, the American blend of industrial might and nearly complete motorization proved sufficient for its worldwide task. The U.S. Army spearheaded the Allied drive to defeat the war-weary German forces in northwest Europe while simultaneously joining naval and marine forces in tightening the noose around the Japanese empire in the Pacific. Indeed, early projections of American troop requirements were continually revised downward.[22] Sixty-one divisions, organized into five armies totaling fifteen corps, were eventually needed in northwest Europe, their ranks filled with 1,700,000 ground combat troops by V-E Day.[23]

The brunt of the fighting across France and Germany in 1944–45 was borne by Bradley's 12th Army Group, which included Gen. Courtney Hodges's "grimly intense" First Army, Patton's "noisy and bumptious" Third Army, and Simpson's "breezy" Ninth Army.[24] Flanked by Montgomery's 21st Army Group to the north and Gen. Jacob L. Devers's 6th Army Group to the south, Bradley's soldiers drove from the beaches of Normandy in northwest France to the banks of the Elbe River in central Germany in eleven months of hard fighting. Eisenhower's "Crusade in Europe" ended at midnight on 8 May 1945. America's cost for this European crusade was 104,812 dead and 377,748 wounded.[25]

Although far from totally perfect in organization, equipment, and doctrine, the American Army's accomplishments nevertheless bear tribute to the nation's remarkable resilience, industry, ingenuity, and leadership. Starting virtually from scratch in 1940, the Army was created—really improvised—during an incredibly short period to produce a war-winning organization.[26]

There were several reasons why this "improvisational" army proved to be ultimately successful on the battlefield against a foe that was usually more experienced, frequently more skillfully handled, and sometimes equipped with better weapons. One overwhelming advantage was in the American Army's exceptional mobility. The decision to motorize the Army almost totally led to combat situations where U.S. units moving quickly over poor roads demonstrated a degree of mobility through motor transport that European armies could only dream about.[27]

Another advantage was its streamlined organization (we might call it "modularizing" today), which simplified command and control, expedited logistics support, eased the problem of repair and maintenance, and facilitated worldwide deployment. The use of a common organization throughout the Army, with the number of "specialized units" kept to a minimum, made training and equipping easier and encouraged the development and implementation of common doctrine.[28]

To all of this must be added ingenuity—inventiveness, mechanical ability, and initiative—with which to capitalize on the overwhelming American industrial capacity spewing forth a seemingly inexhaustible flood of arms, ammunition, and materiel.[29]

But, improvisation or not, the American Army of 1944–45, armed and equipped by the most robust industrial base in the world, and led by competent senior leaders who learned their trade in interwar schools and assignments then honed their skills on the battlefields of Europe, proved to be an outstanding general-purpose combat force.

ORGANIZATION

From the robust but ponderous "square" division of World War I, Gen. Lesley J. McNair, Chief of Staff of General Headquarters until 1942 and thereafter Commander of Army Ground Forces, fashioned a more mobile, leaner, "triangular" division as the building block for the U.S. Army of World War II. Based upon echelons of three (that is, units such as battalions and regiments), this organization was influenced by the concepts of pooling, motorization, and standardization.[30]

McNair had a passion for leanness and flexibility, which led to his adoption of a basic unit configuration that would include only those elements always needed by that unit. Other resources would be maintained in a centralized "pool" to be attached to the division whenever necessary. McNair thought that "what a unit needed only occasionally should be held in a reserve pool under higher headquarters."[31] Specialized units, such as reconnaissance, antiaircraft, and tank elements, were kept in corps- and army-level pools, to be "loaned" to combat divisions when necessary. In practice, however, this concept had mixed results. While it was extremely successful for providing maneuver units with nearly continuously available artillery firepower from the generous field artillery assets "pooled" at division, corps, and army levels, it was less successful with pools of other arms. For example, it was discovered that infantry divisions needed permanent assignment of tank units to ensure any consistent success in combat.[32]

McNair's more successful innovation was the motorization of the U.S. Army. His decision to lavishly supply most formations with motor vehicles and eliminate all horse-drawn transport was one of the most important of the war when its impact on the battlefield is measured.[33] This transformation to a "motorized" U.S. Army was profound, since once American war industry shifted into high gear, it produced millions of military vehicles of all conceivable types. By the end of the war, the U.S. Army provided about every *four* soldiers with a vehicle.[34] The incredible mobility of the American Army, demonstrated time and again from North Africa to central Europe, continually amazed opposing commanders and often made up for inappropriate tactics or sloppy leadership.

In addition to added speed, flexibility, and mobility in combat, motorization had the benefit of requiring fewer critical shipping assets to support it across an ocean. Fodder for draught animals was a major shipping headache to Allied logisticians during World War I and accounted for a disproportionately huge amount of cargo space. Supplies for motor transport required much less maritime support.[35]

Although the U.S. combat division was not "officially" a "motorized" unit, McNair essentially had accomplished that by doing away with all horse-drawn transport. All artillery and heavy equipment was towed by truck or tractor. When this comparative abundance of motor transport is considered, the division was nearly totally motorized for all practical purposes.[36] The addition of six quartermaster truck companies could complete the motorization of an infantry division, but most units found such attachments unnecessary. American divisions posted advances of over 30 miles a day by piling "its infantry on its howitzers, tanks and tank destroyers."[37] The mobility gained by this concept was the U.S. Army's most dominant characteristic in the campaigns in northwest Europe in 1944–45.

A third concept, standardization, developed from McNair's conviction that a standardized, general-purpose force was a more efficient utilization of America's resources. Such an organization, modified only as deemed necessary by the local theater commander, would prove a more effective and flexible organization than an army containing any number of highly specialized, and possibly wasteful, units.[38]

This was a definite advantage in the planning cell, on the training ground, and, most of all, on the battlefield. Compare this American standardization with the situation in the German Army of the same time where "the German Army . . . had a variety of divisions not conforming to standard tables of organization."[39] The potential chaos produced by such diversity of organization could have a disastrous impact on supply, maintenance, and training, as well as on the German commander's tactical control during a battle.

Standardization of U.S. units also facilitated the Army's ability to maximize the continuous flow of war supplies to the fighting front and allow the resulting combat power to be more effectively brought to bear on the enemy. The concept allowed logisticians to customize supplies in "units of fire"—the basic load of ammunition for a "type" battalion (infantry, tank, artillery, etc.) for one day's combat.[40] By facilitating this flow, the streamlining of U.S. formations permitted the more efficient transformation of combat potential into combat power.

Of the eighty-nine divisions that eventually emerged from these concepts, sixty-six were infantry divisions. The National Guard provided eighteen of these infantry divisions with ten Guard divisions serving in northwest Europe by V-E Day.[41] The World War II U.S. Army infantry division comprised a base force of three infantry regiments, a division artillery, an engineer battalion, and the division trains (organic supply units).[42] Forty-two of these infantry divisions formed the bulk of the American Army in northwest Europe in 1944–45.[43]

Despite the official continuance of the "pooling" concept, infantry division commanders in Europe by 1945 controlled considerably more than their divisions' authorized basic strength of 15,000 troops each. Division commanders often had more units in a "permanently attached" status within their divisions than they had organic formations.[44]

Supplementing the sturdy infantry divisions in Europe were the speed and power of fifteen armored divisions.[45] The U.S. armored divisions were basically of two types: an earlier, "heavy" armored division of two tank regiments and one infantry regiment; and a later "combat command" armored division with equal numbers of tank, infantry, and field artillery battalions. Initial organization of U.S. armored units (1940–42) produced the "heavy" three-regiment model. Troop strength numbered over 14,000, with about 5,000 men in tank units, 2,300 in armored infantry units, and 2,100 in field artillery units.[46] Although this organization seems strong in tank forces, many of the unit's 390 tanks were light, reconnaissance tanks—worthless in armored combat against the powerful German panzers.[47] After this type of division's many deficiencies were made painfully apparent in combat against Axis armored formations in North Africa in 1942–43, U.S. armored divisions were reorganized.[48] By 1944, the majority of American armored formations had been redesigned into the "combat command" model; not by coincidence, this streamlining allowed McNair to create more units with the manpower savings. Only two units, the 2nd and 3rd U.S. Armored Divisions, retained the older "heavy" configuration.[49] American armored divisions were able to field 200 percent more armored fighting vehicles than their German panzer division counterparts while using only 85 percent of the authorized manpower strength.[50]

From 1944–45, the U.S. Army fought the war in Europe with these basic organizations (plus a few specialized units, such as the airborne divisions and one mountain division). That it proved adequate to the task is a recognition of the vision of men like McNair and the adaptability of the Army's combat leaders.

MOBILIZATION AND MANPOWER

A significant challenge facing War Department planners and U.S. Army staff officers as the United States entered World War II was the actual *process* of mobilizing the available manpower and properly manning the division organization and structure that McNair had created. The key tasks required by this process were selecting, classifying, training, and deploying personnel for U.S. Army units fighting a global war and, inevitably, replacing soldiers lost in combat operations or to sickness, disease, and accidents. This latter task, replacing combat losses, became a particularly vexing problem after large-scale, high-intensity combat operations began in northwest Europe in the wake of the 6 June 1944 D-Day invasion. Solving it without resorting to draconian, ad hoc methods—such as stripping units in training of key personnel to replace losses in front-line combat units—proved beyond the capability of American planners and staff officers.

Long before replacing massive combat losses reached a crisis level, however, the military Services—Army, Army Air Forces, and Navy (including the Marine Corps)—faced the issue of how to distribute the available manpower needed to fill their respective ranks. During World War II, 16 million Americans served in uniform (40 percent volunteers, 60 percent draftees), and at peak strength in early 1945 U.S. armed forces numbered 12.3 million.[51] Since putting American ground troops into action against Axis forces meant *projecting* that combat power across oceans, there was never any question that the sea Services—Navy and Marine Corps—would get a substantial slice of the "manpower pie." By 1945, the sea Services comprised nearly 4 million personnel (3,380,000 Navy and 475,000 Marine Corps) of the over 12 million total armed forces strength. Army ground forces' chief competitor for manpower, therefore, was the American military's newest Service, the Army Air Forces.

Although the Air Force did not become a separate Service until 1947, during World War II it was essentially treated as such. U.S. Army Air Forces head Gen. Henry H. "Hap" Arnold, not Army Chief of Staff George C. Marshall, ran the "Army" Air Forces. By 1944, 2.4 million Army Air Forces personnel were serving worldwide. Much of the huge investment in manpower committed to the air effort was dedicated to one aspect of airpower—strategic bombing. Air commanders hoped strategic bombing would justify their claim to separate Service status, but its overall impact on winning the war remains a subject of legitimate debate and, therefore, a questionable use of manpower resources.[52] Airpower was a vital component in achieving victory in World War II; but the enormous strategic bombing effort's practical impact on Army ground forces was that it removed huge numbers of badly needed ground combat troops from the available manpower pool. This impact became particularly acute beginning in the last half of 1944 when Army ground forces commanders were scrambling to replace the massive combat losses suffered in the campaigns in northwest Europe.[53] Moreover, as a Service branch requiring a high level of technical skill, the Army Air Forces generally got first pick of the "best and brightest" from the manpower pool, resulting in the air effort having a qualitative as well as quantitative negative impact on Army ground forces.

Indeed, competition with the Army Air Forces was not the Army ground forces' only challenge in the effort to fill its ranks—particularly infantry riflemen—with high-quality personnel. Despite the War Department General Staff's admission as early as 1938 that "the Infantry Division continues to be the basic combat element by which battles are won," this was exposed in practice as being little more than lip service. As Weigley noted:

[T]he American Army of World War II habitually filled the ranks of its combat infantry with its least promising recruits, the uneducated, the unskilled, the unenthusiastic. Those left over after the Army Air Forces, the marines, the navy, the paratroops, and the technical branches had skimmed off the

best of the nation's military manpower were then expected to
bear the main burden of sustained battle."[54]

The Army's system for classifying personnel focused on physical
capacity, intellectual ability, and civilian occupational skill of
inductees; yet its effect was to favor the technical branches at the
expense of ground combat branches (infantry, armor, and artillery).
The result, as Army historians found, was that "the ground combat
arms failed to receive a proportionate share of the high-quality men
assigned by reception centers to the major Army commands."[55] One
sampling of combat soldiers conducted in 1943 found that Army
infantrymen in the sample were well below the Army average in
height, weight, intelligence, and education.[56] Perhaps more important
than quality measures, however, was the low state of infantrymen's
morale—another midwar survey revealed that only 11 percent of
infantrymen would choose to serve in that branch if offered a choice
(compared to 76 percent of Army Air Forces personnel surveyed who
responded that they would stay in their branch).[57] Attempts by Army
Ground Forces commander McNair to convince the War Department
to institute practical policies designed to raise infantrymen's morale
were largely unsuccessful.

Yet, none of the World War II manpower issues confounded U.S.
Army planners and field commanders more than the problem of generating replacement personnel to fill the inevitable gaping holes in
ground combat units caused by the huge number of casualties. It was a
problem that was never satisfactorily solved, and it represented a dual
failure on the part of War Department staff officers—their prewar
casualty assumptions proved woeful underestimates, and the official
system they created for replacing combat losses broke down under the
strain of heavy casualties (particularly infantry riflemen) in mid-1944.
With the system broken, the best that War Department staff officers
could do was to fall back on the same draconian measure taken during
World War I: stripping key small-unit leaders and thousands of soldiers undergoing training in stateside units and shipping them en
masse to casualty-depleted front-line combat units overseas. This
emergency measure not only had a devastating effect on the divisions

undergoing training, but also had a negative impact on the combat units that received the replacements. In general, replacement personnel were inadequately trained to engage in immediate front-line combat and, often, possessed low morale and little motivation. Soldiers sent as replacements under these conditions reported feeling alone, disoriented, and abandoned to their fate by a brutal and uncaring system. One observer reported, "They frequently were thrown into combat with no orientation or advance preparation [resulting in] unnecessary casualties, because the new men did not know how to take care of themselves."[58]

Although McNair's efforts to create the organization of the U.S. Army that fought World War II were extremely effective, much less so were the flawed mobilization and manpower policies and actions of War Department planners to place the "right" person in the "right" position at the "right" time.[59] The result of the Army's policy failures was that the problems of poor quality and low morale among soldiers expected to carry the main burden of combat required exceptionally effective *leadership* at all levels to overcome and achieve battlefield success. That these problems were, in fact, overcome is a tribute to the leadership accomplishments of American commanders, particularly senior commanders at division level and higher.

EQUIPMENT

The equipment used by American infantrymen, tankers, and artillerymen reflected both the strengths and weaknesses of an organization whose guiding principles were mobility, flexibility, and standardization.[60] Blessed with an excellent infantry rifle and superior artillery, the U.S. Army compensated for an inferior tank by capitalizing on its inherent mobility and greater numbers.

The American infantryman was issued the finest shoulder weapon of World War II, the .30-caliber, semiautomatic M1 Garand that, compared to the German rifleman's bolt-operated Mauser 98K, was superior in all respects. In other infantry weapons, however, the American soldier was not as fortunate. In fact, much of the M1's advantage in firepower was overcome by the liberal German issue of machine pistols (submachine guns) to its soldiers.[61] U.S. machine guns also were embarrassingly outclassed by the German light and heavy machine guns. The German MG 34 and MG 42 were well-designed weapons that could fire 850 and 1,200 rounds per minute.[62] The best the ponderous U.S. M1919 Browning could manage was 500 rounds per minute.[63]

In infantry support weapons, the Germans possessed an advantage in their 120mm mortar, and the superb German antitank cannons clearly outmatched their U.S. equivalents.[64] The Germans also held the advantage in rocket-propelled antitank weapons. The infantryman's problem, however, was minor compared to that confronting the American tanker.

By the time of the Normandy invasion in June 1944, the U.S. main battle tank, the 33-ton M4 Sherman with its short-barreled 75mm gun, was clearly inferior to the German PzKpfw V Panther tank and the monstrous PzKpfw VI Tiger. However, it equaled or surpassed the PzKpfw IV, still the most numerous German tank. Although the Sherman possessed a few advantages over the better German tanks, U.S. tankers had to rely ultimately on greater numbers in tank encounters.[65]

The situation for U.S. tankers was frequently worsened by the German "stiffening of the panzers by detachments of fifty-six ton and eventually larger" Tiger tanks—huge monsters mounting the universally feared 88mm gun.[66] American tank destroyers could defeat most German tank armor with well-placed shots. However, because tank destroyers lacked their own armor protection, they were generally failures in their intended role of seeking out enemy tanks, striking them with their high-velocity guns, and destroying them.[67]

In late 1944, American tank designers finally produced an armored vehicle capable of slugging it out on equal terms with the best German tanks (M26 "Pershing" with 4 inches of frontal armor and mounting a 90mm main gun), but it was designed too late in the war to influence armored combat significantly.

The area where the Americans could clearly and consistently outdo the Germans was in field artillery. Available in abundant supply and usually well stocked with ammunition, American artillery weapons were linked by a superior fire control system that facilitated the massing of fires at the critical point.[68] Although the tank had now joined the infantry-artillery team to form a combined arms triad, artillery remained "the outstanding element in the American arsenal."[69] Much as it had in World War I, massed, coordinated field artillery support continued to provide the weight of combat power required to smash an opening in the enemy's defenses, then pin enemy forces down while tanks and infantry exploited the breakthrough.

Excellent communications equipment tied together the entire system of guns, fire direction center, and observers that could produce an enormous volume of fire in an incredibly short period of time. Even a single forward observer could "request and receive the fires of all batteries within range of a target in a single concentrated barrage."[70] The effect of massing the fires of the entire artillery battalion, or even of several battalions, upon a single target was awesome to behold and devastating to endure. The Germans grew to fear and respect American artillery and gave this branch much credit for Allied gains. "On all fronts artillery caused more than half the casualties of World War II battles; but the artillery was the American Army's special strong suit."[71]

In addition to an excellent rifle and superior artillery, the United States was nearly unchallenged in tactical air support. Despite an early lead in both quality of aircraft and tactics and techniques for close support of ground troops, the *Luftwaffe* had been overtaken by the U.S. Army Air Forces in each of these areas by fall 1944, although air-ground teamwork sometimes misfired.

Along with these advantages, as well as other American technological developments that progressed throughout the war, was the overwhelming quantity of U.S. equipment that flooded northern Europe during the last year of the war.[72] American industrial production, untouched and unthreatened by enemy attack, continued to pour forth a stream of rugged, serviceable equipment against which the Germans could ultimately achieve only brief, localized successes.

DOCTRINE

American Army doctrine for conducting the campaigns in northern Europe in 1944–45 was not unlike that used in the last days of the First World War. Indeed, "infantry assault doctrine of World War II

was based on the covering fire tactics of the final phase of World War
I."[73] Russell Weigley explained:

> . . . Each twelve-man rifle squad had a two man scout section
> [Able], a four man fire section [Baker], which included the
> squad's [Browning] automatic rifle, and a five man maneuver-
> and-assault section [Charlie]. Customarily, the squad leader
> would advance with Able to locate the enemy. He would then
> signal his assistant leader in Baker to fire, according to what-
> ever plan the situation suggested. Thereupon, he would join
> Charlie for the maneuver to exploit the cover laid down by
> Baker's fire.[74]

In actual combat, it was not uncommon for the squad leader to be
pinned down with the forward elements, causing the resulting uncoordinated assault to bog down and fall apart.[75] One remedy was the
habitual assignment of tanks to any sizable infantry formation. This
allowed the tanks to engage the enemy strongpoints and centers of
resistance, while the infantry protected the tanks by destroying antitank weapons and enemy infantry.[76] The 102nd Infantry Division
reported that, in the Rhineland and later during the drive into central
Germany, "the usual method of attack across the open ground was for
the infantry and tanks to work closely together." This tactic called for
"small groups of infantrymen [to be] assigned to each tank with
instructions never to desert it and to coordinate their actions with that
of the tank." The 102nd's unit history recorded, "This system worked
to perfection."[77]

Armored units, as well as infantry formations, discovered that
tanks unsupported by infantry were as vulnerable as infantrymen trying to force strongpoints without armored assistance. The 4th Armored
Division relied heavily upon coordinated tank-infantry attacks during
its sweep across France in summer 1944 and found this tactic essential
in forcing any gains at all in the difficult Lorraine campaign.[78] In the
mud and misery of Lorraine during fall 1944, the 4th's slow progress
was achieved only by sending small teams of tanks supported by
infantry forward "to deal with a strongpoint of enemy resistance which

was holding up the advance of the main body or to clean out a village or to hold high ground to safeguard [an] advance."[79] Restricted by the weather, German mines, and a stubborn enemy to advancing on a "one tank front," the foot soldiers and tankers were nearly impotent without each other's support.

Another method of advance used by all types of units was known as the "marching fire offensive," in many ways similar to the massive troop assaults of the First World War.[80] But "marching fire" was perceived by the infantrymen and tankers who were expected to employ it as leading to more casualties among the advancing American troops than the standard "fire and maneuver" assault—thereby making them reluctant to employ it.[81]

Moving beyond the small-unit level up to the division, the doctrine was simple but effective.[82] "Regimental combat teams" (in the infantry divisions) or "combat commands" (in the armored divisions) were established as the basic maneuver element. The regimental combat team/combat command "afforded a method of decentralizing control during fast moving situations."[83] The base for the regimental combat team was an infantry regiment of three infantry battalions. The combat team took its numerical designation from the regiment's number.[84] To this base was added an artillery battalion, a combat engineer platoon, a tank company, and other supporting units, such as tank destroyers, signal, medical, and ordnance. In theory, these regimental combat teams would be dispatched to accomplish some appropriate task in semi-autonomy. In practice, the division commander usually exercised tighter control over his teams in order to better apply the full power of the division against the enemy. Thus the division, not the regimental combat team, became the standard tactical element and focus of combat.[85]

The combat command of the armored division was similar in theory, but was formed on a triumvirate of a tank battalion, an infantry battalion, and a field artillery battalion (as well as supporting units). All these formations emphasized the preferred doctrine of using firepower, normally artillery, instead of manpower. The generous U.S. allocation of ammunition was unachievable by the German Army's artillery by this stage of the war. Mostly horse drawn and always short on ammunition, German artillery support was deficient in every category.[86]

In favorable weather, close air support by Army Air Forces added to the destruction that the American Army could bring down on the German defenses. Fighter-bombers (or *Jagdbombers*, known to Germans as the dreaded "Jabos") had supplemented ground-based firepower as "aerial artillery" since the beginning of the war and by 1944 were important components of American fighting doctrine.[87] Roaming the skies nearly unopposed after the German disasters in the summer of 1944, they were normally assigned to circle behind the front lines waiting for the call from forward ground units to deliver their lethal close support. Dependent upon weather and reliable communications, coordination between the air and ground units improved steadily as the war progressed.[88] Additionally, the Army Air Forces were employed to interdict any enemy forces or supplies moving toward Allied forces, to delay the habitual German counterattack, to strike forces already in contact, and generally to disrupt the enemy through aggressive attacks on roads, rail, towns, and river traffic.[89]

This seemingly lavish use of firepower proved to be the cornerstone of U.S. doctrine in northern Europe during the campaigns of 1944–45. An example of such free use of ammunition can be seen in one infantry division's ammunition expenditures during a time of relative supply austerity. In fewer than 10 days of attack in the Rhineland, the division expended 24,000 rounds of 105mm (artillery) ammunition, 8,184 rounds of 60mm mortar ammunition, and 1,712,550 rounds of small-arms ammunition—more than 1,007 total tons.[90] This high volume of fire from a seemingly inexhaustible supply of weapons was able to make the American Army's unspectacular but sound doctrine unbeatable by the German Army of 1944–45.

LEADERSHIP

The American officers who led the U.S. Army during the last two years of the war constituted a core of about 15,000 prewar regular officers to which had been added nearly 750,000 wartime officers.[91] In a typical infantry regiment, one found the colonel, his executive officer, and one of the three battalion commanders were prewar Regular

Army. The other two battalion commanders were a National Guards-man and a reserve officer. "Probably two-thirds of the company commanders were OCS graduates; the other one-third consisted of Guardsmen with a few reservists."[92] Thus, the burden of small-unit leadership at the tactical level was borne, for the most part, by officers who had been commissioned after the beginning of the war—men who were not products of the prewar Army staff and school system.

But above regimental level, at the division and higher headquarters echelon that "demanded leadership and managerial qualities of an exceptional kind," the majority of commanding officers were Regular Army soldiers.[93] That these officers, who were "exceptional in their skills, as well as character and decisiveness," performed well is a tribute to the Army staff and school system and to the judgment of the men who selected them.[94] Weigley observed:

> Even those officers of high rank who enjoyed a fairly large scope for the exercise of their individual abilities reflected the qualities of the pre-war staff and school system. For most of them had long since been selected by their chiefs and by the instructors in the schools as men who would exercise the highest responsibilities if war should come.[95]

Regardless of the source of their officer commissions—West Point, ROTC, or direct commission—the men who rose to senior command and staff positions in World War II had all progressed through the same system of military education and professional development. The pre–World War II Regular Army officer corps was small enough that most of them knew each other either personally or by reputation, and many had served together during the interwar decades. All of them had attended as students the same levels of military education (Basic Branch Schools, Command and General Staff School, and, most of them, the Army War College) and many had taught in the Army school system as faculty members. Although individually their specific command and staff position assignments varied somewhat, and some of them had World War I combat experience while others did not, in general their career paths prior to the war were similar. As historian Robert H. Berlin noted, by the outbreak of World War II these interwar officers had "developed common professional skills and abilities" gained through schools, service with troops, and as instructors or on staffs.[96]

Yet while their background and preparation seem common, straightforward and systematic, the actual process used to <u>select</u> them for important senior commands is less so. Not since President Abraham Lincoln during the Civil War has a single individual exercised such personal influence over the shaping of the Army's wartime senior leadership ranks as did George Marshall during World War II. The process Marshall and his intimates used to select the lucky officers for higher command was, in effect, a personal sponsorship system that functioned parallel to but outside of the Army's official selection and promotion hierarchy. However inappropriate such a personal sponsorship system might seem today, it was a definite institution at that time.[97]

Most of the key men leading the Battle of the Bulge in the Ardennes had been personally chosen by Marshall for plum assignments and were sponsored by him through at least part of their careers. They were identified by the Chief of Staff early on, and he kept track of their progression, selecting the ones he considered most promising for important positions as the war clouds in Europe gathered.[98] Later, he secured their promotions to high command, then collaborated with them in selecting other promising officers to fill key positions when those assignments opened up. As Thomas Ricks notes, in a 1943 report Marshall explained that he sought generals who were "men who have measured up to the highest standards of military skill, who have demonstrated a comprehensive understanding of modern standards of warfare and who possess the physical stamina, moral courage, strength of character and flexibility of mind necessary to carry the burdens which modern combat conditions impose."[99]

Clearly, those officers chosen by Marshall were fortunate in their timing to be in the right place at the right time to attract his notice. They were certainly not the only capable, competent officers in the U.S. Army when World War II erupted.[100] Their commonality of background and experience in the interwar army with those fortunates whom the Chief of Staff raised to high rank and senior command makes their lack of a "Marshall connection" seem the only thing setting them apart from their luckier contemporaries. Blumenson points this out when he explains the "hitch" in the Marshall method:

> The Marshall method of identifying and rewarding first-rate officers was a system within a system. It worked well so far as it went. For every person entered in Marshall's notebook, there were probably a dozen, perhaps more, who were every bit as good as the ones he listed. The others were simply unfortunate because they failed to come within Marshall's orbit or ken. . . . How many excellent individuals were slighted simply because of their bad luck of never meeting or working with Marshall is, of course, a matter of conjecture.[101]

The very fact that the careers of Eisenhower, Bradley, Patton, and others prior to World War II were, in general, similar to those of their contemporaries is itself a testament to the system that produced them. There probably were a number of other "Ikes" and "Brads" who, if they had been touched by Marshall and received the call to leadership, could have produced a great victory as Ike did. Blumenson, pondering what the American Army of that war would have looked like if Marshall had not been leading it, concluded that, "Most likely, some of our heroes of World War II would have had different names."[102]

By the time of the Ardennes offensive in December 1944, the men Marshall had placed in senior positions in Europe had learned important lessons about command in combat and "gained invaluable experience in battlefield management."[103] During the early campaigns in North Africa, Sicily, and Italy, U.S. senior leaders were given a crash course in modern warfare by an enemy who had honed his skills on numerous battlefields for four years or more before engaging the inexperienced Americans. Complicating matters was the additional strain of fighting with the Allies.

Allied Supreme Commander Eisenhower, in particular, had learned hard lessons on the value of aggressiveness and team play in the very first test of coalition warfare in Tunisia (November 1942 to

May 1943). The abysmally poor performance of the U.S. II Corps and of its commander, Gen. Lloyd Fredendall, demonstrated to Eisenhower that, although prewar "friendship counted for much,"[104] it must not interfere with the relief of any officer who proved indecisive or an early failure. Ike and his senior commanders learned to be quick in relieving subordinates, and they exercised this option with increasing frequency in subsequent campaigns.[105]

Also important to Eisenhower was the concept of "team play." Ike demanded a spirit of cooperation in all his subordinate commanders and learned that his success as coalition warfare commander depended on achieving and maintaining consensus among the Allies. Throughout his exercise of Supreme Command, Ike was an "ally" first and an "American" second. Despite resistance from Patton, Bradley, and, eventually, Marshall, Eisenhower remained faithful to the principle of Allied unity to the end of the war—and as a result became the most successful practitioner of coalition warfare in history.[106] Demanding and receiving cooperation among his Allied subordinates was not always easy, but the fact that his subordinates complied is a recognition of Eisenhower's influence as much as it is a statement of the officers' professionalism.

The campaigns in northern Europe in 1944–45 were clearly marked by Eisenhower's influence and leadership, and he shaped their conduct and outcome. In addition to setting an example for his subordinates to follow, Ike personally selected division, corps, and Army commanders from names supplied by Marshall and McNair (although he often sought the advice of Bradley or SHAEF Chief of Staff Lt. Gen. Walter Bedell Smith).[107]

Marshall facilitated this process by agreeing that Eisenhower "need take no commander unless he had full confidence in him."[108] Subordinate commanders had little latitude in selecting their respective subordinates. For example, Simpson, Ninth Army commander, was allowed to select three officers for his corps commanders from a list of only four names previously approved by Eisenhower.[109]

Eisenhower visited his field commanders frequently but "did not interfere with their conduct of operations . . . usually content[ing] himself with giving [them] a pat on the back and telling them to keep up the good work."[110] Gen. Raymond S. McLain, XIX Corps commander, has written his opinion of how far down the ranks Eisenhower's influence was projected when he wrote, "As a corps commander, I frequently felt his personal influence, and I know, too, that my division commanders and even some of my regimental and battalion commanders, on occasion, also felt his personal presence and influence."[111] The extent of this influence can also be gauged by the celerity with which corps and army commanders relieved their division commanders for timidity, early failure, or "seriously lacking aggressiveness in [their] leadership"—all traits stressed by the Supreme Commander.[112]

The leadership climate established and set by the Supreme Commander in Europe during the final two years of the war, therefore, was characterized by an attitude of aggressiveness at the senior American levels and Allied cooperation, the latter constantly sought by Eisenhower. That this climate produced satisfactory results is attributable, in no small part, to "the 12,000–13,000 officers of the old Army [who] had succeeded in preparing themselves mentally for the transition [to war] to a greater extent than the observer of mounted parades and maneuvers . . . might have suspected."[113] The American Army's staff and school system had proved its worth in the ultimate test.[114]

THE ENEMY

The army the Allies faced in the last two years of the war was not the powerful, confident force that had beaten France in six weeks and had stormed to the gates of Moscow during a furious summer of lightning warfare. Five years of constant war had drained Germany's manpower reserves to a dangerous level and had severely strained combat leadership and other vital resources—but the German Army was far from beaten. Thanks to excellent officers, a core of hardened, battle-wise veterans, and the focusing of Germany's celebrated efficiency into maximizing the potential of the remaining resources of personnel and equipment, the Reich fought on.[115]

Qualitatively, the German Army may still have been the best in the world, even at that late stage of the war. The liberal issue of automatic weapons allowed the German division to maintain "superior firepower [small arms] over its American rival despite having about 1,200 fewer combat infantrymen." Technologically superior equipment (especially tanks, machine guns, and antitank weapons) helped the German soldier compensate for his country's inability to match the overwhelming Allied production rates. And German officers and noncommissioned officers provided leadership that was tough, experienced, and characterized by "superior professional skill."[116]

These advantages, however, could not compensate for all the disadvantages that had accumulated by this stage in the war, nor could they avoid ultimate defeat. The odds were too great to do anything but postpone the inevitable results of attrition: above all other problems, the German Army faced an ever-shrinking manpower pool.

Unceasing warfare on several fronts had seriously depleted the German reserves of personnel, but in just the period June through August 1944, the German armed forces lost almost a million men out of a total ground force of 3 million. Yet, by reducing the authorized levels of existing divisions and stripping training and other specialized units, twenty-five new *Volksgrenadier* divisions appeared on the Western Front alone beginning in September. Nearly 1.5 million new men were called up to fill the depleted *Wehrmacht* ranks during the same period.[117] Prodigious as this effort seems, Germany accomplished this rather remarkable feat only by calling up those men previously exempt from service.

Service schools were stripped of demonstration units in 1944, and the school cadres themselves followed them to the front in 1945. All men between the ages of sixteen and sixty were eligible to serve in the *Volkssturm*, a militia-type organization usually poorly trained and poorly equipped. These units were thrown in late in the war and seldom had heavy weapons.[118] A final source of manpower was wounded or disabled veterans, the so-called "stomach soldiers" who were being called back to active service. By these expedient measures Germany was able to fill its depleted ranks, but deficiencies in training and combat preparation took a toll.[119]

Keeping these units supplied with equipment during the final months of the war was also a serious problem. Although German production figures imply that the manufacture of war materials was not as

devastated by Allied air strikes as was assumed by Allied planners, production could by no measure meet the demands of all fronts.[120] In mid-
1944, at the height of availability, total stocks of German tanks were
approximately 5,000. On the eve of the Ardennes offensive, the Germans had about half that number available in the west, most of which
were committed to the attack. About 45 percent of these were the
excellent PzKpfw V "Panther" and the PzKpfw VI "Tiger" tanks. The
remainder consisted of the inferior PzKpfw IV.[121] These numbers
declined dramatically and consistently and German forces were usually
overwhelmingly outnumbered by Allied armored fighting vehicles.

Tank strength within German panzer divisions also declined
steadily over the course of the war, especially in the last two years. To
compensate, the Germans either decreased the number of tanks in a
company or reduced the number of companies in a battalion (or battalions in a regiment).[122]

A continuing problem for the German Army was its "astonishing
dependence on horse transport."[123] The inventors of the blitzkrieg continued to rely heavily on the horse as the means for moving supplies,
equipment, and most artillery pieces, and German resistance and
morale suffered when they compared their "hobbled" army to the
superior mobility of the American divisions racing across Europe.[124]
Weigley notes, "As the [U.S.] infantrymen promptly demonstrated in
combat . . . the mounting of infantry everywhere conceivable on the
division's trucks and artillery vehicles and the attached tanks [allowed
the division to] readily move on wheels and tracked vehicles. No other
army in the world was so mobile."[125] The German Army of 1944–45
could not match this speed and efficiency.

As the Allies pressed ever closer to Germany and eventually
entered the Reich, the German Army relied increasingly on fortifications to stem the advance. After the drive across France and the
bloody battles in Lorraine, the Germans forced the Allies to breach the
so-called Siegfried Line—the vaunted *Westwall*.

These defenses were never completed as originally planned
because of France's rapid collapse in the spring of 1940, so the final
months of 1944 brought on a feverish spurt of activity to strengthen
them before the Allies attacked. This belt of intertwined fortifications

extended nearly 500 miles from Switzerland to Holland and consisted of "a system of large and small pillboxes and bunkers with three to seven foot walls . . . protected by interlocking fields of fire and reinforced by minefields, fences and lines of obstacles."[126] Supplementing these defenses were antitank ditches, machine-gun nests, and the ubiquitous concrete "dragon's teeth"—the line's most characteristic feature. German engineers took advantage of the rugged terrain in many sectors of the line, using streams and ravines as antitank ditches and flooding low-lying areas to prevent passage.[127] Bunkers of reinforced concrete formed the principal strongpoints of the Siegfried Line.

The Allied assault to break through the Siegfried Line, although interrupted by the German Ardennes offensive, cost an estimated 140,000 Allied casualties and consumed several months—an extremely high price for the small amount of territory gained.[128] That was exactly the purpose of the fortifications, and the German defenders used them skillfully to offset their numerical disadvantage in forces.

The Germans were also skillful at organizing strong defenses around towns and villages, as a way to capitalize upon the concealment and cover offered by the sturdy European buildings and urban areas. Isolated farms and small villages allowed the German defenders to establish strongpoints with excellent fields of fire and good observation across the open, cultivated countryside. Organizing "community diggings," they supplemented deliberate fortifications with thousands of trenches and antitank ditches. By establishing belts of such fortifications and trenches around towns, they made thousands of miniature forts, and each village or farm became a potential strongpoint.[129] As the Allies closed in and crossed the borders of Germany itself, such defenses multiplied, spurred on by the desperation of defending home and family.

Eventually, however, the German Army was forced out of even these fortifications by the Allied advance. Unable to muster sufficient mobile forces to properly defend the Rhine, the last great barrier to the Allied drive into central Germany, the Germans fought the last month of the war in hastily prepared positions as best they could. Finally, its last major field force in western Germany trapped in the Ruhr industrial area by the advancing American columns, the German Army began to surrender in ever-increasing numbers.[130] The German Army finally died as an effective fighting force along the banks of the Elbe River, fleeing the advancing Russians in a last, frenzied attempt to surrender to the Western Allies.

CAMPAIGNS IN NORTHWEST EUROPE, 1944–45

From the initial landings in Normandy on 6 June 1944 until the German incursion in the Ardennes was finally eliminated by the following February, the U.S. Army, chiefly the forces of Bradley's 12th Army Group, established a secure lodgment in Normandy, destroyed German resistance in France, and then survived the major counteroffensive in the Ardennes. In so doing, it accomplished the principal strategic successes of establishing the Normandy lodgment and racing across France to close on the German border.[131] Less than three months after winning the Battle of the Bulge, the Allies had linked up with the Russians in central Germany and conquered a devastated Reich.[132]

Following the landings of the U.S. V and VII Corps along with British and Canadian forces on D-Day, the Allies began pouring in men and supplies, building up the beachhead as fast as possible. The Allies put ashore 314,000 men, 41,000 vehicles, and 116,000 tons of supplies by 19 June. After several weeks of bitter fighting among the daunting hedgerows of the compartmentalized bocage country, Allied forces were able to break out of the Cotentin Peninsula as a result of Bradley's COBRA carpet-bombing breakthrough scheme near St.-Lô on 25 July.[133] The next month brought a remarkable change from the static warfare near the beachhead and saw Allied forces (most notably U.S. Third Army) racing across France.

The Supreme Command's historian, Forrest Pogue, described the dash across France that summer:

> In four weeks the battle of stalemate in the bocage had changed to one of great mobility as the Allied forces searched out the enemy along the Loire and toward Brest, encircled and destroyed thousands of German troops in a great enveloping movement at Falaise, and dashed to the Seine to cut off the Germans and threaten Paris . . . the speed with which the

drives were executed and with which the enemy opposition collapsed west of the Seine followed from the unexpected opportunities which Allied commanders had turned to their advantage.[134]

While the First and Third Armies drove eastward, the newly activated Ninth Army assumed responsibility for the VIII Corps' reduction and capture of the fortified port city of Brest on the Brittany Peninsula. Thousands of casualties resulted and great quantities of supplies were used, but ultimately no usable port facilities remained following the destructive fighting and German demolitions. The decision to capture this stoutly defended citadel, however, has been sharply criticized as detracting from the destruction of the main German forces farther east. Historian Martin Blumenson commented that "If [the Allied leaders] could have seen the bitter battle about to develop at Brest, their decision to take that port would have been a mistake."[135]

Stiffening German resistance and lengthening Allied supply lines caused the swift eastward advance of the Allied armies across France to slow considerably by the end of summer 1944. By mid-September the First Army had swept through Belgium and Luxembourg, and the Third Army had entered Lorraine, driving to the Metz and Nancy areas. By this time, Devers's 6th Army Group had invaded southern France and fallen in on Bradley's right flank. Lt. Gen. Alexander Patch's Seventh Army had driven northward over 300 miles since landing on the beaches of southern France, helping to clear that country of German forces.[136]

Montgomery's 21st Army Group, consisting of British and Canadian forces, anchored the Allied left flank on the English Channel and Holland. Finally clearing the port of Antwerp after desperate German resistance in the Scheldt Estuary approaches, Montgomery's forces eventually opened up badly needed port facilities to the supply-constrained Allies.[137] In September, Montgomery had tried unsuccessfully to establish a bridgehead across the lower Rhine at Arnhem. The resulting MARKET-GARDEN fiasco did more, perhaps, than any single event to cause Eisenhower to maintain the so-called "broad front" strategy of advancing on multiple axes. Certainly, if Montgomery had been successful in putting his British Second Army across the last major natural obstacle to a drive into Germany, and therefore "in a suitable position to be able to develop operations against the north face of the Ruhr,"[138] the Field Marshal's forces would surely have led the main effort of the Allies' dual axis advance into Germany. Failing at Arnhem, however, the 21st Army Group prepared for the difficult fighting in the Rhineland followed by deliberate preparations for forcing the Rhine.[139]

From mid-September until the Germans launched their surprise offensive in the Ardennes on 16 December 1944, the Allied armies waged a bloody battle of attrition from Holland in the north, south to Switzerland. A determined enemy and miserable weather combined to cause a relatively modest advance to the Siegfried Line, this system of fortifications being breached only in the Aachen area. By fall 1944, General Simpson's Ninth Army had been inserted into the Allied line north of First Army and south of Field Marshal Montgomery's 21st Army Group. These battles of attrition in October, November, and into December "were based on the belief that Hitler's forces were still disintegrating and that some lucky push might find a soft spot in the opposing lines which would permit the Allies to advance to the Rhine before the dead of winter. Later, when it became evident that the Germans had reorganized their forces and had succeeded in manning the Westwall fortifications against the Allied offensive, General Eisenhower refused to accept a static policy for the winter, feeling that even minor advances were better than completely defensive tactics."[140]

These "minor advances" included the disastrous Huertgen Forest campaign in which four of the attacking American divisions were nearly destroyed and 33,000 of the 120,000 U.S. troops involved became casualties. Begun as an attempt by Maj. Gen. J. Lawton Collins's VII Corps to "jump" the Siegfried Line on the run, it ended in bloody, frustrating, and fruitless assaults to capture the critical Roer River dams.[141] Two of the shattered divisions, the 4th and 28th Infantry Divisions, were moved to a quiet area of the front to recover—the Ardennes. Allied attention remained diverted elsewhere until, on 16 December 1944, the surprise German offensive riveted SHAEF's focus on the Ardennes.

CHAPTER 2

Eisenhower and the Supreme Command

A ny chance of success for Hitler's Ardennes attack rested firmly on the dictator's assumption that the Allied command would react slowly and deliberately in ordering countermeasures. Indeed, the basic premise for striking at this unexpected time in such an unexpected place was the presumption that the American and British leaders, divided by "nationalistic fears and rivalries,"[1] would haggle for days over the nature of the offensive and how to respond to it. If this went on for as little as forty-eight hours, Hitler hoped to have his forces across the Meuse River and well on their way to splitting the Allied front, possibly isolating the British and Canadian forces in the north from the American Army further south. The Nazi leader, however, badly misjudged the nature of the Allied coalition and the competence and character of the man who led it.

Long before the German attack smashed into the U.S. units in the Ardennes in December 1944, Eisenhower had forged an integrated, effective, totally "Allied" command structure (appendix A) eminently capable of quickly assessing the German attack and reacting appropriately to it. Within hours of the beginning of the assault, Eisenhower and his SHAEF staff had divined the scope of the surprise offensive and had begun to take critical actions necessary to stop its spread and limit its impact on the Allied armies. Sending the first wave of reserves to the threatened region almost immediately, Ike and his SHAEF staff officers continued with a series of critical decisions over the ensuing days that changed the entire nature of the German attack. Eisenhower's prompt actions succeeded in transforming the offensive from a massive breakthrough threatening to split the Allied armies in two to a localized fight for control of the Ardennes region.[2] In so doing, he averted a potential strategic disaster for the Allies and created an opportunity to destroy the bulk of Germany's remaining reserves of manpower and war materiel.

Despite his appropriate actions during this crisis, however, Eisenhower has been criticized for his conduct of the battle as well as for his assumed responsibility for creating the conditions that allowed the enemy the opportunity to launch such an offensive. His critics, both American and British, loudly berated his strategic vision (or lack thereof) for causing the crisis, and second-guessed his decisions impacting on the fight at the tactical level. Field Marshal Sir Alan Brooke, Britain's Chief of the Imperial General Staff, viewed Eisenhower's leadership "with undisguised contempt," charging that Ike's "faulty dispositions and organizations" had caused him to be "thrown off his balance."[3] Even Bradley, Ike's closest friend among his high-ranking subordinates, accused the Supreme Commander of having "an acute case of the shakes"[4] during the offensive and characterized one of Ike's biggest command decisions as "the worst possible mistake"[5] he could have made.

If Eisenhower's leadership is to be judged, it is necessary to examine the development, characteristics, and influence of Eisenhower's command of the coalition warfare he directed in Europe from 1942 to 1945, and to analyze how his battle leadership influenced the Ardennes offensive. The actions of America's most successful practitioner of coalition war,[6] conducting the American Army's greatest battle, provide valuable insight into the American style of battle leadership.

TEAM PLAYER

Dwight David Eisenhower was, above all, a team player. Whether the "team" was the West Point football squad on which he was a star player during his years as a cadet (1911–15), or the 1942–45 Anglo-American partnership he led that became the most successful allied military coalition in history, Ike put the team first and "carefully concealed" his own personal ambition.[7] In fact, as his biographer, Carlo D'Este, reveals, "Eisenhower's easygoing manner and charming smile" was "a disarming façade behind which lay a ruthless, ambitious officer who thirsted to advance his chosen career." It is, therefore, a testament to Eisenhower's remarkable strength of character that he never permitted his sizable ego to interfere with the success of the team—revealingly, years after Eisenhower retired from public life, he explained the secret to his team player success: "I got where I did by knowing how to hide my ego."[8] Ike's ability to be the consummate team player was greatly facilitated by his congenial personality—he consistently came across as personable, likable, and modest. Eisenhower's winning personality was further enhanced by a charismatic smile that helped him make friends easily and to rapidly gain the confidence of virtually all with whom he interacted throughout his career. But, there was steel behind Eisenhower's famous grin.

For all his outward congeniality, Eisenhower proved adept at handling strong-willed subordinates, notably Montgomery and Patton during the 1942–45 campaigns in the Mediterranean and northwest Europe. Both men tried Ike's patience many times; both ended up bending to his will. Although Eisenhower could be personally ruthless when necessary,[9] while he led the World War II allied effort in Europe he had an "enforcer" on his staff to chastise unruly subordinates, allowing Ike to continue playing the genial boss. Eisenhower's SHAEF chief of staff, Lt. Gen. Walter Bedell Smith—known as "Beetle," but whose more telling nickname was "the Barker"—was Ike's attack dog. Smith's job was to ruffle feathers when necessary; after Smith's scolding had achieved the desired effect, Ike would flash his famous ear-to-ear grin and smooth the ruffled feathers back down. It may seem like a simplistic "good cop/bad cop" leadership technique, but it had the singular virtue that it worked.[10] Moreover, allowing Eisenhower to remain above the petty squabbling inevitably present in any large military organization was extremely important to his effectiveness as an allied *coalition* commander, a leadership challenge whose success depended upon team building, gaining consensus, forging compromises, and achieving agreement rather than merely issuing orders.

Another vital key to Eisenhower's success was his high intelligence, a trait that he also admitted that he "hid" and rarely chose to reveal but which, in retrospect, is clearly evident in his accomplishments throughout his military and political careers. Although possessed of a keen "intelligence as icy as has ever risen to the higher reaches of American life,"[11] Ike decided while still a young officer that appearing *too* intelligent might spark jealousy and mistrust among his peers and, particularly, his superiors that could impede his career. Eisenhower, therefore, "went to great lengths to assume the role he had decided to carve out for himself: that of a solid, dependable officer who performed his duties efficiently but without drawing undue attention to himself."[12] Yet, regardless of Eisenhower's efforts to appear merely "solid and dependable" rather than flashy and brilliant—more the steady plow horse than the temperamental thoroughbred—by the eve of America's entry into World War II the attention of senior U.S. Army commanders had, indeed, been drawn to "Ike Eisenhower" through his accomplishments and clearly demonstrated abilities.

Ike's rapid rise from seeming obscurity as America entered World War II in December 1941 to become Supreme Commander of Allied forces in Europe within a few short years has often amazed those who have not carefully studied his pre–World War II career. Although on the surface Eisenhower's career may seem nearly indistinguishable from those of his contemporaries, in fact Ike had impressed his superiors throughout his service in the World War I and interwar army. Despite suffering what at the time seemed a career-killer—no combat experience in World War I—Eisenhower nevertheless progressed steadily with notable accomplishments that by the mid-1930s had gained Ike an Army-wide reputation as "the consummate staff officer, ambitious and all business."[13] Senior Army commanders began requesting Eisenhower by name to join their staffs. Ike's supposed "pre-war anonymity" is a myth.[14] When Army Chief of Staff George C. Marshall brought Eisenhower to join his hand-picked team on the Army General Staff the week after Pearl Harbor in December 1941, he knew very well that he was selecting an officer of proven ability and great promise. And once Ike had been chosen as a "Marshall man," he did not disappoint.

"THE BEST OFFICER IN THE ARMY"

Eisenhower's pre–World War II Army career, during which he evolved from a barely mediocre West Point cadet[15] to become the key officer personally selected by George Marshall—and, eventually, by President Franklin D. Roosevelt—to lead the Allied war effort in Europe, was highlighted by four defining experiences that developed Ike's competence and shaped his character. Each of these experiences contributed to preparing Eisenhower to face his greatest leadership challenge as a World War II coalition commander: the Battle of the Bulge.

First, in 1918, nearly three years after Ike graduated from West Point in June 1915 and following a series of routine initial assignments that provided little opportunity for him to show his future promise,[16] Eisenhower finally got the opportunity to excel in an important position. A year after the United States had declared war on Germany, Captain Eisenhower was assigned to organize and train the 301st Tank Battalion at Camp Meade, Maryland. During those weeks in the spring of 1918, Eisenhower trained his tank battalion for combat, demonstrating to his superiors a remarkable talent for organization and administration that was a telling early indication of leadership qualities he applied to great effect in World War II coalition command. His ability to organize was so impressive, however, that it caused his commander to pull him out of his unit just as it shipped overseas. In what Ike described as "a black mood," he assumed command of Camp Colt, near Gettysburg, Pennsylvania, and began to train the Army's Tank Corps. Although he received two more promotions before the Armistice was signed, Lieutenant Colonel Eisenhower spent the remainder of the fighting war training tankers. Even though Eisenhower missed out on an opportunity to get overseas, the Camp Colt Tank Corps assignment was, in reality, a choice one. It involved great responsibility, relatively independent work in a new and exciting type of warfare, promised speedy promotion, and ensured command of thousands of men—all volunteers. Still, Ike regretted that he had missed battle action. Some years after World War I, Ike met a young officer who had served in France during the war. When the officer complained of the lack of promotions overseas, Ike shot back, "Well, you got overseas—that should be promotion enough!"[17]

Lack of combat experience would continue to embarrass Eisenhower, especially when his British subordinates brought up the subject
later during his World War II command. Nevertheless, Ike's World
War I stateside service had experiences that would help prepare him to
excel as a coalition commander: organizing and training units for war;
early appreciation of tanks and the mobility of armored warfare;
extensive work with civilians and soldier-civilians; and avoidance of
the "Passchendaele" (trench warfare) mentality that characterized the
overcautious attitude of some British commanders in World War II.
Eisenhower had been better served by his noncombat duty than he
suspected.[18]

The second important accomplishment and milestone in Eisenhower's career came as a shock to his fellow officers who underesti-
mated Ike's intelligence. It was particularly surprising to the powerful
Chief of Infantry Branch in Washington, D.C., who controlled all of
that branch's officer assignments—Ike finished first in his Command
and General Staff School class of 1925–26 at Fort Leavenworth,
Kansas. In fact, after Eisenhower had published an article in the
November 1920 Infantry Journal about the role of tanks in future warfare that challenged the "official" position on how tanks were to be
used in combat,[19] Ike was summoned before an angry Chief of
Infantry and told that his ideas "were not only wrong, but dangerous
and that henceforth [he] would keep them to himself." As a result of
straying from the "party line," Ike was continually turned down for
choice assignments (such as the Infantry School) and for further military schooling (primarily the Command and Staff School).[20] Instead,
he shuffled from post to post, usually coerced into coaching the unit
football team. Yet, Ike managed to deftly sidestep his virtual "banish-
ment" by Infantry Branch by becoming the protégé of Gen. Fox Conner, who from 1922 became the younger officer's mentor and guiding
influence. The highly regarded Conner had been Pershing's operations
officer in the Great War and was, Eisenhower asserted, "the ablest man
I ever knew."[21] Conner expanded Ike's intellect by forcing him to read
and study military history and by coaching him in command and staff
duties. When he thought his pupil was sufficiently prepared, Conner
secured Eisenhower a place in the Command and Staff School class of

1925–26, on an adjutant general branch quota (since infantry branch still considered Ike persona non grata). In June 1926, Eisenhower graduated first in his Leavenworth class,[22] a singular achievement that significantly raised his Army-wide profile. Eisenhower's name began to be known to senior leaders, including future Army Chief of Staff then–Lt. Col. George C. Marshall.

Yet, it was the U.S. Army's Chief of Staff from 1930–35 who provided Eisenhower's third defining experience—Gen. Douglas MacArthur. Eisenhower worked under MacArthur for seven years (1932–39), first in Washington, then for four years in the Philippines. This put Ike in daily contact with the Army's top-ranking officer and senior civilian leadership in Washington while MacArthur was Chief of Staff. Ambrose recounts why MacArthur and, later, Marshall, admired and respected Ike:

> Eisenhower did his work brilliantly. It was always done on time. He loyally supported his chief's decisions. He adjusted himself to his chief's time schedules and to other whims. He was able to think from the point of view of his chief, a quality that both MacArthur and Marshall often singled out for praise. He had an instinctive sense of when to make a decision himself, when to pass it up to the boss. MacArthur said of Eisenhower in a fitness report in the early 1930's, *"This is the best officer in the Army* [emphasis added]. When the next war comes, he should go right to the top." In 1942 Marshall showed that he agreed with that assessment by implementing the recommendation.[23]

Although his time working under MacArthur in Washington, D.C., and the Philippines was "among the most frustrating years of his military career,"[24] it not only added MacArthur's "best officer in the Army" efficiency report to Eisenhower's official personnel record, it proved important to Ike's development as a future allied coalition commander.[25] In the Philippines, Ike learned to work as harmoniously as possible with an ally whose culture and background were completely different from his own, forcing him to appreciate the impact of issues from his opposite number's position, not merely his own. Despite the difficulties of the job, the experience helped to prepare Ike for the challenges he later would face commanding the Anglo-American military alliance. The Philippine tour also gave Eisenhower daily lessons in the value and necessity of compromise. To succeed, Ike constantly juggled the demands of his egotistical boss, the Filipino government, an unsympathetic American Army, and his own sense of what was required. Compromises were inevitable and frequent. This job taught another important lesson: how to accomplish extensive missions with limited resources. There were never enough men, equipment, or especially money to do it right. Eisenhower learned to adjust his aims to the resources available, to be opportunistic and flexible, and to do what was affordable when he couldn't do what seemed necessary.[26]

Less than two years after his return from the Philippines in 1939, Eisenhower had a fourth defining experience. In June 1941, three months after Ike was promoted to colonel, he was selected—with the personal approval of Marshall (who had become U.S. Army Chief of Staff in September 1939)—as the Third Army Chief of Staff under Gen. Walter Krueger at Fort Sam Houston, Texas. Krueger had requested Ike by name because he wanted an officer "possessing broad vision, progressive ideas, a thorough grasp of the magnitude of the problems involved in handling an army, and lots of initiative and resourcefulness."[27] Eisenhower's masterful management of Third Army's participation in the landmark Louisiana Maneuvers of 1941 confirmed Ike's superior abilities to Marshall. The Third Army's "victory" in the first large-scale maneuvers for the U.S. Army since World War I was attributed to Ike's tireless work as Krueger's Chief of Staff. Eisenhower not only gained priceless experience in controlling large masses of troops (400,000 took part in the maneuvers) and the equally massive logistical requirements to sustain them, Ike also received his first star when he was promoted to brigadier general in September 1941.[28] More importantly, Eisenhower got the call to report to Marshall for duty on the War Department Staff on 12 December 1941. It was the most important call of his career.[29]

Eisenhower assumed his duties in the War Plans Division on 14 December 1941. This was his first opportunity to work where Marshall could observe him daily, and he made the most of it. By February 1942, Marshall had made Ike the head of War Plans Division. The next month, Eisenhower became the first War Department Chief of Operations, in a general reorganization of the staff.[30] Soon after, on Marshall's recommendation, Eisenhower received his second star. Ambrose relates some reasons why the Marshall-Eisenhower relationship thrived:

> The two men, although ten years apart in age, had much in common. Marshall . . . had been a football player in college. He was a great fan of Fox Conner and a student of military history. Like Eisenhower, he loved exploring the Civil War battlefields and habitually illustrated his points or strengthened his arguments by drawing on examples from past battles and campaigns. The way he exercised leadership coincided nicely with Eisenhower's temperament. He never yelled, never shouted, almost never lost his temper. He built an atmosphere of friendly cooperation and teamwork around him without losing the distinction between the commander and his staff.[31]

Eisenhower completed his apprenticeship for coalition command under Marshall's able tutelage during the hectic, early months of American involvement in the war. Ike especially impressed his chief with his ability to "rise above national rivalries" and work amicably and closely with their new British ally. Starting at the Arcadia Conference and continuing through many U.S.-U.K. meetings, Ike stood out as a fair-minded partner.[32] When Marshall sent Eisenhower to Britain to observe and report on the massive buildup for the eventual attack on Nazi Germany, he was taking the first step toward placing Ike in command of all the Allied forces in the European Theater of Operations. Ike's uncommonly good judgment, quick assessment of the situation, and natural ability to win the friendship and confidence of his British counterparts convinced Marshall he was the perfect choice to lead the American effort. The British, especially, were "impressed by [Eisenhower's] dedication to the Alliance."[33]

EDUCATION OF A COALITION COMMANDER

Absolutely essential to understanding Eisenhower's leadership during the Battle of the Bulge is the knowledge of *how* he developed as an allied coalition commander. Ike had to *learn* how to command an allied coalition. That practical education began in earnest when Eisenhower was selected to lead Operation TORCH, the November 1942 Allied invasion of North Africa.

Ike set out immediately to create an integrated, Anglo-American headquarters to coordinate and control TORCH. Principal staff sections were set up with American chiefs and British deputies, or vice versa. Eisenhower's Allied Force Headquarters (AFHQ) "thus became a balanced collection of British and American officers working closely together to achieve the common aims of the alliance."[34] Significantly, Ike personally set the tone for the command climate he sought to create within his allied headquarters—typical of Eisenhower's leadership, AFHQ was to be a genuine team effort. He tolerated no outward manifestations of national jealousy or parochial pettiness. Instead, Ike worked hard to create "a close-knit organization where differences . . . were insignificant ones."[35] TORCH allowed Ike to learn his trade as a battlefield leader in an environment where his mistakes could not prove fatal to the Alliance or the Allied cause. North Africa became a proving ground for Eisenhower, a laboratory in the conduct of coalition warfare that permitted him to sharpen his skills as an Allied leader in preparation for greater challenges to follow. Forrest Pogue, Supreme Command historian, wrote of Ike's apprenticeship in the Mediterranean:

> The real school for the future commander of Supreme Headquarters Allied Expeditionary Force [SHAEF], . . . was in the Mediterranean Theater where, as Allied Commander in Chief, he came into contact with most of the political and military problems which were to be found later on a greater scale in the European Theater of Operations. It was at Allied Forces Headquarters [AFHQ] in the Mediterranean that he became familiar with the great burdens of a military leader of a coalition. . . . There, if he had not learned it before, the future SHAEF commander learned that war was not a simple matter

of planning and executing tactical operations, but one of balancing many national and international forces against a military objective.[36]

At a desert chokepoint in Tunisia called Kasserine Pass, Eisenhower learned hard lessons about the difficulties of leading allied forces in battle. Ike's teacher this time was German Field Marshal Erwin Rommel, the "Desert Fox."[37] The Battle of Kasserine Pass (14–24 February 1943) deserves closer examination for two important reasons. First, although Kasserine was on a much smaller scale than the massive December 1944 German Ardennes Offensive, Rommel's attack in the Tunisian desert had obvious similarities to the situation later faced by Eisenhower and his armies in the Battle of the Bulge: an overpowering, surprise German assault against U.S. forces that were ill prepared and improperly positioned to oppose it. The more important second reason is that Kasserine revealed to Eisenhower serious problems in leadership, teamwork, and battle command that, in the North African disaster's wake, he immediately set about rectifying. Had Ike *not* learned and taken to heart the hard lessons of Kasserine, his later leadership during the Battle of the Bulge *might* have resulted in a much different outcome in the Ardennes fighting.

The conditions leading to the debacle at Kasserine Pass seem obvious in retrospect. The Tunisian front was hundreds of miles from Ike's headquarters in Algiers. He exercised command through a confusing and convoluted system in which no one seemed certain for whom they worked. Supply lines were woefully overextended and intertwined among nationalities and services. The resulting "teeth" that could be supported by this tenuous logistical "tail" mustered insufficient combat power to smash German-Italian resistance. Above all, the commander of U.S. troops, Maj. Gen. Lloyd R. Fredendall, wasn't up to the task.

Fredendall, Marshall's pick to command the II U.S. Corps in the North African campaign, had performed adequately during the landings at Oran and in the limited fighting that followed. Eisenhower, however, didn't know him personally and was unsure of how he'd react in combat against the stiffer German resistance. He soon heard unsettling reports of Fredendall's openly anti-British attitude as well as evidence of a rather bizarre command style.

Fredendall quickly alienated Ike's British overall ground commander, Gen. Kenneth Anderson, and the two men barely spoke— although Anderson was nominally Fredendall's immediate boss. Worse, Fredendall despised and distrusted his own principal subordinate, 1st Armored Division commander Maj. Gen. Orlando Ward. The American corps commander habitually gave orders directly to Ward's subordinates and continually meddled in details at the division, brigade, and even battalion level. Fredendall also insisted on remaining at his command post far from the front—a heavily fortified bunker chiseled into a remote mountainside. The corps commander seldom left this location and therefore knew little of fast-breaking events at the front.[38] Fredendall made a real disaster seem likely; the battle-wise Rommel made it inevitable.

The German attack smashed into Fredendall's troops on Valentine's Day 1943 and drove them back in disorder. The inexperienced American troops and the incompetent Fredendall made the Battle of Kasserine Pass a disaster for Ike. Fortunately, dissension in the German-Italian high command cost Rommel an opportunity to break the Allied line. Denied the support he needed to achieve a really important breakthrough, Rommel was eventually forced to pull his troops back within the safety of the heavily fortified Mareth Line to await the inevitable Allied assault.

The American tactical defeat was a serious blow to U.S. prestige and to Eisenhower's reputation. Nevertheless, he retained the confidence of Marshall and Allied political leadership (after all, it was Rommel who eventually withdrew, and final Allied victory in the desert was only weeks away). Ike emerged from the ordeal a better leader for the experience—and with the fourth star of a full general.[39]

In addition to the obvious lessons on supply, organization, and command structure, Ike had learned much about the value of aggressiveness and team play in his first test as a coalition commander and battle leader. Fredendall's poor performance demonstrated to Eisenhower that friendship must not interfere with the relief of any officer who proved indecisive or a failure.[40] Ike also learned that senior leadership must be aggressively forward during the critical phase of any operation and not wedded to a command post far to the rear. Later, under Ike's command, a perceived lack of aggressiveness or a tendency for a commander to spend too much time in the rear was justification for immediate relief.[41]

The hapless Fredendall also provided Ike with a stark example of the consequences of violating the first rule of coalition warfare—cooperation and team play with one's coalition partners. Fredendall was despised by his British and French counterparts for his outspokenly anti-Allied posture. Ike could not tolerate such an attitude and learned to place a high value on officers who earned and maintained the respect of their Allied counterparts.[42] General Eisenhower emerged from the crucible of desert fighting with valuable experience in coalition war, improved skills in battle leadership, and increased confidence in himself.

His newly won self-confidence helped Ike to be more assertive with the British Allies and to make constructive changes in his headquarters' conduct for the remainder of the North African campaign (ended 13 May 1943). After the successful invasion and capture of Sicily (July–August 1943) Eisenhower had a first-class team that worked well together (although in the privacy of their diaries, some confided a startling degree of personal animosity toward one or more of the others). Clearly, the driving force behind the coalition was Eisenhower. Historian Pogue wrote that the quality most often stressed about Ike was "the ability to get people of different nationalities and viewpoints to work together," and that "after a year of working with Allied forces in the Mediterranean area, he had demonstrated his knack for making a coalition work."[43] Indeed, when a British politician congratulated him on "his" victory, Ike flashed his famous smile and said, "Ours, you mean, ours."[44]

SUPREME ALLIED COMMANDER

In 1944, President Roosevelt, impressed with Ike's reputation and proven ability to fight a successful coalition war, and professing that he would be "unable to sleep" with Marshall out of the country, selected Eisenhower as Supreme Commander, Allied Expeditionary

Force.[45] Ike's task directive from the Combined Chiefs of Staff read, "You will enter the continent of Europe, and, in conjunction with the other United Nations, undertake operations aimed at the heart of Germany and the destruction of her armed forces."[46]

Despite the inevitable complications (among them a chronic shortage of landing craft and, later, unfavorable weather patterns), Eisenhower's invasion force began to "enter the continent of Europe" by landing troops in France on 6 June 1944. Establishing and expanding the Normandy lodgment was a logistical undertaking without precedent, designed to create an unassailable base to support the subsequent campaigns across France and Germany.[47] Over the next several weeks the beachhead was expanded and secured, and, although German resistance became strong, the Allied Armies broke out of Normandy at the end of July. Pogue attributes the success of the Allied invasion to Eisenhower's "combined Allied command [that] had worked smoothly to bring the full force of naval, air, and ground power to bear on the enemy."[48] It was this unified SHAEF command (appendices B and C), mainly Eisenhower's personal creation, that led to the continuing Allied successes.

The story of the subsequent successful campaigns across France over the next several months is a familiar one. Montgomery's capture of Caen, Bradley's armies smashing the German defensive line at St.-Lô, and the unleashing of Patton's dramatic drive to the Seine and beyond are well known. The conduct of the coalition war that produced these successful campaigns, however, tested Eisenhower's leadership of this "unified command."

The challenge to Ike's coalition leadership that would linger through nearly the entire campaign was the question of an overall ground commander. Field Marshal Montgomery, whose diminutive size concealed one of the war's largest egos, wanted the overall ground command of Allied forces. He held this position, in fact, for the invasion force and only reluctantly gave it up in September when Ike himself incorporated the ground commander duties among the responsibilities of the Supreme Commander. Nevertheless, Montgomery continued to pester him about assuming overall control of the ground war at every opportunity.[49]

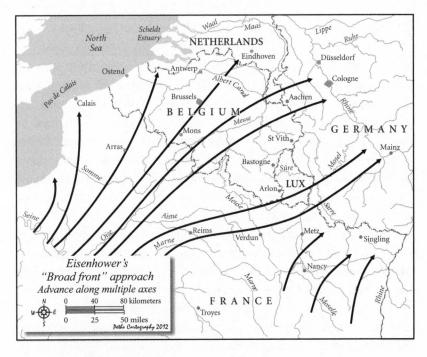

Eisenhower's
"Broad front" approach
Advance along multiple axes

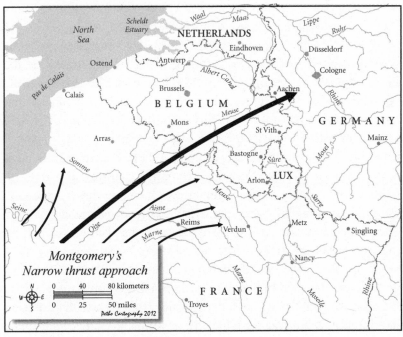

Montgomery's
Narrow thrust approach

Eisenhower also clashed with Montgomery regarding overall Allied military strategy. Monty wanted to lead a "single thrust" of about forty Allied divisions that, he claimed, could strike rapidly across the northern sector, overrun the Ruhr industrial heart of Germany, quickly capture Berlin, and bring an early end to the war. Ike disagreed, worried about logistics, a long, exposed flank, and the German ability to mass against a single thrust.[50] Eisenhower preferred to pressure the outnumbered Germans all along their line in an advance along multiple fronts—derided by Ike's critics as a "broad front" strategy—although he assured Montgomery his would be the main attack of the Allied effort.[51]

Once again, Eisenhower's judgment that it should be an *Allied* victory appears a major consideration in Ike's military strategy. Monty's persistence struck Ike as placing his personal aggrandizement before the best interests of the coalition and would result in a "British" victory, not an Allied triumph. When Monty returned to this theme after the Ardennes offensive, Ike prepared a "him or me" message to the Combined Chiefs of Staff but never had to send it.[52] Montgomery, who realized that Eisenhower, not he, would be the one to stay, finally shut up, relegating his sniping to his postwar memoirs.

Politically, Eisenhower had the challenge of dealing with the combined effects of the two different styles of his American and British bosses. Roosevelt gave both Marshall and Eisenhower little political guidance concerning the running of the war. FDR was not interested in the day-to-day operations of the coalition and provided little information to assist the two soldiers to plan grand strategy.[53] Churchill, on the other hand, was constantly meddling in Ike's business and frequently overloaded the Supreme Commander with both political and military advice. Although such control down to the lowest level was perfectly consistent with the British command system, it often appeared to Ike as little more than nagging. These two conflicting styles caused Eisenhower to demonstrate initiative and assertiveness. In the absence of detailed instructions from his own government, he used initiative to develop politico-military goals for SHAEF, while asserting his independence from Churchill's constant interference.[54] Ike accepted the Prime Minister's advice on many occasions, but he never allowed himself to be bullied by the persuasive British politician.

Yet, Eisenhower's greatest challenge as the military leader of the Allied coalition was the German Ardennes offensive—the Battle of the Bulge. It was during this greatest of all American battles that Ike's field command was put to its toughest test. Buffeted by pressures and demands from his political and military superiors, and sniped at by his American and British subordinates, Eisenhower needed all the leadership skills he had developed over the preceding years to win this conflict.

ATTACK IN THE ARDENNES

When the Ardennes offensive began in the early morning hours of 16 December 1944, it caught Eisenhower and the SHAEF staff completely by surprise.[55] This does not support later claims of several participants that they foresaw the German attack. Ike realized that he had left the Ardennes region vulnerable to a German counterstroke, but he never considered that such an event would occur. The Allies presumed that the German armies in the west had been thoroughly smashed during the war of maneuver fighting of the previous summer, and their remnants had been steadily worn away through the dreary, bitter fall campaigns of attrition. With the Red Army slowly but relentlessly grinding away at the bulk of the *Wehrmacht* on the vast eastern front, Germany seemed on the point of collapse. It may have been only half in jest when, in a 15 December letter, Eisenhower refused Montgomery's demand that he pay off on his £5 bet that the war would be over by Christmas, pointing out that he still had nine days to go.[56]

The thinness of the Allied line in the Ardennes was the inevitable consequence of Eisenhower's military strategy for prosecution of the war on the western front and the American gamble that ninety U.S. divisions would suffice to win a global war.[57] Pressing the Germans everywhere in the knowledge that they could not possibly be strong enough all along their line to stop the superior Allied forces, Eisenhower's multiple axes advance—the strategy approved by the Combined Chiefs of Staff before the Normandy invasion—was ultimately based on the premise that "more is better"—that is, more tanks, more bullets, more beans, more fuel, and above all, more men.[58] "More men," however, was Eisenhower's principal worry on 16 December 1944, not the threat of a German attack. He had no fresh U.S. divisions to put into the line to maintain the momentum of the Allied advance, and even the replacement pool for bringing battle-attrited units back up to fighting strength had nearly dried up.[59] By this stage of the war, there could be no thought of Britain providing any more divisions; that war-weary country was having difficulty calling up even modest numbers of fresh troops.[60] Any large number of new men would have to be American—and America had decided to complete the war with the divisions already formed. The resulting effect on Eisenhower's portion of the World War II global battlefront was his thin front in the Ardennes sector. Weigley correctly analyzed the situation facing Eisenhower:

Eisenhower's dilemma, when in November and early December he fretted over the Ardennes but perceived no satisfactory solution, points to a flaw in American strategy more fundamental than an excessive emulation of the Lincoln-Grant strategy of the Civil war. It was not that the broad-front strategy was wrong; the more basic trouble was that the Anglo-American alliance had not given Eisenhower enough troops to carry it out safely. . . . There were not enough Anglo-American divisions, or enough replacements for casualties in the existing divisions. Eisenhower could not create a reserve unless he abandoned the broad-front strategy. Far from creating a reserve he could not even rest and refit exhausted units like the 28th and the 4th [Infantry Divisions] without risking them in the tissue-thin Ardennes line. More than the misjudgments of the commanders in Europe, the events unfolding in the Ardennes on December 16 indicated that the ninety-division gamble had gone sour. The American army in Europe fought on too narrow a margin of physical superiority for the favored American broad-front strategy to be anything but a risky gamble.[61]

This now-chronic lack of manpower had brought Bradley to Ike's headquarters on 16 December to discuss the problem and plan their strategy for overcoming it. While the two met, received briefings, and prepared to attend the wedding of two members of the SHAEF staff later that day, the lead units of the German attack were crashing into American positions all along the thinly defended Ardennes front. Having begun at 0530 hours that morning, the attack was several hours old before Ike or Bradley received word that something was happening in Troy Middleton's VIII Corps sector. Ike's Intelligence Officer, British major general Ken Strong, brought the word to Eisenhower and Bradley, announcing that "the Germans had counterattacked in the Ardennes and scored penetrations at five places on the VIII Corps front." Strong explained that the attacks had begun early that morning and that the full extent of the attack was still unknown (although he said "the most dangerous penetration seemed to be developing along the V Corps-VIII Corps boundary in the Losheim Gap").[62]

Ike's and Bradley's reactions to Strong's announcement highlight the dramatic differences between the two commanders' battle leadership during the Ardennes crisis and underscore Eisenhower's prompt (and correct) response. Bradley, preferring to regard the German assault as merely a spoiling attack to divert U.S. resources from his own recently begun offensives, thought it could be stopped without difficulty,[63] later writing, "I was not overly concerned."[64] In contrast, Eisenhower seemed to sense immediately that something far bigger had been set in motion. "That's no spoiling attack!" Ike announced.[65]

Eisenhower was the first of all the Allied commanders "to grasp the full import of the attack, the first to be able to readjust his thinking,"[66] and the first to initiate counterstrokes to defeat the unexpected German offensive. After studying operational maps with Bradley and Strong, he directed Bradley to dispatch the 7th and 10th Armored Divisions from their assembly areas in the rear of their respective Ninth and Third Armies to the threatened sector. When Bradley, afraid that Patton would strongly object to losing the 10th Armored, began to demur, Ike "overruled him with a touch of impatience."[67]

The quick decision to rush these two armored units (along with the SHAEF reserve—the 82nd and 101st Airborne Divisions) to the Ardennes was one of Eisenhower's most important decisions of the battle, for it influenced the ultimate outcome of the fighting more than any other single decision taken by a commander on either side.

The doctrinal approach for countering such a breakthrough as the Germans were then attempting in the Ardennes was well known to Eisenhower (who, after all, had graduated first in his Command and General Staff School class) and to Ike's subordinate commanders: Hold the shoulders of the penetration to prevent the enemy from expanding the base of his salient; restrict the advance of enemy forces by interdicting crucial chokepoints and denying full use of routes of advance; and counterattack along the flanks of the penetration to cut off and destroy the advancing enemy forces. It was the classic "Leavenworth solution" to the tactical situation Ike confronted. Carrying out this doctrinal approach successfully, however, was another matter altogether.[68]

The most serious problem facing Eisenhower in his attempt to counter the German attack was where to come up with the reserve forces necessary to launch the counterattacks into the flanks of the penetration. Just as the manpower shortage had created the situation that led to the Germans invading the Ardennes, so was it hindering Eisenhower's reaction to counter the assault—SHAEF had no major strategic reserve forces immediately available. Some weeks prior to the launching of the Ardennes attack, Ike had asked his Army Group commanders to begin assembling a reserve force, but this action had not gone much beyond his request to identify units that could be used as such.[69] SHAEF's pitifully inadequate reserve force on 16 December 1944 consisted of the 82nd and 101st Airborne Divisions, light infantry units lacking tanks and heavy artillery. Both airborne divisions were still resting and refitting after withdrawing from Montgomery's Arnhem-Nijmegen fiasco the past September.

After conferring with Strong, SHAEF Chief of Staff Smith, and his British Deputy Operations Officer, Maj. Gen. J. F. M. Whiteley, Ike ordered the two airborne divisions (organized under Maj. Gen. Matt Ridgway as the XVIII Airborne Corps) placed on alert for dispatch to the Ardennes. By the time the units finally got to the threatened area (and after some understandable confusion), the 82nd, along with Ridgway's headquarters, formed up behind St.-Vith, while the 101st found itself at Bastogne—and was soon surrounded there.[70] Eisenhower also told Bradley "to order his army commanders to alert any division they had which was free for employment in the Ardennes area,"[71] for he realized the two armored divisions and the airborne units were not nearly sufficient to stop the German attack, let alone eliminate the rapidly forming salient. Many more were needed.

Eisenhower's quick appreciation of the scope of the German offensive caused him to realize that successfully defeating it would require a complete reorientation of his three army groups from one of Allied offense all along the line to one of defense in all but the Ardennes sector. SHAEF's focus until the German attack was stopped would have to be on regaining control of the Ardennes. Ike "ordered the cessation of all attacks by the [Allied Expeditionary Force] and the gathering up of every possible reserve to strike the [Ardennes] penetration in both flanks."[72] He directed Bradley and Gen. Jacob Devers to shift forces so that Devers's 6th Army Group on the Allied southern flank could move its boundary northward to cover a large portion of Patton's sector, freeing the Third Army commander to launch an early counterattack into the salient's southern flank.[73] Ike had the SHAEF staff issue a message for his signature, stating:

> The enemy is making a major thrust . . . and still has reserves uncommitted. . . . It appears that he will be prepared to employ the whole of his armored reserve to achieve success. My intention is to take immediate action to check the enemy advance, and then to launch a counteroffensive without delay with all forces north of the Moselle.[74]

Issuing this message on 18 December, Ike supplemented it with instructions that the German line of advance must not be permitted to cross the Meuse River.[75] Major Allied supply dumps were located across the Meuse; if the German offensive reached these critical supplies (especially fuel stocks), the Ardennes attack could explode into a rupture of the entire Allied line.

After sending this message outlining his general strategy on 18 December, Eisenhower summoned his principal American subordinates to a meeting in Verdun on 19 December to issue further orders for countering the German offensive. The meeting was a crucial one; Eisenhower not only outlined his strategy for containing the attack within the Ardennes region, but he also set a tone of optimism and opportunism.[76] Ike's personal leadership stabilized the chaotic situation. Ambrose recorded:

> Eisenhower's reaction [to the German Ardennes offensive] was crucial. If he had panicked, shouting orders on the telephone and pulling units from various sectors to throw them piecemeal into the battle, he would have spread panic all down the line. But he was calm, optimistic, even delighted at this seemingly ominous development . . . [writing to General Somervell on another subject on 17 December, Ike wrote,] "If things go well we should not only stop the thrust but should be able to profit from it."[77]

At the meeting Eisenhower showed his true character in the face of such serious, potentially catastrophic adversity.[78] He immediately set the positive tone he wanted his subordinate commanders to adopt by announcing, "The present situation is to be regarded as one of opportunity for us and not of disaster. There will be only cheerful faces at this conference table."[79] Clearly, Ike was not only planning to merely halt the German offensive, he intended to trap and utterly destroy the enemy that, in his opinion, had foolishly thrust out from the protection of the formidable German Siegfried Line defenses. Patton, realizing Ike was referring to the opportunity to destroy this last major reserve of German forces in the west, quickly rejoined, "Hell, let's have the guts to let the sons-of-bitches go all the way to Paris, then we'll really cut 'em off and chew 'em up!"[80]

Lest anyone think the general laughter following Patton's quip indicated approval of his facetious suggestion, Ike said, "George, that's fine. But the enemy must never be allowed to cross the Meuse."[81] The most dramatic part of the discussion came when Patton replied to Eisenhower's query as to how soon the Third Army could launch a counterattack into the south of the German salient. Now at center stage (and no doubt relishing every second of it), Patton announced that his army could attack "on December 22nd with three divisions!"[82] Not realizing that Patton had been quietly preparing for this shift in orientation for several days, the others in the room expressed disbelief. It seemed impossible that Patton's army could shift 90 degrees from a major offensive to the east to one toward the north in such a short time. To Eisenhower, however, Patton's dramatic announcement seemed to indicate the Army commander was underestimating the actual strength of the German offensive—clearly three divisions would not be sufficient combat power to execute successfully the kind of thrust Ike knew would be necessary to cut off the advancing German formations.[83] After Patton explained that he would follow up his initial three-division attack with one of three more soon after, Eisenhower approved the plan.[84]

By the end of the day, Eisenhower and the SHAEF staff had set in motion most of the important elements necessary to isolate the German penetration and ultimately defeat it: The few immediately available reserves had been rapidly dispatched to the threatened area; actions to create more reserves and fling them against the salient had been initiated; and the plan to begin the crucial counterattacks into the flanks of the penetration had been put in motion. Eisenhower's prompt actions on the first two days of the offensive were beginning to show positive results, but it was still early in the battle, and German forces continued to gain ground and push westward. Jacques Nobécourt, a Frenchman who wrote a well-balanced, nonpartisan view of Eisenhower's leadership during the Ardennes crisis, summed up the situation facing the Allies on 19 December:

The decisions he [Ike] had taken on December 16 were beginning to pay off; the flanks of the German salient were holding and resistance was firm at the vital communications points. In the center there was still a gap of 25 miles between the two airborne divisions and the German armor was pouring through it. But already there were signs the offensive was running out of steam.[85]

To complete the isolation of the Ardennes battlefront and prevent the German attack from rupturing the Allied line, Eisenhower realized that firm control needed to be established all along the threatened sector. His northern two armies now separated from Patton's army by the force of the attack, Bradley obstinately refused to relocate his headquarters.[86] Worse, yet, Bradley had made no effort to visit First Army headquarters to make a personal assessment of the rapidly-evolving tactical situation and, more importantly, to provide support and guidance to the shaken First Army commander and staff. Although Bradley assured Ike that he could control the battle by telephone and radio from his Luxembourg City army group headquarters, Bradley's claim likely only evoked in Eisenhower bitter memories of Fredendall's similar failure that contributed to the Kasserine Pass fiasco. Therefore, one more essential command decision had yet to be made—should the northern half of the bulge remain under Bradley's command? Eisenhower's decision on this question became the most controversial one he made during the battle, but it epitomizes more than any other his firm grasp of the true nature of an *allied* command. Eisenhower shifted command of the Ninth and the rest of the First (all forces north of the Bastogne area) to Montgomery.[87] Despite Ike's close friendship with Bradley and bruised American egos, he knew it was the right thing to do to save the Allied cause. Historian Chester Wilmot, openly pro-British and not noted for being pro-American, wrote, "In all his career as Supreme Commander there was perhaps no other time when Eisenhower revealed so clearly the greatness of his qualities."[88] The decision was bitterly resented by Bradley, who continued until his death to claim that it was unnecessary.

Given the extent of the German penetration of the American front and Bradley's stubborn refusal to either relocate his Luxembourg City command post or to visit forward headquarters, Eisenhower felt he had no alternative. David Eisenhower wrote:

By the night of the nineteenth, a command transfer was inevitable and imminent. After Eisenhower's long, cold drive back to Versailles from Verdun, reports reached SHAEF describing an alarming deterioration in the Ardennes . . .

Word arrived that 10,000 [sic] men of the . . . 106th [Infantry Division at St.-Vith] . . . had surrendered, the largest battlefield surrender of American troops in the [European] war. . . . By midday the 101st Airborne at Bastogne had been in contact [with numerous German units] . . . opening the seesaw siege for the city . . . [and Ike] learned of the near capture of the fuel dumps at Spa, which Bradley had assured him would not be located south of the Meuse.[89]

When Eisenhower's British deputies, Strong and Whiteley, had finally convinced a reluctant Smith of the necessity to alter the command arrangements, the SHAEF Chief of Staff placed the recommendation before the Supreme Commander.[90] Eisenhower immediately approved it and personally phoned Bradley to tell him of his decision. With the SHAEF staff still present, Ike passed the order to his reluctant subordinate, listened to Bradley's protests, then said sharply, "Well, Brad, those are my orders."[91] This short conversation, more than any other action taken by Eisenhower and the SHAEF staff during the battle "discredited the German assumption that nationalistic fears and rivalries would inhibit prompt and effective steps to meet the German challenge."[92] It meant that Hitler's gamble had failed.

Ike next called Montgomery to inform him of the command change and "confirm that he now commanded two American armies."[93] Monty immediately set out in his typically thorough manner to regroup and reorganize the northern half of the Ardennes battlefield. A master of planning and attention to detail, the 21st Army Group commander had no equal in organizing a "tidy show." Moving Horrocks's XXX British Corps to blocking positions along the west bank of the Meuse River, he visited both of his new American Army headquarters to coordinate personally the reorganization.[94]

What Montgomery found at Hodges's First Army headquarters was disturbing. Hodges and his First Army staff were confused and disorganized, contact with subordinate units was intermittent, and the situation seemed to be rapidly spinning out of control. Moreover, it was then four days into the battle, and Montgomery was appalled to find that neither Bradley nor any member of his 12th Army Group staff had visited Hodges's command post to assess the situation or issue instructions, and the telephone or radio could not substitute for personal contact during such a critical time.[95] Hodges seemed to Montgomery to be on the verge of total collapse, and it took personal intervention by Eisenhower and Bradley to prevent Hodges's being relieved from command of First Army.[96]

Despite problems with Hodges and the First Army staff, Montgomery successfully brought order to the northern sector of the battlefield and effectively stabilized the previously fluid situation. Within days of the 20 December command change (appendix D), the Allies began to stem the German onslaught and take control of the battle. Unfortunately, Montgomery proved bitterly disappointing to Ike in carrying out the crucial counterattacks that Eisenhower had intended to use to destroy Hitler's last remaining mobile reserves.

His inability to trap the mass of the German panzer and grenadier units outside of their Siegfried Line defenses with well-placed, coordinated counteroffensives on the south and north flanks was perhaps Eisenhower's greatest failure in the Ardennes battle. Eisenhower's main intention was to launch early coordinated and comprehensive counterattacks of such scope and magnitude that the great bulk of German forces would not only be defeated, they would be trapped.[97] Eisenhower adopted this position from the beginning and clearly laid out his intention at the Verdun meeting of the senior commanders on 19 December.[98] His brief annoyance with Patton's dramatic announcement to launch an attack from the south of the salient in only three days was not directed at the early timing or premature nature of the assault, but only at its seemingly insufficient strength to accomplish Ike's intention to "bag" the bulk of the German forces. In the end, however, it didn't happen the way Ike and the SHAEF staff envisioned, and the German forces, though defeated, were not annihilated. Although Patton was true to his boast and launched his counteroffensive from the south in a nearly unbelievably short time, there came no corresponding counterattack from the north of the salient. Montgomery wasn't ready.

Despite Bradley's command failures and weak leadership to this point in the battle, Patton, his principal subordinate (indeed, his only subordinate army commander by this time), was fully capable of the task of driving a timely, armored-tipped assault into the southern flank of the German offensive. The battle-proven 4th Armored Division, along with the 26th and 80th Infantry Divisions, jumped off on 21 December from Arlon in an attack toward Bastogne. Three days later, Patton's XII Corps launched a similar attack along the right flank of the earlier one.[99] There was, however, no counteroffensive from Montgomery's command, even as Patton's troops drove steadily into the southern flank of the German offensive. Montgomery felt he had good reason to delay his inevitable counteroffensive: He feared the Germans had uncommitted units with which to continue their offensive (at least seventeen and perhaps as many as thirty divisions); he doubted that American units, smashed by the full weight of the German offensive, had the resiliency to shake off their initial shock and counterattack without a complete and methodical reorganization; and he thought that Manteuffel's 5th Panzer Army could easily contain Patton's southern flank thrust and be prepared to help Dietrich's 6th Panzer Army defeat any Allied counteroffensive on the northern flank.[100] Unwilling to commit troops to what he regarded as a premature counterattack, Montgomery continued his methodically efficient battlefield reorganization. "Sharply critical of Montgomery's overcaution," American commanders like Maj. Gen. J. Lawton Collins, aggressive commander of the U.S. VII Corps, pulled uneasily against Monty's restraint.[101]

Eisenhower also chaffed at Montgomery's slowness to launch a counterstroke. He could sense the moment slipping away when the two-pronged attack against the German salient would trap the bulk of German forces. Weigley reports that, when an increasingly frustrated Eisenhower heard an oral report that Montgomery was ready to consider a counterattack, he exclaimed, "Praise God from whom all blessings flow!"[102] Unfortunately, Ike's praise was premature; Monty had only agreed to pull Collins's VII Corps out of the line in order to allow it to *prepare* for a counterattack—he still wasn't ready for the real thing.

Weigley suggests that Eisenhower and Montgomery differed fundamentally on the issue of destroying the enemy forces in the Ardennes. Eisenhower was intent on using this unforeseen opportunity to crush the last of the German mobile reserves. Montgomery, it seems to Weigley, remained focused on his own scheme of leading a single Allied thrust to the Ruhr and beyond; defeating the enemy in the Ardennes was secondary to the larger issue of this long-pursued goal. The Ardennes fighting was, to Montgomery, only a means for achieving his quest of becoming the overall ground commander. Weigley explained:

> Montgomery was not thinking about the Ardennes in terms of an offensive. His whole interest was in eliminating the Ardennes involvement to permit a prompt return to the offensive in the north. . . . Montgomery sought a counterattack, not a counteroffensive; he would pursue a tactical victory and proposed nothing larger. . . . Eisenhower had something more in mind for the Ardennes than a tactical victory. . . . [He] wanted to exploit the opportunity created by the enemy in the Ardennes to destroy the German army west of the Rhine.[103]

Finally, on 3 January 1945, over a week after Patton launched his attack from the south, Montgomery's counteroffensive in the north began in earnest. But instead of being launched to cut off the enemy at the very base of the salient, the Allied attacks struck at the nose and waist of the bulge.[104] The poor road network near the base of the salient, the bitter winter weather, and the skillful German withdrawal (practiced, after all, countless times under similar conditions of weather and superior enemy forces on the vast Russian front) combined to limit significantly the overall "bag" of forces Eisenhower had hoped to achieve. It was not until 16 January 1945 that the northern and southern pincers linked up at Houffalize, Belgium—halfway along the length of the "bulge"—and was only on 7 February that the front line was returned to its original position of 16 December 1944.[105]

The Allied victory in the Ardennes was not as thorough and satisfying as it could have been, nor did it eliminate completely the last of the German mobile reserves in the West. It did, however, drain the *Wehrmacht* of precious resources of manpower, equipment, and fuel that could have been better used to slow the inevitable Allied offensives to the Rhine and beyond. It also changed the nature of the final Allied offensives against Germany, because it left a German vacuum and an American concentration in the Ardennes-Eifel region, encouraging Eisenhower to let Bradley's 12th Army Group conduct a major drive into central Germany and not simply play out the remainder of the war in limited supporting offensives guarding Montgomery's flank.[106] More than anything else, the Ardennes victory was Eisenhower's victory. Just as he shouldered responsibility for creating the conditions that led to the surprise German attack, so should he receive the credit for defeating it.

ANALYSIS OF BATTLE LEADERSHIP

The Battle of the Bulge brought out attributes of leadership in Eisenhower that have often been overlooked by his postwar critics and analysts. Some of his severest detractors, American as well as Allied, were surprised by Ike's decisive command and firm grasp of the mantle of leadership that began at the first moments of the Ardennes fighting. No mere vacillating delegator of authority—no genial but ineffectual "chairman of the board" who lacked strategic vision, as Ike's critics often maintained that he was—could have so quickly assessed the scope and magnitude of the German attack, then taken appropriate and immediate actions to defeat it as Eisenhower did. As D. K. R. Crosswell, Smith's biographer wrote, "Opening with portents of disaster, the Battle of the Bulge turned into SHAEF's finest moment."[107] The Allied commander most responsible for that "finest moment" was the Supreme Commander Dwight David Eisenhower.

THE SUCCESSES

Ike's decisive leadership during this battle could not have been as effective as it was, however, were it not for his creation, over the previous months of combat and preparation for combat, of a smoothly functioning, totally integrated Allied headquarters at SHAEF. It was this organization, manned by proven performers and led by Ike, that permitted Eisenhower the flexibility and responsiveness to assess and deal rapidly with the German attack. Despite SHAEF's poor showing during the logistics crisis of the previous summer, when it "proved incapable of responding to rapidly changing conditions,"[108] several more months of combat had significantly improved its responsiveness and effectiveness.

SHAEF was, after all, an evolving organization, created during an ongoing war, with unprecedented operational and strategic responsibilities. The Supreme Command's historian, Forrest Pogue, provides a summary of those headquarters responsibilities:

> In the SHAEF organization one finds the most ambitious effort made in modern times to control the military operations of Allies in the field and deal with political and diplomatic problems bearing on military campaigns. Not only did the Supreme Commander direct the military operations of one British, one Canadian, one French, and five American armies in battle, but he also acted as Theater Commander of more than three million American troops . . . and was responsible for the planning and executing of civil affairs and military government responsibilities in five liberated countries and Germany. His duties involved acting for the United States and Great Britain on crucial diplomatic issues. Both the Allied governments called on him for recommendations and advice as to the settlement of questions of political, as well as military, import. So great were [Ike's] tasks and so extended [SHAEF's] functions that some historians have asked whether or not such a burden should be imposed on a commander in another war.[109]

By the time the Germans opened their Ardennes offensive, Ike had created a "truly integrated staff" in which a staff officer could act "for the general Allied good" without regard for the petty national interests of the officer's nation of origin. Pogue asserts that "in [Ike's] insistence that no one should be able to determine when examining a decision of SHAEF whether it was given by a British or American officer"[110] rested Eisenhower's decisive contribution to Allied victory. In creating this instrument, Ike made it possible for his leadership during the Ardennes crisis to actually be decisive.

That decisiveness was the predominant characteristic of the Ardennes offensive and had the greatest impact on the outcome of the battle. Ike realized from early reports of the German offensive that it was "no spoiling attack"; this immediate recognition of the scope and strategic implications of the attack caused him to take one of the key actions of the battle—the dispatch of the 7th and 10th Armored Divisions to the threatened area. The timely arrival of these two mobile, powerful units at the two key road junctions of St.-Vith and Bastogne prevented the German attack from swiftly overrunning the towns and allowed the Allies to gain control of the rate of the German advance. Had the decision to dispatch the two units been delayed for even a few hours, it seems unlikely that the crucial road junctions could have been saved from being quickly captured.

It seems clear that if Eisenhower had left the decision to Bradley, the 12th Army Group commander would have deferred making it. Bradley erred badly at the beginning of the battle by assuming it was only a limited attack, aimed at disrupting his own offensive to capture the Roer River dams. Ike had to direct him to send the tank divisions to the Ardennes, and in the case of the 10th Armored, he very nearly had to give him a direct order because Bradley, dreading Patton's inevitable rage at having a unit taken from him, tried to demur. Ike's immediate, decisive action here was crucial to the early stopping of the German attack.

Further, Eisenhower's early orders to send the two airborne units to the Ardennes and to completely reorient and reorganize the Allied front from Holland to Switzerland were critical ones whose delay could have helped the Germans reach the Meuse in force. Although the immediate dispatch of all available reserves to the threatened sector was the obvious Allied course of action, it was because of Eisenhower's quick appreciation of the scope of the attack and his decisive, immediate action that total disaster was averted.

An important, often overlooked characteristic of Eisenhower's battle leadership during the Ardennes fighting is the impact of Ike's calm, reasoned, unpanicked response to the crisis. His personal example of steadiness and unflappability affected the entire SHAEF organization as well as his immediate subordinate commanders. His personal leadership was infectious and desperately needed in the early hours of the confusing and overwhelming attack. One need only contrast the positive impact of Ike's personal example with the negative impact of Hodges's panic at First Army headquarters to see the difference. SHAEF reacted superbly to the challenge of the German attack, while First Army headquarters was clearly overwhelmed. Isolated and stunned by the suddenness and power of the offensive, the First Army was very nearly combat ineffective for a time, regaining its bearings only after Montgomery's reorganization. Eisenhower's steady, optimistic personal example set the tone for the leadership climate within his command and created an environment for his commanders to achieve success.

Ike's firm grasp of the overall strategic situation and the quick realization of the significance of the German attack are other important aspects of Eisenhower's battle leadership. His strategic vision was crucial to his rapid response to the assault and was essential in assisting him to determine the correct reactions to counter the attack. Indeed, this aspect of his battle leadership is the single prerequisite to all the other demonstrated attributes. Had he not correctly perceived the true nature and scope of the attack, he could not have accurately determined the way to stop it.

Eisenhower's strategic vision not only recognized the extreme danger his armies then faced—he also clearly saw the unprecedented opportunity presented by the German attack. Throughout the fall Eisenhower had wrestled with the problem of concentrating enough combat power at some place along his extensive front to achieve a significant breakthrough. Indeed, one premise of the multiple axes advance strategy is that an outnumbered enemy cannot be strong enough everywhere to resist a breakthrough somewhere. The truly significant breakthrough, however, continued to elude him, because nowhere along the Allied line did the German forces seem weak enough to permit such a breach. Even if a breakthrough of the German front could be achieved, the enemy still possessed significant mobile reserves that could be hurled against the flanks of an Allied penetration to limit its success or thwart it completely.

Now, however, the Germans themselves had voluntarily pushed their last significant mobile reserves out from behind the security of the Siegfried Line defenses and into the open. Moreover, they were creating a salient into the Allied lines and would soon find these last, precious, mobile reserves surrounded on three sides by Allied armies. When the skies cleared, they would also be exposed to punishing air attacks. Such an opportunity seemed almost too good to be true. Eisenhower quickly announced that the theme of the Allied counterattacks would be to *trap* the German forces in the bulge salient. He wanted no repeats of Argentan-Falaise the previous summer, where thousands of Germans escaped the Allied trap.[111] With Patton already committed to attacking early from the south, Ike needed only to energize Montgomery to launch a coordinated counteroffensive from the north to eliminate the bulk of German mobile reserves remaining on the Western Front.

The discrepancy between Ike's intentions to destroy the German forces in the bulge salient and Montgomery's intentions to merely "see them off" illustrates the fundamental difference in strategic vision between the two commanders on this subject.[112] Although Montgomery and his supporters argued that his "single-thrust" plan to knife quickly through the heart of Germany to Berlin was the correct strategic plan to end the war rapidly, Monty's obsession with leading this final campaign obscured his vision of the opportunity presented to the Allies by the German Ardennes offensive. He was so preoccupied with gaining approval of his single-thrust offensive in the north (and receiving overall command of Allied ground forces) that he treated the Ardennes counteroffensive as a sideshow, to be finished with the least possible effort and expenditure of resources, thereby not detracting from his real priority—the final campaign into Germany. Montgomery's attitude after he assumed command of the northern sector of the Ardennes constantly frustrated Eisenhower's attempts to launch an early, coordinated counteroffensive. When he was finally ready to attack (not until 3 January 1945, ten days after Patton began his attack in the south),[113] it was too late to trap the mass of German forces. Ike's strategic vision in this case was 20/20, but Monty's myopic view blinded him to the strategic possibilities in the Ardennes.

Ironically, it was Eisenhower's unselfish appointment of Montgomery as commander of the northern sector of the Ardennes that was the most controversial and most significant manifestation of his overall leadership during the Battle of the Bulge. This decision, more than any other action Ike took during the battle (or, indeed during the entire war), proved his greatness as an *allied* commander, not merely an *American* one. It was not only simply the correct course of action for the Supreme Commander to take given the circumstances at that point; this transfer of command of the northern sector to Montgomery placed Eisenhower in a category by himself as a genuine "coalition commander." It defined Ike's leadership and revealed the depth of his understanding of the nature of the coalition warfare he was fighting. Nobécourt explains:

> Eisenhower took the decision on his own, merely reporting the matter to the Joint Chiefs of Staff in Washington, without asking for authorisation. . . . The American generals, who considered that they had been betrayed by Eisenhower, failed to take into account the timing of these various steps. They forgot, moreover, that Eisenhower's staff was truly "integrated," and that Whiteley and Strong were merely giving proof that in their view the interests of the Alliance outweighed any national considerations.[114]

Bradley railed against the decision in his memoirs and always insisted the command change was unnecessary. However, his weak initial reaction, his refusal to move his Luxembourg City headquarters to a location better suited to managing and coordinating the defensive phase and subsequent counteroffensive, and his failure to even make an attempt to visit First Army headquarters during the battle's first crucial days gave the Supreme Commander no choice. Further, when Bradley admitted to Smith that the command change would make sense "if Monty's were an American command,"[115] he effectively decided the issue in Montgomery's favor.

Forrest Pogue wrote, "Among the many burdens of the SHAEF commander one must list the problem of dealing with some of the field commanders," because of their "misunderstanding . . . of the nature of the war which was being fought under the Supreme Command."[116] This is exactly the point in the Montgomery-Bradley command change issue. Eisenhower was fighting a true coalition war and made decisions as a coalition commander, not as an American commander of coalition troops. Subsequent arguments on this issue by Ike's critics miss this crucial point, criticizing him solely from an American perspective. These arguments focus completely on what was best for the American commanders involved, or look at the results of the battle only from the American position. By so doing, these critics ignore the first rule of coalition warfare—team building and achieving consensus among Allies that will produce a plan "most likely to bring military success"[117] to the Alliance. When Smith briefed Eisenhower on the SHAEF staff recommendation to place Montgomery in command of most of Bradley's forces, the Supreme Commander never hesitated to make the change.

THE FAILURES

Even the best commanders, however, make mistakes in their battle leadership, and Eisenhower was no exception. His leadership during the Ardennes crisis, surely his finest hour as a Supreme Commander, nevertheless must be criticized on at least three major points: his warfighting strategy, his failure to predict the attack, and his inability to close the trap on the bulk of German forces.

Warfighting Strategy. Eisenhower's strategy to prosecute the war in France and Germany by attacking along several major lines of advance all along the Allied line was not a bad idea. Given the ever-shrinking size of the German manpower pool and the overwhelming superiority of the Allies' industrial production capacity, attacking an inferior enemy everywhere in the (reasonable) expectation that he will break somewhere is a proven war winner.[118] But Eisenhower's plan for prosecuting the war against Germany depended upon a continual superiority in manpower and a constant flow of replacements for the tremendous number of casualties such a strategy produces. He could not attack everywhere and at the same time expect to keep losses to a minimum. The American Army's decision to field only ninety divisions, however, risked Eisenhower not having the manpower necessary to make his military strategy work; by December 1944, the replacement crisis had forced Ike to maintain only a hollow shell defense in the Ardennes. By insisting on a strategy of general assaults all along the Allied line, Eisenhower created the very conditions that made the German Ardennes offensive possible.

Certainly, Eisenhower knew the U.S. Army's mobilization schedule and that, by the early months of 1945 at the very latest, no new Army divisions would be forthcoming. The obvious question then is: Why did Ike persist in a manpower-intensive military strategy when manpower would become increasingly limited? The first reason—and a vitally important one—was that the military strategy Eisenhower implemented of advancing along multiple axes was the one that had been approved by the Combined Chiefs of Staff before the Normandy invasion. Despite Monty's pestering to change that strategy, Ike was persevering in what had been approved by the Combined Chiefs. Any change in the approved military strategy—particularly to Montgomery's proposed "single thrust" which Ike considered risky—would require overwhelming reasons as justification to the Combined Chiefs of Staff. Still, the manpower crisis that erupted in the fall of 1944 might reasonably have provided Ike with those "overwhelming reasons" to make a military strategy change. The most likely answer as to why Eisenhower did not consider a strategy change is that Ike thought his strategy would win the war *before* his armies ran out of divisions and the pipeline bringing new divisions and replacements to Europe dried up. Eisenhower was far from alone among senior Allied commanders in believing that the German armies, defeated decisively in France the previous summer and brutally battered during the fall campaigns, was a spent force lacking any significant personnel and war materiel reserves to stop the Allied juggernaut. Many Allied commanders at all levels thought "one more big push"—or, in the case of Ike's military strategy, a general offensive featuring multiple "pushes"—would crack through the thin veneer of enemy defenses and open a clear way into the heart of Germany. Bradley's reaction to the surprise German attack likely expressed the opinion of most Allied commanders when the Ardennes Offensive hit: "I don't know where the SOB has gotten all his strength!"[119]

Failure to Foresee. Clearly, Ike and the SHAEF staff were completely surprised by the timing, location, and magnitude of the Ardennes attack. Although Eisenhower and his subordinate commanders were leaving the Ardennes vulnerable to an enemy surprise assault, they never really expected that German forces could mount so powerful and devastating an attack at this stage in the war. The soldiers of Middleton's understrength VIII Corps paid a stiff price in blood for the blunder.[120]

To Eisenhower's great credit, he never attempted to avoid any of the blame for the Ardennes surprise. He accepted all blame for the debacle, saying the fault lay with him and not with his subordinate commanders. Ambrose recorded that:

> Eisenhower accepted the blame for the surprise and he was right to do so, as he failed to read correctly the mind of the enemy. Eisenhower failed to see that Hitler would take desperate chances, and Eisenhower was the man responsible for the weakness of Middleton's [VIII Corps] line in the Ardennes, because he was the one who had insisted on maintaining a general offensive.[121]

Ike confessed his failure to Marshall in a 21 December cable, admitting to the Army Chief of Staff that "all of us, without exception, were astonished" by the offensive.[122] In his postwar memoir, *Crusade in Europe*, Eisenhower categorically removed whatever lingering doubt may have remained about his own responsibility for the surprise and the weakness of the Ardennes defenses by writing:

> The responsibility for maintaining only four divisions on the Ardennes front and for running the risk of a large German penetration in that area was mine. At any moment from November 1 onward I could have passed to the defensive along the whole front and made our lines absolutely secure

from attack while we waited for reinforcements. My basic decision was to continue the offensive to the extreme limit of our ability, and it was this decision that was responsible for the startling successes of the first week of the German December attack. . . . The fighting during the autumn followed the pattern I had personally prescribed. We remained on the offensive and weakened ourselves where necessary to maintain those offensives. This plan gave the German opportunity to launch his attack against a weak portion of our lines. If giving him that chance is to be condemned by historians, their condemnation should be directed at me alone.[123]

The Open Trap. Eisenhower's greatest failure during the Battle of the Bulge was, ironically, a consequence of one of his greatest leadership successes—the transfer of command of the northern sector to Montgomery. Ike's inability to energize Montgomery into a timely, coordinated counteroffensive from the north, and thereby maximize Patton's attacks from the south, allowed the Germans to shift their forces within the salient to oppose the Allied counterattacks most effectively. By the time Monty finally got moving, the skillful Germans were in a position to escape successfully.

Despite the early high hopes Eisenhower held for the complete destruction of the German forces within the salient, he had to settle for less than total elimination of Hitler's last mobile reserves in the west. It is clear that Eisenhower intended for Montgomery to attack much earlier than the Field Marshal eventually did, so that the bulk of German forces in the bulge would be trapped. As early as 20 December, Ike sent Monty a cable asking for his "personal appreciation of the situation on the north flank," with intention to "shorten our line and collect a strong reserve for the purpose of destroying the enemy in Belgium."[124] That same day, he sent a message to all three senior commanders (Montgomery, Bradley, and Devers, with information copies to the American, British, and Combined Chiefs of Staff) outlining his intentions regarding the Ardennes situation. In it, Ike said he intended to take "immediate action to check the enemy's advance and to launch counteroffensives without delay on each side of the enemy salient with all available forces."[125] For Monty's northern group of armies in particular, he directed that the Field Marshal "launch a counteroffensive against the enemy's salient," requesting the submission of a plan outline "to include strength, direction, and time."[126] It seems impossible that Montgomery did not understand what the Supreme Commander wanted him to do. Montgomery, the "Master of the Battlefield," would attack in his own time, in his own way.

Part of Eisenhower's problem must undoubtedly be the significant difference between the British and American styles of leadership and command. Under the British system, subordinate commanders are rarely given the freedom of action that is routine under the American system. While American senior commanders give their subordinate commanders broad, general missions and leave the details of accomplishing those missions to the subordinates, British orders often include the "how" as well as the "what." Surely by this point in the war Eisenhower realized this most basic difference and made allowances for it. After suffering through Monty's "deliberate" approach in Tunisia and Sicily; at Caen, Argentan-Falaise, and the Scheldt Estuary; and during MARKET-GARDEN (among others), Ike must have known it would require more than just stating his "intentions" to get Monty moving.[127] Why, then, not simply "order" Monty to attack? Eisenhower's refusal to "get tough" with Montgomery until it was too late to influence an early counteroffensive in the north is not only the result of Ike's preferred command style, it is due to the very nature of exercising allied coalition command. Eisenhower did not bark orders at subordinates and force them to his will. Although he could make tough decisions when necessary, these tended to be the solitary, agonizing, Supreme Commander decisions, such as pressing on with the Normandy invasion in the teeth of uncertain weather or the decision to remove two-thirds of Bradley's command and give it to an egotistical Briton. As an allied coalition commander, Ike led by reaching general agreement among all the participants, not by fiat.[128] This is why he was so successful as a coalition commander, as success in allied command requires a commander to build consensus carefully, delaying action until all parties are ready to commit. As a coalition commander, Eisenhower was constrained to wait until Montgomery was prepared to take the action Ike wanted. Had he tried to force Monty to do something he was not yet prepared to do, Ike risked jeopardizing the coalition by fomenting "confusion and debate that would . . . certainly damage the good will and devotion to a common cause"[129] that had so far characterized the Anglo-American coalition. In short, until Montgomery finally backed him completely into a corner and gave him no choice, Eisenhower had to content himself with restating his "intentions" in order to protect the coalition structure he had so carefully built over the previous months.

CHARACTER OF A COALITION COMMANDER

The Battle of the Bulge brought "out the steel in Dwight Eisenhower's"[130] character, and any assessment today of Eisenhower's battle leadership is quite different from the one some of his postwar critics created. His headquarters, SHAEF, was never a British-dominated, weak organization with the purpose to foil subordinate commanders' quests for decisive action. On the contrary, it was a totally integrated, cohesive entity that, by the time of the Ardennes offensive, had evolved on the battlefield into a highly effective organization with wide, unprecedented responsibilities for prosecuting the greatest allied war ever fought. The critics who have asserted otherwise do not understand the demands and requirements of prosecuting coalition warfare. Eisenhower, along with his able Chief of Staff, Smith, and other talented, dedicated subordinate staff officers, was directly responsible for its creation.[131]

Far from being weak and uncertain, from the very beginning of the Battle of the Bulge Eisenhower showed his true strength of character, and his battle leadership was notable for Ike's decisiveness and immediate action. He set the example with a calm, optimistic, opportunistic approach to countering the German surprise attack that significantly aided the Allies in putting together a coordinated defense and structuring a massive counteroffensive. Eisenhower demonstrated great moral courage when he took away two-thirds of his friend and West Point classmate Omar Bradley's 12th Army Group, in effect sidelining Bradley for the remainder of the battle.

Eisenhower's understanding of the demands of fighting a coalition war places his battle leadership high above that of some of his more highly praised subordinates, especially his difficult British Army Group Commander, Field Marshal Montgomery.[132] Any comparison of the two commanders' performances and character in the latter stages of the Ardennes, as Weigley has written, points out, in contrast to Ike, "the defects of character that crippled Montgomery as a coalition commander."[133]

Smith's biographer, Crosswell, has provided an excellent wrap-up of Ike's leadership and strength of character:

Eisenhower's strength rested not in the traditional realm of strategist or heroic leader but rather in his ability to handle people and avoid divisive problems. . . . Beneath the amiable "Ike" existed the hard-minded operator. . . . He did emerge . . . as an excellent choice for supreme commander. Indeed, it is difficult to imagine anyone better suited for the role. . . . Eisenhower's virtue as a commander rested in his ability to broker competing national, personal, and strategic sensitivities and susceptibilities. His role as coordinator—more political than military—obliged him to seek compromises rather than provide decisive leadership from above. . . . The one constant in Eisenhower's approach was the effort to preserve Allied harmony. . . . By all accounts he inspired those around him not by force of character but by his simplicity, his commonsense Kansas approach to men and events, and his naturalness and genuine sense of humor. . . . His chief duties involved the preservation of the integrity of the Allied command and the execution of the strategic decisions of the coalition. This required a set of intimate personal skills that gave positive substance to the rhetoric of Allied cooperation and teamwork. These traits Eisenhower possessed in profusion.[134]

Eisenhower was an outstanding coalition commander, one uniquely suited to exercise Allied command. When thrust onto the world stage in an unprecedented position, Ike made a complex coalition work effectively. His battle leadership of this coalition during the Battle of the Bulge is a masterful application of command in a difficult, demanding role. Ike led "the greatest Allied army in history" and won, according to General Marshall, "the greatest victory in the history of warfare." Overcoming "every conceivable difficulty incident to varied national interests and international political problems of unprecedented complications," Eisenhower triumphed.[135] Historian Martin Blumenson concluded: "America's greatest field commander in World War II, Eisenhower represented more than anyone else the new leadership and the new American role in world history. His achievement was great. His military stature assured."[136]

CHAPTER 3

Bradley and the 12th Army Group

On 20 December 1944, Lt. Gen. Omar N. Bradley—acclaimed as America's "soldier's general"—was, in effect, relieved of army group command for the remainder of the Battle of the Bulge by his West Point Class of 1915 classmate and good friend, Supreme Allied Commander Gen. Dwight D. Eisenhower.[1] On that day, British Field Marshal Bernard L. Montgomery was given command of all U.S. forces north of an east-west line drawn midway between the vital Ardennes' crossroads towns of St.-Vith and Bastogne. The command rearrangement gave Monty control of the U.S. Ninth Army and nearly all of the U.S. First Army. Bradley and his 12th Army Group staff were left with only shattered elements of one First Army corps (Maj. Gen. Troy H. Middleton's VIII Corps) and Gen. George S. Patton's Third Army—and Patton needed little help from Bradley to command Third Army.[2]

In fact, Bradley's serious lapses in leadership and command during the critical first days of the Battle of the Bulge had prompted Eisenhower's decision to sideline him. Frantically trying to stop the unexpected, powerful German offensive threatening to shatter his thinly held line in the rugged Ardennes region, Ike reacted decisively to Bradley's weak leadership by putting the good of the U.S.-British coalition ahead of friendship and national pride.[3]

Bradley, the man whom Ike would later call "the greatest battle-line commander" of the war,[4] therefore, spent the rest of the U.S. Army's largest and bloodiest battle of the European campaign stewing on the sidelines, bitterly resenting the fact that Eisenhower had replaced him with the irritating, egotistical Briton, the Allied commander Bradley most despised. In his memoirs, Bradley wrote that this was "the darkest of times" of his entire career and that "never in my life had I been so enraged and so utterly exasperated."[5]

Yet, three months after Ike benched him during the Battle of the Bulge, Bradley was promoted—upon Eisenhower's strong recommendation to U.S. Army Chief of Staff George C. Marshall—to four-star General rank.[6] Moreover, Bradley finished the war as field commander of the largest concentration of American soldiers in history (1.3 million men), his fame as the "soldier's general" and as one of the key architects of victory in the European Theater intact. Historian Joseph R. Fischer summarized Bradley's enduring reputation:

[I]n truth, no American field commander ever faced his challenges or possessed his knack for commanding the respect of soldiers. . . . To superiors, he was a loyal subordinate while at the same time a vocal advocate on behalf of his men. Ernie Pyle summarized the men who waded ashore at Normandy as simply "Brave Men," and so they were, made so by their soft-spoken commanding general.[7]

Chiefly due to that "soldier's general" and "greatest battle-line commander" reputation—and with his only real Army competitor, Eisenhower, opening the way by turning to a political career—in the post–World War II years Bradley rose to the pinnacle of military rank and command. He became U.S. Army Chief of Staff (1948–49), was appointed the first Chairman of the Joint Chiefs of Staff (1949–53) and, in September 1950, was the last U.S. Army general promoted to five-star General of the Army rank.[8] Bradley was "the last of the great World War II commanders" who "soldiered on for another dozen years as a living legend."[9]

But, during the Ardennes crisis, at the moment when Bradley's reputed loyal, steady, and reliable commandership was needed most, his leadership and character had failed the toughest test in combat that he faced in the entire war. How, then, should Bradley's failures in the Battle of the Bulge affect his popular image and lasting reputation? A critical examination of Bradley's demonstrated leadership in the Ardennes—indeed, a probing inspection of the key influences in his pre–World War II Army career and his wartime command prior to the Battle of the Bulge—is required to answer that question.

"GETTING THERE"

Historian Russell Weigley captured Omar Bradley's enduring popular image when he wrote that it was one of "Lincolnesque, homespun kindliness [that] readily inspired devotion"[10] among his staff, American soldiers, and the public at large. Indeed, Bradley's humble Midwest origins, self-effacing demeanor, and rise to high rank from an impoverished childhood evoke comparison to America's Civil War president. In truth, as Rick Atkinson points out, Bradley's carefully "cultivated image of homespun humility . . . was not so much wrong as incomplete; he also possessed an intolerant rectitude and a capacity for dissimulation" and "could be simple, direct and ruthless."[11] From the moment his Army career began, Bradley had his energies chiefly focused on "getting there"—achieving advancement and promotion.[12]

Preferring a Field Artillery or Engineer branch commission ("owing to the more rapid promotion" in those branches, he claimed), when he graduated from West Point in 1915 Bradley instead received his third choice, Infantry. He assuaged his disappointment at missing out on the branches that promised speedier promotions by telling himself that, as a member of the largest branch in the Army, an Infantry officer "has the best chance of reaching the topmost positions."[13] He elected to join the 14th Infantry Regiment in Spokane, Washington, in an attempt to avoid "the rough and disagreeable duty" on the Mexican-American border where many of his classmates were headed in response to troubles caused by Mexican revolutionary, Pancho Villa. The ploy didn't work, since the 14th was dispatched to the

border in 1916 where Bradley endured "miserable" conditions performing "routine and boring" duties.[14]

Like Eisenhower, Bradley never made it to France during World
War I, lamenting that his lack of combat experience meant that he was
"professionally ruined" and "could only look forward to a career lifetime of dull routine assignments and would be lucky to retire after
thirty years as a lieutenant colonel."[15] Yet, Bradley actually had a
chance to get some valuable combat experience in 1919, receiving
orders to take command of a 1,000-man U.S. Army unit and lead it to
Vladivostok as part of the Allied intervention during the Russian Civil
War. But this wasn't the kind of promotion-enhancing combat he
sought, and he was appalled at the prospect of "another miserable and
unhappy assignment." Bradley shamelessly ducked the Russia assignment, speciously using the cover that he was then on a list of officers
who could be selected—if called upon—to serve on a court martial
board, thereby avoiding the posting on a technicality. While his contemporaries, like future World War II Pacific Theater army commander, Robert L. Eichelberger, were leading American troops facing
attacks by swarms of Bolsheviks, Bradley taught ROTC students in
South Dakota.[16]

In fact, throughout his pre–World War II career, Bradley was more
schoolteacher than warrior. Following his 1919–20 ROTC assignment,
Bradley taught mathematics at West Point for four years (1920–24),
served as an instructor at Fort Benning's Infantry School (1929–33),
and returned to West Point in the Tactical Department (1934–36). He
explained, "In later years some writers would observe that I had the air
of a schoolteacher. . . . I was in fact officially a teacher for thirteen of
my first twenty-three years of commissioned service."[17] Bradley might
have added more years to his classroom assignments, as during that
time he also attended as a student the Infantry Officers Advanced
Course (1924–25), the Command and General Staff School (1928–29),
and the Army War College (1933–34). Although extremely pleased to
attend the Command and General Staff School because, he wrote, it
seemed certain to guarantee him "promotion to Colonel before retirement,"[18] he initially balked at War College attendance, fearing relega-
tion to low-ranking staff positions. He quickly changed his mind when

he discovered that the War College, in Bradley's words, "was beginning to carry weight in the selection of general officers."[19]

From 1919 until 1942, Bradley served in exactly one troop assignment—in Hawaii with the 19th (briefly) and 27th Infantry Regiments
(1925–28). Even that short stint with troops included a year as liaison
officer with the Hawaii National Guard, a job Bradley considered "a
dead end."[20] Bradley's most important interwar assignment, however,
had nothing to do with troops—it had everything to do with George C.
Marshall.

Bradley's acceptance of an offer of assignment to the Infantry
School faculty in 1929 was, he recalled, "the most fortunate decision of
my life"[21]—at that time, Col. George C. Marshall ruled the Infantry
School as Assistant Commandant, personally approving all assignments. Bradley served his first year as a member of the Tactics Section
and so impressed Marshall with his attention to detail that the next year
he was chosen Chief of the Weapons Section. Bradley considered Marshall's selection to be "the highest possible personal honor," and spent
four years at Benning, three directly under Marshall's observation.
Bradley was delighted when Marshall wrote him, "I very much hope
we will have the opportunity to serve together again; I can think of
nothing more satisfactory to me."[22] Given the dramatic impact it would
have on his career, it proved highly satisfactory to Bradley, also.

None of the officers that Marshall, as Army Chief of Staff beginning in September 1939, selected for senior leadership positions in
World War II benefited more from the "Marshall method" of personal
sponsorship than did Omar Bradley. Assigned to the Personnel Division of the General Staff in Washington, D.C., in 1938, Bradley was
transferred to the Chief of Staff's office at Marshall's request in 1939.
The next two years under Marshall were Bradley's trial by fire as the
new Chief of Staff mobilized his subordinates to exert superhuman
efforts to prepare an embarrassingly *un*prepared U.S. Army for the
coming war.[23]

Testing his carefully chosen subordinates by constantly challenging them with ever-increasing demands for flawless performance,
Marshall rewarded those who passed each test with promotions and
positions of greater responsibility. However, if any failed even once to

produce the results Marshall demanded, he usually cast them aside, replacing them with other names from his "little black book." Bradley passed Marshall's tests and in early 1941 got his reward.

In February 1941, Marshall chose Bradley as Commandant of the Infantry School. Most pleasing to Bradley, however, was that the assignment came with a promotion to brigadier general. He crowed that he was "the first man in my class to make it!" when recalling his feelings at pinning on the star.[24] At Benning, Bradley created the Infantry branch's Officer Candidate School and his successful leadership of the Infantry School led to Bradley's second star and command—in training—of the 82nd Division (for three months) and 28th Division (for seven months).[25]

Although slated to assume corps command,[26] Bradley was instead dispatched by Marshall to North Africa in February 1943. Bradley's West Point classmate, Eisenhower, had requested that Marshall send him a trusted officer to act as Ike's "eyes and ears," and had listed Bradley's name among a dozen officers that he would accept for the sensitive mission.[27] The debacle at Kasserine Pass, where Rommel's *Afrika Korps* had pummeled the II U.S. Corps (February 1943), exposed serious problems in American leadership and Ike needed help in evaluating what went wrong and how to remedy the problems.[28] Soon placed under Patton's command, however, the II Corps steadily improved and Patton convinced Eisenhower to assign Bradley as his deputy corps commander. When Patton handed over corps command in April 1943 to begin planning the Sicily campaign, Bradley replaced him and led II Corps in combat during the remainder of the Tunisian Campaign (ended 13 May 1943) and in the July–August 1943 invasion and conquest of Sicily.

"ZERO DEFECTS"

Bradley owed his famous reputation as the "soldier's general" to George Patton. Had it not been for Patton's egregious "slapping" incidents in August 1943 during the Sicily campaign, Bradley most likely would have finished out World War II as merely one among a large number of many other competent but mostly anonymous U.S. Army commanders at the corps or perhaps field army level. But, when the story inevitably leaked that Patton had slapped two hospitalized, shell-shocked soldiers—a story that Bradley initially had conspired to suppress—Eisenhower was desperate to redeem the Army's tarnished image amid the public relations disaster that Patton had created.[29] Ike used the power of the media itself to counteract the media firestorm—he sent beloved, highly respected war correspondent Ernie Pyle to "go and discover Bradley."[30] It was journalist Pyle, not the men whom Bradley led, who christened him "the soldier's general," but the nickname stuck. Therefore, when Patton "slapped" his way out of contention for the Normandy invasion's senior U.S. ground command that month, Bradley (suddenly famous and now battle-tested) was in the right place at the right time—and with the right nickname.[31] In a World War II example of what today is called "branding," the label "soldier's general" read much better in the headlines than "Old Blood & Guts" to the folks back home worried about the fate of their loved ones serving in combat.

On 1 September 1943, Marshall informed Ike of his decision to name Bradley as the commander of the American combat army for Operation OVERLORD, the Normandy invasion. His cable read, "Thanks for your generous attitude regarding Bradley. Have him make preparations to leave for England [and] tell him that he will head an Army headquarters and will also probably have to develop an Army Group headquarters. . . ."[32] On 8 September 1943, Bradley left Sicily en route to England. He had just over eight months to create the U.S. First Army and prepare it to enter battle on the beaches of France.[33]

Bradley's preparations for D-Day and subsequent invasion activities have been characterized as not overly bold but effective and workmanlike. He lobbied successfully for the inclusion of the major airborne operations as part of the invasion plan, despite British warnings that the risky undertaking could experience casualties of up to 70 percent.[34] Bradley is also credited with advocating (and getting) another American landing area—Utah Beach—to put, as Ike phrased it, "enough wallop in the initial attack."[35] Considering the bloody near-fiasco that V Corps experienced on Omaha Beach on D-Day, it was fortunate that U.S. forces had the additional landing area. Even more important than operational plans, however, was the selection of subordinate corps and division commanders, the choosing of the senior leaders to command the American effort. Marshall gave Eisenhower free rein in the final selection of these important subordinates, but Ike discussed each with Bradley and SHAEF Chief of Staff Bedell Smith. If any of the three disapproved, the man was rejected.[36]

Lt. Gen. Bradley, as commander of the First U.S. Army, oversaw the D-Day landings on 6 June 1944 from the bridge of the cruiser USS *Augusta*. While the news from Utah Beach was positive and optimistic, Omaha Beach looked bad. Bradley, feeling helpless on the ship, recorded his thoughts and actions:

> The whole of D-Day was for me a time of grave personal anxiety and frustration. I was stuck on the Augusta. Our communications with the forces assaulting Omaha Beach were thin to nonexistent. From the few radio messages we overheard . . . I gained the impression that our forces had suffered an irreversible catastrophe. I sent my chief of staff, Bill Kean, and [aide] Chet Hanson to the beach for a firsthand look. Their report was more optimistic than I dared hope for. The situation everywhere on the beach was still grave, but our troops had forced one or two of the draws and were inching inland. Based on their report, I gave up any thought of abandoning Omaha Beach.[37]

By that evening, Bradley had pushed 35,000 U.S. troops ashore on the two beachheads at a cost of about 2,500 casualties among the U.S. soldiers assaulting the beaches (most of these suffered at Omaha Beach). On the First Army's left, the British and Canadians had gotten 75,000 troops ashore, reporting 3,000 as casualties. Bradley moved his command post to Normandy on 10 June, D+4.[38]

Bradley's command of the battles in the Norman hedgerows and the subsequent breakout from the beachhead revealed a ruthlessness that belies his more benign "soldier's general" reputation. German resistance in the tough bocage country hedgerows proved surprisingly strong in the weeks following the invasion,[39] prompting Bradley to resort to draconian measures to produce even the smallest gains at an appalling cost in casualties. He ruthlessly relieved numerous regiment and division commanders, including one unlucky division commander whom Bradley sacked after only *four days* in command—shortly afterward, Bradley fired the unfortunate commander's replacement.[40] Bradley was especially ruthless with division commanders who were not personally touring front-line units, and he once relieved a division commander upon discovering him and his assistant division commander both in the command post at the same time—one of them, Bradley strongly felt, should have been at the front getting a firsthand feel for the battle's progress.[41]

Soldier-historian Daniel Bolger described the command climate Bradley created in First Army as one of "zero defects"—no mistakes tolerated—claiming that the "soldier's general" exercised command in a hostile and brutal manner. Bolger asserts Bradley's "zero defects" style was an understandable legacy of the man who selected him for command—George Marshall, a leader who "rarely granted a second chance." Bradley, and his successor at First Army, fellow "Marshall man," Lt. Gen. Courtney H. Hodges, relieved many more subordinates than "Old Blood & Guts" George Patton ever did.[42]

Numerous command reliefs, of course, did not evoke criticism from Marshall—nor did they from Eisenhower, for that matter. Anyway, by 1944 plenty of officers waited in the wings to take over where others had failed. However, Bradley's own failure at a critical juncture shortly after the Normandy breakout had a more significant impact on operations than did sending home in disgrace a few colonels and generals.

On 1 August 1944, the Third Army became operational in France under command of the now-rehabilitated George Patton. This caused the contingency for which Bradley's staff had been planning to implement—the activation of the 12th Army Group. Bradley's forces consisted of the First Army on his left flank (now commanded by Hodges), with Patton's Third Army on the right. Terrain, circumstances, and Patton's aggressive temperament combined to create a campaign characterized by a rapid, sweeping right wheel by Patton's army, and a slower, steadier sweep on the left by Hodges's forces. Complementing a British-Canadian advance on the Allied far left

(Montgomery's 21st Army Group), the American attack began to rapidly drive across France.[43] Along with the phenomenal success, however, Bradley's tentative leadership helped cause the failure in August
1944 to rapidly close the Falaise Pocket at Argentan, thereby allowing a
large part of the trapped German Army to escape. As a direct result of
Bradley's over-caution in closing the Falaise-Argentan Gap on the
retreating German army, thousands of enemy soldiers escaped to fight
again. When the German Mortain counterattack had collapsed on 13
August 1944, Patton's Third Army rushed to cut off the retreat by
advancing toward Canadian forces moving south from Montgomery's
21st Army Group. Patton boldly instructed his subordinates to drive
past previously established Army Group boundaries and make contact
with the Canadians to close the narrow enemy escape route out of the
pocket between Falaise and Argentan. But Bradley timidly counter-
manded him, ordering Patton to pull back and wait.[44] Although the
pocket became a killing ground for thousands of German soldiers as
well as a repository for nearly all that army's heavy weapons and most
of its vehicles, thousands more soldiers slipped through the gap and
joined the defenses at the *Westwall*. Included in these German escapees
were many of the higher-level unit staffs, key to rebuilding new units.
Bradley later admitted that "a golden opportunity had been lost," yet
insisted that the decision—and ultimate responsibility—"was mine and
mine alone." Less publicly, however, Bradley shifted the blame to
Montgomery for advancing too slow from the north.[45]

   In autumn 1944, after the dramatic sweep across France to the
German border spearheaded by Patton's Third Army, Bradley's battle
leadership again failed. This time, it cost thousands of the "soldier's
general's" GIs their lives and wounded thousands more. As German
defenses stiffened amid the mud and misery of Lorraine when the
Allied armies closed up on Germany's border, Bradley's bold attempt
to jump the Siegfried Line on the run was an ill-conceived, costly disaster. The densely wooded, strongly fortified Huertgen Forest, with
its primitive road net, was not an opportune area for a major offensive, yet Bradley pushed Maj. Gen. J. Lawton "Lightning Joe"
Collins's VII Corps into this nightmare because he overoptimistically
believed it could crack open the *Westwall* defenses. Eventually, six

entire American infantry divisions were chewed to pieces in the "Passchendaele with tree bursts," and none of them was totally fit for combat in time for the Ardennes offensive several weeks later.[46] Collins later seemed somewhat philosophical about the ordeal, saying that "someone had to cover that sector," and VII Corps got the mission.[47] Critics have rightly chastised Bradley for allowing six divisions to be destroyed in an operation that gained virtually no objectives. Bradley's weak counterargument was that no other area that could reasonably have been assaulted offered any better opportunity. Coming on the heels of Monty's September 1944 "bridge too far" disaster at Arnhem, it forced the Allies to regroup their forces in preparation for the final push into Germany. Meanwhile, several of the units broken in the Huertgen fiasco were sent to a quiet sector to refit—the Ardennes.[48]

ATTACK IN THE ARDENNES

When the German attack in the Ardennes began on 16 December 1944, the 12th Army Group's commander was much more concerned with the overall manpower shortage hobbling his armies than he was about the threat of an enemy breakthrough. Bradley later wrote that the "alarming crisis in manpower" totally preoccupied him, and "the possibility of an enemy attack through the Ardennes" seemed remote. Later that day, while Middleton's VIII Corps was reeling backward from the force of the powerful armored and infantry attacks against the overextended American lines, Bradley was motoring over icy roads to meet with Eisenhower at SHAEF headquarters to discuss the infantry replacement crisis.[49] Even when Ike's intelligence officer interrupted their discussions later in the evening with news of the German attack, Bradley was not alarmed. His own V Corps (First Army) had recently initiated an attack to seize the critical Roer River dams, so Bradley incorrectly assumed that the German assaults were in reaction to this offensive: "My initial reaction to these fragmentary and unclear reports was that von Rundstedt had launched a limited spoiling attack through the Ardennes in an effort to force Hodges [First Army] and Patton [Third Army] to slow down or pull back. I was not overly concerned."[50]

Eisenhower, however, sensed the seriousness of the assault almost immediately. The scope of the German offensive seemed to confirm to Ike that the enemy was capitalizing on "the badly stretched condition of our troops" that had existed for some time.[51] It was Eisenhower, not Bradley, who quickly ordered the dispatch of the 7th and 10th Armored Divisions to help bolster Middleton.[52]

The prompt dispatch of the two armored divisions—the 7th to St.-Vith and the 10th to Bastogne—was one of the most critical decisions the American command took during the entire battle. It is significant that Eisenhower—not Bradley—was the commander who initiated that decision, because it emphasizes the differences in the manner in which the two men conducted the defense in their respective commands. Ike seemed to grasp the developing situation immediately, to reach critical decisions quickly, and then to act forcefully to carry out those decisions. Bradley, perhaps indulging in some wishful thinking, was slow to comprehend the extent of his ruptured front, allowed Ike to take the lead in reacting to the attack, and initially seemed more concerned with placating Patton over losing 10th Armored Division than with stopping the German assault. Writing of the early hours of the Ardennes attack in his autobiography, Bradley admits:

> It gradually became apparent—Ike sensed it before I did—that this was . . . an all-out offensive by three German armies. . . . Urged on by Ike, who had correctly diagnosed the full extent of the danger, I made telephone calls . . . to order the 10th Armored and the 7th Armored to turn north and south, to close in on the base of the enemy salient. . . . We had been caught flat-footed.[53]

Bradley later claimed that he had feared a German attack through the lightly defended Ardennes and had discussed defensive reactions to such a situation with Middleton. He knew very well that Middleton's VIII Corps was spread much too thinly over the extended Ardennes lines but felt he could not continue offensive action in other sectors of the 12th Army Group (appendix E) if he gave Middleton any more help. Bradley referred to this situation as a "calculated risk" he was willing to take in order to continue the attack in other areas.[54] It seems obvious, however, that Bradley's "calculated risk" was never considered very risky by the 12th Army Group staff or its commander. The reactions of 12th Army Group and First Army to the German offensive show absolutely no evidence of any prior planning for such a contingency, despite Bradley's later claims. Perhaps equally telling physical evidence that Bradley had concocted his "calculated risk" excuse after the fact is that, in direct violation of SHAEF instructions, large supply depots, including huge amounts of petrol, were located directly behind the most threatened sector of VIII U.S. Corps' front. In truth, Bradley never thought the Germans would ever launch a strong offensive in the Ardennes region (or in any region, for that matter) and therefore Bradley's "calculated risk" excuse for stripping the Ardennes of the means of conducting a cohesive defense seems hardly credible when all hindsight is removed. It smacks of face-saving—after all, it is more acceptable for an enemy to call one's bluff than to be completely fooled by him. If his risk had indeed been as "calculated" as he later claimed, his reactions to the German attack surely would have been quicker, more aggressive, and initiated by the 12th Army Group, not SHAEF. Bradley was completely fooled by the size and location of the German offensive, and he reacted slowly.

It was Eisenhower who began the process of sending other reserve forces to the threatened area, but the number of reserves available was pitifully small. The XVIII Airborne Corps, consisting of the 82nd and 101st Airborne Divisions, was rapidly dispatched to assembly areas in the Ardennes—the 82nd to Houffalize and the 101st to Bastogne.[55] Their arrivals at the respective towns were timely; they just managed to beat the advancing German forces and secure the important road junctions against capture.[56]

The doctrinal response to the German breakthrough was no secret to the American command—hold the "shoulders" of the enemy penetration, give ground slowly, gather reserves for strong counterattacks to cut off the enemy advances—and SHAEF began immediately to carry it out.[57]

One key factor to successfully conducting this "doctrinal response"[58] was maintaining close and uninterrupted communications between units and commands at all levels. Bradley's headquarters, located south of the Ardennes and quite near the front lines at Luxembourg City, was in a terrible position from which to control the overall reaction of 12th Army Group. Yet, when Eisenhower suggested that Bradley relocate his command group to the better-situated Verdun, Bradley balked. To move his headquarters to the rear in reaction to the German assault "would be a sure sign of weakness—to the Germans, the Luxembourgers, and [his] own troops. A panic would ensue." Bradley told Ike, "I will never move backwards with a headquarters, there's too much prestige at stake."[59] While perhaps admirable in its brave attempt to maintain troop morale, this refusal to relocate led directly to the situation Bradley described as "the darkest of times" for his professional career—Bradley's relief from army group command for the remainder of the Battle of the Bulge.[60]

The location and momentum of the German attack split the 12th Army Group between St.-Vith and Bastogne. To the south, closer to Bradley's Luxembourg headquarters, was a portion of VIII Corps and all of Patton's Third Army. Remaining in the north of the expanding bulge was most of Hodges's First Army and all of Simpson's Ninth Army.[61] While Bradley and his staff maintained sometimes tenuous radio and telephone contact with all their subordinate army headquarters, only with difficulty could Bradley himself visit these locations physically for crucial face-to-face contact and coordination with his subordinate commanders, and he could not carry out personal reconnaissance of critical portions of the battlefield. Historian Russell Weigley, writing of Ike's command style, noted that "it is essential that a commander should be able to visit his principal subordinates, to feel the atmosphere at their headquarters and hold free and lengthy discussions."[62] Frequent visits to forward units and subordinate commanders had been such an emphasis of Bradley's command up to this point that it is inconceivable that he actually proposed to Ike that he could command the toughest battle to be faced in the European war solely by telephone and radio. Given Ike's experience in combat to date, it seems impossible that Eisenhower would agree to such a command-and-control arrangement.

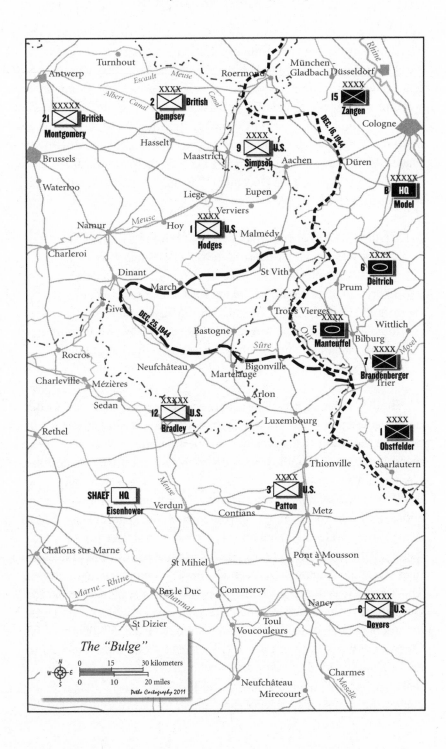

The "Bulge"

0   15   30 kilometers

0   10   20 miles

Petho Cartography 2011

Eisenhower, perhaps thinking back to the disastrous battle at Kasserine Pass in Tunisia in February 1943 and remembering the hapless Fredendall's failure to leave his command post and visit any unit, was not comforted by Bradley's insistence that he could adequately control his units in the north by radio and telephone. Ike, setting aside all issues of "national pride" as Supreme Commander, therefore placed Montgomery in command of all U.S. forces north of the St.-Vith/Bastogne split on 20 December.[63] Bradley raged at the decision in his memoirs:

> Giving Monty operational control of my First and Ninth armies was the worst possible mistake Ike could have made. Owing to Monty's caution and conservatism, it practically assured that we would fail to cut off the German salient with a bold thrust from the north. The enemy would escape in force as it had escaped from the Falaise Gap. We were going to lose a golden opportunity to destroy the German war machine.[64]

Bradley's concern that the command change would lead to the failure to completely cut off the German forces in the bulge appears to be more hindsight than foresight. At the time Ike gave Monty command in the north, Bradley was still trying to find a way to stop the German attack, not cut it off. Indeed, his outrage seems more the result of hurt pride than of missed tactical opportunities in future operations, as he did concede that he would not object to the change if 21st Army Group were commanded by an American.[65] The shift in command left Bradley and his 12th Army Group staff sitting on the sidelines while the American units under Monty's command and Patton's Third Army executed the maneuver portions of the battle to stop the Germans and eliminate the salient. To facilitate Patton's drive against the southern edge of the bulge, even the remnants of Middleton's VIII Corps, Bradley's only remaining First Army unit, were attached to Patton. Not the kind of subordinate who easily tolerates his superior looking over his shoulder, Patton and the Third Army staff accomplished the complicated shift of direction of the Army's attack and the difficult relief of Bastogne without assistance from 12th Army Group.[66]

The celebrated 90-degree turn of Patton's Third Army to attack into the southern half of the bulge was suggested by Patton, not Bradley. Patton, who had noted as early as 25 November that First Army dispositions invited a German attack, had ordered his Third Army staff to prepare contingency plans to counter a strong enemy thrust into the Ardennes. Once Patton noted the power and extent of the German attack, he realized it was the major enemy offensive whose possibility had concerned him. After rebuffing Bradley's early attempts to prepare to shift some Third Army units northward to help VIII Corps, Patton had reconsidered and finalized his own counter-attack plan by 18 December, presenting it to Eisenhower and the assembled commanders at the Verdun meeting the following day. Bradley, according to Weigley, "remained uncommonly impatient and irritable" at the conference, and allowed his aggressive subordinate, Patton, to do much of the talking for the Army Group.[67] Certainly it was Patton who took the lead in presenting his counterattack plan, and Bradley, apparently, was content to let him carry the ball by himself. D'Este wrote that Bradley "realized that the only principal players were Eisenhower and Patton" and that "Bradley's role was largely reduced to that of an observer; the battle was Patton's to mastermind and control."[68] Patton's "masterful design, masterfully executed" was a Patton–Third Army staff creation, with little credit owed to Bradley and his 12th Army Group staff.[69]

Despite the 20 December shift in Army Group boundaries, Bradley claimed that he "kept in close touch with Simpson and Hodges by telephone" throughout the remainder of the Ardennes fighting,[70] letting them know that he intended to return them to 12th Army Group command as soon as Eisenhower would agree. However, although the First Army returned to 12th Army Group on 17 January 1945, Simpson's Ninth Army remained under Montgomery's 21st Army Group command until nearly the end of the war, 3 April 1945.[71]

By the end of December, the German advance had been stopped— short of its objective of crossing the Meuse River—but Eisenhower's plan to cut off the bulk of enemy troops within the "bulge" before they could successfully withdraw from the salient failed to produce the dramatic result that he sought. Instead of pinching off the German salient at its base with a First Army attack from the north and Third Army striking from the south, "the two wings [met] in Houffalize, halfway down the length of the Bulge."[72] In his postwar memoir, Bradley blamed the failure on Montgomery's "stagnating conservatism"[73] that unnecessarily postponed the First Army thrust from the north side of the salient:

> Monty's penchant for tedious planning, the massive buildup and the "set-piece" battle were only too well known . . . it seemed to me that he talked like a man who had lost touch with reality. Every scrap of intelligence we had available . . . indicated beyond doubt that . . . Hitler's last great, ill-advised gamble had failed . . . Now was the time to hit back. Not three months from now.[74]

Bradley's protests, however, seem disingenuous. Written decades after the fact, they not only represent another self-serving criticism of Eisenhower's decision to place Montgomery in command of two-thirds of Bradley's army group, they ignore the fact that, as Atkinson points out, at the time "Bradley also favored pinching the enemy at Houffalize."[75] Certainly, Montgomery's failure to launch the northern pincer in a timely manner was a great frustration to Eisenhower, and the result resembled the Falaise Gap of the previous summer; again, thousands of German troops, this time with much of their equipment, managed to escape. Reorganized and reconstituted into new formations, they joined the defenses at the boundary of Germany and along the Rhine.[76] Yet, Montgomery's tardiness in launching the counterstroke from the north of the bulge[77] that only succeeded in angering Ike,[78] confirmed his original position that he could never support Montgomery as his deputy for ground operations.[79] The result also greatly benefitted Bradley, however, because Ike promptly returned the First Army to his operational control the day following the 16 January 1945 linkup.[80]

   Although the Battle of the Bulge was a trying and frustrating time for Bradley personally, the battlefield performance of units that had been 12th Army Group formations had, at times, been magnificent. Middleton's delaying actions with his shattered VIII Corps saved Bastogne and the southern shoulder. The 7th Armored's defense of St.-Vith and the stand of the First Army units on the northern shoulder effectively choked to death the German main attack. And Patton's rapid counterstroke into the southern flank of the salient to relieve Bastogne was masterful. Yet, each of these portions of the Battle of the Bulge was fought primarily as individual actions by the commanders on the scene with little, if any, assistance from Bradley and 12th Army Group.

ANALYSIS OF BATTLE LEADERSHIP

The commander who emerges from an examination of Bradley's leadership in the Ardennes fighting and the battles of France and Germany is a much more complex individual than the shy, farmer-boy image the Bradley legend perpetuates. There is abundant evidence that aspects of Bradley's exercise of command rest rather uncomfortably alongside his more benign popular image: He was known as a patient and supportive commander, yet he ruthlessly relieved subordinates in the Normandy fighting; it was claimed by Eisenhower numerous times that Bradley was always a "loyal team player," but he could be jealous and petty when dealing with his coequal Army Group commanders, Montgomery and Jake Devers; he was credited with bold, aggressive leadership in the OVERLORD landings, the St.-Lô breakout, and the drive across France, yet he proved to be overcautious and unimaginative in his timid control of the Brittany campaign, the failure to close the Falaise Gap in a timely manner, and in standing by while his GIs were slaughtered in their thousands in the Huertgen Forest debacle; he had the reputation of firmly backing Ike as a supporter of the Anglo-American alliance, but he reacted to Montgomery's expanded command of U.S. troops during the Ardennes crisis with resentment, hurt pride, and pique; and he could display a calm, steadying command presence who recovered quickly in the heat of battle, but during the Battle of the Bulge he completely misjudged the strength and location of the attack, displayed little initiative in moving troops to the threatened area, and reacted slowly in devising efforts to stop the German drive.

Any accurate overall assessment of the influence of Bradley's battle leadership on the Ardennes fighting and the campaigns of France and Germany must lie somewhere between Eisenhower's judgment that he was the war's "greatest battle-line commander" and Patton's condemnation that Bradley was an "insufferably orthodox . . . nothing."[81]

Bradley's greatest strength as a leader of large formations of citizen-soldiers was the ability of his "soldier's general" reputation to motivate and inspire the common soldier with confidence in the top-level leadership of the American Army. The tag line "soldier's general" seems entirely appropriate for a commander whose overall success, to a large degree, must depend upon convincing the 1.3 million soldiers in his charge that he really did care deeply about their lives and welfare. Once war correspondent Ernie Pyle christened Bradley with the nickname, it stuck to the point that Bradley was able to project that "soldier's general" image even when he was promoted to higher levels of command (First Army, then 12th Army Group) where interaction with the common soldier was rare. To his credit, Bradley continually visited units at or near the front lines during a battle, several times narrowly missing being wounded by bombs or shells.[82]

Bradley took pains to ensure that his troops didn't think he was wedded to his command post during a battle. He made sure his subordinate division commanders did the same, going so far as to relieve one division commander during the hard fighting in the hedgerows of Normandy when he and Eisenhower found both the division commander and his assistant at their command post at the same time during an operation.[83] Bradley regularly visited his subordinate commanders, even during the rapid sweep across France in the summer of 1944, refusing to let distance or difficult terrain keep him away.

It is inexcusable, then, and out of character when he broke from this pattern during the Ardennes fighting. Although his tactical headquarters location in Luxembourg City (designed to facilitate his control of Patton's upcoming Saar offensive) was isolated by the terrain and the German breakthrough, he never seemed to even try to overcome these difficulties to visit his hard-pressed commanders. When Montgomery visited the visibly shaken and nervous Hodges at First

Army headquarters on 20 December, he noted incredulously that "neither Army Commander (Hodges and Ninth Army's Simpson) had seen Bradley or any senior member of his staff since the battle began, and they had no directive on which to work."[84] Although Bradley claims to have kept in telephone and radio contact with all his subordinate headquarters throughout the battle, the telephone and radio cannot substitute for personal contact and on-scene observation of actual conditions.[85] In his autobiography Bradley tried to justify his failure to visit Hodges:

> I intended to fly to Spa that day [18 December 1944] to see Hodges and brief him on the change in strategy. But Hodges' First Army had been hit by the full weight of the Sixth Panzer Armee. Gerow's V Corps, as well as Middleton's VIII Corps, was under severe attack. Hodges himself was in the process of retreating, moving his headquarters rearward from Spa to Chaudfontaine, outside Liège. It became clear in several telephone conversations with Hodges and Bill Kean [First Army Chief of Staff] that part of the First Army was in a bad way. . . . Hodges was in no shape to mount a counterattack. It would take all of his planning and resources merely to hold the northern shoulder.[86]

Far from providing Bradley a good excuse for not visiting Hodges, these reasons seem to demand even greater energy on Bradley's part to get his calm, steadying presence to Hodges's side as quickly as possible. Had Bradley visited Hodges's headquarters during the first few days of battle, demonstrating to Eisenhower that he could effectively maintain personal control of all his units despite the German breakthrough, Ike would probably not have deemed it necessary to give Monty command of the northern half of the bulge. (Eisenhower and his chief of staff, Smith, had reacted negatively to the Monty suggestion when it was first made in the early part of the battle, yielding only when Bradley declined to move his headquarters.[87]) Bradley's excuse—that he could not move his headquarters to the rear during the battle without panicking the troops and the locals—seems to miss the point. The real issue seems to be not so much the location of his headquarters but where he himself chose to be during the battle.

As the fighting wore on and the Allied countermaneuvers began to develop, Bradley and the 12th Army Group staff became more and more superfluous in their headquarters at the southern half of the salient. The only major troop formation Bradley controlled at that point, Patton's Third Army, was attacking northward into the German flanks with little assistance required from Bradley and his staff. A few days prior, however, Hodges and his Army staff could have greatly benefitted from Bradley's calm leadership and sound tactical advice. In fact, Hodges kept insisting that Gerow, V Corps commander, continue his recently launched offensive throughout 16 December and into 17 December—an incredibly poor appreciation of the true tactical situation that could have proven disastrous for the defense of the crucial northern shoulder on Elsenborn ridge if Gerow had complied.[88] By disregarding one of his own basic tenets of battle leadership— regular personal visits to front-line units and commanders—Bradley not only jeopardized the cohesion of his defense of the Ardennes area but also undoubtedly precipitated the shift in command that so enraged him.

Bradley's battle leadership throughout his World War II commands—II Corps, First Army, and 12th Army Group—greatly benefited from superb subordinates. When he was supported by talented, aggressive division, corps, and Army commanders, Bradley's wise technique of "holding the reins loosely" proved extremely successful. Middleton, Manton Eddy, and Lucian Truscott, as division commanders in Sicily; Collins of the VII Corps in Normandy; and, of course, Patton in the sweep across France, are all notable examples.[89] And all contributed immeasurably to Bradley's postwar reputation as the Army's "greatest battle line commander" and a key architect of victory.

One alleged strength of Bradley's leadership during the campaigns of the Mediterranean and of France—his commitment as an Allied "team player" who firmly supported Ike as SHAEF's commander— was absent throughout the Ardennes battle. Bradley deeply resented the decision to give Monty command of his northern armies, despite his own admission during the battle that the logic behind Ike's decision was apparent—that is, he agreed with the necessity of rearranging the command setup, but only if an American took over.

The arguments Bradley uses to justify his opposition to Montgomery's assumption of command of the two U.S. armies seem especially disingenuous because they center around Bradley's supposed fear of Monty's unnecessary delay in launching a counteroffensive.[90] If, as Bradley claims, he held these misgivings at the time the change in command was made, then his failure to take action to firmly establish his own personal control and contact with his two armies in the north appears even more damning. Indeed, Bradley himself was not pushing Hodges or Simpson to organize a counteroffensive in the north at the time Monty assumed command, and it was Patton, not Bradley, who initiated the thrust into the southern part of the bulge. His arguments seem to be the result of damaged pride more than of any genuine fears held before the command change.

In addition, Bradley's criticisms seem even pettier because he fails to acknowledge the positive aspects of Montgomery's timely assumption of command in the north. Lacking Bradley's presence in the north (or any of his 12th Army Group staff, for that matter), Hodges, Simpson, and their subordinate commanders fighting desperately to stop the German drive welcomed Montgomery's arrival (along with his numerous and highly active liaison officers and other 21st Army Group staff). Brig. Gen. Bruce C. Clarke, who, along with the remainder of the 7th Armored Division, was conducting a magnificent defense of St.-Vith with no help or guidance from any higher headquarters, reflected that he was elated when the Field Marshal arrived on 20 December. Clarke and his division commander, Brig. Gen. Bob Hasbrouck, reported that Montgomery raised their own self-confidence and had a positive effect on the morale of their battle-weary troops.[91]

Although Monty has been criticized for emphasizing a "tidy show" too much over a rapid counterattack, it cannot be denied that he brought needed order and discipline to a confused and chaotic situation. By 18 December, Hodges's First Army headquarters was in a shambles, his staff having abandoned their command post in Spa in such a panic that Hasbrouck's staff, newly arrived in the sector to coordinate 7th Armored's opposition to the German assault and trying to find anyone from First Army who could give them information about the battle, discovered the deserted command post with secret documents and classified operational maps left scattered about.[92] Monty's presence (and that of his British XXX Corps units, which he positioned to guard the previously undefended Meuse River bridges) helped to remedy this panicky situation by steadying the shaken Hodges and freeing his staff to concentrate on the conduct of their defense. On the other hand, by allowing his personal pride to overcome his ability to act unselfishly as an Allied team member, Bradley had no positive impact on the northern defenses and the Ardennes outcome.

Bradley could show boldness and initiative in his battle leadership—and sometimes not. During the planning for the Normandy invasion, he was a leading advocate of a major airborne operation to precede the landings. This risky undertaking was opposed by many in the Allied camp, but Bradley's firm support of it convinced Eisenhower to let it proceed.[93] His willingness in July and August of 1944 to let Patton's Third Army race off across the French countryside, trailing a long, exposed right flank was also risky, but it helped the Allied armies get hundreds of kilometers and several weeks ahead of the preinvasion schedule.[94] And later in the war, when the 9th Armored Division presented him with the ultimate prize—an intact bridge across the Rhine at Remagen—Bradley exploited it.[95]

These successes, however, were counterbalanced by failures to capitalize on the possibilities they presented. After the Normandy breakout, Bradley seemed content to follow blindly the preinvasion plan to turn west and capture the Brittany ports, despite some of his more perceptive subordinates' urging to the contrary. He allowed his armored strength to be diverted to the west, into Brittany, instead of driving quickly east to attack the main enemy forces.[96] This conventional approach to the campaign unnecessarily delayed Patton's offensive. Later, after supporting the bold plan to swing Patton's army northward to trap the German Army in the Falaise Pocket, Bradley suddenly became more orthodox and tentative in his exercise of command and prevented Patton from closing the gap in a timely manner. This allowed a great number of the enemy troops to escape from the trap that Allied initiative had created.[97] In the Ardennes, initiative and boldness deserted him completely.

A weak argument can be constructed that Bradley's boldness was a factor leading to the early success of the German Ardennes attack, for it was partly because of his decision to hold the Ardennes with a thin line of worn-out or green divisions (his so-called "calculated risk" to permit offensive action in other areas) that allowed the enemy to crack American defenses. However, this theory presumes that Bradley's "calculated risk" explanation for the thinness of the Ardennes sector holds up to scrutiny—but it doesn't.[98] Bradley never really thought there was any chance the Germans would launch a mobile counteroffensive, and he certainly didn't think any German counterattack would strike the Ardennes. This time boldness was not a factor.

Once the German attack began, Bradley's battle leadership displayed no initiative at all. He allowed Eisenhower to take the lead in reacting to the German attack and was slow in getting his own headquarters into the fight. His principal subordinate, Patton, devised the bold counterstroke delivered by the Third Army, with Bradley content to let events sweep him along.[99] Although he was correct in letting his talented subordinate Patton execute the southern drive without interference from 12th Army Group, a bolder Bradley might have played a greater guiding role in its creation. If he had taken the initiative to visit Hodges, he surely could have assisted the overwhelmed First Army commander in sorting out a proper defense and would likely have avoided the galling command change. Despite Bradley's postwar harping on Montgomery's slowness to begin a counterattack in the north, it was Bradley's own lack of action that was a big contributor to the reverses. Had he displayed any aggressiveness and risk-taking, Bradley would have had a good chance of trapping the bulk of German forces in the salient. Instead, Bradley's leadership during the Battle of the Bulge failed to justify his inflated postwar reputation.

DARKEST OF TIMES

As a final insight into Bradley's demonstrated battle leadership during the Ardennes fighting, it is revealing to delve into his personal character, to examine the image of the simple farmer boy suddenly raised to fame and glory by fate and circumstance. Not surprisingly, much of this image appears to be more perception than reality. Bradley's simple beginnings notwithstanding, he emerges as a much more complex individual than the Bradley legend perpetuates. If his *A General's Life* autobiography is accurate, Bradley was concerned with "getting there," achieving rank and prestige, from his earliest days in the service. He describes his failure to get to France in World War I in terms of reduced promotion possibilities in future years[100] and actually turned down a combat command in Siberia because it offered no chance for advancement.[101]

He selected unit assignments for the sought-after positions they offered and accepted schooling if it promised chances of future promotions.[102] Bradley exults when he receives a plum assignment and is positively ecstatic when Marshall offers him command of the Infantry School in 1941 because it comes with a brigadier general's star.

Bradley's resentment of Montgomery's assumption of command during the Ardennes seems to be that of a man who has been personally humiliated, not that of an Allied commander who thinks Ike has made an error that will damage the coalition. Further, Bradley likely feared his relief from army group command—even a temporary one— placed his upcoming promotion to four-star rank in jeopardy.[103] Whatever his actual motivation, it is evident in his own and other witnesses' writings that the reassignment of his First and Ninth Armies to Montgomery was personally devastating to his pride and ego. The unconcealed bitterness in his autobiography bespeaks a man watching his career being destroyed, and when he writes in response to Ike's decision that "I prayed for the souls of the dead American GI's,"[104] the overdramatic imagery seems contrived and lacks sincerity.

Therefore, the failures in Bradley's leadership evident in the Ardennes fighting can, at least in part, be explained by his personal character—his shock and disappointment at having the bulk of his command given to a man whom he despised, because of an attack he never imagined would be launched.

Comparing Bradley's demonstrated leadership and character throughout his career, in the 1944–45 campaigns he led in France and Germany, and particularly during his "darkest of times," the Battle of the Bulge, provides ample evidence that the Bradley reality doesn't fit the Bradley legend. Yet, despite all of the evidence to the contrary, revising Bradley's reputation to fit the facts is a difficult, perhaps impossible, challenge. In the countless books and articles written about World War II that refer to Bradley, his name is nearly habitually paired with his "soldier's general" nickname—thus cloaking Bradley, deserved or not, in all of the positive images that label evokes. Indeed, even Eisenhower, who witnessed firsthand Bradley's failures in the Bulge, could still overrate Bradley's wartime accomplishments by writing this glowing evaluation to Marshall on 30 March 1945:

> [Bradley] has never once held back in attempting any maneuver, no matter how bold in conception and never has he paused to regroup when there was opportunity lying on his front. His handling of his Army Commanders has been superb and his energy, common sense, tactical skill and complete loyalty have made him a great lieutenant on whom I can always rely with the greatest confidence.[105]

A more honest and accurate assessment of Bradley's character and accomplishments in command of 12th Army Group is contained in Thomas Ricks's *The Generals*, his insightful examination of the evolution of American generalship from World War II to current operations. Ricks concludes that "during the war [Bradley] had run an unhappy headquarters, one that during 1944–45 had developed a reputation for 'irritable suspiciousness.'"[106] And regarding Bradley's enduring reputation as one of the architects of victory in Europe, Ricks points out that despite the "extreme advantages" Bradley's forces held over his German opponent—he "had more men than his foe . . . enjoyed a twenty-to-one advantage in tanks . . . [and] . . . overwhelming air superiority"—"Bradley took months to force his surrounded, outnumbered foe to capitulate."[107] Victor Davis Hanson wrote an even more damning indictment of Bradley's command of 12th Army Group: "Bradley's timidity and caution, passed off in the popular press as caring for the GI, would repeatedly—at Falaise, at the Seine . . . in the Lorraine, and afterward at the Bulge—bring on the most horrific fighting of the war in the winter of 1944–45."[108]

One reason why Eisenhower's exaggeration of Bradley's wartime performance has, in the decades following World War II, become the lasting "conventional wisdom" is the fact that Bradley's longevity served him well—it allowed him to elevate his own claimed accomplishments by getting in the last word at the expense of his two main rivals for fame in the European Theater. By the time of his 1981 death, Bradley had outlived Eisenhower by a dozen years and Patton by nearly four decades. Therefore, when he savaged both men in his *A General's Life* autobiography, neither was still around to defend himself or his reputation. Jonathan Jordan, in his one-volume triple biography of all three, noted that "the aura of his two more famous brothers in arms . . . gnawed at him when he pictured his place in history."[109] Jordan judged that the "thought that Brad's wartime legacy had become an appendage to the greater legends of Patton and Eisenhower whetted his feelings into a sharp resentment toward [Patton] and a muted contempt for Ike." He added:

> In the last full decade of his life, [Bradley] decided to set the record straight, as he saw it. Bradley's second autobiography— a work completed by his collaborator [Clay Blair] after his death in 1981—portrayed Eisenhower as a political wizard but a tactical bumbler who was better at directing a conference than an army. Referring to [Patton] as "the most fiercely ambitious man and the strangest duck I have ever known," Brad's postscript depicted George Patton as a deeply flawed, insecure man whose brief explosions of genius were bookends to long pauses filled with depression, egotism, and ineptitude. Physically and mentally robust until the day he died, Bradley claimed the last word in a story written over three decades of idealism, frustration, resentment, and mutual respect.[110]

It remains to be seen if Bradley will continue to be allowed to have the last word on his wartime leadership and accomplishments, or if historians will "set the record straight" by more closely and critically examining his battle command—particularly during his "darkest of times," the Battle of the Bulge.[111]

CHAPTER 4

Simpson and the Ninth Army

The fighting power of Lt. Gen. Omar Bradley's 12th Army Group was contained in the three American field armies deployed along the Army Group front (appendix E). Stretching nearly 200 miles, from Holland in the north, through Belgium and Luxembourg, then south to the Lorraine region of France, the long, twisting battle line was manned by nearly a million soldiers.[1] The three armies in which these soldiers served reflected, in many ways, the characters and personalities of their three very different commanders.

The First Army, the senior formation of the three, a "temperamental" unit that had "trudged across Europe with a grim intensity" through the summer and fall of 1944, was commanded by Lt. Gen. Courtney H. Hodges.[2] Commissioned from the ranks in the pre–World War I Army, Hodges was a battlefield hero of that war and a crony of Marshall from their Fort Benning Infantry School days. Described by Bradley as his "idea of the quintessential 'Georgia gentleman'" who was a "faultless . . . military technician,"[3] Hodges has also been described, less flatteringly, as "the model of a rumpled, unassertive, small-town banker," who allowed much of the day-to-day running of First Army to be conducted by his Chief of Staff, the "prickly" Maj. Gen. William B. Kean Jr. Under Kean's direction, First Army headquarters became "critical, unforgiving, and resentful of all authority but its own."[4]

The Third Army was commanded by the most famous of Bradley's subordinates—Lt. Gen. George S. Patton Jr. "Fiercely ambitious" and hungry for publicity, Patton created the Third Army in his own image.[5] Historian Russell Weigley described Patton's product: "At its headquarters . . . Third Army was a cavalry army, with movement and pursuit the passions not only of the commanding general but of the whole army command."[6] Surrounding himself with like-minded cavalrymen, Patton created a "noisy and bumptious"[7] freewheeling army that had "advanced further and faster than any Army in the history of the war" the previous summer. Unlike First Army, "Patton left no one in any doubt as to who was in command of the Third Army."[8] And also unlike First Army, it was Patton, not his Third Army Chief of Staff, Maj. Gen. Hobart R. "Hap" Gay, who controlled the unit's day-to-day operations and gave it its unique "cavalry army" personality.

The Ninth Army, the junior formation of Bradley's three armies, also reflected the personality of its commander—Lt. Gen. William H. Simpson. A "lanky six-foot-four, egg-bald Texan" with an ever-present smile, Simpson guided the Ninth Army from its inception and training through the campaigns of France and Germany. A West Point classmate of his more famous friend, Patton, the modest Simpson created an organization Bradley admitted "was in some respects superior to any in my command."[9] Ably assisted by his outstanding Chief of Staff, Brig. Gen. James E. Moore, Simpson skillfully applied the techniques, principles, and procedures he had been taught over the years at the Army's schools to build a unit that was a model of efficiency, organization, and staff administration. Simpson, described by Bradley as "big, bald and enthusiastic," earned for himself and his Ninth Army a reputation for dependability and disciplined duty performance that spread to the highest echelons of the Allied command.[10] Eisenhower paid Simpson a high compliment by reflecting, "If Simpson ever made a mistake as an Army Commander, it never came to my attention."[11] Ninth Army's smooth execution of even the most difficult assignments earned Bradley's praise that the "Ninth remained uncommonly normal."[12]

Each of Bradley's three armies and their much different commanders were deeply involved in the Ardennes offensive, and each army reacted to the German attack in a manner consistent with its unique character and personality. One of them, Hodges's First Army, bore the full brunt of the initial enemy assault and was sent reeling by the force of the offensive. The other two—Patton's Third and Simpson's Ninth—were called upon to implement the U.S. Army's doctrinal response for countering such a massive attack. This chapter examines the leadership of these commanders, with a greater emphasis on the "uncommonly normal" battle leadership of General Simpson.

SIMPSON'S CAREER

Born 19 May 1888—"the son of a Confederate cavalryman"—and raised in the north-central Texas town of Weatherford,[13] in the shadow of Fort Worth, William Hood Simpson developed a respect for the frontier values of hard work, determination, and a cheerful calmness in the face of adversity. Despite what would soon painfully emerge as extremely poor academic preparation, Simpson received an appointment to the United States Military Academy at West Point in 1905.[14] He entered the Academy that summer, joining the other members of the Class of 1909, including a "turn-back" from the Class of 1908— George S. Patton Jr. Patton and another member of the Class of 1908, Courtney H. Hodges, had failed mathematics during Plebe (freshman) year. Patton had been allowed to re-enter West Point with Simpson's class; Hodges, however, was not allowed to re-enter and he enlisted in the Regular Army as a private.

Simpson became a popular, well-liked member of the class and was noted for his good nature if not for his scholarship.[15] The 1909 *Howitzer* (class yearbook) describes him as "Cheerful Charlie," and the entry includes this description of his usual demeanor: "The slow cracking of that aboriginal visage terminates in a beaming countenance of good will that no glumness can withstand."[16] This outstanding trait would serve him well in later years and would be remarked upon by virtually all who worked for him.

After four years at West Point, during which his poor secondary educational background put him constantly in danger of failing,[17] Simpson ranked 101 out of the Class of 1909's 103 graduates.

Commissioned a second lieutenant of Infantry, he was assigned to the 6th Infantry Regiment at Fort Lincoln, North Dakota, following his graduation leave.[18]

In January 1910, Simpson accompanied his regiment to the Philippines where he saw some combat in the bloody, nasty, and confused fighting against the Moro insurgents.[19] He served with the 6th Infantry on Mindanao until posted back to the States in 1912. After spending two years at the Presidio, San Francisco, the 6th Infantry moved to El Paso, Texas.[20] In 1916, Simpson and his regiment, like many U.S. Army units scattered over the West in small, isolated posts, were dispatched to the Mexican-American border to deal with Pancho Villa's irregulars and the troubles caused by the turmoil of the Mexican revolution. From his base in El Paso, Simpson participated in General Pershing's Mexican Punitive Expedition into the Mexican interior, winning a promotion to first lieutenant on 1 July 1916.[21] Like his classmate Patton, Simpson saw some combat action in Mexico, as he had on Mindanao.

When the United States entered World War I, Simpson was still serving in El Paso. By spring 1917, however, he had been assigned as aide-de-camp to Maj. Gen. George Bell Jr., the El Paso Military District commander.[22] This fortunate assignment proved to be Simpson's ticket to France—and combat duty.

Unlike Eisenhower and Bradley, Simpson managed to get overseas and into the fighting when his boss, Bell, assumed command of the 33rd Infantry Division at Camp Logan, Texas, in July 1917.[23] Nicknamed the "Prairie Division," the 33rd Infantry Division was an Illinois National Guard outfit training at Camp Logan, filling its ranks with draftees and "enlisted"[24] men prior to shipping out for France. While the unit trained and prepared for its movement overseas, Captain Simpson (promoted May 1917) accompanied his division commander on a tour of the British, French, and American Armies in France.[25] This observation tour assisted him in his duties as commander of the 33rd Division's School of Arms from December 1917 to April 1918. Simpson escorted the division to Brest, France, in April 1918, and soon after attended the Army General Staff School of the American Expeditionary Forces at Langres, France.[26]

Major Simpson (promoted June 1918) gained invaluable experience during his unit's time in France, especially after assuming duties
as the Division Operations Officer in August 1918. He added immeasurably to his knowledge of high-level staff procedures by serving as
the division's Chief of Staff from the Armistice in November 1918
until he returned to the States in June 1919.[27] After serving the final
months of overseas service as a temporary lieutenant colonel (promoted November 1918), Simpson reverted to his permanent rank of
captain on 20 June 1920. However, the following day Simpson was
promoted a permanent major, where he would stay for the next four-
teen years.[28]

Simpson's experiences between the wars are similar to those of
most of his contemporaries and include a combination of staff, command, instructor, and student assignments. Immediately upon his
return to the States in June 1919, Simpson served as the chief of staff
of the 6th Infantry Division in Camp Grant, Illinois.[29] This was the
period of rapid disintegration of the large, wartime American Army,
and divisions like Simpson's melted quickly away in the pacifistic,
antimilitary environment of the times. By the time Simpson was
assigned to the Office of the Chief of Infantry in Washington, D.C.,
the Army barely numbered 150,000. Despite the Army's pitiful size,
the chiefs of the branches wielded considerable power and prestige.
Simpson's assignment to the Chief of Infantry's office, therefore, was
a significant and positive step in his career.[30]

After two years as an assistant executive officer in the Infantry
Chief's Training Section, Simpson was rewarded with attendance at
the Advanced Course at the Infantry School in Fort Benning, Georgia.[31] In those days, this course was a nine-month preparation for
promising infantry officers for future attendance at the Command and
Staff School at Fort Leavenworth, Kansas. An attendee at the following year's Infantry Officers Advanced Course, Omar Bradley,
described the Georgia post:

> Fort Benning—the Infantry School—was then a mere six
> years old . . . [it] soon grew far beyond musketry training. It
> evolved into the "home" of the U.S. infantry, a broad-gauge

school dedicated to the task of producing the best-trained infantry leaders in the world. In 1922, Congress decreed Benning a "fort," and . . . two years later, a massive construction program was under way. . . . The reservation itself was enormous—some 97,000 acres, about half that in valuable yellow pine, the rest open and suitable for military maneuvers.[32]

Simpson did well enough during his attendance at the Infantry Advanced Course to secure for himself a place at the following year's class at the Command and Staff School at Leavenworth; he reported for this year-long assignment in July 1924.[33] His class was only the second one-year course since the consolidation of Leavenworth's School of the Line and General Staff School the previous year.[34] Mark Bender describes the "Leavenworth doctrine" of warfighting in Simpson's era:

To avoid trench warfare, school doctrine directed strong and aggressive offensive action to envelop or penetrate enemy defensive positions. Follow-on pursuit required units to push both friendly and enemy troops to the limit to deny the enemy time to reorganize. Mobility and finesse were keys to the offense, rather than concentrated brute force, which required a greater investment of men and materiel. Surprise was also advantageous, because the attacker was able to choose the time and place of attack. While a commander in the defense could choose ground and buy time, doctrine considered the defense as a temporary expedient until the offense could be resumed. Furthermore, extended periods of defense forfeited freedom of maneuver and had a negative impact on troop morale.[35]

Learning this common doctrine was important to Simpson and his contemporaries, for it provided them all with a shared base of understanding and a "common language of war."[36] This common doctrine proved its worth in the campaigns of France and Germany in 1944–45 and was especially critical in assisting the American commanders to react to halt the German Ardennes offensive. The Army school system, epitomized in courses such as the Command and Staff School Simpson attended that year, was crucial to forging the battle leadership of the American commanders of World War II.

Following graduation, Simpson finally returned to troop duty and was assigned as the battalion commander of the 3rd Battalion, 12th Infantry Regiment, reporting to that unit in June 1925.[37] Simpson's battalion was then stationed at Fort Meade, Maryland, located in the sleepy, rural Maryland countryside between Baltimore and Washington, D.C. Six weeks after he assumed command, however, Simpson moved his battalion to Fort Washington, Maryland. Major Simpson assumed the additional duty of Post Commander when he arrived at the smaller post with fewer "tenant" units. He held this position for two years, then received orders sending him back to school again— this time to the Army War College.[38]

Major Simpson arrived at the Army War College in Washington, D.C., in August 1927. Along with him reported his new War College classmate, Maj. Dwight D. Eisenhower.[39] Although most officers would serve in later "academic environments," such as teaching positions at West Point or in ROTC, the War College was usually the last time these officers would be students.[40] Eisenhower's biographer, Stephen Ambrose, described the course Ike and Simpson attended that year as "a pleasant sabbatical."[41]

After graduation from the War College in June 1928, Simpson was assigned to the War Department General Staff.[42] His position was in the military intelligence division of the general staff in that division's Latin American section. The following year, in the summer of 1929, Simpson became the executive officer of the military intelligence division, a position held until he was reassigned in June 1932.[43]

Like his contemporaries in the small, interwar officer corps, Simpson drew an assignment as a professor of military science and tactics in a civilian university's ROTC unit. Also like his contemporaries, his tour was lengthy; he spent the next four years at Pomona College in Claremont, California. At the conclusion of his ROTC duty, Lieutenant Colonel Simpson (promoted October 1934) remained in an academic environment.[44]

Simpson returned to the Army War College in Washington, D.C., in August 1936, this time as an instructor on the school faculty. A year later, Simpson became the director of the military intelligence division of the War College faculty, capitalizing, no doubt, on his several years' service in military intelligence on the War Department General Staff. While serving in this position, he became Colonel Simpson, pinning on his eagles 1 September 1938.[45] During his four-year tour at the War College, the Army began its long road back to preparedness, as the war in Europe erupted, then threatened to involve other nations—including the isolationist United States. George Marshall and other men of vision started to rebuild America's military forces and rectify the nearly two decades of shameful neglect.

Simpson benefitted from the increasing size of the American Army when he was selected to command the 9th Infantry Regiment at Fort Sam Houston, Texas, in June 1940. Less than four months later he became a brigadier general, and with the promotion came an increase in responsibility. Simpson was transferred to Camp Wolters, Texas, to assume command of the Infantry Replacement Training Center.[46] By April 1941, training camps and division posts across the country were beginning to swell with draftees and volunteers as the prewar buildup got into full swing. Simpson must have continued to demonstrate outstanding performance of duty in his several assignments because in October 1941 he received one of the highest compliments a soldier can get—the two stars of a major general and command of a division.

Simpson assumed command of the 35th Infantry Division, then forming up for its initial training at Camp Robinson, Arkansas, in October 1941.[47] Continuing to build his fine reputation as an outstanding trainer of troops, Simpson began a rapid succession of training commands. From October 1941 until September 1943, he commanded the 35th Division in Arkansas and California, then the 30th Infantry Division at Fort Jackson, South Carolina, and finally the XII Corps, also at Fort Jackson. Each of these units was, for him, a training command—someone else would take them into combat.[48] Simpson, however, wanted to capitalize on his combat experience from the Philippines, Mexico, and World War I France. In October

1943, he began a command tour that would eventually lead him into combat, taking charge of the Fourth Army—later to be redesignated the Ninth Army.

TRAINING COMMAND TO COMBAT COMMAND

In October 1943, upon assuming command of the Fourth Army, Simpson received his third star and promotion to lieutenant general.[49] Simpson's association with the unit he would lead into combat actually began in San Jose, California, when he received command of the Fourth Army as another training outfit. But, unlike his previous three commands, Fourth Army headquarters was formed at double normal strength to permit the subsequent activation of a combat army. Simpson's Fourth Army was to be deployed to the European Theater in spring 1944, then used in combat as a follow-on unit to the cross-channel invasion forces.[50] Simpson couldn't have been happier—but there remained one hurdle.

Even though Simpson had formed, trained, and activated this Army, it was by no means a foregone conclusion that he would lead it into combat. As late as March 1944, Eisenhower, preferring seasoned combat leaders to promote to Army command, wrote to Marshall:

> [O]n the subject of providing us with battle experienced commanders. To take up first the question of next Army headquarters, I much prefer Simpson to Fredendall. I think it is possible that our coming operations [cross-channel attack and subsequent campaign in France] will bring to light some corps commander whose promotion to Army command might become obviously desirable. I am thinking of such prospects as Collins [VII Corps], Middleton [VIII Corps], and [Charles H.] Corlett [XIX Corps].[51]

Nevertheless, Marshall continued to support Simpson's presence at the head of the next combat army. The Chief of Staff did so not just because Simpson had proven himself to be an extremely capable commander, but also, apparently, "to assure generals who trained large formations in the states . . . that they did not face dead ends, that they were not altogether excluded from leading their armies into combat."[52] In addition to fulfilling his long-time personal ambition to lead a unit into combat, Simpson would be an encouragement to a whole class of officers. Eisenhower, admitting that the time available effectively precluded waiting for corps commanders to prove their mettle in the upcoming campaigns, bowed to Marshall's wishes. It seems fortunate that he did, for as Weigley noted, "In his army's first test in combat, Simpson began repaying Marshall's trust."[53]

The smartest thing Simpson did while preparing his unit for combat service was to select Brig. Gen. James E. Moore to be his Army's Chief of Staff. The relationship between the two men proved to be the key to influencing and directing the performance of the entire organization. Simpson and Moore had worked together in several units in the past and had a comfortable and effective working relationship. Simpson's biographer, Thomas R. Stone, described Moore as "an intelligent, thorough, dedicated and loyal staff officer [who] well complemented Simpson."[54] In return, Simpson "was careful to enhance Moore's position" by passing his guidance and questions through the Chief of Staff, and having him "sit in on his discussions with the staff officers" and commanders.[55] Stone says:

> [T]hey understood, trusted and admired each other. Moore usually could anticipate Simpson's reactions while Simpson gave Moore a great deal of latitude. Often while Simpson was in the field, Moore would issue orders in the Commander's name, then tell Simpson later. So closely did the two work together that in many instances it is impossible to sort out actions taken or ideas conceived.[56]

Simpson and Moore initiated the difficult process of structuring an effective organization through which to focus and direct the efforts of their army by establishing the tone and tenor of the unit early in its history. They built their team well, and, while an attempt was made to nominate officers from the Army at large, Simpson had Moore do much of the actual selecting as Moore knew the Army's younger officers. With very few changes, these officers served in their original

Army headquarters positions throughout the European campaigns. Mostly infantrymen, the men who made up the Army organizational structure began focusing their group effort toward the goal of preparing the Army for combat operations in fall 1943 while still a part of the Fourth Army's expanded staff.[57]

After organizing the staff, Simpson and Moore proceeded to train it to function in a manner designed to produce the best results in combat.[58] They rejected any trick ideas or those that promised to be only temporarily effective, preferring sound, proven procedures that gave a positive answer to the question, "Would it work effectively in combat?"[59] Simpson established the training of his staff as an early top priority task, and both he and Moore "made it a practice to monitor closely the training" of the staff sections.[60] During stateside preparations for overseas deployment, the army staff participated in highly beneficial map exercises lasting more than a month. This allowed for a number of problems in staff functioning to be identified and addressed. Such intensive training could not, however, identify or cover all the practical aspects of each staff section's broad scope of responsibility.[61]

Upon arriving in England in May 1944, a number of other problems were identified. Solutions were found by closely studying the manner in which other headquarters had approached problems, through reading their directives and procedures and sending staff officers on temporary duty with deployed armies to obtain practical experience.[62] This prompted the practice of sending observers from Simpson's staff across the channel to France (after D-Day) to gain firsthand experience in the way the deployed armies' headquarters were dealing with battlefield procedures. These observers, upon returning to headquarters in England, conducted night schools to teach the new procedures to other staff members.[63]

These visits to the already-deployed Army headquarters served also to emphasize to Simpson some fundamental differences in the three armies. First Army, probably reflecting its Chief of Staff Kean's suspicion and resentment of outsiders, would allow only Simpson and his chief of staff to visit his headquarters and staff sections. On the other hand, Simpson's West Point classmate, Patton, allowed anyone from Simpson's staff to visit his army—all were welcome at Third Army headquarters.[64]

Training of the staff did not end when the now-redesignated Ninth Army[65] moved to France and began combat operations in September 1944. The staff continued to reappraise and adjust working methods during the unit's initial combat operations, and later, any break in the action was seized upon by Simpson or Moore to refocus the organization on the ultimate goal by refining and aligning procedures.[66]

After staging and training in England for nearly three months, Simpson's Ninth Army headquarters moved to France on 27 August 1944[67] and entered combat on 5 September 1944. Units under Ninth Army command were the 2nd, 8th, 29th Infantry Divisions besieging Brest, and the 83rd Infantry Division and the 6th Armored Division guarding a long, exposed flank.[68] The Ninth Army assumed command responsibilities for combat operations currently under way in the Brittany peninsula, which included Middleton's VIII Corps assault on the fortified port city of Brest.[69] After a bloody siege, VIII Corps successfully captured Brest on 18 September, but was rewarded with only a smashed, unusable, rubble-strewn shell of a town. The German defenders had rendered the port useless for months to come. The fall of the fortress, however, ended the Army's combat operations in Brittany, and a shifting of units to the Allied front in Belgium began shortly thereafter.[70]

Although the Brittany campaign became controversial later because of the amount of precious resources expended, there occurred two incidents involving Simpson that shed light on his leadership and character. The first was his unflagging personal support to Middleton while the VIII Corps commander was deeply involved in the frustrating, unglamorous task of reducing the fortress at Brest. Although Eisenhower, Bradley, and others became impatient with the drawn-out siege, and pestered Simpson and Middleton to hurry and complete it, the Ninth Army commander was steadfast in his support of his harried subordinate. Simpson protected Middleton from harassment from higher command as much as he could and went so far as to assume personal control of the 83rd Infantry Division and 6th Armored Division to allow VIII Corps (his only corps headquarters) to concentrate fully on the siege.[71] The other incident occurring during the Brittany campaign serves to demonstrate the difference between Simpson and his classmate, Patton. Ricks writes that "Simpson liked to have his subordinate commanders publicly accept the surrender of German generals, giving them the credit and the appearances in newspaper photographs." In one such example, Simpson demonstrated his loyalty to subordinates and his non-publicity-seeking nature by refusing to personally accept the surrender of some 20,000 German soldiers—an event that promised extensive news coverage. Stone wrote:

> Simpson could have taken [the German] surrender personally, but he had chosen to miss the ceremony, for he felt that as representatives of the 83rd Division had made contact with the Germans and had handled the entire operation, [Maj. Gen. Robert C.] Macon [83rd Division commander] was entitled to the limelight. Such an action would not make the Army commander's name a household word, but it would help earn the loyalty of his subordinates. Thus, Simpson attended to Brest, while the newsreel cameras whirred at the Beaugency Bridge [site of the surrender].[72]

It seems highly improbable that Patton, given the same circumstances, would have taken Simpson's actions. A short time later, when Brest finally fell, Simpson repeated the gesture, allowing Middleton to accept the German surrender.

With the conclusion of the Brittany campaign, the Ninth Army began to move eastward to take up positions along the Allied front. On 2 October 1944, Ninth Army headquarters opened for business in a former teacher's college in Arlon, Belgium.[73] Located in the quiet Ardennes sector of the front, Ninth Army's portion of the line was eventually to be the site of the great German offensive two months later. The Ninth Army sector was manned by the 2nd, 8th, and 83rd Infantry Divisions and was generally the same area later held by Middleton's VIII Corps in December.[74] But Simpson's stay in the Ardennes proved to be short lived.

In less than two weeks, the 12th Army Group commander, Bradley, ordered the Ninth Army headquarters to pack up once more, this time moving to the far left flank of the American line—to Maastricht, Holland. Bradley, anticipating Eisenhower's eventual shifting of a U.S. Army to the control of Field Marshal Montgomery's British 21st Army Group, reasoned that the relatively green Ninth Army could more easily be spared than the veteran First. Bradley also perceived that Simpson's easygoing temperament made him a better choice to serve under the egotistical Montgomery. Certainly Simpson was a better choice than Hodges to survive service under the Field Marshal—and there could be no thought of Patton ever submitting to Montgomery's command. Bradley wrote that "Simpson and his staff had not yet been subjected to Monty's megalomania and were, on the whole, more diplomatic and adaptable."[75]

Before Simpson and the Ninth Army staff moved north, however, another incident occurred that demonstrated the commander's genuine concern for the well-being of his troops, even those who would soon transfer to another command. As Simpson prepared to shift his headquarters north, just prior to the approach of the wet, miserable fall and winter weather, he personally "directed the initiation of a massive supply effort designed to issue winter clothing" to the 83rd Infantry Division.[76] Even though he would soon leave this division behind to be looked after by another army, Simpson felt a responsibility to the men who had served him well. This kind of loyalty was appreciated by the men in the foxholes.

By the time the November offensive began on the sixteenth, Ninth Army was in position as Bradley's left flank unit. It consisted of two corps, the XIII and XIX, comprising the 29th, 30th, 84th, and 102nd Infantry Divisions, and the 2nd Armored Division.[77] This first major offensive for Simpson and the Ninth Army turned into an ineffective, plodding slog through the mud and misery of western Germany. The 102nd Infantry Division's official history describes the terrible conditions:

During an average year, rain falls . . . 15 days in November, but in 1944 precipitation was recorded for 28 days. This excessive rain and almost constant cloudiness frequently grounded our air forces. Overcast skies likewise reduced the small amount of evaporation that normally occurs, so that fields became bogs, foxholes turned into wells, trenches into stagnant canals. Vehicles were often roadbound. Unimproved thoroughfares quickly disintegrated. Artillery observation was reduced to short ranges; and infantrymen, directed to guide on various landmarks could not locate them in the mist and fog. Weapons were clogged and jammed with mud in spite of all precautions and always the troops were wet, miserable and cold.[78]

The weather was not the only enemy during this drive to close up on the Roer River. The German soldier, for the first time defending his Fatherland, took every advantage of observation and fields of fire that the open and cultivated countryside offered, fortifying each small town and village with trenches, mines, and antitank ditches.[79] By the time the Roer was reached at the end of November, Ninth Army was ready for a rest and a chance to recuperate before the assault crossings of the river were undertaken.

Ninth Army's role in the November offensive, which involved each of Bradley's three armies, has never received much recognition, being overlooked in favor of Hodges's bloody fiasco in the Huertgen Forest, or Patton's problems in Lorraine on Bradley's right flank. But the Ninth's fighting in this first real incursion into Germany was just as significant. Harold Leinbaugh and John Campbell, fighting with the 84th Infantry Division, described the terrible but typical combat during Operation CLIPPER, their regiment's attack to seize the high ground east of the Rhineland city of Geilenkirchen in the final two weeks of November 1944:

The three rifle platoons [of K Company, 333rd Infantry Regiment] had been thoroughly clobbered trying to advance beyond the chateau. The concentration of German firepower was absolutely overwhelming with its violence, surprise and intensity. Artillery fire, 88s and 75s from hidden tanks, and

120 mortars with apparently limitless supplies of ammunition hit us. Machine-gun fire whipping in from pillboxes across the Würm seemed almost an afterthought. The noise, the shock, the sensation of total helplessness and bewilderment, the loss of control, the sudden loss of every familiar assumption—nothing in civilian life or training offered an experience remotely comparable. The barrage went on and on. The company had lost the initiative and taken several quick casualties. Men scooped slit trenches in the mud; others grabbed cover wherever they could find it. Our new-boy illusions of the past two days dissolved in a moment.[80]

The horror of this kind of grinding combat continued into the first two weeks of December as Simpson's troops attempted to close up on the Roer River. Initially it was envisioned that this offensive would possibly drive on to capture the important city of Cologne and reach the Rhine. This optimism vanished in the mud and mire along the banks of the Roer River. Weigley's assessment of the Ninth's first combat performance stated, "Like Hodges' First Army, Simpson's Ninth had achieved nothing resembling a breakthrough."[81] But he also observed that "in its first major campaign, Ninth Army had advanced more rapidly" than First Army, "produced no major mistakes," and began to claim Bradley's affections as "the army he could count on."[82]

ATTACK IN THE ARDENNES

Bradley's decision in October to move Ninth Army to his left flank had put Hodges, not Simpson, directly in the path of the German offensive. While the Ninth Army was still rebuilding units and recuperating from its November offensive in the Rhineland, the First Army (appendix F) had already begun another corps-sized attack, launching Gerow's V Corps on 13 December to seize the vital Roer River dams.[83] Farther to the south, on Bradley's right flank, Patton's Third Army was nearly ready to launch its own offensive to close up on the Rhine. In the early morning hours of 16 December 1944, however, the carefully made plans of all three American Army commanders were radically altered by the three German Armies crashing into the Ardennes.

The main German attack, "Sepp" Dietrich's 6th Panzer Army, was carefully planned to hit Hodges's lines at their weakest point—just along the V Corps–VIII Corps boundary.[84] Lightly defended by scattered units of the 14th Cavalry Group, the point of attack was the so-called "Losheim Gap," the classic invasion route through the Ardennes region. Although termed a "gap," the 9,000-yard-wide corridor defended by the cavalry group was heavily wooded and only slightly less rugged than the surrounding Ardennes.[85] Just as Rommel's panzer division had done in the blitzkrieg of 1940 over this same ground, Dietrich's tanks and grenadiers overran their lightly armed opposition, driving west toward the Meuse River.[86]

To the north of the Losheim Gap, in the V Corps sector, is an area of high ground known as the Elsenborn Ridge. The desperate but successful defense here anchored the bulge's northern shoulder.[87] Units from Dietrich's attacking forces hit the U.S. 99th Infantry Division, forcing it back onto the Elsenborn Ridge and, ironically, placing the unit in positions better suited to halting the German attack. The 99th, like its southern neighbor in the VIII Corps sector, the 106th Infantry Division, was inexperienced and new to combat. But unlike the unfortunate 106th, the 99th did not allow itself to be surrounded and broken by the German assault. Instead, it joined with the veteran 2nd Infantry Division in executing one of the key defensive stands of the battle.[88] This important stand, however, owed little to the battle leadership of Hodges and the First Army staff.

Hodges and his staff were slow to recognize the German offensive for what it was, wasting precious time before responding to it. Concerned primarily with Gerow's V Corps offensive, launched three days before the German assault began, First Army refused to believe early reports of the size of the enemy attack. Historian Charles B. MacDonald, an infantry company commander during the fighting on Elsenborn Ridge, wrote of Hodges's reaction to the attack:

Full realization of what was happening in the Ardennes had been slow to come at headquarters of Courtney Hodges' First Army, located in the Hotel Britannique in the once fashionable watering place of Spa, the same hotel from which

Hindenburg and Ludendorff had directed the German armies in World War I. Because the opening artillery bombardment had knocked out most telephone lines to forward units, and because not all units resorted promptly to their radios, reports from some sectors were slow to come. Emanating mainly from the northernmost divisions, the first reports seemed to indicate only a local spoiling attack designed to upset the 2d Division's drive on the Roer dams.[89]

Hodges persisted in his mistaken belief that this was only a limited attack throughout the first day of the German offensive. Gerow, whose V Corps was discovering that its attack toward the dams had been preempted by the massive German assault, tried unsuccessfully to convince Hodges and his staff to call off the V Corps attack. Hodges, however, told Gerow that he "did not intend to dance to the Germans' tune" and ordered the attack on the dams to continue.[90] Receiving no orders to the contrary from Bradley's headquarters until late afternoon, Hodges insisted that Gerow continue to attack. Fortunately for the American defense of the Ardennes, Gerow and the 2nd Infantry Division's commander, Maj. Gen. Walter Robertson, disobeyed First Army's orders.[91]

Gerow, described by Weigley as "the epitome of the meticulous, painstaking staff officer,"[92] had no combat experience prior to assuming command of V Corps for the Normandy invasion. Considered by some to be a risk when Ike placed him in command of V Corps, Gerow had proven himself to be a steady, tireless, competent combat leader who "possessed an admirable feeling for the ebb, the flow, the portents of battle."[93] Gerow, along with Eisenhower, was one of the first of the American commanders to realize the German attack was a full-blown offensive, not a local counterattack. Yet, he could not convince Hodges (or Kean, the "gray eminence" at First Army[94]) that any attempt to continue his offensive was not only futile, it was dangerous. Continuing to drive east was only putting V Corps' neck further into the German noose, risking the loss of the whole corps. Hodges still stubbornly refused to recognize the true situation, so Gerow took responsibility upon his own shoulders and ordered Robertson to stop the attack. He ordered the 2nd Division's reserve regiment to move to back up the hard-pressed 99th Division, holding precariously to positions around the Elsenborn Ridge. At the same time, Gerow took another action that would have just as important an effect on the successful defense of the critical high ground—he directed all available artillery units to the threatened area.[95]

V Corps and, later, First Army artillery units, were critical to solidifying the American defense of the Elsenborn Ridge and holding the northern shoulder of the bulge. In the Army's official history of the battle, historian Hugh Cole assessed the overall impact of the artillery units in the north:

> At Monschau [near the eastern end of the ridge] the artillery stopped the attack cold, effectively narrowing the German assault front. In the 99th Division sector the division artillery held its ground until the close of the 17th when the V Corps artillery groupment at Elsenborn took over the fight with such a weight of metal that one infantry battalion was covered by a defensive barrage of 11,500 rounds during the night of 17 December. . . . The Americans fired about 1,255,000 artillery rounds during [the battle] and by 23 December had brought a total of 4,155 artillery pieces into action.[96]

This concentration of American artillery battalions on and behind the Elsenborn Ridge was not only crucial to holding the valuable terrain against the German onslaught, it was also instrumental in applying the Army doctrine for slowing and stopping the overall enemy offensive—restricting the attacker's mobility. Because the impenetrability of the Ardennes is largely due to its limited road network, denying the enemy unrestricted use of the roads by maintaining nearly continuous artillery fire on them was critical to implementing this doctrine. The massed artillery units positioned along the ridge maintained a torrent of shellfire on the 6th Panzer Army's advance, effectively choking it.[97]

By midmorning of 17 December, the second day of the attack, Hodges had finally begun to realize the full extent of the German offensive. He permitted Gerow to withdraw Robertson's forward regiments from their attack positions (Gerow had stopped the attack on his own initiative but had not yet moved the entire division) and sent them to join their reserve regiment and the 99th on the Elsenborn Ridge. Soon other reserves were rushed to back up the 2nd and 99th Divisions, and the vital high ground was saved.[98]

Meanwhile, Hodges's other threatened corps, Middleton's VIII, was in serious trouble just to Gerow's south. Like Gerow, Middleton suspected early on that the attack all along his thinly defended front was more than a local spoiling attack. By 1000 hours on 16 December, elements of sixteen different German divisions had been identified among the attackers, and the 14th Cavalry Group was disintegrating in the face of Dietrich's main attack.[99] Yet Hodges and First Army headquarters were as slow to come to Middleton's aid as they had been to listen to Gerow. Exacerbating Hodges's problem with VIII Corps was the nature of the German assault.

The attack of the 6th Panzer Army, striking nearly directly along the V Corps–VIII Corps boundary, was effectively splitting Hodges's First Army in two. From the Losheim Gap/St.-Vith area southward (the sector containing the bulk of Middleton's command), the area was being isolated from First Army control. This left Middleton on his own. Rallying his broken units and making the most effective use of his pitifully small reserve forces, the VIII Corps commander began to conduct a skillful and successful defense, holding the key road centers until outside help arrived.[100]

Neither Hodges nor his Army Group commander, Bradley, was responsible for sending the much-needed help to Middleton. First Army's contribution to the VIII Corps defense was to allow Middleton the use of several First Army combat engineer battalions in his makeshift delaying actions along the corps front, but these units were already working in the VIII Corps sector when the battle began, and it was Middleton, not Hodges, who initiated their use. First Army merely acquiesced to Middleton's appropriation of these valuable assets.[101] Additionally, First Army had no role at all in dispatching the units that became Middleton's greatest saviors in rescuing his defensive line—the 7th Armored Division (from Simpson's army) and the 10th Armored Division (from Patton's army).

More than anything else, it was Eisenhower's nearly instant appreciation of the scope of the German offensive that started the two armored divisions on the road to the Ardennes. Rejecting Bradley's conclusion that it was merely a spoiling attack, Ike directed the 12th Army Group commander to "send Middleton some help."[102] Bradley reluctantly did so at Eisenhower's direction, not "urging."[103] Bradley made two calls to get the two divisions moving on the roads to the Ardennes: one to his Army Group chief of staff, Maj. Gen. Leven C. Allen, and one to mollify a skeptical Patton.[104] Bradley also called Hodges at First Army and issued orders for him "to stand by to move other available divisions to reinforce the armor."[105] At that time, Hodges was still adamant that Gerow continue his futile attack to capture the dams. Perhaps it was Bradley's phone call that alerted him to the gravity of the situation, for by the next morning, 17 December, he permitted Gerow to forget the Roer dams and concentrate his forces on the defense of the Elsenborn Ridge.[106] Bradley's phone call to Patton, on the other hand, seems to have been a more difficult one. The 12th Army Group commander described the call in his autobiography:

> Patton scoffed [at the order to move 10th Armored Division]; he thought [as I had at first] that it was merely a spoiling attack and that Middleton could handle it. I was compelled to give Patton a direct, unequivocal order to get the 10th Armored moving. He did so reluctantly, logging: "Bradley admitted my logic but took counsel of his fears and ordered . . . the move. I wish he were less timid."[107]

Patton had been reluctant to give up his 10th Armored Division at first, but, once committed, he threw his Third Army staff into the fight with seemingly limitless energy. Patton had suspected a German offensive for the past several weeks, going so far as to order his staff to prepare a counterattack plan for Third Army along three possible axes of advance into a supposed southern flank of an enemy salient in the Ardennes.[108] By the time Patton met with Eisenhower and Bradley on 19 December, his staff had already begun the "masterful feat" of disengaging from Third Army's own offensive, swinging a large part of the army a full 90 degrees, and preparing to attack toward

Bastogne.[109] Although initially just as reluctant as Hodges to terminate his army's ongoing offensive, Patton and the Third Army staff proved much quicker at recognizing the need for action and much more adaptable at generating and applying combat power in stopping the enemy. Chester Wilmot, an ardent Montgomery supporter and therefore no fan of Patton, nevertheless praised the Third Army commander by writing: "There was no holding back on his part now [after 19 December]. He was not losing divisions; he was being given a new chance to fight and there was nothing he liked better."[110] Wilmot goes on to claim that Patton had no "equal on the Allied side in the rapid deployment of troops."[111] A keen observer of what was taking place at that time at Ninth Army headquarters to the north of the bulge might take issue with Wilmot's claim.

Whereas Bradley had been forced to order Patton to send the 10th Armored to the Ardennes, no such order was necessary in Simpson's case. Bradley's chief of staff, Allen, had notified Simpson of the need of the 7th Armored in VIII Corps' sector, and the steady, reliable Simpson had the unit alerted and ready to roll in record time.[112] The Ninth Army G-3 After Action Report for the first day of the German assault reads:

> On 16 December 1944 a major German attack began in the First U.S. Army zone in Luxembourg and Belgium. . . . Ninth U.S. Army immediately began to regroup its forces in order to release elements for movement to the south to aid First U.S. Army in holding the German advance. The 7th Armored Division was alerted on 16 December at 1745A hours to move south as soon as possible. An advance party departed at 1930A hours to report to the Commanding General of the VIII Corps. . . . On 17 December both the 7th Armored Division and the 30th Infantry Division were attached to First U.S. Army and started movement to the First U.S. Army area.[113]

Simpson's unselfish and competent battle leadership was shown continually throughout the European campaign, but no instance demonstrates those qualities of his command ability more clearly than the Ninth Army's response to the Ardennes offensive. During this critical time, Simpson was quick to appreciate that a team effort was desperately needed to turn back the German assault and, as John S. D. Eisenhower noted in his book, *The Bitter Woods*, "it was unnecessary to make personal explanations to . . . General Simpson" as Bradley had done with Patton.[114] Simpson and Moore began immediately to refocus their army's actions on applying the unit's considerable combat power to stopping, then countering, the German offensive. First priority was to get the 7th Armored Division to the VIII Corps sector.

As soon as Ninth Army headquarters received the call from the 12th Army Group to dispatch the armored division, the unit was placed on alert. Brig. Gen. Robert W. Hasbrouck, the 7th's commander, called the commander of his Combat Command B, Brig. Gen. Bruce C. Clarke, and ordered him to report to Middleton at the VIII Corps command post in Bastogne, explaining that his unit would be sent to follow as soon as road clearance was obtained. Clarke, who was just then about to depart for a much-needed weekend pass to Paris, immediately began the long drive south to find Middleton.[115]

Sent by Middleton to St.-Vith to rescue the crumbling situation at that key crossroad, Clarke's combat command arrived the afternoon of 17 December—literally with no time to spare, as the Germans closed in on the outskirts of St.-Vith.[116] Ninth Army's prompt reaction (delayed only by First Army staff's inability to get the proper road clearances in a timely manner)[117] saved the vital crossroads. Clarke's inspired defense of the town and surrounding area over the next week was, according to Weigley, "the battle . . . that bought the time required by Allied generalship to recapture control of the [overall] battle."[118] If Simpson's only contribution to the Battle of the Bulge had been getting the 7th Armored to St.-Vith in time to save it, he well deserved a place in the history books. As it was, Simpson and the Ninth Army contributed much more.

Simpson and Moore's early realization of the scope of the German offensive was similar to Eisenhower's. On their own initiative, they began to reconfigure the Ninth Army's defensive posture in order to send more badly needed combat units to the Ardennes. Shortly after receiving the call from 12th Army Group to send the 7th Armored south, Simpson personally called Hodges at First Army and offered to send him the 30th Infantry Division and the 2nd Armored Division as well.[119] Maj. Gen. Raymond McLain, commander of XIX Corps in Ninth Army recalled, "Big-hearted Simpson voluntarily offered Hodges [one of my divisions] to cover the critical situation developing at Spa [First Army headquarters], and I soon received an order to send the 30th Infantry Division through Spa to meet the oncoming Germans and to prevent the latter from swinging around toward Aachen."[120]

Within the first six days of the battle, Simpson had sent five full divisions to Hodges's assistance—two on the very first day, the third a day later. By the end of the tenth day of the German attack, seven Ninth Army divisions were in combat against the enemy.[121] Facilitating this, as Cole noted, was Simpson's unselfish spirit of cooperation and team play: "In many cases, the transfer of units would be accomplished in simple fashion by telephone calls and simultaneous agreement between the higher commanders concerned."[122]

Before the end of December, there were four infantry divisions and three armored divisions as well as twenty-eight nondivisional combat units from Ninth Army fighting in the First Army sector against the German main attack. This prodigious effort compares more than favorably with the better-known and much-heralded contribution by Patton's Third Army.[123]

In addition to sending the majority of the Ninth Army's combat power to the Ardennes region, Simpson and Moore reorganized and regrouped the remaining units in order to provide a viable defense along their long front. Shifting the army boundary southward to encompass the former sector of the First Army's VII Corps, Simpson now had an extended front of over 40 miles to defend.[124] In his characteristically well-organized and thoughtful manner, Simpson had his Ninth Army staff methodically "turn its thoughts from an impending drive across the Cologne plain and devote its energies to . . . cope with this threatening surprise move."[125] He continued:

> In a Letter of Instruction dated December 19, the Army had set forth detailed directives for the organization of the ground and defined defensive lines to be prepared by the corps.

Priority for work on various defensive positions was laid down and coordination between adjacent units provided. An engineer annex supplemented the general instructions with specific details in regard to mines, wire, and demolitions. Overlays showing the locations of vital highway and railroad structures were issued to corps, and priorities were established for the destruction of the installations if this should become necessary. In addition, the Army developed counterattack plans which included the use of the 5th Armored Division, which would be made available . . . if needed, and various British units whose operational control would be exercised from time to time during the ensuing month.[126]

Ninth Army reaction to the surprise German offensive does seem "uncommonly normal" when compared to the near panic at First Army headquarters and a command level "beset by conflicting pressures" at Third Army.[127] Simpson's remarkable ability to cause his army to react in what seems to be an ordinary manner in such an extraordinary situation is a great compliment to his battle leadership. His personal reaction to Eisenhower's decision on 20 December to place the Ninth Army and most of the First Army under Field Marshal Montgomery's command compliments Simpson's character and sense of duty as well.

Most American senior commanders below the Supreme Commander deeply resented Eisenhower's decision to give the egotistical British field marshal command of all Bradley's forces on the northern half of the salient. Bradley was outraged, writing later that it "was the worst possible mistake Ike could have made."[128] Patton, who probably despised Montgomery more than any other American general, suspected the move was due to "the machinations of the Prime Minister [Churchill]," and wrote disgustedly in his diary, "Eisenhower is unwilling or unable to command Montgomery."[129] Hodges, visibly shaken by the German attack and appearing to be on the verge of breaking down completely, barely escaped being relieved of command by Montgomery after the latter visited First Army headquarters the day he assumed command. He kept his job only through Ike's and

Bradley's intercession.[130] Simpson, however, was nearly alone among the senior American commanders in complying with Eisenhower's instructions to "respond cheerfully and efficiently to every instruction [Montgomery] gives."[131] Weigley records that, during the battle, Simpson sent the following message to Ike:

> I and my Army are operating smoothly and cheerfully under the command of the Field Marshal. The most cordial relations and a very high spirit of cooperation have been established between him and myself personally and between our respective Staffs. You can depend on me to respond cheerfully, promptly and as efficiently as I possibly can to every instruction he gives. . . . The Field Marshal paid me a visit and at his request I took him to the headquarters of my XIX Corps where I had all of my Corps and Division Commanders assembled to meet him. After all had been introduced to him, he made us a splendid talk on the present situation.[132]

Simpson's professional and straightforward attitude toward Montgomery and his willing obedience to the field marshal's commands stand out in stark contrast to his contemporaries' undisguised loathing and antipathy. Appreciative of this attitude, Ike later wrote a personal message to Simpson, thanking him for his outstanding leadership, noting "I have been particularly gratified to note that your relationships with our British friends, including your seniors . . . have been based on mutual respect and friendly cooperation."[133] Eisenhower, dismayed that Bradley's "12th Army Group was getting as difficult to work with as [Monty's] 21 Army Group,"[134] must have welcomed Simpson's refreshing attitude and been delighted to find a kindred soul.

After the German offensive had run its course and the three American armies had stopped the westward movement of the panzers and grenadiers, the campaign to reduce the bulge and return the front to its original position began. Both First and Third Army headquarters were heavily involved in this phase of the Ardennes battle; Ninth Army staff, however, had little impact on the counteroffensive. Although the majority of Ninth Army combat units continued to fight on in the First

Army area, they remained under Hodges's operational command until the battle ended. Simpson and his Ninth Army staff spent the remainder of the Ardennes battle protecting their wide front against any possible German threat to their area and also preparing detailed plans for their upcoming offensive—the Rhineland Campaign, to begin in February.[135]

First Army, under Montgomery's 21st Army Group, and Third Army, under Bradley's 12th, executed the Allied counteroffensive to reduce the German salient. Hodges, kept under tight rein by Monty, chafed under the field marshal's heavy hand until returned to Bradley on 17 January. Patton, now Bradley's only subordinate, fought his usual aggressive and successful battle.[136]

ANALYSIS OF BATTLE LEADERSHIP

Bradley's characterizations of his three army commanders, written later after years of reflection, seem extraordinarily appropriate descriptions of their three, very different approaches to battle leadership.[137] The Ardennes offensive served, like a magnifying glass, to enlarge these commanders' differences and point out exactly how their differing leadership approaches affected each of their armies and the outcome of the battle. The strengths and shortcomings of each man stand out, in many ways, as strengths and shortcomings of the overall American leadership in the European campaigns.

THE FIRST ARMY

Lieutenant General Hodges was overwhelmed by the German offensive that cut his First Army in two during the early days of the attack. The impact of the attack striking his forward units produced something akin to a physical shock to him personally, and his command reaction reflected it. Weigley reports that, when Montgomery visited First Army headquarters on 20 December, the field marshal "soon judged that under the strain of the battle Hodges was on his way to becoming one of the 'cardiaques' who used to frequent the spas now inhabited by the First Army," hinting to Eisenhower that Hodges might have to be relieved of command.[138] That Hodges continued in command of First Army is undoubtedly because of the intercession of both Bradley and Eisenhower. When Montgomery realized that he was stuck with Hodges, however, the field marshal couldn't resist taking the credit for turning Hodges around. On 23 December, Montgomery sent Ike an "eyes only" message reading: "Hodges was a bit shaken early on and needed moral support and was very tired. He is doing better now and I see him and Simpson every day. First Army is now reorganized and in good trim and we will fight a good battle up here."[139]

Bradley felt protective of the man who had taken over from him as First Army commander and was more inclined to excuse his shortcomings—especially now that Montgomery's assumption of command in the north implied criticism of all American senior leadership:

One important factor in determining [SHAEF's] position [to give Monty command in the north], I believe, was a sudden temporary loss of confidence in Courtney Hodges. Hodges had been under immense pressure for four days [by 20 December] and he was exhausted. He was not a man like Patton, who naturally radiated unbounded confidence and dogged determination. In fact, even in the most optimistic circumstances he had an air of caution. Now, as I knew, Hodges was sounding more and more depressed at a time when we needed Pattonesque bravado.[140]

Others involved in the desperate fighting in the First Army's area were not as sympathetic with Hodges's lack of strong leadership and firm control of the battle. Hasbrouck, commander of the 7th Armored Division, fighting fiercely to keep control of the vital St.-Vith area, became disgusted with First Army's lack of support (or even knowledge) of his hard-pressed unit. Years later, he wrote that "Hodges was a poor excuse for an Army Commander. He was too old and too frail."[141] Hasbrouck went on to write contemptuously of "how First Army HQ fled from Spa, leaving . . . top secret maps still on the walls," and how finally, in desperation, he "had to send an officer to find them."[142] It must be concluded that Hasbrouck and Clarke's masterful mobile defense of St.-Vith and the surrounding area was brought off successfully *despite* Hodges and his First Army staff, not because of them.

Further, the outstanding defenses created by V Corps on the Elsenborn Ridge and VIII Corps in front of St.-Vith and Bastogne were the direct result of the efforts of the local commanders and not those of Hodges and the First Army. In the case of Gerow's V Corps, Hodges's stubborn insistence that the attack toward the Roer River dams be maintained all through that critical first day of the German offensive seriously threatened the defense of the northern shoulder and nearly doomed Gerow's entire corps to being cut off and destroyed. It is true that the lack of reports from front-line units restricted the amount of information relayed to Hodges and the First Army staff; nevertheless, the commander on the ground, Gerow, had attempted to set them straight most of the day. That the army commander and his staff refused to believe Gerow's reports is an indication of how little faith and trust Hodges's staff had in the judgment of their subordinate commanders. Hodges's justification for his insistence on continuing the V Corps attack—"He did not intend to dance to the German's tune"[143]— sounds more like an excuse for his headquarters' well-known penchant for being "resentful of all authority but its own."[144]

Part of the confusion and lack of appreciation in Hodges's headquarters may be due to the absence of guidance or direction from Bradley's 12th Army Group. Out of his headquarters for nearly the whole day on 16 December, Bradley, too, was still unconvinced of the scope of the attack when he called Hodges later that day.[145] It is difficult to determine exactly what kind of signals Bradley gave Hodges in these conversations. Over the next several days Bradley did not see fit to visit Hodges's headquarters at all (although he contacted him by telephone several times during that period).[146] Wilmot records that Montgomery was justifiably amazed to note on 20 December that "Hodges had been left without clear direction. Since the German offensive began, [Hodges] had seen neither Bradley nor any senior member of Bradley's staff," receiving "only the briefest orders, many of which were out of date by the time they reached [First Army]."[147]

But there were other headquarters, at army, corps, division, and lower, who needed no detailed guidance from their higher commanders to instruct them on what to do during this critical, confusing time. First Army was Bradley's senior Army headquarters and, therefore, his most experienced, yet their reaction to the initial German assault was poor. Perhaps too used to having things their own way, the First Army commander and his staff were unable to adapt quickly to the changing conditions on the battlefield. Even later, after the initial shock of the enemy attack had passed, Hodges seemed to persist in an inappropriate response to countering the German drive.

Perhaps echoing Bradley's earlier refusal to move his exposed headquarters to the rear, Hodges demanded that no First Army unit be allowed to withdraw from positions already held.[148] Despite Montgomery's suggestions that he withdraw from some of the more exposed positions, Hodges refused to order a retreat. While holding fast was exactly the correct action for the units on the Elsenborn Ridge, it was suicidal a few days later for the 7th Armored Division's combat units who were trying to escape the German trap at St.-Vith. Having conducted a brilliant mobile defense of St.-Vith and the surrounding area for nearly a week, Clarke's combat command was now ready to withdraw to safety behind the Salm River. First Army (and XVIII Airborne Corps commander Maj. Gen. Matthew B. Ridgway) thought that Clarke should stay put and conduct a static defense like the defenders of Bastogne, an action sure to cause the armored unit's destruction.[149] Fortunately for Clarke, Montgomery stepped in this time and overruled Hodges and Ridgway. Clarke's division commander, Hasbrouck, later wrote that "Montgomery . . . saved us from Ridgway's crazy idea."[150]

First Army's successes during the battle are more the result of the initiative of its subordinate commanders and other units rather than its own. Gerow began the crucial massing of units on the Elsenborn Ridge, not Hodges. Without prompting from Hodges, Middleton requested the use of the First Army combat engineer units already in his area to flesh out his meager reserves. It was Middleton again who asked for the return from V Corps of Brigadier General Bill Hoge's Combat Command B, 9th Armored Division, which he used to bolster the defense near St.-Vith; First Army merely acquiesced.[151] Eisenhower initiated the timely dispatch of the 7th Armored Division to the

VIII Corps area before First Army even acknowledged that it was needed. And it was Simpson who called Hodges to begin the process of sending the bulk of Ninth Army's combat power to the First Army area. Weigley assessed First Army as having "a competent staff [that] needed a cool . . . and dominant commander."[152] Clearly Hodges was not that man.

THE THIRD ARMY

The battle leadership of the Third Army fares much better compared with the First Army—hardly surprising given the obvious abilities of its famous commander. Lt. Gen. George S. Patton Jr. was in his favorite element during the desperate, fluid, mobile warfare in the Ardennes. With his army situated well out of the path of the German attack, Patton accepted the "cavalry to the rescue" mission seemingly tailor-made for his Third Army—"a cavalry army, with movement and pursuit [its] passions."[153] Initially disappointed that his own offensive had to be cancelled, Patton warmed to the task when he realized he could now play the hero once again, driving his tanks to the relief of the "gallant defenders" of besieged Bastogne. He could hardly have written a better script for himself.

Third Army's rapid, 90-degree shift from its offensive facing east, to an attack into the southern flank of the German salient reflected both the strengths and weaknesses of an army built around Patton's personality. Weigley examined Third Army's staff and concluded:

Any weakness in Patton's staff lay less in individuals than in organization. It was occasional bursts of individual exertion and ability that had to compensate for the lack of a consistently effective organization, which failed to manage the day-to-day activities of the Third Army with the consistency of staff supervision in the First or Ninth Army. This absence of constant, detailed, untiring staff work at Third Army headquarters was at the same time a corollary of the personalized command that Patton exerted over his army in contrast to Hodges or Simpson. It was not Patton's design that his army should be directed by anonymous staff officers. . . . The Third

Army was commanded by George S. Patton, Jr., in person or through his Household Cavalry.[154]

The dynamic Patton could slash through the "staff inertia" normally found in large organizations, quickly imposing his will. If this over-personalized control of the Third Army was a shortcoming in some situations, it seems a definite strength in permitting the army to react rapidly to the German attack. Assisting in this procedure was Patton's prescient planning for just such a situation.

Admirers of the Third Army's rapid reaction to the German attack usually fail to appreciate the amount of prior planning Patton conducted in the days leading up to the decision to launch the Bastogne counterattack. Suspecting that the Germans were preparing an attack in the Ardennes region, Patton had already devised a counterplan to strike into the flank of such an attack. As early as November Patton became worried about the "static" VIII Corps front on his army's left flank, with its "newly arrived" or "tired units."[155] When Patton was briefed the week before the offensive began that "the Germans were possibly . . . concentrating forces opposite Middleton," Blumenson records "he set his staff to plan to 'be in position to meet whatever happens.'"[156] Third Army staff preparations "included surveying the roads and bridges" along likely counterattack routes the army might use.[157] When Bradley alerted him to the need to help rescue First Army, therefore, much of the staff work had been initiated.

Patton's proposal to "attack within a mere three days with three divisions,"[158] however, seems somewhat of a miscalculation of the actual scope of the German attack. As Eisenhower realized from the moment Patton made the dramatic offer at the meeting in Verdun on 19 December, three divisions would not be sufficient combat power to smash through the enemy's southern flank. As it turned out, "Patton's initial fast-moving narrow thrust . . . misfired."[159] Although one of 4th Armored Division's tank-infantry-artillery task forces actually entered Bastogne unopposed on 20 December, it was rapidly withdrawn back to the division's lines to avoid "a piecemeal commitment of [the] division."[160] Even so, Patton's initial three divisions were not powerful enough to force their way through to Bastogne. It required six divisions from Third Army's III and XII Corps, plus the remnants of Middleton's VIII Corps to finally lift the siege on 26 December.[161]

Weigley writes that although "the Third Army turn to Bastogne was effectively enough administered by the Third Army staff,"[162] the inherent weakness of Patton's style of battle leadership—his overpowering dominance of his staff—actually delayed the relief of the town. "Patton tried to do too much and thereby crowded his strategic and tactical vision with too many details," Weigley concluded.[163] By establishing himself as indispensable, Patton created his army's great strength as well as its principal weakness. While he could order (and get) sudden, rapid shifts in his army's focus, doing too much by himself could hamstring his staff's efforts. One of Patton's contemporaries observed that "Patton can get more good work out of a bunch of mediocre staff officers than anyone I ever saw,"[164] But this is more a critique of one of the principal drawbacks of Patton's style of battle leadership than it is a criticism of his staff. Although forced to work constantly in the shadow of "the Great Man," the Third Army staff "had individual members capable of rising to a demanding occasion,"[165] who, when allowed to do their jobs without undue interference from their army commander, produced excellent results.

THE NINTH ARMY

Lt. Gen. William H. Simpson seemed to blend all the favorable qualities of a sympathetic, inspiring leader whose Ninth Army staff operated as an extension of his own thoughts and will. The "uncommonly normal" functioning of Simpson's staff seems to be a textbook example of the procedures and techniques taught in the American Army's service schools. The healthy relationship between Simpson and the highly competent Moore produced a responsive, smoothly operating headquarters that seemed a model of staff organization and administration.[166]

Far from being disrupted and disoriented by the German attack (as the First Army was), the Ninth Army quickly adapted to the changing nature of the battlefield in order to bring the maximum possible amount of the army's combat power to bear on the enemy offensive. And while it was primarily the force of Patton's personality that got

Third Army quickly oriented on the Ardennes, Simpson's success in rapidly getting his divisions into combat in the First Army area seems more the result of his army's coolly efficient organization. When most other American commanders were wasting time worrying about their reputations when Montgomery assumed command in the north, Simpson was cooperating cheerfully with the British commander.

Of the three army commanders, Simpson seems to have been closest to Eisenhower in his appreciation of the scope of the German offensive. Hodges, certainly, was completely in the dark during the initial part of the German attack, only recognizing the danger after Bradley (on Ike's direction) alerted him. Although Patton correctly surmised that some kind of German attack was in the offing in the VIII Corps area, and planned accordingly, he seemed to misjudge the massive extent of the attack initially. His hurry-up counterattack of three divisions toward Bastogne was shown to be not nearly powerful enough to force a corridor and keep it open. Simpson, on the other hand, must have quickly realized the huge scope of the offensive, as his subsequent actions are those of a commander who knows that all his combat power will be necessary to stop it.[167]

That Ninth Army's seven divisions and twenty-eight nondivisional combat units were instrumental in stopping, then defeating the German offensive is obvious in retrospect. The stand of Ninth Army's 7th Armored Division at St.-Vith is, by itself, reason enough to heap praise on Simpson's units. It is also significant that Simpson surmised the necessity of sending his units south before Hodges even asked for them. It was Simpson, on his own initiative, who called Hodges and offered his units; and the Ninth Army commander, unlike the "headstrong" Third Army commander, needed no personal appeal from Bradley to get his armored division moving to Hodges's aid. Once Eisenhower directed the 7th Armored be sent to help Middleton, Simpson began action on his own to speed his other combat units to the threatened area. And, despite Patton's prior planning and admirably rapid shift of focus, Simpson actually got more Ninth Army units into combat than did the Third Army—and faster as well.[168]

It is primarily Simpson's personal nature that has prevented recognition of his army's significant achievements in the Battle of the

Bulge (and Ninth Army's outstanding performance throughout the remainder of the war). Selfless and steady, Simpson placed teamwork and mission accomplishment above publicity and personal recognition. Had he sought the limelight, like the better-known Patton, or had he been more colorful, it seems highly probable that Ninth Army's significant accomplishments would have been more widely reported. As it was, by the time Simpson and the Ninth Army became operational in Europe and began to achieve significant successes, there seemed to be only one army commander and only one army to stir the war correspondents' imagination and generate headlines—George Patton and his Third Army. Simpson, who seemed actively to avoid publicity, remained in the background, identified in reporters' dispatches as "the Ninth Army commander" and rarely by name. This contrasts to the reporters' habit of virtually always referring to Patton's unit as "Patton's Third Army."[169] To Simpson, such personal recognition was unnecessary.

Simpson's ability to get his combat power into action during the Ardennes offensive while simultaneously shifting his army boundary and establishing a cohesive defense of a longer, thinner front must be credited to the superior performance of the Ninth Army staff—clearly the best organized, most effective staff of any army in the theater. The amazement with which the Ninth Army's consistently normal operation, even in times of crisis, was observed is eloquent testimony of its preeminence. The command climate in Ninth Army headquarters created by Simpson and Moore established the kind of staff organization and functioning that produced these outstanding results.

In contrast, First Army was, at heart, "an unhappy headquarters."[170] Weigley wrote that "the prickly General Hodges presided over a staff headed by the prickly General Kean, and over an army so accustomed to being first in priority . . . that First Army headquarters treated primacy as a natural right."[171] Such a command climate creates a staff attitude hardly suited to rapidly adapting to reverses like the German attack in the Ardennes, but it does help explain Hodges's reluctance to believe Gerow's sound advice to stop the Roer dams attack. Third Army, incapable of maintaining a "consistently effective organization,"[172] could manage to produce brilliant feats in the short run, such as the dramatic 90-degree shift, but it could sometimes be hobbled by Patton's personalized, heavy-handed control over the long run. Neither the First nor Third Army could match the day-to-day efficiency and effectiveness of the Ninth Army. Their operations during the Ardennes offensive clearly bring this out. Simpson's operations officer credits his army commander for why the Ninth Army staff worked so well:

> General Simpson's genius lay in his characteristic manner, his command presence, his ability to listen, his unfailing use of his staff to check things out before making decisions, and his way of making all hands feel that they were important to him and to the Army. . . . I have never known a commander to make better use of his staff than General Simpson.[173]

Ninth Army's success in all its operations, including the Battle of the Bulge, is directly attributable to Simpson's ability to form, train, and direct his team toward its well-defined goal.

The battle leadership displayed by Patton, and, most notably, Simpson reflected many of the strengths that seem common to the best American combat leadership during the European campaign:

- A calm steadfastness under pressure.
- A nearly instinctive appreciation of the situation and what it required.
- An aggressive spirit that demanded offensive action.
- An understanding of the importance of tactical mobility.
- An ability to focus overwhelming firepower on a threat.
- A sound education in a common doctrine of warfare that allowed the rapid coordination of the combat power of several commands.

The reaction of the army commanders contained all of these to greater or lesser degrees. Their combined application of the "doctrinal response" required by the massive German attack in the Ardennes effectively doomed the enemy offensive within days of its commencement. Certainly the nearly instantaneous responsiveness of Patton and Simpson in rushing reinforcements to the First Army area was decisive to the outcome of the battle, condemning the Germans to failure even as they continued to gain ground.

There were also shortcomings in the battle leadership, particularly prevalent in the First Army's reactions:

- A failure to predict the timing and location of the massive assault.
- A stubborn resistance to alter existing plans when confronted with a changing battlefield situation.
- A slow appreciation of the scope of the enemy offensive; an attitude that prohibited any tactical withdrawal, even when warranted.
- A dangerous anti-Montgomery jealousy that put "American" interests above "Allied" ones.

THE "UNCOMMONLY NORMAL" NINTH ARMY

When measured against all these strengths and shortcomings, it is clear that Simpson's "uncommonly normal" Ninth Army fares best. It could be argued that, because the First Army had to bear the brunt of the attack, it only follows that their reaction would naturally be more confused and less orderly. Yet, this seems to ignore the truly outstanding reactions of some of their subordinate units, such as V and VIII Corps, who actually bore the full impact of the offensive. These subordinate units would seem to have an even greater claim on such an excuse, but their actions don't require one.

The great difference seems to come back to the battle leadership of the army commanders. Simpson's showed an abundance of leadership strengths, Hodges's did not. The First Army's reaction to the crisis was characterized by many of the shortcomings pointed out, while Ninth Army's showed few of these weaknesses. Simpson and his Chief of Staff Moore created a command climate in their organization that greatly facilitated their army's outstanding response to the demands of the Ardennes offensive. Hodges and his Chief of Staff Kean had, by the time of the Battle of the Bulge, produced a command climate in First Army within which a real battlefield disaster was highly likely. Patton, whose headquarters showed both strengths and shortcomings during the battle, had created a Third Army staff so dependent on his own persona that it is difficult to separate the two. Still, Third Army demonstrated more strengths than shortcomings, clearly outperforming First Army, and Patton's abilities purely as a battle leader are legend.

As an army commander, however, Simpson demonstrated battle leadership during the Battle of the Bulge that was difficult to top. His mixture of common-sense command style with a textbook staff organization produced a smoothly functioning headquarters, remarkable for its efficiency and consistency. Perhaps the best summation of Simpson's leadership was made by Maj. Gen. Alvan C. Gillem Jr., who commanded the XIII Corps, Ninth Army, when he wrote:

> We see leadership best reflected, for example, when firmness is substituted for harshness, understanding for intolerance, humanness for bigotry, and when pride replaces egotism. General Simpson's every action exemplified the best of these traits of character. His integrity inspired a high degree of loyalty. His conduct on all occasions was scrupulous, and his associates of all ranks found him to be patient, impartial, courageous, sympathetic, and confident. They also found him equally loyal to seniors and juniors alike. He was an able, respected commander for whom all were willing to give their best endeavors.[174]

Possibly the only fault which can, in retrospect, be attributed to Simpson is that he never allowed himself to garner the publicity due him and his unit. Sadly, Simpson is "the most forgotten American field army commander of the Western Front."[175] If better known, his outstanding battle leadership could have provided later generations of Army officers with a better example than Patton's often bizarre personal leadership style.[176]

CHAPTER 5

Middleton and the VIII Corps

The man whose command was most directly affected by the sixteen German divisions crashing through the Ardennes was sound asleep in his headquarters at Bastogne when the barrage began on 16 December.[1] Maj. Gen. Troy Houston Middleton, a fifty-five-year-old infantryman, had commanded the VIII Corps since its introduction into the Normandy fighting on 12 June 1944. He had an Army-wide reputation as an excellent tactician and as a tough, experienced fighter whose demeanor in desperate combat was described as "cool as an icicle."[2] Eisenhower had personally selected him to lead VIII Corps in combat. Once the U.S. Army's youngest regimental commander, Middleton inspired George Marshall to describe him as "the outstanding infantry regimental commander on the battlefield in France" during World War I.[3]

Although outwardly he reminded observers of a fatherly, bespectacled college professor, the VIII Corps commander possessed a steely resolve and stubborn tenacity of purpose that allowed him to relieve overly excitable or unsuccessful subordinates without hesitation. Middleton used all the tactical knowledge, sound judgment, and shrewd sense of his troops' capabilities he could muster to retain a semblance of control over his shattered corps during the Battle of the Bulge—but it was primarily the calm leadership he displayed in the eye of this manmade hurricane that will stand as his greatest achievement.[4]

MIDDLETON'S CAREER

Troy Middleton was born on 12 October 1889 in Copiah County, Mississippi, the fifth of nine children. After a childhood in this rural section of the country, Middleton finished his formal education at Mississippi A & M, graduating in 1909. Just missing out on an appointment to West Point, he enlisted as a private in the 29th Infantry Regiment in March 1910.[5]

During his nearly three years as an enlisted man, Middleton gained much valuable practical experience as well as an insight into the common soldier's perceptions and attitudes. He successfully completed a commissioning exam while stationed at Fort Leavenworth, Kansas, in 1912 and was commissioned a second lieutenant of infantry in 1913. Posted shortly thereafter to the Mexican border, Middleton saw service in Texas until the United States entered the First World War.

Middleton accompanied the 4th Infantry Division to France in spring 1918 and was promoted to major in June. He took a battalion into the line, ready for combat in July. Middleton led his battalion throughout the intense combat at St. Mihiel and Meuse-Argonne, learning his job as he went. His coolness under fire and obviously quick grasp of the elements necessary for success in this style of infantry combat led to his rapid promotions to lieutenant colonel and then colonel by October. He assumed command of the 39th Infantry Regiment on the battlefield on 11 October 1918, becoming the youngest regimental commander in the U.S. Army. His regiment continued to score resounding successes until the Armistice halted its advances on 11 November. After a brief tour of occupation duty, Middleton returned to the United States in early 1919.[6]

In the rapid demobilization at the conclusion of the war, Middleton reverted to his peacetime rank of captain and assumed duties as an instructor at the Infantry School in Fort Benning in July 1919. After several years as an instructor during which he further enhanced his reputation as a tactician, Middleton was selected to attend the Command and General Staff School in 1923, where he became an Honor Graduate. He remained at Fort Leavenworth on the staff school faculty from 1924 to 1928. Many of the men who would lead the U.S. Army to victory in World War II, including Eisenhower, were taught by Middleton during his tenure as an instructor.[7] Following this tour as a teacher, he became a student once more, attending the Army War College in 1928–29. After brief service in the 29th Infantry Regiment at Fort Benning, Middleton was selected as Commandant of Cadets for the ROTC program at Louisiana State University (LSU) in 1930. He remained there for the next six years. Promoted to lieutenant colonel near the end of his stay at LSU, he was sent to the Philippines as an inspector general in 1936. It was while serving in the Philippines that Middleton wrestled with the decision to remain in the service or to retire and accept a lucrative position—dean of administration at an annual salary of $5,400—with LSU. While trying to decide, he sought the advice of Eisenhower, also serving in the islands. Ike urged him not to resign. He argued that a future war was unavoidable and that with Middleton's record from the First World War, he was certain to receive high command, maybe even a division. Despite Eisenhower's advice, Middleton retired and accepted the position at LSU.[8]

Ike was right of course. Middleton enjoyed the comfortable academic life, but when war engulfed the United States, he wrote Marshall to volunteer for active duty. The Chief of Staff quickly accepted the offer, promoted Middleton to brigadier general, and assigned him as assistant division commander of the 45th Infantry Division, then training at Fort Devens, Massachusetts, in 1942. Later that year Middleton was appointed division commander of the Oklahoma-Texas National Guard outfit and prepared to lead the 45th into its first combat in the invasion of Sicily.[9]

Bradley, Middleton's superior for this invasion, didn't know him personally but had heard of his reputation, "which was very, very good."[10] The 45th's initial combat performance completely validated Bradley's confidence in its commander, as it executed well throughout the Sicilian campaign. Middleton led his division into Italy and continued his outstanding performance until November 1943, when he was forced to give up command of the 45th to enter a hospital at Naples because of a chronic and painful knee injury. Eventually this recurring ailment forced his evacuation to Walter Reed Hospital in Washington, D.C. The condition was serious enough that it nearly led to Middleton's permanent stateside assignment, but his combat reputation was so outstanding that Ike asked for him for corps command during the Normandy invasion.

Proven combat leaders were still in acutely short supply in the American Army, and continued British skepticism of the competence of senior U.S. commanders forced Ike to insist that only those who had demonstrated combat excellence would get OVERLORD commands. As D-Day approached, Middleton prepared his corps to enter the fighting war. He would go back into combat "despite the gimpy knee."[11]

NORMANDY TO THE ARDENNES

The VIII Corps' initiation to combat at D+6 days was a bloody, frustrating struggle through the hedgerows of Normandy's Cotentin Peninsula. Middleton's progress was kept at a crawl more by the marshy, unyielding terrain than the determined German defenders. Advances were measured in hundreds of yards, causing observers to characterize the fighting as a "dismal failure."[12] In spite of Middleton's almost ruthless relief of several subordinate commanders, his corps made little real progress. This rather inauspicious beginning was soon followed by resounding success, however, when the First Army's COBRA operation finally blasted a hole in the German defenses. The operation's carpet-bombing devastated the area surrounding St.-Lô, but it allowed J. Lawton Collins's VII Corps to break through the crust of German resistance. Free at last from the restrictive confines of the beachhead area, Middleton's VIII Corps swept rapidly forward as the right flank unit of the U.S. front. Throughout the remainder of July and August, Middleton's attack gained momentum. Led by the 4th and 6th Armored Divisions, VIII Corps units were advancing farther and faster than anyone had thought possible. The corps' bag of German prisoners nearly overwhelmed their capacity to guard them, and the two armored divisions were slashing forward at an unprecedented rate.[13]

At the beginning of August, in compliance with OVERLORD plans to logistically expand the Normandy lodgment area, VIII Corps units turned westward into the Brittany Peninsula and headed for the port cities of Lorient and Brest. This decision to route an entire corps of 50,000 troops away from battle against the principal German forces

to the east and send them in the opposite direction has been surrounded with controversy and second-guessing. Nevertheless, in compliance with Bradley's orders, the VIII Corps' spearheads, the 4th and
6th Armored Divisions, drove rapidly into the Brittany Peninsula,
besieging the two major port cities of Brest and Lorient. By this time,
Middleton's corps was assigned to Patton's Third Army, eager to roll
against the main German strength; soon, however, the VIII Corps lost
its premier armored division, Wood's 4th, to the drive across France.
Back in Brittany, Middleton moved his infantry divisions up to begin
the assault upon the fortress city of Brest.[14]

Securing Brest was difficult, and the costly, frustrating siege warfare took nearly a month and 10,000 American casualties. The result
of this "knockdown, dragout, slugging contest over a secondary objective" was the capture of a devastated port, now useless as a supply
base, and resulted in the debatable allegation that Brest's capture had
a serious negative effect on the pursuit across France.[15] At any rate,
Middleton's battered corps was withdrawn from the Brittany Peninsula in September and eventually moved to a quiet sector of the Allied
front in order to refit, recuperate, and recover its full combat abilities.
During October, the VIII Corps was moved into positions in the dark
forests and twisting narrow roads of the Ardennes.

VIII CORPS IN THE ARDENNES

For Middleton and the VIII Corps, the Ardennes remained a quiet sector through November and into December as the fighting war swirled
around it on both sides. In this haven for played-out, exhausted units
or troops fresh from the States, by 16 December the VIII Corps
(appendix G) had four divisions to secure an 85-mile "long, desolate
front."[16] This is three times the frontage a corps was doctrinally
expected to defend, but it was a logical and expected result of Ike's
strategy to advance along multiple axes. The units assigned to Middleton's command at this time were a mixed bag of understrength veteran units and untried recent arrivals.[17]

His two experienced infantry divisions, the 4th and the 28th, had
been nearly destroyed in the nightmarish debacle in the Huertgen Forest (October–November 1944). The 28th Infantry Division, which

began the war as a Pennsylvania National Guard outfit, was especially roughly handled at the battle of Schmidt and other phases of the Huertgen attacks. Afterward, its grim-humored GIs referred to the unit as "the bloody bucket," finding that epithet a macabre but apt description of its red, keystone-shaped shoulder patch.[18] Despite its battered, understrength condition, the division had two exceptional leaders in key positions who were to prove invaluable during the upcoming fight. Maj. Gen. Norman "Dutch" Cota, the 28th's commander, had been in tough combat since he landed on Omaha Beach with the 29th Infantry Division on D-Day. In command of the 28th since August, he was unlikely to panic easily. The other leader was Col. Hurley Fuller, commander of the 110th Infantry Regiment, which occupied a critical position in the 28th's overextended line. An irascible, argumentative, pugnacious World War I vet, Fuller would prove to have just the right temperament for the upcoming struggle.

Middleton's other veteran unit was the 4th Infantry Division, under Maj. Gen. Raymond O. Barton. Also a battered survivor of the Huertgen, the 4th had lost over 6,000 troops to the Germans and the weather in the forest fighting. Two weeks after being relieved by the 83rd Infantry Division, it was far from full strength. It was, however, on the far right of Middleton's thin corps front, not in the path of the main German panzer assault. Nevertheless, in its depleted state it would find itself hard pressed by the infantry forces of the German Seventh Army.[19]

Arguably, in the worst position of all of Middleton's units was the brand-new 106th Infantry Division. It had never seen combat and had been "in the line" only four days before the German assault began. The "Golden Lions" of the 106th had taken over the northern portion of the VIII Corps line from the veteran 2nd Infantry Division, now part of the V Corps assault to capture belatedly the Roer River dams. The 106th relieved the 2nd foxhole by foxhole, constrained to occupy every fighting position the 2nd had held.

Although the 106th's commander, Maj. Gen. Alan W. Jones, felt that some of these positions, especially those on the Schnee Eifel plateau, were too exposed to offer a proper defense, he was not allowed to change any dispositions.[20] The Schnee Eifel positions were actually part of the Siegfried Line, and any withdrawal from those hard-won bunkers would not play well on the home front. Adding to Jones's difficulties was his unit's proximity to the Losheim Gap, the "classic" invasion route through the Ardennes. Not only was this a primary armored avenue of approach, it was also defended by the weak 14th Cavalry Group, a unit more suited to screening than defending against a determined panzer attack. To top it off, the V Corps–VIII Corps boundary ran through the northern portion of the gap. Because unit boundaries are particularly vulnerable to enemy assault, it was doubly unfortunate for the 106th and the VIII Corps to be saddled with these dispositions.[21]

Middleton had one additional unit with which to defend his impossibly wide front, one combat command of the 9th Armored Division (another was detached to V Corps to assist in its offensive). Middleton used his armored combat command to plug a gaping hole in his defensive line, inserting it between the 28th and the 4th. The third portion of the 9th, Combat Command R, was in reserve near Marnach (although not primarily a "maneuver unit" like Combat Commands A and B, it could be used in a pinch).[22] Middleton's only other potential reserves were four engineer combat battalions within the VIII Corps area of operations.

Total troops available to Middleton and the VIII Corps on the early morning of 16 December 1944 were 68,822, or about one soldier for every 2 meters of defended front—hardly a formidable force. As the Ardennes attack eventually gained strength, the Germans were able to achieve an eight-to-one advantage in infantry, and a four-to-one advantage in tanks against the VIII Corps front.[23] Bad weather became a German ally, grounding the Allied air forces and neutralizing the strong Allied air arm.

THE INITIAL GERMAN ASSAULT

The full force of the German attack fell on the veteran 28th Division in the center and the untried 106th Division in the north of the VIII Corps sector. Not surprisingly, the Germans were once again using the Losheim Gap as a main axis of attack. Over the course of the next few days, both infantry divisions were destroyed as effective fighting forces, and Middleton was compelled to use every asset at his command to try to slow the German advance.

The disruption caused by the overwhelming attack made the maintenance of a cohesive defense impossible. As the panzer and panzergrenadier spearheads slashed farther to the west, Middleton found it increasingly difficult to exercise control over his northernmost units from his command post in Bastogne. Ultimately, he lost effective control of those units, because he had his hands full trying to react to the attacks on his units immediately in front of Bastogne. As the 28th Division continued to disintegrate under relentless German pressure, Middleton exercised personal command and control over the disposition of each precious unit, ordering individual tank-infantry-engineer teams to threatened sectors to parry each German thrust.[24]

When the guard awakened Middleton in his headquarters van that early morning of 16 December, the corps commander could hear the German barrage rumbling in the eastern distance. Although Middleton was not particularly alarmed at first, a steady stream of reports from subordinate units that they were under attack by German infantry, tanks, and artillery flooded into the VIII Corps headquarters throughout that morning, and by 1000 hours elements of 16 German divisions had been identified among the attackers. Middleton realized that this enemy assault clearly was no demonstration or spoiling attack to relieve the pressure of V Corps' offensive. This was a major German offensive slamming into the weakest sector of the entire Allied line.[25]

Middleton's ability to rapidly grasp the implications of the German attack allowed him to focus the efforts of the corps staff quickly to make maximum effective use of his corps' battered units. The problem was obvious: how to regain control of the battle to a sufficient degree to stabilize the front long enough for reserves (from outside the corps area) to counterattack into the flanks of the assault. Solving the problem was another matter. By the evening of the first day of the attack, the VIII Corps no longer had a "front" in the strict military sense. Instead, it consisted of a large number of individual units or parts of units, in varying stages of disintegration, some clinging to important road junctions or strongpoints, some fleeing westward.[26]

While Middleton and his staff certainly realized the immensity of the attack by this time, it appears unlikely that they as yet were aware of the precarious position of most of their units. For example, the corps commander thought he had made clear to the 106th's commander, Alan Jones, that his two exposed regiments on the Schnee Eifel should be withdrawn to more defensible terrain. Instead, Jones thought Middleton wanted his two units to stand fast and await relief by an armored counterattack. The result was the largest single surrender of U.S. troops in the European Theater, as the 8,000 men of the 422nd and 423rd Infantry Regiments were turned over to the enemy by their commanders on 19 December.[27] The loss of two-thirds of the combat power of his only full-strength division was a serious, and nearly fatal, blow to Middleton's defense.

By the evening of the first day's attack, VIII Corps was in an extremely bad situation along the major portion of its "front." In the north, the main German attack had shattered the weak 14th Cavalry Group, and panzergrenadiers were about to encircle the two ill-fated 106th Division regiments. The 28th Division in the center was clinging to strongpoints and road junctions, but giving ground slowly and inexorably. In the south the news was slightly better. The 4th Infantry, along with the combat command of the 9th Armored, was having an easier time against the infantry attacks of the German Seventh Army.[28] How Middleton and his corps staff reacted from this point on clearly reveals Middleton's leadership and character.

COMMAND REACTION AT VIII CORPS HEADQUARTERS

"One did not have to be a genius to know that St.-Vith and Bastogne were critical points during the Battle of the Bulge." So wrote Middleton in 1967 in his assessment of command reaction during the battle. All one had to do, he pointed out, was look at the map.[29] Or even without a map, all you had to do was watch the advancing German spearheads, and they would show you these same critical points. Those would-be "geniuses" who rushed forward after the battle wanting to claim credit for picking Bastogne and St.-Vith as critical hubs of the fighting were far behind Middleton and the VIII Corps staff in realizing the obvious.[30]

Middleton appreciated from the beginning that he would have to hold the two critical communications centers if he were to slow the German advance. To carry out any workable delay, Middleton was forced to use tactics not always consistent with doctrine. His frontage was too extended and too pierced to use a conventional defense, so he counted on his subordinate unit commanders to make the best use of the restrictive terrain and their meager resources to establish "islands of defense [to make] the Germans pay a disproportionate price for their moves against [the VIII Corps]."[31] Units had to react piecemeal, and Middleton began almost immediately to grab any unit he could find to "plug the yawning gap in [his] front."[32] Historian Hugh Cole, writing in the Army's official history, described this effort:

The story of the units that were retained under tactical control and employed directly by General Middleton in the attempt to form some defense in depth in the VIII Corps center has been partially recorded. . . . The effect that these units had in retarding the German advances, a course of action evolving extemporaneously, must be considered along with the role played by the uncoordinated front-line formations in the haphazard sequence of delaying actions. . . . With the very limited forces at his disposal . . . the VIII Corps commander found it physically impossible to erect any of the standard defenses taught in the higher Army schools or prescribed in the field service regulations. The best he could do to defend the extended front was to deploy his troops as a screen retaining local reserves for local counterattacks at potentially dangerous points. . . . Under the circumstances there could be no thought of an elastic defense with strong formations echeloned in any depth . . . [He had to] attempt to plug a few of the gaps in the forward line, slow the enemy columns on a few main roads, and strengthen by human means two or three of the natural physical barriers deep in the corps rear area.[33]

Beginning to sort some order out of the mass confusion, Middleton and his staff dispatched units to critical portions of the line, reacted to enemy advances as best they could, and continued to try to stay current with the extremely fluid situation. Almost immediately, the direction of the main German attack combined with the poor road network began to sever Middleton from his northernmost unit.

The most important decision Middleton made to influence the fighting in the north and the resulting defense of St.-Vith was his dispatch of Brig. Gen. Bruce C. Clarke to the 106th Division's command post in the early morning hours of 17 December. Clarke had sped on ahead of his Combat Command B, 7th Armored Division, to locate the VIII Corps headquarters and determine where Middleton wanted his armored force to enter the battle. The VIII Corps commander calmly told Clarke that, "Alan Jones is having some trouble at St.-Vith—grab something to eat and a little sleep and go to him . . . if he needs help give it to him."[34] So began the 7th Armored Division's epic defense of the crucial northern crossroads.

The other major input Middleton made to the 106th's defense was not as helpful, for it contributed to the disastrous surrender of the two regiments on the Schnee Eifel. Middleton's command style was such that he deferred decisions, whenever possible, to the subordinate commander "on the spot." He believed, usually correctly, that the commander on the ground had the best overall picture of the tactical situation at his location and was therefore the best judge of action most appropriate for the moment.[35] At St.-Vith on 17 December, however, Jones and his unit were totally inexperienced and had been in the line only four days prior to the German assault. In this situation, the combat-experienced corps commander with an Army-wide reputation as a premiere tactician should have provided much stronger guidance to the less-experienced subordinate. Instead, Middleton let Jones make the final decision regarding the two regiments, with terrible results.[36]

Other factors also contributed to the debacle, including Jones's much too sanguine reporting of the situation in a controversial phone conversation with Middleton late on the sixteenth (and again on the seventeenth), as well as a completely unreasonable expectation of the arrival time of the bulk of Combat Command B at St.-Vith. To further muddle an already confusing situation, the switchboard operator

during the phone call on the sixteenth mistakenly unplugged the connection for a few critical moments, thus allowing each commander to
believe the other had concurred in exactly the opposite course of
action each assumed. This entire episode could be cited as a textbook
example of Clausewitz's "friction" or "fog of war," and remains today
a highly controversial incident.[37]

Beyond these two critical episodes, Middleton exercised little
impact over the outcome of the fighting at St.-Vith. Indeed, he lost
even the nominal control he had over his northern units on 20 December, when Eisenhower divided command responsibility for the bulge,
placing Montgomery in command of American units in the north half
of the Bulge with the St.-Vith units coming under command of Ridgway's XVIII Airborne Corps.

Events therefore rapidly evolved to cause VIII Corps' defensive
efforts to be concentrated on the 28th Division's sector immediately in
front of Bastogne. As Cole related, this inaugurated "the period of
'piecemeal reaction' . . . when Middleton's VIII Corps was trying to
plug the yawning gaps in its front with rifle platoons of engineers and
mechanics, and before an American riposte could be made in force."[38]
Col. Hurley Fuller's 110th Infantry Regiment, spread out along the
wide, empty frontage of "Skyline Drive," got the worst of it in the
28th's sector. As Fuller's overwhelmingly outnumbered units slowly
yielded ground, Middleton tried to organize the best defense he could
given his meager reserves.

While Fuller's front collapsed, the VIII Corps commander
grabbed his only armored reserve, Combat Command R, 9th Armored,
and sent mobile teams to critical road junctions east of Bastogne. The
fate of Task Force Rose, one of these teams, is illustrative of the desperate nature of the fighting and the paucity of reserves available to
VIII Corps. It also shows Middleton's personal involvement in the
fighting details.[39]

Middleton ordered Col. Joseph H. Gilbreth, commander of Combat Command R, 9th Armored, to dispatch two task forces to two critical road junctions on the eastern approaches to Bastogne after the
corps commander received word of the German success against the

110th Infantry at Clervaux. Middleton personally selected positions guarding crossroads commanding approaches to the main paved road from St.-Vith to Bastogne. Capt. L. K. Rose of Combat Command R had a company of tanks and one of infantry, bolstered by an armored engineer platoon to try to defend the northernmost of the two road junctions.[40]

Task Force Rose got the order to move out for the crossroads village of Lullange at 2140 hours on the seventeenth, just ten minutes after the corps found out that German columns had cleared Clervaux and were heading for the same road junction. Gilbreth was told to establish the roadblocks "without delay," as the enemy was crossing the Clerf River only 5 miles away. Indeed, enemy fire was already falling around Lullange. Rose and his force were in position on the hills commanding the approaches to the junction shortly after midnight.

By midmorning on the eighteenth, German reconnaissance elements, backed up by two panzer battalions, began to appear along the road in front of Rose. The task force, aided by the fires of the 73rd Armored Field Artillery Battalion, kept the enemy at bay throughout the morning and into the early afternoon, but by 1400 hours Rose was in trouble. His infantry company swept away by the panzers, Rose and his tanks were hemmed in on three sides and about to be surrounded. If Task Force Rose was to extricate itself, it would have to move immediately. The decision was Middleton's. Cole relates that, at 1405 hours, VIII Corps received the following message from Combat Command R's Gilbreth:

TF Rose . . . is as good as surrounded . . . have counted 16 German tanks there . . . TF is being hit from 3 sides. Recommend that they fight their way out. They could use 2 platoons of A/52d Armd Inf Bn . . . everything else is committed. . . . Did not commit any of the TDs [Tank Destroyers], will wait until the over-all plan is known. Plan to push TF Rose toward the other road block. If the decision is to stay, some units will be sent there to help them out.[41]

Middleton not only couldn't allow Rose to withdraw, but also couldn't even permit Gilbreth to attempt to reinforce the doomed task force. He knew that any force sent to assist Rose would itself be overwhelmed by the overpowering numbers of panzers and grenadiers swarming down the St.-Vith–Bastogne road. The corps commander needed every tank and rifle to establish new roadblocks at other critical locations all along the disintegrating front. The armored infantrymen Gilbreth proposed to send to Rose's aid were the last infantry reserves in Gilbreth's command. Committing them in a hopeless cause was out of the question. At 1430 hours, word was received at Combat Command R headquarters that Task Force Rose had been overrun.[42]

This scenario was repeated many times during the critical hours that Middleton tried to slow the advancing Germans while his senior commanders at SHAEF, Army Group, and Army rushed to assemble reserves from outside VIII Corps. The fact that the corps commander himself was personally ordering and approving the dispositions of company and battalion task forces emphasizes the gravity of the overall situation. But, more importantly, the sum of all these actions clearly demonstrates Middleton's personal command in this critical situation and establishes, irrefutably, his impact on the course of the battle.

As Gilbreth's painfully inadequate forces were slowing, if not stopping the Germans who had broken through the 110th Infantry, fresh troops were arriving in Bastogne to help Middleton. On 16 December, Eisenhower had directed Bradley to rush two armored divisions from the First Army's flanking units to the threatened area. The 7th Armored Division moved from reserve positions in the Ninth Army area and was assembled at and behind the St.-Vith roadblock. Now, late on 18 December, the leading combat command of the 10th Armored Division began to reach Bastogne. Rushing north from Patton's Third Army, Col. William Roberts's Combat Command B was arriving just in time to allow Middleton to continue to delay the enemy advance.[43]

Almost immediately upon arrival at Middleton's headquarters in Bastogne, however, Roberts and the VIII Corps commander clashed. The issue was the "proper"—and most effective—employment of Roberts's combat command to stop the Germans. Roberts naturally wanted to fight his force as a single unit. Armored warfare doctrine, seemingly proven in the unprecedented dash across France the previous summer, called for the weight and shock power of the tank-infantry-artillery team to be maximized by the combat commands operating as a single combined-arms team unit. Middleton, on the other hand, wanted Roberts to break his command into small company teams and battalion-sized task forces scattered across the VIII Corps front at critical locations as the ill-fated Task Force Rose had done. The very idea was anathema to the true tanker.[44]

Middleton, the former Staff College teacher and tactics instructor knew very well the proper doctrine stipulated by "the book" for employment of armor, and he completely understood Roberts's objections. However, he also appreciated much better than the newly arrived Roberts the utter hopelessness of attempting any "conventional" defense or "textbook" deployments in the nightmarish situation his battered corps occupied. Middleton later recalled:

I went against the book and broke up our armor into task forces. When Bill Roberts came up to Bastogne on December 18 with his combat command, I asked him how much strength he had. Then I told him to break up his fine outfit into three task forces. Bill didn't like it at all. He told me, "Troy, that's no way to use armor." And I told him that I knew it as well as he did. But we weren't fighting any textbook war there. Without some armor to back up our roadblocks, we couldn't have stopped anything.[45]

Luckily for the defense of Bastogne, the corps commander won the argument. Roberts's assets proved to be key to both buying time to allow the 101st Airborne Division to reach Bastogne and later assisting the paratroopers in holding the town. Without the defense of the key road junctions (as well as the 28th Infantry Division's gallant but piecemeal fighting further east), Bastogne would have fallen long before the 101st Airborne moved up to occupy it. It is highly unlikely that the 101st could have fought its way into the town against the German forces then rushing toward it.

The last "major" reserve force Middleton had to help slow the attackers was also a source of controversy after the battle. These were the engineer units assigned to VIII Corps or working in the corps area when the offensive began. Middleton had four engineer combat battalions under his command, and an additional Engineer Group of three engineer combat battalions from First Army was in direct support in his corps area.[46] Although engineer troops are trained to accomplish the mission of "fighting as infantry" when necessary, this is not the most effective use of these trained technicians; the situation in VIII Corps was one of those necessary times, however.

The first to be put into the fight was the 168th Engineer Combat Battalion. Middleton gave this unit to Jones at St.-Vith on the sixteenth in an attempt to stabilize the rapidly deteriorating situation in the north. The next day, he sent the 44th, another of his engineer combat battalions, east to back up the crumbling 28th Division sector, and a third engineer unit, the 159th, was given to Barton's 4th Division and headed south. By late afternoon on the seventeenth, of his corps units he had only the 35th Engineer Combat Battalion uncommitted.[47] The 35th, along with one of the First Army engineer battalions, was also soon committed, as it became part of the defensive line established east of Bastogne. This line, extending from Foy to Neffe, was suggested to Middleton by his corps engineer officer and served as a virtual "last ditch" infantry barrier to hold Bastogne long enough for the arriving paratroopers to get into position. These units did the job along with Roberts's tankers from the 10th Armored and Cota's infantrymen in the 28th. Delayed long enough by numerous small-unit actions, German forces were unable to enter Bastogne before the 101st Airborne Division arrived in strength on the night of 18–19 December.[48]

Many of Middleton's remaining engineers were used in more traditional engineer roles, such as demolition, minefield emplacement, and obstacle construction as VIII Corps attempted to establish a corps barrier line. The "VIII Corps Barrier Line," if the scattered collection of obstacles built (and also defended) by Middleton's engineers can be called that, extended from the general vicinity of Houffalize in the north to south of Bastogne. It was neither a barrier nor a true "line" but consisted mainly of isolated positions at road junctions, river crossings, and other critical points in the path of the German drive. Middleton tried to lay down the barrier line across the front of the advancing German columns, but the speed of the enemy advance forced the efforts to be concentrated more along the edges of the penetrations. Nevertheless, the combined effect of the engineer effort contributed considerably to the German delay and frustrated many of the enemy's efforts to seize crucial bridges and road junctions quickly.[49] The ongoing argument, however, continues to focus on the most effective use of engineer forces to delay a rapidly advancing enemy. Cole sums up the question well in his official history of the battle:

> Students of the retrograde action fought by the VIII Corps between 16 and 22 December will wish to examine the question as to the most profitable use of engineer troops who formed the backbone of the rear area defense in such circumstances. The "magnificent job" which General Middleton later ascribed to the engineers credits the engineers in their role as infantry. The VIII Corps engineer and the various engineer group commanders at that time and later believed the engineer battalions and companies could have done more to impede the German advance if they had been denied the eastern firing line and employed in a tactically unified second line of defense in the western part of the corps area. For this latter purpose General Middleton would have had some 3,300 engineers in addition to those organic in the divisions. But it is questionable whether the 7th Armored Division would have had time to establish itself at St.-Vith, not to speak of the 101st Airborne Division at Bastogne, without the intervention of the engineer battalions.[50]

While Middleton and his beleaguered staff were fighting the piecemeal delaying actions to buy some precious time, forces were assembling at Bastogne which would ultimately prevent its capture. The first reinforcements to arrive at Bastogne were the elements of Roberts's Combat Command B of the 10th Armored. These were now

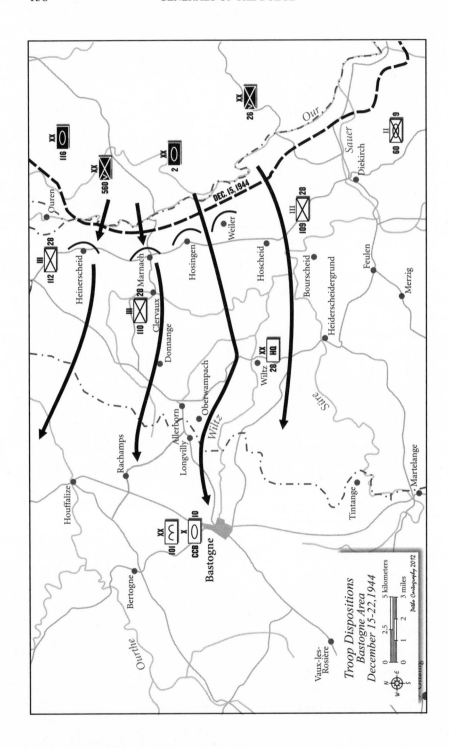

Troop Dispositions
Bastogne Area
December 15–22, 1944

An American soldier walks along a deserted road in the Luxembourg area of the Ardennes. U.S. ARMY

M4A3 Sherman tank, the principal armored fighting vehicle of World War II. Although often outclassed by some of the later German panzers, American assembly lines produced about 50,000 of these sturdy tanks during the war, a number the Germans could never hope to achieve. U.S. ARMY

M2A1 105mm howitzer, the ubiquitous U.S. artillery piece of World War II and a key element in a fire control system that made American artillery the most feared killer on the battlefield. U.S. ARMY

M7 self-propelled 105mm howitzer. Integrating firepower and mobility, the M7 consisted of a 105mm howitzer mounted on a modified M4 tank chassis. Lt. Col. Roy Clay's 275th Armored Field Artillery Battalion used these weapons to good effect during the fighting around St.-Vith. U.S. ARMY

A 155mm howitzer, manned by African-American soldiers. The critical manpower shortage, exacerbated by the huge Ardennes casualty lists, led Eisenhower to issue a circular calling for infantry volunteers "without regard to color or race." Unexpectedly large numbers of African Americans volunteered—almost 5,000 in the first month— which helped to reshape attitudes toward the Army's policy of racially segregated units. U.S. ARMY

The "Red Ball Highway" was the U.S. response to keeping the rapidly advancing Allied armies sufficiently supplied with the "sinews of war" as ever-lengthening lines of communication put increasing strains on the overburdened logistics system. Truck convoys rolled over this highway day and night, moving supplies from the beachheads to the fighting front. U.S. ARMY

This captured German combat photo shows advance elements of the Sixth Panzer Army at an Ardennes crossroads between Malmedy and St-Vith, 17 December 1944. NATIONAL ARCHIVES

In a posed propaganda photo taken a few kilometers from St.-Vith early in the battle, an SS trooper gestures to comrades to move forward past abandoned and burning U.S. jeeps and half-tracks (probably from the 14th Cavalry Group).
NATIONAL ARCHIVES

General of the Army Dwight D. Eisenhower, Supreme Allied Commander, wearing the five-star insignia of a General of the Army and the unit patch of the Supreme Headquarters Allied Expeditionary Force (SHAEF). The photo was taken shortly after the conclusion of the Battle of the Bulge. NATIONAL ARCHIVES

Supreme Command, Allied Expeditionary Force meets for the first time in London on 1 February 1944. Seated, left to right: Air Chief Marshal Sir Arthur Tedder, General Eisenhower, and Gen. Sir Bernard Montgomery. Standing, left to right: Lt. Gen. Omar N. Bradley, Adm. Sir Bertram Ramsey, Air Chief Marshal Sir Trafford Leigh-Mallory, and Lt. Gen. Walter Bedell Smith. NATIONAL ARCHIVES

Ike visiting senior U.S. commanders, 10 October 1944. Left to right, front row: Lt. Gen. George S. Patton Jr., Lt. Gen. Omar N. Bradley, Eisenhower, Lt. Gen. Courtney H. Hodges, and Lt. Gen. William H. Simpson. Visible in the second row are Maj. Gen. Leonard T. Gerow (between Ike and Hodges) and Maj. Gen. Elwood R. Quesada (between Hodges and Simpson). NATIONAL ARCHIVES

Standing in the ruins of Bastogne, Bradley (left) looks on as Ike and Patton (right) have a serious discussion about the recently concluded Battle of the Bulge. U.S. ARMY

Lt. Gen. Courtney H. Hodges, First Army commander during the Battle of the Bulge. U.S. ARMY

Lt. Gen. William H. Simpson, Ninth Army commander during the Battle of the Bulge.
NATIONAL ARCHIVES

Maj. Gen. Troy H. Middleton, VIII Corps commander.
NATIONAL ARCHIVES

Maj. Gen. Alan W. Jones, 106th Infantry Division commander.
U.S. ARMY

Brig. Gen. Bruce C. Clarke, Commander, Combat Command B, 7th Armored Division. U.S. ARMY

Senior allied commanders Field Marshal Sir Alan Brooke, Chief of the Imperial General Staff (left), Eisenhower, and 21st Army Group commander Montgomery near the end of the war. 12th Army Group commander Bradley is on the right. NATIONAL ARCHIVES

Ike and Middleton share a light moment during a visit by Eisenhower to the VIII Corps area in the "quiet" Ardennes sector, 9 November 1944. A little over a month later, the smiling stopped. NATIONAL ARCHIVES

Eisenhower and Bradley (second from the right) visit Lieutenant General Hodges (second from left) and some of Hodges's subordinate commanders following the Battle of the Bulge. Rear, Maj. Gen. Clarence R. Huebner, V Corps; center, Maj. Gen. Edwin P. Parker Jr., 78th Infantry Division; and right, Maj. Gen. Matthew B. Ridgway, XVIII Airborne Corps. NATIONAL ARCHIVES

Generals of the Bulge. Some of the U.S. senior leaders who fought at the Battle of the Bulge join Eisenhower shortly after the end of the war in Europe. Left to right, front row: Simpson; Patton; Gen. Carl A. Spaatz, U.S. Army Air Forces Europe; Eisenhower; Bradley; Hodges; and Lt. Gen. Leonard T. Gerow, Fifteenth Army. Second row: Brig. Gen. Ralph F. Stearley, IX Tactical Air Command; Lt. Gen. Hoyt S. Vandenberg, 9th Air Force; Lt. Gen. Walter Bedell Smith, SHAEF Chief of Staff; Maj. Gen. Otto P. Weyland, XIX Tactical Air Command; and Brig. Gen. Richard E. Nugent, XXIX Tactical Air Command. NATIONAL ARCHIVES engaged at numerous critical locations, helping Middleton keep the Germans out of the town. The next units to arrive which would play an important role in the city's defense consisted of several artillery battalions (or parts thereof). Most of these units were withdrawing from the fighting to the east after supporting the 28th Division's futile efforts to stop the enemy advances.

The artillery units would be especially useful to the 101st in its defense of Bastogne, because the airborne troopers' organic artillery consisted of only three battalions of short-ranged light artillery and one battalion of 105mm howitzers. Brig. Gen. Anthony C. McAuliffe, the 101st's acting commander and himself an artilleryman, eventually had several additional artillery battalions and collections of guns to help support his lightly armed paratroopers. These included the 155mm guns of the 755th Armored Field Artillery Battalion, sent from outside the sector, and the 969th Field Artillery Battalion, which straggled in after firing for the 28th Division. They joined Roberts's 420th Armored Field Artillery Battalion of the 10th Armored and parts of other units such as the 58th and 73rd Armored Field Artillery Battalions who fought their way rearward from the east.[51]

The last significant group to join the Bastogne defense was the survivors from the 28th Division and other units who had fought the battle to the east. There is no way to determine the number of soldiers who thus complemented the 101st's defense of the city, but in this desperate fight, every man counted. These tankers, gunners, infantrymen, and others added 12,000 defenders to the 11,000 or so officers and men of the 101st at Bastogne, and they played an important, if unheralded, role in the defense.[52]

While this force assembled in Bastogne, Middleton began moving his VIII Corps headquarters to safer ground to the southwest. Although Middleton himself remained in Bastogne for two more days to complete the coordination for the city's defense, on 18 December the bulk of the corps headquarters moved 18 miles southwest to Florenville about 10 miles from the town of Neufchâteau, out of the path of the main German attack.[53]

As he drove away from the soon-to-be-surrounded city, however, Middleton left behind a further point of controversy. Much like the situation at St.-Vith, Middleton had neglected to establish firmly and unquestionably a command structure for the conglomeration of units defending Bastogne. Instead, he had merely requested that the two senior officers, McAuliffe and Roberts, "cooperate" in the conduct of the battle. Such an ambiguous command setup in a confusing fight, involving as it did multiple units from several different parent commands, was unacceptable. Middleton belatedly realized this and appointed McAuliffe (who was anyway the senior officer present) as overall commander in Bastogne.[54]

Middleton's departure from Bastogne by no means ended his participation in the Battle of the Bulge. Instead, under Patton's Third Army after Ike's splitting of command responsibility, Middleton and the VIII Corps continued to be instrumental in ultimately defeating the German attack. He helped supervise the relief of Bastogne by the 4th Armored Division on 26 December and, with his newly reorganized VIII Corps, led one of the initial counteroffensives to throw back the Germans to their original jumping-off positions.

Middleton's counteroffensive in the south of the bulge began as early as 30 December, but its effectiveness was crippled by the ever-cautious Montgomery delaying any offensive action in the north until later in January. Middleton later blamed Montgomery's tardiness for seriously reducing the potential capture of German prisoners and allowing much German equipment to be withdrawn.[55]

Middleton and the VIII Corps finished out the war in the Third Army, winning well-earned respect from this famous army's renowned commander. Near the end, Patton wrote a personal note to Middleton, saying, "None of us will ever forget the stark valor with which you and your Corps contested every foot of ground during von Rundstedt's attack. Your decision to hold Bastogne was a stroke of genius."[56] This last praise came from the same man who had earlier ranted at Middleton for allowing the 101st Airborne to become surrounded. Apparently, cooler reflection on Middleton's commandership caused the famous but volatile Patton a greater appreciation of the opportunities presented by the unprecedented situation in the soon-to-be-famous city.

ANALYSIS OF BATTLE LEADERSHIP

An attempt to assess the impact of an individual's actions upon a seventy-year-old event is difficult, but especially so when the event in question has become surrounded by legend, and aspects of the battle, such as the 101st Airborne's defense of Bastogne, have become military icons. Over the years, the legend has become the reality. And legend, although inspiring, has little substance with which to instruct later generations of soldiers who may benefit from the experiences of those who led the fighting. The task is to demystify the event by examining the actions of the commanders and then attempt to draw some conclusions from the demonstrated battle leadership. In the case of Middleton, we must determine the characteristics of his battle leadership and how they affected the conduct of the Ardennes fighting.[57]

Middleton's most outstanding characteristic, remarked upon time and again by those observing his leadership in battle, was his overpowering calmness. His ability to remain cool and collected while the absolute worst was happening was probably the single most important aspect affecting his conduct of the defense.[58] Indeed, Middleton's great asset during the entire war was his unflappable calmness in adversity. He singled out this trait in a postwar questionnaire on senior leadership, advising would-be commanders, "Be calm. Guard against becoming excited. . . . Calmness is one of the greatest virtues. Every officer I relieved during the war could be classed among the excitable and jittery. The good Lord gave every person his share of common sense, the commander who does not use this valuable commodity is doomed."[59]

Middleton displayed this trait consistently during his battle command, but in no instance was it better demonstrated or more critically needed than during the dark days of the Battle of the Bulge. Even amid the most difficult and crucial phases of the fighting, Middleton remained "completely calm and in command of himself."[60] While rallying his shattered units and confidently directing their desperate delaying actions, Middleton was outwardly "calm and optimistic."[61] This steadying influence was exactly what was needed in this unprecedented situation, and in what was probably Middleton's finest hour it was his greatest contribution as a battle leader.

This superb attribute was not always viewed positively by his superiors, however. During the difficult fighting in Normandy on the Cotentin Peninsula, Eisenhower would have preferred a more out-wardly enthusiastic, aggressive reaction from Middleton, and wrote, "Middleton does not display the enthusiasm in his leadership that do the others." Ike admitted, however, that "he is tactically sound and a very fine, straightforward workman."[62] Despite misgivings concerning his enthusiasm, Eisenhower retained confidence in Middleton's steady, undramatic ability to command his corps skillfully and accom-plish the mission.

This unflappability and apparent lack of aggressiveness may also be what caused Matt Ridgway, the XVIII Airborne Corps commander, to relate on 19 December that he assessed the VIII Corps headquarters to be completely unaware of the total situation.[63] There is little doubt that the VIII Corps staff was exercising no real control of the events occurring around St.-Vith (nor in the 4th Infantry Division sector, for that matter), but Middleton and his staff had as complete a picture as any higher headquarters did of the fluid situation at the time.[64] Mid-dleton's undramatic demeanor and lack of stormy aggressiveness could have been interpreted by the flashy paratrooper as being out of touch with events. Ridgway's concern is understandable, however, as his mission was to bring the defense of the northern area, including St.-Vith, under command of his corps, and he was rushing to sort some order out of a totally confusing situation. But he would have to get the information he needed to establish his defense from the on-scene commanders at St.-Vith—Hasbrouck, Clarke, and Jones—not from Middleton.

The importance of Middleton's calm and steadying influence on the VIII Corps defense in the Ardennes cannot be overemphasized, because it formed the bedrock upon which the critical decisions affect-ing the conduct of the battle rested. Middleton's refusal to panic pro-vided the VIII Corps staff with an outstanding personal example as well as giving them unyielding support to initiate the best defense pos-sible in a completely confusing and fluid environment. The defense permitted by the units available to the VIII Corps commander was characterized by immediate and disciplined responses to each of the

German threats as they developed. A calm and steady appraisal of each of these threats, coupled with a realistic utilization of the meager reserves, was crucial to the piecemeal delaying tactics that Middleton was forced by circumstances to employ. He had to coolly evaluate each impassioned request from his hard-pressed subordinates before allowing any of his tiny reserve to be committed.[65] Middleton may have wished desperately to send reinforcements to save Captain Rose and his outgunned task force, but he had to resist that temptation. It was not in his nature to play the blustering showman in this critical situation, nor would it necessarily have proven effective. What proved useful was his calm, measured, and workmanlike response in this fight.[66]

Middleton's steadying calmness provided the atmosphere for another of the demonstrated leadership characteristics he employed to good effect in the fighting—his flexibility. Middleton's ability to adapt his defense to the nature of the German assault was a critical factor in the VIII Corps' efforts to slow the advance in its sector. Mixed with large measures of initiative and innovation, plus a generous dose of moral courage, Middleton's adaptability proved essential to the overall defense.

It may be argued that the inherent weakness of the VIII Corps initial dispositions, coupled with the overwhelming nature of the German assault, necessitated the type of defense eventually used, but this reasoning ignores the tactical choices available to the corps commander. For example, Middleton was under no order or obligation to hold Bastogne, and as mentioned earlier, Patton initially chided Middleton for allowing the 101st Airborne to become surrounded in the key city. Further, Middleton's decision to fight for time by delaying with small task forces at each critical road junction seemed to orthodox tankers to fly directly in the face of the proper doctrine of the time. Armored warfare doctrine demanded concentrating the maximum available tank and mechanized forces for a decisive counterattack against the enemy's vulnerable point, thus Roberts of the 10th Armored resisted when Middleton told him to break up his combat command into smaller task forces and scatter them across the landscape. Middleton realized, however, that the unprecedented situation demanded that he adapt any textbook tactics to the realities of the situation. If the enemy could not be delayed immediately, then Bastogne would be lost and the VIII Corps front quickly overrun.[67]

Even prior to the German attack, Middleton had used his adaptability to maximize the defensive potential of his available troops. Hurley Fuller of the 110th Infantry received Middleton's permission to abandon any attempt to hold an uninterrupted line along his impossibly wide sector. Instead, he planned to delay any enemy assault by clinging as long as possible to each of the critical road junctions his widely scattered units garrisoned. When put to the test, Fuller's plan worked, justifying his corps commander's approval. In fact, this became Middleton's strategy as well.[68]

A final example of Middleton adapting tactics to resources must be the controversial employment of the engineer combat battalions. Middleton has been criticized for his initial use of these engineer battalions to fight as infantry. As Cole has pointed out, however, it is doubtful if either the 7th Armored or the 101st Airborne could have gotten into their respective defensive positions without the time bought by the engineers. To argue that they could have gained more time by being employed purely in an engineer role demonstrates a lack of understanding of the desperate tactical situation facing VIII Corps at the time and a poor appreciation of Middleton's flexibility.[69]

Fortunately, Middleton displayed an outstanding ability to adapt his tactics to the actual threat. As he told his biographer years later, "If the method you're using doesn't work, try something else. The fellow who wrote the book couldn't think of everything." Although Middleton didn't write the book, he spent several years teaching it at the Command and General Staff School and the Infantry School. His refusal to follow blindly what he termed the "Leavenworth solution" was a triumph of his good common sense coupled with a keen appreciation of what was necessary at the time.[70]

To be fair, Middleton's battle leadership did not always feature the flexibility it demonstrated in the Ardennes fighting. During the hedgerow combat in the early phases of VIII Corps' European campaign, for example, Middleton's units were uninspired and unimaginative. Persisting in an attempt to force well-prepared positions using orthodox tactics, despite heavy casualties, the corps failed to achieve its objectives. Middleton's principal effort at a solution was to relieve several of his subordinate division and regimental commanders, including one who was in command for only four days.[71] Nothing worked, however, until the massive COBRA carpet-bombings blasted a gap in the German defenses.

The Normandy breakout provided another instance in which Middleton's adaptability and flexibility didn't seem to measure up to his Ardennes performance. Freed from the confines of the Cotentin Peninsula and the frustrating hedgerow fighting, the VIII Corps' two fine armored divisions, Wood's 4th and Gerow's 6th, raced through the crumbling German resistance and ranged far ahead of the remainder of the corps. Although Middleton was perfectly content to use oral orders and other informal techniques to control his units, he was definitely uncomfortable when the speed and distance of his advancing units took them out of radio and telephone contact for relatively long periods.[72] This problem was particularly acute during the race across the Brittany Peninsula. The two armored commanders "regarded themselves as belonging to the Patton school of thought," and they and "their units became infected with an enthusiasm and self-confidence . . . perfectly suited to exploitation but proved . . . a headache to those who sought to retain a semblance of control."[73] Middleton was gravely concerned about his ability to manage these units effectively as they became more and more independent of his corps command. The situation was never satisfactorily controlled by VIII Corps and improved only when the armored units reached the limits of their advance at the shores of the peninsula. Middleton's battle leadership never adapted an effective means of managing the activities of these rapidly moving units.

The seeming disconnect between Middleton's outstanding ability to adapt his tactics during the Ardennes fighting and his failure of flexibility in Normandy and Brittany could perhaps be answered by the differing types of combat involved. In Normandy and Brittany he was attacking, seeking to find his opponent's weakness and exploit it. In the Ardennes, Middleton was reacting to the overwhelming enemy assault. The Germans held the initiative, and Middleton, like an overmatched boxer, was counterpunching for all he was worth. It may be, simply, that the infantryman in Middleton was more capable of defending against an armored assault than he was of conducting and controlling such a mechanized attack. After all, the defense he ultimately employed was primarily infantry oriented, using tanks as support for infantry-engineer roadblocks. He rejected (and rightfully so it would seem, given the situation in the Ardennes) any bold and over-ambitious use of larger armored formations when those units were available. Middleton's outstanding ability to adapt tactics to fit the dire circumstances he faced during the Battle of the Bulge indisputably proved to be exceptionally effective.[74]

In addition to calmness and flexibility, Middleton's battle leadership exhibited other positive characteristics that had an important, albeit lesser, effect on the battle: his talents as a tactician and organization of his staff. Middleton's technical competence as a tactician, and the common background and understanding this allowed him to have with his superiors who, like himself, were all infantrymen, was important because it permitted all the primary senior commanders involved in countering the German attack to work quickly toward a common end with roughly the same strategy.[75]

Bradley asserted postwar that he and Middleton had discussed and agreed upon a plan for defeating just such an attack in the Ardennes as the Germans launched, but this certainly is Bradley using hindsight. Nevertheless they both must have realized beforehand that holding the "shoulders" of the penetration and restricting the flow of enemy forces at crucial chokepoints while awaiting counterattack by outside reserves was the proper doctrinal response.[76] The problem, however, was not figuring out what Middleton was supposed to do—it was how to come up with the necessary forces with which to counterattack into the flanks of the German thrust. It was Middleton's predictability at the operational level that provided the advantage.[77]

Middleton's organizational leadership and management of his staff directed his corps to institute and employ management techniques and procedures that emphasized standard and well-established practice. This permitted an uncomplicated and simple approach to fighting the corps for Middleton's staff members.[78] Having a simple and stream-lined system for conducting operations is a definite advantage in a confusing and rapidly moving situation like the Ardennes fighting. Middleton was right when he wrote after the war, "Avoid complicated maneuvers. To expect results from large numbers of men the operations must be kept simple."[79] Such ideas seem to show perfect understanding of Clausewitz's observation that "in war everything is simple; but the simplest things are difficult to accomplish."[80]

Certainly there were also negative aspects associated with Middleton's battle leadership. The most glaring example of the leadership failings exhibited by the VIII Corps commander was his incredible reluctance to appoint an overall commander in several situations that desperately required one. Notably at St.-Vith and again at Bastogne, he refused or delayed placing one officer in overall command, weakly requesting the men on the spot to "cooperate" with each other.[81] Such a failure could have created a fatal confusion through lack of unity of command, especially at St.-Vith. If Bruce C. Clarke had been less willing to assume responsibility for the crumbling defense of St.-Vith, or had Alan Jones been more willing to cling to control of a situation that had already overwhelmed him, a disaster could have resulted. As it turned out, and with no thanks to Middleton, command unity devolved upon Clarke and later, Hasbrouck, his division commander.

In fairness to Middleton on this issue, there were some mitigating circumstances present. Hasbrouck's and Clarke's unit, the 7th Armored Division, belonged to Simpson's Ninth Army and were outside Middleton's normal chain of command. Additionally, before departing the Ninth Army area to move to the Ardennes, the tankers had been given only a vague, incomplete picture of what was going on in the VIII Corps sector and what their ultimate mission was to be.[82] Formal operations orders and detailed plans were out of the question in this situation, and probably would have been out of date within hours of their issue anyway. Further complicating matters was a seniority problem among the three generals. Jones, a major general and the ranking officer, had the smallest and weakest unit, while Hasbrouck, although commanding a full-strength armored division, had not yet been promoted and was still a brigadier general. While there was no question that Hasbrouck outranked Clarke, his direct subordinate, before Hasbrouck arrived on the scene, Jones had voluntarily turned over command of all troops in the St.-Vith area to the junior brigadier, Clarke.[83] As if that wasn't confusing enough, the 9th Armored Division Combat Command B commander, Bill Hoge, also a brigadier general, arrived in the St.-Vith area and joined the defense. Despite all the confusing factors present at St.-Vith (or, precisely *because* of the confusion), Middleton should have quickly appointed an overall commander, assuming responsibility as the ranking officer in the overall area whose headquarters was charged with coordinating the entire defense. Instead, he merely asked the several commanders to "carry the ball" for him—hardly what could be characterized as definitive guidance.[84] If he felt he lacked the authority to place Simpson's subordinates under command of one of his own unit commanders, he could have phoned Bradley. (He spoke to his Army Group commander several times during this period, which shows that communications was not a factor.)[85] It is highly doubtful that Bradley would have said no, as he sent the 7th Armored to Middleton in the first place. At any rate, the genial and cooperative Simpson was no stubborn Patton, and the Ninth Army commander would not have fought the command arrangement.[86]

Middleton never did establish command unity at St.-Vith. When responsibility for the defense of St.-Vith transferred to XVIII Airborne Corps on 20 December, the issue was still undecided and had to wait for Ridgway to sort it out. When John S. D. Eisenhower wrote that, "Middleton's preference for cooperation rather than unity of command caused less confusion than might be imagined," he was not complimenting Middleton.[87]

Nearly the same situation was repeated at Bastogne, although this time temporarily. Middleton spoke to Tony McAuliffe, acting commander of the 101st Airborne, and Roberts of the 10th Armored and "asked the men to cooperate, with neither in charge."[88] In this instance, both units involved came from outside Middleton's corps, but at least there was no seniority question, McAuliffe was the only one with stars on his collar. This time, however, Middleton corrected his mistake in a short time. He called Roberts in and told him McAuliffe was in sole command. There is evidence that Middleton took this action after receiving advice to do so from the 28th Infantry Division's commander, Dutch Cota, who with his division staff had just passed through Bastogne after being run out of Wiltz by the advancing Germans. When Cota observed the confusion and lack of overall direction in the town, he called Middleton and made the suggestion.[89] Whatever the motivation, Middleton's establishment of command unity in Bastogne was propitious and necessary. Nevertheless, he rightfully deserves criticism for failing to appoint an overall commander sooner at both critical locations. It was a major flaw in his battle leadership in the Ardennes.

Although Middleton's failure to establish unity of command quickly at critical locations had the greatest potential for disaster during the battle, the one failing that actually resulted in a serious setback took a slightly different form. Alan Jones and the 106th Infantry Division were new to VIII Corps and the Ardennes and had never seen combat. In addition to the unit's inexperience, it suffered from being in a weak location and occupying exposed positions. Yet Middleton failed to provide Jones or his staff with anything close to proper guidance or advice the critical situation would seem to demand. Instead, the battle-wise, veteran corps commander allowed his completely inexperienced subordinate to flounder on his own mistakes. As a consequence, the two regiments in the Schnee Eifel positions were lost, the largest single surrender of American troops in the European theater.[90]

Middleton's defense is anchored on his belief that the commander actually on the ground was the best judge of the situation and therefore should make the final decision. He wrote that he felt the senior commander should not unduly interfere with the subordinate's attempts to carry out a mission, and he "followed the principle that once you have assigned a task to a person leave him alone. If he needs advice he will come to you . . . there is no need for constant interference."[91] While this belief is laudable in general, Jones's specific situation in the Ardennes warranted more direction from Middleton than he received. During the inevitable postmortems on the disaster, Middleton allowed Jones to shoulder the blame for the surrender, while excusing his own actions with the magnanimous pronouncement that "although Jones made the wrong decision, he made it in good faith, based on information then available to him."[92] That may sound fine and high principled, but it lets Middleton off too easily, especially considering the fact that Middleton had expressed grave concern about the exposed positions on the Schnee Eifel long before the German attack began. According to one source, "Several times General Middleton requested permission to withdraw from this penetration of the German defensive positions [the exposed area] to straighten out his line along more tenable positions."[93] Because Middleton knew the vulnerability of Jones's dispositions well prior to the attack, he should have insisted clearly and unambiguously that Jones withdraw the two regiments, instead of leaving the ultimate decision to the less knowledgeable division commander.

After the battle, Middleton rather forcefully expressed his opinion that, had the veteran 2nd Infantry Division still occupied the northern flank instead of the untried 106th, "they'd never have broken through!"[94] This is revealing, as it shows Middleton admitting that the 106th was far from up to the standards needed to stop the Germans. Knowing this then, he had a duty to exert more control over the green 106th and its inexperienced commander. Ultimately, the primary responsibility for failing to ensure the regiments were swiftly withdrawn to more defensible terrain was Middleton's, not Jones's.

"MIDDLETON DID IT MAGNIFICENTLY"

Assessment of Middleton's battle leadership and strength of character clearly shows that his successes outweighed his failures. Above all, his calm and steady guidance of the VIII Corps in an almost hopelessly confusing situation was exactly what was needed to maintain the best possible defense under the circumstances. Members of his staff, subordinate commanders, and outside observers all noted this important influence and remarked upon it in later years. It seems that they would all agree with Middleton's aide, who wrote, "I never knew a man who had such equanimity under stress and who had the ability to master all the details with such apparent ease . . . everyone had complete confidence in his ability."[95]

Although his failures of command had potentially serious consequences, they did not affect the ultimate outcome to the same degree as his successes. The surrender of the 106th's two regiments, although a disaster for the nearly 8,000 soldiers involved, was counterbalanced by Middleton's dispatch of the 7th Armored Division to St.-Vith. Likewise, his failure to establish command unity quickly at St.-Vith and Bastogne was mitigated by the initiative and cooperation of excellent subordinates. Finally, Middleton's flexibility in adapting his tactics to the nature of the German threat created just the right defense needed to delay the attackers for the maximum amount of time possible.

Middleton's battle leadership was an important element in the American victory in the Ardennes. Although the 101st Airborne's defense of Bastogne has emerged as the popular image of this greatest of all American battles, without Middleton's steady leadership there would have been no siege of that famous city. Indeed, much more can be learned about command in combat by analyzing Middleton's battle leadership than by focusing totally on the defense of Bastogne. One of Middleton's subordinates, who himself became a highly respected corps commander in World War II combat, has written as good a bottom line on Middleton in the Ardennes as can be recorded: "His objective, with his crippled corps, was to slow down the German armies. Middleton did it magnificently, and has never been given adequate credit for his great performance."[96]

CHAPTER 6

Jones, Clarke, and the Defense of St.-Vith

If there is one lamentable figure among the senior American commanders in the Battle of the Bulge, it must be Maj. Gen. Alan W. Jones of the ill-fated 106th Infantry Division. His unit was destroyed as a cohesive fighting force so rapidly and so decisively that, at the darkest moment during the defense of St.-Vith, he remarked to Brig. Gen. Bruce C. Clarke, who had just arrived with his reinforcing armored command, "I've lost a division quicker than any division commander in the U.S. Army."[1] Indeed, when his two surrounded regiments on the Schnee Eifel capitulated to the Germans after fighting only four days, they represented the largest single surrender of American troops in the European Theater of Operations.[2] Such a disaster for American arms in such a key portion of the Ardennes could have been fatal to the entire U.S. effort had it not been for one of the heroes of this same battle— Brig. Gen. Bruce C. Clarke of the 7th Armored Division.

JONES'S CAREER
The Beginnings
At age twenty-two, Alan Walter Jones was commissioned a second lieutenant of infantry after graduating from the University of Washington. This was in 1917, the first summer of the Great War for the United States and the beginning of the buildup of our tiny, constabulary Army into a major fighting force.[3]

Appointed at Fort Leavenworth, Kansas, as a member of the 43rd Infantry Regiment, Jones joined the regiment in Camp Douglas, Utah, in October 1917. Although anxious to see combat overseas, Jones shared the fate of Eisenhower and Bradley and remained in training in the United States throughout the war. Unlike Middleton, who won fame and rapid promotion on the battlefield in France, First Lieutenant Jones served in more mundane places such as Camp Pike, Arkansas, and Pensacola, Florida, winning only a modest promotion to temporary captain in summer 1918. Even that rank was lost a year later when, like all officers in the rapidly demobilizing American Army, Jones reverted to his permanent rank, first lieutenant, in October 1919.

As quickly as it had grown, the powerful American Army stood down, becoming once again a small, professional force performing mostly policing duties in widely scattered locations such as the Philippine Islands, a Pacific outpost and remnant of the "Big Stick" days of the beginning of the century.[4] By the early 1920s, Captain Jones had regained his World War I rank and was in Manila with the 45th Infantry Regiment. For the 15,000 or so officers who led the Regular Army in those years between the world wars, service in the Philippines was a pleasant posting. Families routinely accompanied Army officers serving in the islands, and cheap native labor promised many amenities otherwise hard to afford on a captain's meager salary.[5]

Jones's next assignment was a fortunate one, for it took him to the Infantry School at Fort Benning during the years when George C. Marshall reigned as Assistant Commandant. Marshall kept a close eye on all officers passing through the school, personally selecting or approving all officers who served on the school faculty. The future Army Chief of Staff made notes to himself about those officers who impressed him and would later call on these men to fill the important command and staff positions during the war.[6] Jones's rapid rise after American entry into World War II seems likely to have been at least partly the result of favorably impressing Marshall during those years. If so, Jones was in good company, joining the likes of Bradley, "Vinegar Joe" Stilwell, J. Lawton Collins, Matthew Ridgway, and Walter Bedell Smith.

Apparently, Jones had impressed others as well, for his next assignment was to attend the Field Artillery Officers' Advanced Course at the Field Artillery School at Fort Sill, Oklahoma. This early version of cross-fertilization within branches of the Army was usually restricted to above-average performers who showed promise. Jones's selection also indicated that he scored higher than his infantry officer contemporaries in mathematics, otherwise he would not have been allowed to attend.[7]

Jones's next tour of duty was with the 12th Infantry Regiment at Fort Washington, Maryland, in 1931. Just over a year later, he was reassigned in the Washington, D.C., area to the Office of the Chief of Infantry, an influential and important assignment for Major Jones. Favorably impressing one's branch chief was not only a ticket to higher schooling (e.g., Command and Staff School and Army War College), but also an avenue to a choice command or staff assignment.[8] It is hardly surprising, then, that Jones's next assignment was as a student at the Command and Staff School at Fort Leavenworth, Kansas, in the Class of 1936.

After graduation from the Staff School, Jones returned to Washington State, joining the 7th Infantry Regiment at Vancouver Barracks in summer 1936, before returning to Washington, D.C., to attend the Army War College the following summer. After Jones completed the War College in the summer of 1938, he was reassigned to the 19th Infantry Regiment in Schofield Barracks, Hawaii. Duty in Hawaii was another choice assignment in the prewar army. Jones spent nearly three years there, advancing to lieutenant colonel on 1 July 1940.[9] By this time the war in Europe was nearly a year old, and the French Army—the largest army in Western Europe—had been humiliated by Germany in six weeks of "lightning war." Marshall and others of foresight were frantically trying to rebuild the pathetically small American Army into some kind of credible fighting force before it was too late.[10]

As part of his efforts to restructure and revitalize the American Army, Marshall was gathering around him in the War Department and the Army Staff those young, competent, and capable officers he had identified in the years between the wars. Jones was among those summoned to Washington, D.C., to report for duty in the Office of the

Assistant Chief of Staff, G-3, in 1941. On Christmas Eve of that year, just over two weeks after the United States had officially entered the war, Jones pinned on the eagles of a full colonel.[11]

By April 1942, Colonel Jones had transferred from the Army Staff to Gen. Lesley J. McNair's Army Ground Forces Command, located in Washington, D.C. Next to Marshall, McNair had the greatest impact on the creation of the American Army that fought in World War II. The "triangular" division organization, standardization of like units, "pooling" of assets (such as artillery), and nearly complete motorization of army units were all McNair innovations.[12] Jones was fortunate to serve under McNair at a time of such change and must have learned many valuable lessons from the association. It must be assumed that McNair was also suitably impressed with Jones's performance, because Jones gained the single star of a brigadier general barely six months after his promotion to colonel.[13]

Jones could now reflect on his quarter century of Army service with justifiable pride in achieving the top levels of his chosen profession. He had much in common with other soon-to-be famous infantrymen like Eisenhower and Bradley. They had all missed out on combat in World War I but shared similar schooling and career assignments, such as duty in the Philippines and Army Staff G-3 (Eisenhower) and Fort Benning's Infantry School and Hawaii (Bradley).

His preparation to meet the challenges he would face on the battlefield, so much like that of his near-contemporaries, would seem in retrospect to suggest that he, like them, would succeed in the test of battle.[14] But the cruel circumstances of combat following hard on the heels of stateside decimation of his division for replacements would single out Jones for disaster.

THE 106TH DIVISION

General Jones continued to progress in rank and responsibility through the next few months in the rapidly expanding Army. He was appointed Assistant Division Commander of the 90th Infantry Division and was clearly being trained and groomed (and evaluated) for higher command. He held the assistant position until January 1943, when he was entrusted with the post that all his contemporaries strove to achieve—command of a combat division. Jones took command of the 106th Infantry Division at Fort Jackson, South Carolina, in January, and on 16 March 1943 received his promotion to major general.[15]

Units comprising the 106th Division began arriving at Ft. Jackson on 29 November 1942, and it was formally activated on 15 March 1943. Its components came from all the various branches to Fort Jackson to complete a rigorous and comprehensive training program that would take the better part of two years. General Jones led the unit and trained it hard to prepare for combat in Europe. In the unit's history, *St. Vith: Lion in the Way*, Col. R. Ernest Dupuy explained the purpose of the training:

> The theory was that each of these new divisions would begin and end as homogeneous groups—recruits brought in around a hard core, called a cadre, gathered from already trained units. The training, laid down by Army Ground Forces, would be progressive from the beginning, balanced and coordinated, to the end that when each division moved to the battle front it would be a team. Its officers and men would know one another, would know their business. The only thing lacking would be that first thirty minutes of combat.[16]

After nearly two years of diligent training (including participating in the Second Army maneuvers in Tennessee in early 1944), the 106th Infantry Division became a reasonably well-trained outfit of 708 officers, 42 warrant officers, and 12,523 enlisted men.[17] The division had demonstrated it could operate effectively as a combat team, and small-unit leaders among the soldiers had been identified and placed in key positions. The unit was nearly ready to enter combat. Jones must have been confident of his unit's ability to perform its job on the battlefield with the team he had trained. In April 1944, however, after the unit had completed the Second Army maneuvers and moved to Camp Atterbury, Indiana, it was picked apart.

Thousands of Jones's men were reassigned out of the division, primarily because of mounting casualty lists in the European fighting. The manpower crisis was also, indirectly, a result of such things as the huge Army Service Forces structure, the decision to limit the number of ground combat divisions (vice the air effort, for example), and the suspicion of planners that the war was winding down.[18] In April, 3,100 enlisted men were ordered out of the 106th and shipped overseas. By August 1944, a total of 7,247 had been shipped out. To make matters worse, most of the infantrymen taken from Jones were the aggressive, capable small-unit leaders occupying key positions—the very men a trained unit can least afford to lose and still maintain combat efficiency.[19]

Regardless of how well trained a unit is, it cannot lose over 60 percent of its best and brightest and retain a high level of combat efficiency. By the time the 106th moved to Massachusetts and its port of embarkation in October 1944, it had regained its full number strength by transfers from the Army Air Forces, Specialized Training Program, Army Service Forces, and other noninfantry fields, but the division could in no way quickly make up for the staggering loss of trained, key infantrymen. Nevertheless, the war would not wait on the 106th to retrain itself, so the division shipped out for the European Theater in mid-October. General Jones collected his rebuilt division in England at the end of October, and he and the division staff began to oversee the unit's drawing of equipment in preparation for the impending movement to combat.[20]

Drawing equipment was about all the 106th had time to do before beginning its shift to the combat zone on 1 and 2 December 1944. Winter conditions on the English Channel were unpleasant and made worse by having to endure several shipboard days either crossing or waiting on storm-tossed troopships around the Channel ports before disembarking. Once they finally landed, troops still had to contend with the bone-jarring trip to the front in Belgium in wet, freezing weather. Dupuy describes the miserable conditions:

> Days of rain, snow and mud; days of misery for the men packed in trucks as they rumbled through France and into Belgium, were prelude for the 106th's entry into battle. Inability to change clothing or footgear sopping and soggy with icy water is not conducive to the joy of living. When

such things precede the vital test, when the discomfort and misery are added to the uncertainty of battle, the men undergoing them must be of tempered caliber, men so inured to the rigors of discipline they subordinate personal matters for teamwork. And the combat teams of the 106th, unfortunately, were not yet of that caliber; the Division was paying for the frequent drain on it for replacements, with constant influx of new personnel.[21]

Awaiting the officers and men of the 106th was the ominously quiet section of the Allied line referred to as the "Ghost Front" by those combat-weary soldiers who were manning it. If it lived up to its name, it might be just the place for the new unit filled with new replacements to learn the ropes and ease itself into combat. Jones must have hoped so as his unit was trucked wearily toward the weakest part of the entire line.

The "Golden Lions" of the 106th Infantry Division began taking over the 22-mile wide section of the Ardennes front from the veteran 2nd Infantry Division on 10 December, accomplishing most of the handover on 11 December in accordance with the VIII Corps Letter of Instruction. Although the third and final infantry regiment (the 424th) did not complete its occupation of the southernmost part of the division sector until 12 December, Jones assumed responsibility for the area at 1900 hours, 11 December 1944.[22] He had barely four days before the main effort of the German attack slammed into his green, untried unit.

CLARKE'S CAREER
The Beginnings
Bruce C. Clarke's path to the crossroads at St.-Vith differed in many ways from that Jones had followed. Clarke was several years younger, a former enlisted soldier, West Point graduate, and engineer-turned-tanker. Perhaps most important, he had fought his way across the battlefields of France to reach the beleaguered Belgian town. In the critical early hours of the fight to hold St.-Vith, Clarke's combat leadership (and Jones's inexperience) would prove decisive.

In 1918, the year after Alan Jones was commissioned an infantry lieutenant out of college, the seventeen-year-old Clarke sought out a recruiting sergeant in Watertown, New York, and enlisted in the U.S. Army.[23] The former farm boy signed enlistment papers and drew his first uniform at Fort Slocum, New York, in April 1918. Eager to see combat before the war ended, Clarke must have been disappointed that he remained in the United States in training for the final few months of the war.[24] This taste of military life seemed to please him, however, for Clarke retained a military connection after he was mustered out of the Regular Army:

> I had been an enlisted man in the Army in 1918, long enough to complete basic training. In 1920, I joined a New York National Guard artillery battalion in Buffalo, New York (the 106th Field Artillery Battalion). I rose to Corporal. From there I applied to take the competitive exam of the National Guard for West Point. I passed and entered on July 1, 1921 in the Class of 1925.[25]

Clarke did well at West Point, both academically and militarily, serving in cadet leadership positions in three of his four years there. Almost as soon as his Plebe (freshman) year was completed, Clarke was chosen a Cadet Corporal and served in that rank for the next two years. In his final year, he was a Cadet Captain and company commander—among the highest-ranking cadets in his class. He progressed well enough to tutor some of his classmates who were having problems, and he graduated high enough (33 of 248) to earn his first choice of branch. Clarke chose the Corps of Engineers and was commissioned in that branch on graduation day, 12 June 1925.[26]

Newly commissioned (and newlywed) Second Lieutenant Clarke reported to the 29th Engineer Topographic Battalion at Fort Humphreys, near Washington, D.C., and assumed duties as a platoon leader. He spent the next year learning the responsibilities of a small-unit leader and familiarizing himself with the tools and equipment of a junior officer in the Engineers.[27] More importantly, Lieutenant Clarke began in earnest a study of leadership, commandership, and soldiership, which became a consuming passion for the rest of his life. Beginning here and continuing through each successive unit, Clarke turned his assignments into "leadership laboratories" in which he tested his ideas on leadership and commandership and sought to draw lessons for improvement in his next unit. He wrote later of these early experiences and some of the lessons he learned about small-unit leadership:

> I had fixed in my mind . . . principles in handling men. Many years ago I wrote we cannot produce outstanding units from the ordinary run of personnel unless we train, coach, and develop our squad leaders, platoon sergeants and platoon leaders to look well after the men in their units and mold them into proud and winning teams under the direction of good commandership from above. . . . The key words are *teams* and *motivation*.[28]

Clarke must have impressed his superiors with his early performance, for after only a year in his first army unit he was selected to attend Cornell University and complete a degree in civil engineering. He accomplished that academic mission and returned to the military post in summer 1927. For the remainder of that summer, Clarke commanded the Engineer School Colored Detachment, then attended the Engineer Officer's Advanced Course. He remained on post after completing the Advanced Course, and returned for duty in his old unit, the "29th Topo" through 1928 and into 1929. Lieutenant Clarke's next posting was to the 3rd Engineer Regiment in Schofield Barracks, Hawaii.[29]

In Hawaii, Clarke mixed "line" duties as a platoon leader, with one of the few staff assignments of his career during the three-year tour in the islands. He served for a time as the regimental supply officer of his engineer regiment, but predictably, the lessons he carried with him from Hawaii continued to be those of leading and motivating soldiers. In 1932, he witnessed an example of "motivation" for the unit's annual qualification rifle range in which the company first sergeant won the top award (and the lion's share of $85 from the company fund). Clarke wondered how such a system motivated the

"Bolos" (soldiers who shot so poorly they failed to qualify with their weapon). He wrote later about this:

Awards that motivate only the top men are of little value in raising the ability of a unit. It takes awards to motivate the lower third to do that. A unit is measured by the ability of the lower third personnel in it to carry their part of the load.[30]

Upon his return from Hawaii, Clarke became the junior member of the Reserve Officer Training Corps (ROTC) detachment at the University of Tennessee. Because ROTC duty was commonplace among the officers in the pre–World War II army, assignments of four years or even longer to civilian schools was not uncommon. So, like many others, including Bradley and Middleton, Clarke took up his post as assistant professor of military science and tactics.[31]

In addition to his military duties, which included serving as the detachment's adjutant and administrative officer, Clarke refereed football games, coached the university wrestling team, and in his spare time studied for and obtained a law degree from LaSalle Extension University. He recorded later that, although he had no intention of practicing law, the LL.B. "balanced my education."[32]

After four years of ROTC duty, Clarke was ordered to the Galveston Engineer District on the Texas coast in 1936. Clarke continued to perform in an outstanding manner, putting his civil engineering training to work. He described his duties:

I was . . . in charge of surveying the rivers of Texas for Congress for navigation, flood control, water power and water conservation. I created a new organization of 50 professional engineers, surveyors, draftsmen and field crews covering practically the whole state of Texas. During the next three years we submitted over 40 reports to Congress on Texas.[33]

Although Clarke (now captain) had been away from a troop assignment for seven years, his record must have been viewed as superior by engineer branch, for he was selected to attend the Command

and General Staff School in 1939. His was to be the last class until after World War II. When Captain Clarke reported to Fort Leavenworth to begin the Staff School, the standard nine-month course of instruction was in effect. However, with Europe at war and Marshall frantically trying to retrieve the American Army from decades of unpreparedness and neglect, Clarke's class was cut to five months, and the Staff School, closed for the duration of the war. On 1 February 1940, Clarke graduated. It was the last Army school he ever attended.[34]

Clarke's next assignment was the most important one of his career because it began his association with the branch in which he would achieve his greatest successes and in which he would make his greatest battlefield contributions. Clarke was assigned to Brig. Gen. Adna R. Chaffee's newly formed 7th Mechanized Brigade at Fort Knox, Kentucky. His association with the fledgling U.S. Armored Force had begun.

Clarke was ordered to organize the 47th Engineer Troop (Mechanized) and serve also as Brigadier General Chaffee's brigade engineer in this largely experimental armored brigade. By April 1940, Clarke's troop of two lieutenants and ninety-one enlisted engineers was in Louisiana with Chaffee's 7th Mechanized Brigade conducting war game maneuvers against the 1st Infantry Tank Brigade from Fort Benning, Georgia.[35] Much rode on the outcome of these maneuvers, for a separate American armored force was still only an idea of visionaries like Chaffee. The infantry still officially owned all the tanks.

The result of the maneuvers was a smashing victory for Chaffee's armored brigade, validating his theories. No small part of the victory was due to Clarke's innovative and creative use of his engineer troop. He demonstrated to Chaffee that he understood perfectly the aggressive, slashing tactics that a powerful armored force could use to overwhelm a less mobile enemy—the same tactics the Germans were unleashing against the Anglo-French forces.[36] On 1 July 1940, Chief of Staff Marshall officially created the American armored force and activated the 1st and 2nd Armored Divisions. For the armored force engineer, Chaffee chose Clarke.[37]

Clarke, still a junior officer, was actually the "acting" armored force engineer, commander of the 1st Armored Division's 16th

Armored Engineer Battalion, and division engineer. Eventually, senior officers would arrive to bump Clarke out of these jobs requiring higher rank. Before this happened, Chaffee appointed Clarke to serve on the board that developed the first Table of Organization and Equipment for the armored division. Chaffee's guidance was that the armored division be "a balanced team of combat arms and services . . . of equal importance and equal prestige"[38]—good guidance, since the eventual result was the versatile, mobile, yet powerful armored "Combat Command" divisions that led the race across France and the battlefields of Europe in 1944 and 1945.

With the outbreak of real war in Europe, events proceeded at a fast pace. Clarke listed his duties and assignments over the next year and a half:

> Follow[ing] in rapid order was duty as Armored Force Engineer; Commanding Officer of 16th Engineer Battalion, 1st Armored Division; official observer with the British 1st Armoured Division that had come out of Dunkirk; orders to Pine Camp [New York] to create the 24th Armored Engineer Battalion [4th Armored Division]; Chief of Staff, 4th Armored Division during Major General [Henry W.] Baird's and Major General [John S.] "P" Wood's time as Division Commanders. . . . I went from Captain in February 1940 to Major, Lieutenant Colonel and Colonel on 1 February 1942—a two year period.[39]

The unit Clarke helped prepare for war in the pine barrens of New York was to become one of the most famous of the entire war in the European Theater of Operations. Once it was unleashed on the Germans after the Normandy breakout, it led the way in the Allied race across France. In the process, the 4th Armored Division helped create the legend of George Patton as a genius of armored warfare. Commanding the vanguard and leading the way was Colonel Clarke.[40]

THE 4TH AND 7TH ARMORED DIVISIONS

For more than two years, the 4th Armored Division had trained long and hard in the snows of Pine Camp, at the blistering Mojave Desert

Training Center and the proving ground of the Tennessee maneuvers. Under its aggressive, dynamic commander, Maj. Gen. John S. "P" Wood, the division was molded into a superb fighting organization. Unlike the unfortunate 106th Infantry Division, the 4th Armored was not picked apart to provide replacements, and it entered combat as a well-trained team of men who had been working together for many months.[41] Clarke had helped oversee the long months of training as the division Chief of Staff. In that position, he learned much about leadership, commandership, training, and morale from Wood (and his predecessor Baird). As the division entered combat, Clarke took command of one of its principal fighting elements, Combat Command A. He would lead its triumvirate of tanks, artillery, and armored infantry from Normandy to Lorraine in an American blitzkrieg of unequalled power and mobility.[42]

Clarke's commander, "P" Wood, was a big, athletic, inspirational leader whose enthusiasm and drive seemed almost limitless. Wood established himself as one of the premier division commanders in Europe as he drove the 4th Armored Division farther and faster than anyone thought possible once the St.-Lô breakout sprung his unit from the hedgerows of Normandy. The division's official history describes the unit's operating mode:

> Under General Wood, the Fourth Armored's style of fighting was set. . . . It was a daring, hard-riding, fast shooting style. The division's front was as wide as the roads down which it sped. The recon men out front kept going until they hit resistance too hot to handle. Teams of tanks and armored infantrymen swung out smoothly in attack formation under the protective fire of the quickly emplaced artillery. The division broke the enemy or flowed about them, cutting the German lines of communication and splitting apart the units.[43]

In the lead were Clarke and the soldiers of Combat Command A. Although the division's race across France was initially delayed by a brief (and ultimately futile) diversion west into Brittany in an attempt to capture intact some badly needed port facilities, by early August Wood had Clarke and the rest headed east.[44] Within the month, Clarke had driven his command across the Seine and had closed up on the Moselle River at Commercy. The rapid advance had covered about 1,000 miles. The 4th Armored sent 11,000 German prisoners to the rear, losing about 1,100 of its own from all causes.[45] Unfortunately, by the end of August, all along the Allied line, fuel supplies dried up because the advance had been so successful. By supreme effort, including the phenomenally successful "Red Ball Highway," a few days later supplies of fuel flowed once again. Unfortunately, the brief respite gave the Germans enough time to regain their balance and stiffen their defenses by the time the 4th Armored, including Clarke's Combat Command A, began to roll.[46] Clarke's objective was to cross the Moselle River and cut off the German forces holding out in the fortress city of Nancy. He succeeded in a smashing victory for Combat Command A and the rest of the 4th Armored. Clarke later referred to the encirclement of Nancy, including the subsequent tank battles in the vicinity near Arracourt, as his "greatest victory"[47] (despite his much-heralded success later at St.-Vith). Indeed, the operations of Clarke's Combat Command A, the 4th Armored, and its parent unit, the XII Corps, around Nancy and Arracourt have been studied at the Command and General Staff College as early examples demonstrating the principles of modern airland battle maneuver warfare. This is a lasting tribute not only to Clarke's skill as an armored warfare tactician but also to his demonstrated battle commandership.[48]

Of importance to this study is the way the conduct of the fighting around Arracourt resembled the later German attacks (and Clarke's defense) at St.-Vith. A monograph prepared by CGSC's Combat Studies Institute describes that fighting:

> The Fifth Panzer Army . . . bypassed Lunéville and was moving north to strike at CC'A's exposed position around Arracourt. The battle that resulted was one of the largest armored engagements ever fought on the Western Front. . . . CC'A' held Arracourt with an extended tank infantry engineer outpost line supported by tanks, tank destroyers and artillery. At 0800 on 19 September [1944], company sized elements of the 113th Panzer Brigade penetrated the outposts . . . of CC'A's

salient. Two tank destroyer platoons and a medium tank company engaged the panzers in a running fight that extended into the vicinity of CC'A's headquarters where a battalion of self-propelled 105mm howitzers took the panzers under point-blank fire. The Germans discovered that the fog, which gave them tactical surprise and protected them from U.S. aircraft, worked to their disadvantage by negating the superior range of their tank guns. As the fighting surged back and forth through the fog, CC'A's tank and tank destroyers utilized their mobility to outmaneuver and ambush the large panzers. . . . Colonel Clarke unleashed two medium tank companies on a sweep that took the panzers in flank and rear. . . . According to the Germans, the panzer assault cost them fifty precious tanks and accomplished nothing. . . . From 20 to 25 September, the Fifth Panzer Army fed the 111th Panzer Brigade and the understrength 11th Panzer Division into a series of attacks against the Arracourt position. Each assault followed the pattern set on 19 September. The panzers attacked under the cover of fog only to be disorganized by CC'A's mobile defense.[49]

The account reads like a dress rehearsal of Clarke's later fighting at St.-Vith. The weather, tactics, equipment, and even the enemy unit involved, the 5th Panzer Army, commanded by Gen. Hasso von Manteuffel, were the same or similar to the later, larger battle in the Ardennes. The outcomes were also similar, as the Americans scored a great success against the attackers. The entire 4th Armored Division, including Clarke's Combat Command A, which bore the brunt of the fighting, toted up an impressive 281 German tanks destroyed, 3,000 enemy killed, and another 3,000 taken prisoner against 626 friendly casualties.[50] It was the largest American tank battle prior to the Battle of the Bulge. Clarke was clearly doing exceptionally well in this particular "leadership laboratory."

Although Clarke had ably demonstrated his readiness for a promotion by his superb battlefield performance, he would have to leave the 4th Armored in order to receive it. Armored divisions were allotted one brigadier general and one major general (the division commander). The 4th already had its brigadier general, Holmes Dager (commanding Combat Command B). Clarke was reassigned to another armored division where he could receive the star he had earned. On 1 November 1944, Clarke reported to the 7th Armored Division, a part of Lt. Gen. William Simpson's Ninth Army in Holland, as the new commander of Combat Command B—a unit that was having problems.[51] As Clarke said, "The 7th Armored Division was in bad shape on 1 November 1944."[52]

Reflecting in the third person in postwar memoirs, he went on to describe what confronted him and his old friend, the also newly appointed division commander, Brig. Gen. Robert Hasbrouck, as they arrived at the 7th Armored:

> When Clarke went from the 4th Armored Division to the 7th Armored Division on 1 November 1944, General Hasbrouck and he replaced generals who were relieved, reduced to Colonel, and ordered home. They found a division that had been under the command of a former infantry officer who did not understand [the correct] employment of armored forces. He had three fixed combat commands. Their composition never changed. All three were normally engaged in the classic "two up, one back" formation. There was little flexibility and the battalions were inadequately maintained, physically and mentally depleted, and about 50 percent effective.[53]

Hasbrouck and Clarke reorganized the unit along the proper lines, making it a flexible, mobile organization like the 4th. They initiated an intensive training program to instill confidence and competence into the leadership at all levels. There was nothing wrong with the soldiers in the 7th, but the unit as a whole had suffered from poor "generalship and commandership" from the top. After six weeks of intensive training, Clarke and Hasbrouck were beginning to see some positive results. Clarke's promotion to general finally arrived on 7 December 1944,[54] nine days before the Ardennes attack.

ATTACK AT ST.-VITH

As newly promoted Brigadier General Clarke continued to train Combat Command B, 7th Armored Division, in Holland and mold it into an effective fighting force, Jones was attempting much the same thing with his 106th Infantry Division in Belgium (appendix H). But while Clarke had nearly six months of recent combat leadership to draw upon, Jones had none. In fact, none of Jones's subordinate unit senior commanders had any worthwhile recent combat experience.[55] Further, while Clarke had six weeks to work with the 7th while it sat out of the combat line, Jones had only four days to season his troops as they manned a huge sector in the Ardennes front. This woefully inadequate period of preparation, so closely following the long and tiring journey across the Atlantic, the Channel, and then Belgium, left Jones's division obviously unprepared for the German attack in mid-December.

The 106th Division's sector was probably the most difficult to defend of all sectors in Middleton's overextended VIII Corps line. Impossibly wide for a single division to defend, it meandered for some 22 miles along the broken terrain of the German-Belgian border. Although his right (southern) flank rested in a somewhat defensible area of "innumerable watercourses" and "jumbled hills" near the 28th Infantry Division's positions, Jones's left (northern) flank abutted the V Corps–VIII Corps boundary in the Losheim Gap, the region's classic invasion route.[56] To his front, Jones was constrained to place the bulk of his combat power on the high plateau of the Schnee Eifel, with those particular positions extending into the Siegfried Line.[57]

To defend what amounted to an 8-mile-deep, 22-mile-wide salient into the German lines, Jones had the following: an infantry division of nine battalions of riflemen; two squadrons of cavalry (the attached 14th Cavalry Group); five battalions of field artillery; one battalion of tank destroyers; one battalion of antiaircraft artillery; and (potentially) the fires of nine battalions of VIII Corps field artillery units that were in the vicinity. In all, Jones had about 14,000 of his own soldiers, to which he added about 1,000 cavalrymen and another 1,200 or so from the tank destroyers, antiaircraft artillery, and other attached support troops.[58] Given the extent of the sector, this total of approximately 16,000 troops was hardly a formidable force.

Jones's headquarters was in a school in the town of St.-Vith itself. Described as "an average Belgian town, with a population of a little over 2,000,"[59] it had sufficient billets to hold a division head-quarters and associated support troops. More importantly, it sat at the center of a road net that tied together the roads that ran around the barrier of the Schnee Eifel plateau 12 miles to the east. Six roads crossed at the St.-Vith hub, then connected to the road nets running to the north (Malmedy), south (Bastogne), and west (Vielsalm). Like Bastogne, 25 miles to the south, St.-Vith constituted a major choke-point for any attack through the Ardennes[60]—that is, if it could be successfully defended.

Jones may have been lacking in combat experience, but he knew enough to be uncomfortable with the defensive positions his units had been obliged to take up. The 106th had been ordered to relieve the 2nd Infantry Division in place, occupying each of the 2nd's pillboxes and positions. The bulk of Jones's combat power, the 422nd and 423rd Infantry Regiments, held these positions. They were too exposed for Jones's liking, because a determined German thrust to either flank of the plateau could put the two regiments in danger of being surrounded and cut off.[61] Jones's superior, Middleton, didn't like the exposed positions on the Schnee Eifel for the same reasons and felt the same; in fact, on his own initiative he had earlier withdrawn units of the 2nd Infantry Division from some of the most exposed of the Siegfried Line positions and had the pillboxes destroyed.[62] Nevertheless, most of the positions on the plateau remained, now manned by Jones's men.

The four days prior to the launching of the German offensive were relatively quiet ones in the 106th Division's sector. The unit After Action Report describes the division's activities for each of the days in three short sentences. Typical is this entry for 13 December 1944: "Defensive positions maintained and improved in all sectors. Enemy activity during period consisted of artillery fire and minor patrol activity. Seven infantry battalions and one squadron of cavalry [reinforced] engaged during period."[63] But if the lack of significant enemy activity had convinced Jones and his unit to think that the so-called "Ghost Front" would mercifully live up to its name, they soon lost this illusion.

16 DECEMBER

At 0530 hours on 16 December, U.S. artillery forward observers looked east as "the whole horizon erupted" before their eyes. For 45 minutes, nearly 2,000 artillery pieces and mortars of all types and calibers (up to giant 14-inch guns) kept up a sustained barrage that blasted front line positions, interdicted road junctions, and cut wire lines between headquarters and forward units.[64] All along the 80-mile Ardennes front, units were pounded with tons of shells in preparation for the German assault. Before the guns had stopped their barrage, German infantry, supported by panzers, advanced against the American positions.

Despite many of the wire lines being cut, the 106th headquarters received enough reports of ground action to indicate the attack was a general assault all along their overextended line. The 422nd and 423rd Regiments both reported enemy attacks early in the day, and the lightly armed cavalry troops of the 14th Cavalry Group in the Losheim Gap were being pushed back by spirited attacks.[65] Some of the 14-inch shells fell in St.-Vith, and while they did little damage, they helped lend credence to the subordinate units' battle reports.[66]

Jones's headquarters, which had barely enough time to establish itself as a functioning division command entity since it arrived in St.-Vith, must have quickly become overwhelmed by the countless reports of numerous German attacks on virtually all of its deployed units throughout the morning hours of that first day. Nevertheless, Jones and his staff reacted to the increasing number of assaults by ordering units from the division's meager reserve forces to each of the threatened areas and by keeping Middleton and the VIII Corps staff informed of the developing (and deteriorating) situation.

By 1145 hours, one of the 424th's battalions in division reserve had been released to the regiment to help hold its line, and at 1200 hours one of the division's engineer companies had to be committed as infantry to block further penetrations of the 423rd's sector. Jones threw in most of the rest of his reserve forces later in the afternoon as other areas were threatened. The 422nd committed its regimental reserve in the morning but needed help from the division reserve by 1700 hours.[67] The 32nd Reconnaissance Squadron was brought up from group reserve to help the hard-pressed 14th Cavalry Group, which was quickly "unravelling."[68]

Middleton, Jones's boss, tried to help his subordinate when it became obvious that the German assault was a serious threat, but even the corps commander had few assets in reserve to influence the action. He released a large portion of his precious armored reserve at 1120 hours that morning when he assigned Combat Command B, 9th Armored Division, to the 106th. But the badly needed armored combat command, still at Faymonville in the V Corps sector to the north, would take several hours to reach St.-Vith.[69] Nevertheless, Jones set his staff to work developing a counterattack plan using this unit.[70] He would use it, of course, to try to keep his two regiments on the plateau from being surrounded. The immediate question facing Jones, however, was whether to pull back those two regiments and their supporting units while he still could. This was the single most important question Jones would address in his entire career, and his decision would decide the ultimate fate of his unit. The combat-inexperienced Jones received scant help in making his decision from his battle-hardened corps commander, Middleton. Instead of *ordering* Jones to withdraw the bulk of his division from the exposed positions, Middleton left the final decision to his new subordinate. After a confusing and controversial phone conversation on the evening of 16 December, each man thought the other had agreed to just the opposite course of action—Middleton thought Jones was pulling the units back, but Jones believed his corps commander had approved his decision to leave them in place. This disaster was nearly catastrophic for the entire American defense of the Ardennes, for Jones had made the wrong decision. By leaving the units in place, he destroyed his division.[71]

17 DECEMBER

Jones's decision to keep the units in place on the plateau may have rested on his expectation of an early morning arrival of Combat Command B, 7th Armored (appendix I), on 17 December. He hoped to use the tanks and armored infantry to keep the roads to the east open and therefore keep the Germans out of St.-Vith.[72] But when the 7th

Armored had not arrived by 0930 hours, 17 December, Jones had to take some action to stop the enemy from rapidly closing on the St.-Vith hub. Like Middleton was doing at Bastogne, Jones turned to his only remaining reserve force—combat engineers.

Jones and his staff gave the mission of delaying the enemy and defending St.-Vith to Lt. Col. Tom Riggs, the big, ex-football star from the University of Illinois who commanded the 81st Engineer Combat Battalion—the 106th's division engineer unit. Riggs described how he received his critical mission:

> My orders to command a task force for the defense of St.-Vith were issued by Maj. Gen. Jones in the division CP at about 0930 on 17 December. We had just finished a division staff meeting focused on the lack of any resistance to the German advance in the northern sector defended by the 14th Cav. Gp. A German tank and infantry force was reported to be moving west on the Schoenberg-St.-Vith road. Col. Baker, chief of staff of the 106th, helped to designate and notify the attachment to the task force of [VIII] corps units: 168 Engr. Cbt Bn. and a platoon from the 820 Tank Destroyer Battalion.[73]

By dispatching Riggs's patchwork force (it included the division's band) to defend the approaches to St.-Vith, Jones (described at this time by Riggs as "an increasingly frustrated man") had fortunately taken the correct action to prevent the hard-pressed crossroads from being overrun. Riggs's force was completely destroyed over the next few days, but it kept the enemy out of St.-Vith during the critical hours before help arrived.[74]

While Jones was desperately trying to assess the overall situation and do what he could to patch up his punctured front, events were occurring elsewhere that would ultimately prevent the destruction of the 106th Division from severely hampering the overall defense. As Jones and his staff tried to keep their heads and react appropriately in the unfamiliarity of combat and the chaos of the overwhelming attack, Eisenhower had assessed the situation and concluded that Middleton needed help. He alerted the 7th Armored Division to move to the

Ardennes to give Alan Jones some much needed (and combat-experienced) assistance.

On the evening of 16 December, Clarke was about to start out on a much-deserved rest trip to Paris when his division commander contacted him from the command post. Clarke later recalled what happened:

> At 2000 I received a telephone call from General Robert W. Hasbrouck, Commanding General, 7th Armored Division, saying that the division had received orders to march immediately south to Bastogne to report to the Commanding General of the VIII Corps. What we were to do when we got to Bastogne was unknown. He told me that the division would march as soon as road clearances could be obtained. General Hasbrouck directed that I proceed immediately to Bastogne and report to [General Middleton] to get information on the situation. My combat command would lead the division on its march of 60 to 70 miles south.[75]

Clarke grabbed his Operations Officer, Maj. Owen Woodruff, and set off immediately with two enlisted drivers.

The trip south to the VIII Corps headquarters at Bastogne was a miserable one in the fog over icy roads, but at 0400 hours the next morning, 17 December, Clarke found the VIII Corps Commander quietly reading in his headquarters van at Bastogne.[76] Middleton then made his greatest single contribution to the defense of St.-Vith when he told Clarke, "Alan Jones is having some trouble at St.-Vith—grab something to eat and a little sleep and go to him . . . if he needs help give it to him."[77] By dispatching the 7th Armored to bolster Jones, Middleton ensured the vital crossroads would become a chokepoint for the German drive and not a funnel into the Allied rear.

The situation in the 106th's area was growing worse by the minute as Middleton spoke with Clarke, but the corps commander's natural calmness and understated directive failed to convey the true situation to the armored commander. Clarke, who arrived at St.-Vith about 1030 hours, was appalled to find that confusion and chaos were rampant within Jones's headquarters staff.[78] As Clarke sought out Jones to learn what was happening, he directed Woodruff to find out all he could from the 106th's staff. Years later Woodruff described the panicked situation:

> The 106th Division Headquarters was set up in a school building in St.-Vith. I was told the G-3 section was located on the top [3rd] floor of the building. [Clarke] told me to find out what the situation was while [he] conferred with General Jones. Unfortunately, as I was going up the stairs to the 3rd floor the G-3 section was coming down the stairs with bits and pieces of their equipment. The room that had contained the operation maps and other paraphernalia . . . was disintegrating. The operations sergeant was busy burning classified documents and otherwise destroying the maps with their acetate covers. I asked him what they were doing and he said something about the Germans are almost here and we are getting out. I tried to talk to anyone who would stand still long enough to answer a question. . . . I never found anyone from the G-2 section to talk to . . . the net result of this chaos was my failure to obtain any detailed information and I never was able to find a map with troop dispositions. . . . We acquired little or nothing in the way of information from the 106th Division staff.[79]

Meanwhile, Clarke had found Jones in his office, told him who he was, and asked to be briefed on the situation as it was known. Jones seemed extremely agitated and apprehensive, especially since his son, Lt. Alan Jones Jr., was serving as a staff officer in one of the cut-off regiments.[80] When Jones told Clarke as much as he knew—a major German attack had surrounded his two regiments on the Schnee Eifel and was pressing in on St.-Vith from three sides—the armored commander knew it was a "serious breakthrough." Clarke also concluded that the 106th's overall knowledge of the situation (both enemy and friendly) was "very hazy."[81]

Jones urged Clarke to attack to the east to relieve his cut-off troops, but when Clarke asked to speak to the surrounded commanders to coordinate the operation, the division commander said he couldn't reach them by wire or radio (although intermittent radio contact was maintained until nearly the end).[82] Jones and his staff had also neglected to appoint one overall commander for the two surrounded regiments; this would not only make it difficult to work with them from the point of view of any counterattack, but would also plague the efforts of the units themselves to coordinate their attempts to break out on their own. Moreover, the 106th had prepared no counterattack plan, offering the weak excuse that the VIII Corps had not issued its directive to prepare one until the day before the German assault[83]—not a convincing excuse from a unit that had expressed grave concern over its exposed regiments since the day it took over its sector. Earlier, on 16 December, the 106th staff had begun to plan a counterattack using Combat Command B, 9th Armored, after that unit was attached to them that day, but instead sent the 9th's tankers to the southern part of the 106th's sector on the mistaken belief the 7th Armored was arriving early on 17 December.[84] Judging from the 106th staff's chaotic state when Clarke arrived, it seems unlikely that they would have been able to coordinate a successful counterattack for the 9th Armored late on 16 or early 17 December even if they had tried.

It soon became painfully evident to Clarke that the 106th couldn't maintain enough control of the panicked traffic on its roads even to ensure the prompt arrival of Clarke's desperately needed combat command. Clarke's Combat Command B, 7th Armored, was inching its way over narrow roads clogged with fleeing vehicles in an agonizingly slow crawl toward St.-Vith. It began to look as if the rapidly advancing German columns from the east would arrive at St.-Vith before the tankers and armored infantrymen could force their way into town from the west.[85]

As Jones's staff continued to pack up and move their operation westward, the 106th Division commander remained in his office, fretting over the impossible predicament in which his unit found itself, but seeming to exercise little control over any efforts to salvage the situation. Clarke said that he never observed anyone from Jones's staff (including Colonel Baker, his Chief of Staff) make any attempt to contact Jones for instructions, directives, or advice, nor did he notice that Jones called for any staff officer. Clarke remembered that, "General Jones was apparently in a state of apprehension, and he kept remarking . . . about his son who was a Lieutenant in one of the surrounded battle groups [regiments]. It, of course, bothered him."[86]

At about 1300 hours Clarke witnessed an incident upsetting to him. Jones received a call from his corps commander, Middleton, inquiring as to the situation in St.-Vith. As the shocked armored commander listened in disbelief, Jones told his superior that, "in general, things are looking up. . . . Clarke is here [and] has troops coming. . . . We are going to be all right." After he had hung up, Clarke confronted Jones to ask him why he had not told his corps commander the truth about the situation. Jones explained, "General Middleton had enough troubles already."[87] To Clarke this deliberate misrepresentation of the actual situation was inexcusable, whatever its motivation and regardless of how upset Jones was over the plight of his division and his son.

The two men continued their vigil in Jones's office, awaiting the arrival of Clarke's troops and hoping the fresh tanks and troops would get there before the Germans. These troops were still on the road from Vielsalm, pushing eastward against the tide of fleeing vehicles surging west. Around 1400 hours, hearing "what seemed like small arms firing from the east"[88] the two commanders went to the third floor to investigate. From that vantage point they thought they could detect German soldiers coming out of the woods to the east. This seemed to be the last straw for Jones. As Clarke reported, Jones turned to him and said, "You take command, I'll give you all I have."[89] It was then that Jones made his sardonic quip that he'd set a record for "losing a division quicker than any commander in the U.S. Army."[90] Jones quit his responsibilities at 1430 hours on 17 December and, according to Clarke "apparently his headquarters had quit before that."[91] Alan Jones's attempts to influence the outcome of the defense of St.-Vith and save his overwhelmed unit thus ended in chaos and despair. Bruce Clarke now assumed that mission, and the odds appeared poor.

LEADERSHIP IN A MOBILE DEFENSE

The situation confronting Clarke at 1430 hours on the afternoon of 17 December 1944 was discouraging from the armored commander's point of view. He had precious little armor and very few other troops to command, let alone to lead on a successful defense of the St.-Vith crossroads. On his left flank (north), the 14th Cavalry Group was being scattered by overpowering panzer and grenadier assaults. To his front, the bulk of the 106th Division (two regiments) was surrounded on the Schnee Eifel plateau with little prospect of a successful break-out. The right flank (south), defended by the 106th's remaining infantry regiment (the 424th Infantry) supported by Bill Hoge's Combat Command B, 9th Armored, was only in slightly better shape[92] but it soon got a boost from the 112th Infantry Regiment of the 28th Infantry Division when that unit was pushed into the St.-Vith area by the force of the German thrust toward Bastogne.[93] Protecting the immediate approaches to St.-Vith was Tom Riggs's pathetically small force of combat engineers, bandsmen, and other support troops. It seemed unlikely that the hard-pressed engineer officer could keep the Germans out of town much longer.

Clarke could expect no staff support from the 106th division to help him control the battle, as Jones's staff was scurrying westward. Even Clarke's operations officer, Major Woodruff, was unavailable to help him plan a defense—he was futilely trying to direct chaotic traffic at the crossroads in town.[94]

During the chaos, a lieutenant colonel wearing the crossed cannons of a field artillery officer approached Clarke: "General, I'm Roy Clay. I have a separate battalion of self-propelled 105's, the 275th Armored Field Artillery. We've got some ammunition left and we're ready to work. 'God bless you, Clay!' [Clarke replied,] 'You're all the artillery we've got. Head out the ridge east of town and support those two engineer companies dug in there.'"[95] This was the first good news Clarke had received since leaving Holland; Clay's offer to stay and fight was heartening as well as badly needed. A few other units (and bits and pieces of units) had also chosen to fight it out rather than join the retreat. In that regard, Clay's story is an instructive example of how some of these units managed to get to St.-Vith and continue to fight.

16 DECEMBER

Clay's gunners (attached to the 106th Division Artillery) had begun the battle as the only artillery in direct support of the 14th Cavalry Group defending the division's left flank in the Losheim Gap. When the German barrage began at 0530 hours on 16 December, shells hit the 275th's five forward observation posts, manned twenty-four hours a day to provide maximum coverage to the thinly spread cavalry troopers. Although the shelling severed all wire communications with the front-line elements, the forward observers switched to their radios to contact the battalion fire direction center and quickly received effective fire on the masses of enemy troops attacking along the entire front.[96]

As the German assault infantry and armored vehicles pushed the cavalrymen before them, they quickly cut off and surrounded most of the forward observation posts, but the observer parties continued to call in mission after mission, sometimes directing rounds onto their own positions. Clay's 275th fired furiously all through that long day and into the night, expending the equivalent of two complete basic loads of 105mm artillery ammunition in less than a day. Firing more than 4,000 rounds in less than 24 hours, gun crews reported that water poured down the muzzles to cool the weapons emerged only as steam through the breech, and heat-blistered paint peeled from the barrels. Frantic calls for assistance to the 106th and 99th Division Artilleries went unanswered, as those units were busy responding to German assaults on their own supported units. Finally, the 106th Division Artillery Commander, Brig. Gen. Leo McMahon, called the 275th and said, "You're on your own. Good luck."[97] No help at all could be expected through "normal" channels.

The lightly armed cavalry troopers were no match for the German assault waves. By 1530 hours, the 275th found itself on the front line with no infantry support between it and the enemy. Withdrawing in two columns to a less exposed position, the battalion continued to answer calls for fire.[98]

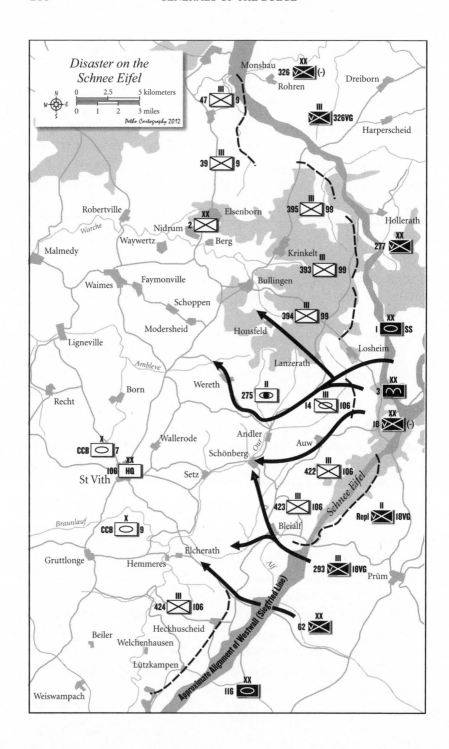

Disaster on the Schnee Eifel

17 DECEMBER

The 14th Cavalry Group, disorganized and confused by the furious onslaught, frustrated Clay's gunners for much of 17 December by refusing to allow them to fire toward the east, fearing that cut-off American troops could be killed in the shelling. This situation ended in the afternoon on 17 December when the battered and dazed 14th Cavalry Group was forced to withdraw for the last time and finally disintegrated as an effective fighting force.[99]

This situation led to Clay's dramatic offer to Clarke and his approaching Combat Command B, 7th Armored. Clay recalled, "No one had to tell me I was under Clarke's command. I assumed it."[100] For the next two critical days, Clay's 275th Armored Field Artillery Battalion constituted the entire artillery support for Clarke's troopers manning the St.-Vith roadblock—a stand that gained Clay's gunners a Presidential Unit Citation. This battalion, and units like it that drifted into the St.-Vith salient, provided the help Clarke desperately needed to patch together a viable defense.[101]

Shortly after Clarke dispatched Clay to provide much-needed support to Riggs's tiny force, portions of the 7th Armored began to trickle into St.-Vith. Troop B, 87th Cavalry Reconnaissance Squadron, was the first 7th Armored unit to force its way through the packed roads. Clarke immediately sent it to fall in on Riggs's left flank. As other units arrived, they too were moved to defensive positions ringing the eastern approaches to the town. The 38th Armored Infantry Battalion, the 23rd Armored Infantry Battalion, the 31st Tank Battalion, and the 33rd Armored Engineer Battalion were all in the St.-Vith vicinity by midnight, and most were in combat hours before that.[102] Clarke recorded how he disposed his forces and organized the defense:

> As [the combat command] arrived, which continued until after dark, I sent help to [Lieutenant Colonel] Riggs, established a direct fire force with my tank destroyer company, established a counter-attack force of 2 tank companies and sent troops forward to the northwest and southeast locations of St.-Vith with instructions to stop the Germans. My small staff and I were up all night getting the situation organized.[103]

While the armored units were trickling into St.-Vith on the afternoon and evening of 17 December, General Hasbrouck, the 7th's commander, arrived in town in the late afternoon. After a brief meeting
alone with Alan Jones, who was still in St.-Vith, Hasbrouck briefed
Clarke on how he saw the mission.[104] Clarke, of course, was to stop
the Germans from entering St.-Vith, or delay them for as long as possible. Hasbrouck, commanding the entire 7th Armored Division,
would attempt to do the same for the whole northern sector. From his
headquarters in Vielsalm, west of St.-Vith, Hasbrouck and the 7th
Armored Division staff planned and conducted the defense of that portion of the VIII Corps line formerly held by the 106th Infantry Division. Hasbrouck had Clarke and his Combat Command B defending
St.-Vith. To Clarke's north, Combat Command R, 7th Armored, protected the left flank of the division. Bill Hoge's Combat Command B,
9th Armored, along with the 424th Infantry Regiment of the 106th and
the 28th Division's 112th Infantry Regiment, was fighting to the south
of St.-Vith on the division's right flank. Hasbrouck placed his remaining combat command, Combat Command A, southwest of St.-Vith
where it could respond to any breakthroughs as division reserve.[105] But
the key to the entire 7th Armored's defensive line was Clarke's command at the St.-Vith hub.

Drawing on his considerable combat experience and, it would
seem, recalling the lessons of the successful tank battles around Arracourt, Clarke prepared to conduct a mobile defense of the St.-Vith
area. This entailed not just resisting each German attack with a brittle
crust of tanks and infantrymen, but also meeting each of those thrusts
by counterpunching with a mobile, powerful tank reserve. And unlike
besieged Bastogne, where a chiefly infantry force held a thin line
while surrounded, Clarke was willing to give ground, when necessary,
to maximize the delay inflicted on the enemy. Such defensive tactics
were meant to capitalize on the speed and power of his armored
forces, not simply to hold terrain.[106]

17–18 DECEMBER
Commencing the night of 17–18 December and continuing with little
respite through the next week, Combat Command B, 7th Armored,

and its attached units reacted to assault after assault by German panzer and grenadier forces determined to take St.-Vith. Clarke, who got little sleep until his unit finally withdrew from the St.-Vith pocket on 23 December, closely controlled American reactions to the enemy attacks and stayed nearly constantly on the move to threatened areas.[107] This report of the action of 18 December, prepared by the U.S. Army Armor School after the war, gives a good account of how Clarke's mobile defense reacted to the German attacks throughout this period:

> The Germans continued their "squeeze play" on the St.-Vith area during the cold, misty morning [of 18 December] when at 0800 they hit CC'B' with a well-coordinated attack by infantry supported by tanks. From the north the attack moved in on Hunningen and from the east against the line across the Schoenberg road. Hunningen was lost temporarily but an aggressive counterattack was mounted by CC'B', using three medium tank companies and one tank destroyer company. . . . The crossroads was recaptured at a cost to the Germans of seven tanks and one armored car destroyed and over 100 infantry killed. On the east, CC'B' restored the line with a counterattack by two medium tank companies after initial penetrations had been made. Such counterattacks, carried out by CC'B' with aggressiveness and determination, were characteristic of the defense of St.-Vith and must have caused the Germans to think the defenders were in greater strength than was the case.[108]

In fact, the German 5th Panzer Army commander, Manteuffel, told Clarke after the war that he thought his German forces had engaged an armored *corps* at St.-Vith and not merely a brigade-sized element. Clarke explained to the German commander that, instead of facing an American tank corps, "You were seeing the same tanks over and over again . . . in different places . . . our mobile reserve."[109] Such a defense required at least two conditions: a steady flow of fuel and ammunition, and the ability to trade ground for time. Therefore, if

Clarke's troops became surrounded like the defenders at Bastogne, his mobile defense would grind to a halt and become ineffective.

20–22 DECEMBER

By 20 December, the defenders of the St.-Vith salient held "the easternmost position of any organized nature in the center sector of the Ardennes battleground,"[110] but their situation was becoming tenuous as the German attack swept around them on both sides. The 6th Panzer Army in the north had penetrated miles to the west of St.-Vith (although restricted to a narrow corridor by American units holding the Elsenborn Ridge). Manteuffel's 5th Panzer Army was 25 miles southwest of St.-Vith, driving westward.[111] Although the German spearheads to the rear of Clarke had not yet linked up, that seemed to be only a matter of time. Soon the decision would have to be made either to withdraw Clarke's forces from the St.-Vith salient or let them become surrounded.

On the night of 21 December the overpowering German forces finally battered their way into St.-Vith itself, pushing Clarke's defenders out of the nearly destroyed town. The Americans, however, retained control of the surrounding area and continued effectively to deny unrestricted use of the road network to the German columns.[112] In fact, allowing the enemy into the town turned into something of an advantage for the defenders since the "traffic jam thus created" effectively knotted the roads, and by midmorning 22 December "the flood of [enemy] vehicles streaming into St.-Vith was out of control."[113] For several hours the German columns could move neither forward nor backward. Stalled within the St.-Vith traffic grid, they seemed, ironically, the victims of their own success. Although Clarke and his subordinate commanders appreciated the respite, they knew it couldn't last forever, and that the enemy columns would soon continue their westward advance. By 1100 hours on 22 December, Combat Command B was again being hard pressed by enemy units exiting the St.-Vith traffic jam.[114] Clarke was holding, but just barely.

Despite the success Combat Command B's mobile defense was having around St.-Vith, the prospect of fighting surrounded inevitably arose as the overpowering German attacks whittled down Clarke's outnumbered forces. The defensive lines of the area between Vielsalm and St.-Vith, east of the Salm River, were slowly forming into a goose-egg shape, but an exit across the river remained open. With German pressure increasing, it wouldn't stay open much longer, and encirclement loomed. Clarke's refusal to allow his forces to be encircled (and turning his tanks into "iron pillboxes") was vigorously supported by Hasbrouck. It nearly got them both relieved of command.[115]

The success of the 5th Panzer Army's attack had effectively cut off the northern sector of the VIII Corps line from General Middleton's control. To counter this, Eisenhower had given command of the northern half of the bulge to Field Marshal Montgomery on 20 December, leaving Bradley with control of the area from Bastogne south. As a result of this command rearrangement, at 2230 on 20 December, the 7th Armored in the St.-Vith area came under command of Maj. Gen. Matthew Ridgway's XVIII Airborne Corps, then being rushed from a "theater reserve" position to the threatened sector.[116] Ridgway, a paratrooper used to fighting surrounded, was not inclined to approve any withdrawal. On 22 December matters had come to a head. Ridgway wanted the 7th to remain east of the Salm River in the "fortified goose-egg" and fight surrounded.[117]

To a paratrooper, fighting encircled by the enemy is not unusual; in fact, it's how they normally start most battles after their "vertical insertion." Because of his previous airborne infantry combat experience, Ridgway thought, not illogically, that Clarke's forces could continue to resist within the goose egg, supplied through the Allied-controlled skies. After all, the 101st Airborne was exercising this exact tactic at the other critical roadblock, Bastogne. Why, Ridgway wondered, couldn't the 7th Armored do the same thing in the St.-Vith area? Hasbrouck answered Ridgway's question in a message received at XVIII Airborne Corps headquarters at 1150 on 22 December, outlining several reasons why Clarke's troops (and the other defenders, including Hoge's Combat Command B, 9th Armored) should be withdrawn to safety across the Salm River: restricted supply lines, attack from enemy artillery from all sides, an inadequate road net to fight a mobile defense, imminent loss of existing supply sources, and a force only 50 percent effective after nearly a week of combat. Primarily, the differences between the 7th Armored at St.-Vith and the 101st Airborne at Bastogne were the seriously attrited condition of the tankers (after a week's fighting) and the necessity for the armored unit to fight a mobile defense rather than simply endure a static siege. As a dramatic postscript to his message, Hasbrouck added that he had just received word of renewed heavy attacks against Clarke's troops.[118] Time was short.

Ridgway remained unconvinced. A charter member of the "airborne club," he knew neither Hasbrouck nor Clarke and suspected their motives. As far as he knew, they could be as panicked as some of the other officers he had met since the battle started, giving up on an otherwise salvageable situation. Further complicating matters, Alan Jones and the 106th Division staff (by now reduced to commanding their own 424th Infantry Regiment and exercising loose control over Hoge's Combat Command B, 9th Armored, and the 112th Infantry Regiment of the 28th Division) were sending Ridgway mixed and confusing signals about the situation. Ridgway went to Hasbrouck's command post to see for himself. What he got was more frustration. Although Hasbrouck once again laid out all the right reasons for withdrawal, Jones (much to Hasbrouck's disgust) seemed to change his earlier opinion and agree with Ridgway that an encircled defense was possible.[119] The corps commander, now seemingly more than ever needing to see for himself, grabbed Hasbrouck and headed for Clarke's command post. He left Jones behind.

Ridgway desperately wanted someone who knew what the actual situation was to tell him what he really wanted to hear—that is, the goose-egg defense was practicable. He wouldn't hear it from Clarke, however. Clarke told him his force was only about 40 percent effective, and would soon become combat ineffective it if wasn't withdrawn and reconstituted.[120] Even now the strong-willed corps commander was unconvinced and would remain so until someone he knew and trusted told him his plan wouldn't work. Fortunately for the battle-weary St.-Vith defenders, Ridgway had known Bill Hoge since their cadet days at West Point and therefore trusted him to tell the absolute truth about the condition of the defense. Hoge, who was still en route to Clarke's command post, spoke to Ridgway on the radio and set up a rendezvous. The two old friends met by the side of the road, and Ridgway finally realized that Hasbrouck and Clarke had been presenting the true picture. Hoge confirmed all that the 7th Armored tankers had related.[121]

While the two men were meeting, however, the order for Clarke and the other defenders to withdraw behind the Salm was being received at 7th Armored headquarters. Field Marshal Montgomery, now Ridgway's senior commander at 21st Army Group Headquarters, had independently evaluated the viability of continuing the defense east of the Salm (with the help of his "phantom" communication-liaison officers visiting many U.S. command posts) and concluded, "They can come back with all honor. . . . They put up a wonderful show."

At 1500 on 22 December, 7th Armored received a message from XVIII Airborne Corps headquarters stating that the "request of CG, 7th Armored Division, for withdrawal had been approved."[122] This (plus the talk with Hoge) forced Ridgway to accept the withdrawal. It also forced Ridgway to realize that something would have to be done formally about Jones before his contradictory actions, now issuing from Vielsalm, further complicated the situation. Upon his return to Vielsalm, Ridgway held a closed meeting with Jones, Hasbrouck, and the corps deputy Chief of Staff, Colonel Quill. Ridgway had Quill write out an order relieving Jones of his command.[123] Although the 106th Division unit history reports that Ridgway made Jones his Deputy Corps Commander in an effort to clarify the genuinely confusing command situation, this seems to be only polite fiction, meant to salve hurt feelings. Ridgway had had enough of Jones's equivocating and could not afford to subsidize any further mistakes. Later that same night, Jones was medically evacuated after collapsing with a heart attack.[124] The nightmare was over for the former 106th Division commander. For Clarke, however, it hung on through that long night.

The news that permission had been granted for Combat Command B, 7th Armored, and the other defenders in the goose egg to withdraw across the Salm to safety was received with somewhat mixed emotions at Clarke's headquarters. Receiving permission to withdraw was one thing; actually disengaging in the midst of a

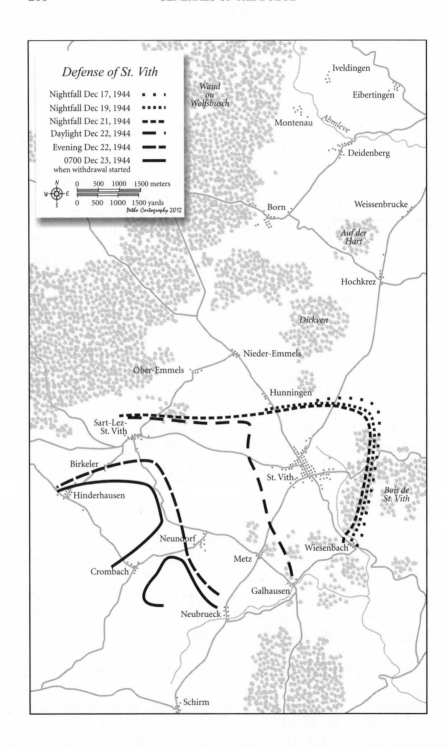

Defense of St. Vith

Nightfall Dec 17, 1944
Nightfall Dec 19, 1944
Nightfall Dec 21, 1944
Daylight Dec 22, 1944
Evening Dec 22, 1944
0700 Dec 23, 1944
when withdrawal started

0   500   1000   1500 meters
0   500   1000   1500 yards
Petho Cartography 2012

desperate fight and getting safely across the river would be difficult. In fact, unless the temperature dropped enough to sufficiently freeze the sticky mud that threatened to bog down his armored vehicles, Clarke might be literally stuck on the east side of the river.

23 DECEMBER

Mercifully, the weather turned cold late that night. The soggy ground froze sufficiently to support the tanks and armored vehicles and allow them to initiate a fighting withdrawal under pressure.[125] However, Clarke encountered relentless enemy attacks all around the rapidly shrinking perimeter. As the long hours of darkness slowly slipped away, enemy forces in contact kept Clarke from breaking clear completely. Finally, at 0500 on 23 December, Hasbrouck sent a message informing Clarke and the others in the goose egg that "it will be necessary to disengage, whether circumstances are favorable or not, if we are to carry out any kind of withdrawal with equipment."[126] Beginning with Hoge's Combat Command B, 9th Armored, at 0700, the defenders began to disengage. Under the protective fires of Clay's 275th Armored Field Artillery Battalion and other artillery units that had gotten across the river during the night, and with a pickup covering force of a tank company, an infantry company, and a tank destroyer company guarding the rear, Clarke and the rest moved safely across the Salm on 23 December.[127]

The movement back across the Salm, a maneuver that would not have been easy even in peacetime, was accomplished in a surprisingly smooth and organized manner—despite the fact that Clarke, once more, was called on to play traffic cop. Clarke and the remnants of Combat Command B, 7th Armored, moved into an assembly area near Xhoris by 2300. They were instructed to refuel, re-arm, and prepare for action in the morning.[128]

ANALYSIS OF BATTLE LEADERSHIP

It is tempting, but neither fair nor illuminating, to conclude that Clarke was a success and Jones a failure. Such an approach doesn't do justice to either man and would obscure many lessons that could be drawn from a careful and thoughtful analysis of the action. Of course, Clarke's leadership created a successful mobile defense from a rapidly disinte-grating situation, just as Jones's leadership failures contributed in large measure to the confused and panicky situation in St.-Vith. These con-clusions, however, tell only part of the story and do little to instruct stu-dents of the fighting as to how Clarke's and Jones's demonstrated battle leadership influenced the outcome of the St.-Vith defense. To accom-plish that, one must look beyond the superficial and examine their leadership in the context of their experience, their units, their tactical sit-uations—and fate. Above all, it should be recognized that Jones was certainly more victim than failure in the events leading up to and culmi-nating in the destruction of his unit at the St.-Vith crossroads. Clearly, he and his green division were the victims of adverse circumstances over which they had no control. Some of these circumstances read like a listing of the weaknesses of the entire U.S. Army in World War II.

Infantry replacement shortages probably had the greatest impact on the performance of the 106th Infantry Division in its short-lived combat stint. By April 1944, Jones and the other leaders of the "Golden Lions" had built a combat team of infantrymen who had lived and trained together for over a year. They knew and trusted each other, and the key leadership positions at all levels were filled with trained and proven performers. The replacement shortage caused the War Department to grab infantrymen from any source available and the 106th was stripped of over 60 percent of its riflemen, wiping out the division's small-unit leadership.[129] Although the 106th had been brought up to strength by the time of its deployment to Europe, these new men (most with noninfantry backgrounds) had not been fully trained or completely integrated, and none could replace the lost key leaders in the short time available. To make matters worse, the drain and fill was stretched out over the entire spring and summer of 1944, causing what would seem to the 106th's leaders as a continual state of disruption and turmoil—a terrible training environment. There seems to be little that Jones or any member of his staff could have done to alleviate this problem except, as they did, to train and integrate the newcomers as quickly as possible.[130]

Once Jones and his division arrived in Belgium, they were again the victims of circumstance—the Supreme Command's decision to attack along a broad front. This decision (along with the national strategy to mobilize only eighty-nine U.S. Army divisions) resulted in an exceptionally thin Allied line, so thin that the only "strategic reserves" available to SHAEF when the Ardennes offensive began were the two airborne infantry divisions, recuperating from the MARKET-GARDEN fiasco.[131] The effect of all this on the 106th Division, therefore, was to mandate that it hold an active section of the long Allied line, instead of completing its training within the theater of operations but safely behind the lines. Moreover, it had but four days in its assigned sector of that line and was still getting settled when the attack started. Although the high command had intentionally given the new 106th the quietest section of the entire front, such good intentions backfired when the full force of the German assault slammed into that very sector. Instead of the safest part of the line, it turned out to be the most dangerous.

Even within the Ardennes line itself, Jones's sector was arguably the worst to try to defend, given the restrictions placed on the unit from its higher headquarters. Unfortunately, the 106th had to contend with a corps boundary, a flank sitting astride a principal invasion route (the Losheim Gap), and a large portion of its unit confined to an exposed position on the Schnee Eifel plateau. In addition, it had been constrained to occupy defensive positions selected and prepared by another unit.[132] Although the leaders at First Army and VIII Corps must have had some misgivings about the overall dispositions and preparedness to fight of the 106th Division, it seems that no one really believed the untried unit would actually be attacked on the "Ghost Front." Had Jones been plugged into the line at any other point outside the Ardennes, he may have had sufficient time to season his troops and prepare them better for their first combat. It seems unarguable that the 106th would not have been destroyed had it not been shoved into the path of a powerful offensive that no one thought even a remote possibility. Eisenhower, Bradley, and all the rest of the high command must share the blame for being totally fooled by the timing, location, and intensity of the German attack. Later claims by Bradley and others of a "calculated risk" notwithstanding, the Allies were surprised by the Ardennes attack, and the chief victims of that surprise were Jones and his division.[133]

A further vulnerability of the 106th, shared with each of the other infantry divisions in World War II, was the lack of tanks as part of the permanent organization of the infantry division. McNair's "lean and mobile" vision for the wartime army he created led him to include within the "standard" infantry division only those formations it would always need, regardless of where in the world it fought. Tanks and other specialized units or equipment were to be assigned from "pools" when the tactical situation warranted.[134] In Europe, it was realized too late that the tactical situation nearly *always* warranted the attachment of some armor, and by the end of the war, nearly every infantry division had at least a tank battalion more or less permanently attached.[135] As a standard infantry division, however, the 106th was not expected to be fighting enemy armor for some time and had no tank units assigned to it when the attack began (apart from the lightly armored 14th Cavalry Group). The speed and power of even a tank company might have significantly helped Jones in the early stages of the battle. Its presence would certainly have provided Jones a powerful force to maneuver against what was, at least initially, an infantry-heavy German attack.

Alan Jones deserves no blame for any of these situations and could have done nothing to prevent or alleviate them, given the time available and the circumstances then existing. If these conditions are set aside, however, how did Jones help or hinder his crippled unit? Given the awful circumstances in which they found themselves, how did the actions and decisions he and his staff made affect the outcome of the fighting? What were the characteristics of Alan Jones's battle leadership and how did they affect the conduct of the fight for St.-Vith?

Jones could have done much more to restore the shattered morale of his staff by maintaining calmness within his rapidly deteriorating headquarters. Observers of Jones during that critical period described his demeanor as "extremely agitated and apprehensive," and that outwardly he appeared to be "an increasingly frustrated man."[136] In contrast to the unflappable coolness of Middleton, his corps commander in Bastogne, Jones's personal leadership during the hours of greatest crisis seemed to visibly lack these traits. Clarke reported that Jones gave the impression that his knowledge of the situation was hazy,[137] and that he appeared to be consumed with worry about his son who was serving in one of the surrounded regiments. Clarke later related that Jones returned again and again to the concern for his lost son and sometimes seemed to be thinking of little else.[138] This concern of a father for the safety of his son is certainly understandable, but when that father is also responsible for the safety of 16,000 other sons, he has a duty to ensure those men perceive their commander as a competent and confident leader. By his inability to project outwardly that competence and confidence, regardless of his reasons, Jones denied his staff and soldiers that image and unintentionally fired their panic. As the division commander—the man all the "Golden Lions" looked to for inspiration and support in this crisis—Jones should have steeled his nerves and at least outwardly have shown a confidence-inspiring image. When Jones's nerve failed him, it also failed those around him. This lack of a calm steadfastness was one of the biggest failures of his battle leadership at St.-Vith.

Jones's failure in personal leadership exacerbated his apparent weakness in organizational leadership—that is, a commander's ability to influence the unit's total performance by directing and focusing the efforts of the unit staff toward a common goal.[139] One day into battle found the 106th Division staff in turmoil. Panic had set in, and no one seemed to be in charge. By the time Woodruff arrived, he found the entire staff frantically abandoning its headquarters and effective control already lost. Clarke reported that no staff officer came to see Jones and that he did not send for one during one of the most critical phases of the battle; this serves to confirm that events had moved beyond Jones's ability to influence, much less control, his division.[140]

Outside, in the vehicle-jammed streets of St.-Vith, near-total chaos reigned with no apparent attempt at traffic control. For a unit supposedly pinning all its hopes of rescue for its trapped regiments on the early arrival of the 7th Armored, these conditions seem unacceptable. The 106th's staff appears to have been completely unprepared either to receive the promised reinforcements or to utilize them properly once they arrived. Taken altogether, this points to a near complete breakdown of organizational leadership and a clear failure to maintain control of the staff, primary responsibilities of a division commander and his chief of staff. How much of this failure should be attributed to Jones and how much to his chief of staff, Colonel Baker, is not possible to ascertain, but it is the division commander who has final responsibility for the performance of his staff.

Jones's battle leadership at St.-Vith also seemed to be crippled by a lack of decisiveness at critical times. In several instances, it seemed as if Jones didn't know what needed to be done, let alone how to go about doing it. The lack of a counterattack plan to rescue his trapped regiments, the failure to appoint one overall commander to coordinate the attempted breakout of those regiments, and missing the opportunity to try a linkup with them using Hoge's Combat Command B, 9th Armored, when it became available are all examples of missed opportunities and botched chances. As Clarke observed upon his arrival in St.-Vith on 17 December, Jones seemed content to remain in his office and worry about the situation instead of trying to make something happen to change it. Later on, when Ridgway sought Hasbrouck's and Jones's opinions about defending the "fortified goose-egg," Jones exasperated both men by vacillating from one position to the other, remaining the only local commander to recommend what would have been the most disastrous action, defending the goose egg. This last example of indecision was too much for the dynamic and decisive Ridgway—he relieved Jones shortly thereafter.[141]

When reviewing Jones's actions, it may be possible that he was even then suffering the preliminary symptoms of his impending cardiac seizure a few days later. Extreme depression, confusion, apprehension, and an inability to make decisions are all typical manifestations of this condition, which could have certainly been brought on by the incredible stress Jones was under. If true, it may go a long way toward explaining Jones's extreme agitation and confused state of mind when Clarke arrived.

But the instance of indecision by Jones that had the single greatest impact on the destruction of his division should actually not have been Jones's decision at all. This decision, of course, was the one to pull back the exposed regiments on the Schnee Eifel plateau before they became surrounded. This decision should rightfully have been made by Jones's corps commander, Middleton. The VIII Corps commander was an experienced, battle-hardened veteran of campaigns in Sicily, Italy, and France who had an Army-wide reputation as an expert tactician. Moreover, Middleton had expressed concern about the exposed nature of the Schnee Eifel positions well prior to the attack, and he admitted later that he knew the 106th was not up to the standards required to stop the German assault.[142] Middleton claimed he was deferring judgment to the man on the spot, Jones. Jones, however, inexperienced and new to the area, could not have made a decision as informed and tactically sound as the experienced Middleton would have. By making no decision, Jones left the troops in place, thereby dooming them to being surrounded and captured. However, it is Middleton's failure to order the regiments to be withdrawn, leaving Jones to decide, that must bear the principal blame.

Amid the mistakes made by Jones and his staff during this critical time, there are at least three bright spots in their performance. First, Jones's use of his rather small reserve forces early on the first day of the assault was the right response to the threat, as it was then developing. The 106th Division headquarters seems to have quickly realized the massive extent of the enemy attack and wasted no time in releasing reserves for use against each threatened sector. In this regard, they seem to have been ahead of their counterparts at VIII Corps headquarters in divining the German intention and reacting quickly to it, showing none of the command inertia that seemed prevalent later on. While their reactions were undoubtedly helped by the slowness of the German attack to develop its full force, their actions nonetheless were correct.

A second positive note in the gloom was Jones's dispatch of Riggs and his small force of engineers and support troops to defend the eastern approaches to St.-Vith on the morning of 17 December.[143] No positive action Jones took during the entire battle was more important to its overall success than when he ordered this tiny group to deploy and attempt to keep the enemy away from the vital crossroads. Though born of desperation, it nevertheless prevented St.-Vith from being overrun and allowed Clarke and Combat Command B, 7th Armored, to get into position to conduct their mobile defense. Much like Middleton

was doing in front of Bastogne with his corps engineers, Jones had recognized that he had to use this engineer-turned-infantry roadblock to
buy some much-needed time. It worked.

The final example of good battle leadership displayed by Jones
was, ironically, his voluntarily handing over of that leadership to
Clarke. Whatever Jones's state of mind was by 1430 on 17 December,
he retained enough appreciation of the overall situation to realize that
the junior Clarke, who would soon have his fresh armored combat
command in the fight at St.-Vith, could better conduct the kind of
defense necessary if he alone were in charge. Although the offer startled and surprised Clarke, it made good sense from Jones's point of
view and probably was key in making Clarke's mobile defense possible. By this time in the battle, Jones may have realized his greatest
contribution was simply to get out of the way.[144]

Clarke turned out to be just the right man in exactly the right place
to salvage a creditable defense from a deteriorating situation. This
propitious circumstance—part luck, part design—gave the combat-
experienced armored commander a perfect opportunity to become one
of the genuine heroes of the Battle of the Bulge. Clarke quickly seized
upon that opportunity and never faltered.

Two other commanders made crucial decisions that sent Clarke
and his unit to the vital crossroads: Eisenhower and Middleton. Ike's
quick assessment of the scope of the German attack led to his directive to Bradley on 16 December that got Clarke on the road to Bastogne later that same night.[145] Once at VIII Corps headquarters, he
received Middleton's understated directive to "go to [Jones] . . . if he
needs help, give it to him."[146] The two senior men had sent him to the
right place, but once he got to St.-Vith, Clarke was on his own.

In later years, Clarke frequently wrote and remarked that two of
the primary skills of a commander were to know what needed to be
done, and then have some idea of how to go about accomplishing it.
Clarke's battle leadership during the defense of St.-Vith is one of the
best examples of the practical application of these skills which one
can find. With no advance knowledge of the situation at St.-Vith, and
practically no definitive orders or directives from higher authority,
Clarke organized, conducted, and commanded a superb mobile

defense of one of the most critical portions of the Ardennes battle-field.

What should be done about the confused and desperate situation confronting Clarke when he arrived at Jones's headquarters was by no means obvious. Jones, naturally enough, was fixated solely on rescuing his trapped regiments on the Schnee Eifel plateau and pleaded with Clarke for a counterattack to free his units without delay,[147] but was unable to put him in contact with the leadership of the surrounded units or provide any details Clarke could use to coordinate a counterattack. With German troops threatening the outskirts of St.-Vith while Clarke's command was still trying to fight its way through, it may have occurred to observers of the situation that the sensible course of action would have been to abandon St.-Vith altogether. Establishing a more defensible line along the west side of the Salm River, anchored around Vielsalm, had some immediate advantages.

Clarke, however, rejected any course save a vigorous defense of what he quickly realized was a vital road hub. As an experienced armored commander who had fought his way across France, he knew that denying the enemy free and unrestricted use of the extensive road net around St.-Vith was the best way to slow, if not stop, a sweeping mechanized assault.

Because much of the impenetrability of the Ardennes is actually due to its poor road network, denying an invader free use of the few good roads couldn't help but slow his advance. Clarke surely must have agreed with Middleton's postwar statement about not having to be a genius to know that St.-Vith and Bastogne were critical points during the Battle of the Bulge.[148] Trained early in his career as a topographic engineer, Clarke had learned to appreciate terrain and its effect on the battlefield. Clarke realized the importance to the German drive of the St.-Vith road hub and in maintaining combat mobility and the momentum of attack.[149]

Clarke's extensive experience as a combat commander in the battles across France the previous summer—especially, it seems the Arracourt tank battles—showed him the value of capitalizing on the mobility and flexibility of his armored unit to create a mobile defense. Later he described how he conducted this defense:

My mission was to stop or slow down the [enemy advance] until more U.S. troops could be assembled west of the Salm River. My combat command, which was a flexible organization now [compared to its weak organization prior to 1 November 1944] varied as the division commander added and took away battalions as he needed them to take care of the division's crises. My basic tactic was to keep my units mobile with a mobile counterattack force of two companies of tanks, and to give ground as necessary so as not to lose my command or any portion of it.[150]

These are nearly exactly the same tactics Clarke had used to repel Manteuffel's 5th Panzer Army attacks at Arracourt the previous September; the success they demonstrated there must have convinced Clarke they would work at St.-Vith. Now that he and Hasbrouck had reorganized the 7th Armored along the more flexible, mobile lines of the extremely successful 4th Armored Division (in which they had both held commands), Clarke had just the right weapon he needed to carry out the type of mobile defense he realized was necessary. The final element needed for Clarke to prosecute the fighting in the manner he knew was necessary was for him to be given free rein in conducting it. Jones did that at 1430 hours on 17 December when he told Clarke, "You take command."[151]

Not every commander in Clarke's position that afternoon would have been eager to be placed in charge of what appeared to be a rapidly disintegrating, losing cause. But one of Clarke's most dominant leadership characteristics, clearly demonstrated here, was a supreme and total self-confidence. Anyone who knew Clarke had to realize early on that he never doubted his own abilities, nor was he ever shy about stepping forward to take charge or expressing his opinion about any military subject. Never a braggart, he had a forceful and dynamic personality that frequently caused others to defer to him. Clarke inspired confidence in his staff and his soldiers and always seemed to exude optimism and competence. In this, he seems to have projected just the opposite image that Jones was then projecting. Given the state of affairs in St.-Vith at that time, such confidence and optimism were sorely needed.

Clarke's conduct of the defense of St.-Vith is not, however, without criticism. Some have charged that his battle leadership caused mistakes that had serious consequences for the 106th Division. Primarily, these issues revolve around the surrounded regiments on the Schnee Eifel plateau and the attempts to rescue them.

The first such criticism to emerge is the charge that the "late arrival"[152] of Clarke's Combat Command B, 7th Armored Division, was instrumental in dooming the surrounded regiments of the 106th Division to capitulation. Those, like Dupuy, who make this claim point out that Jones's corps commander, Middleton, had personally told Jones that the 7th Armored was scheduled to arrive at St.-Vith by 0700 hours on 17 December, thereby causing Jones to base his rescue plans on that information.[153] When Clarke's unit failed to arrive until late on the afternoon of that day, it was too late to save Jones's trapped units. This, they say, was the single, crucial mistake that ultimately forced the units to give up. Dupuy, in his book, *Lion in the Way*, a defense of the 106th, writes, "One comes right back to the point that the nonarrival of Combat Command B, 7th Armored Division, at 7:00 A.M. that morning was the crux of the situation."[154] Because Clarke was the commander of the unit ordered to support Jones at St.-Vith, he must be responsible.

Examination of this criticism, however, fails to show where any blame for the timing of the arrival of the 7th Armored Division could be Clarke's. Indeed, the announced arrival time of the 7th Armored Division at St.-Vith (0700 on 17 December) was unreasonably early for anyone to expect that the entire unit—marching almost 70 miles over icy roads, clogged with fleeing vehicles, across the path of the German offensive—could possibly be in St.-Vith at that time. Historian Russell Weigley observed, "Anyone believing this [arrival time] was not looking carefully at his maps." Acting on convoy information provided by the First Army staff, Middleton told Jones that a combat command of 7th Armored Division would "arrive at 0700 hours" on 17 December. Uncritically accepting this information, therefore, Jones anticipated an early counterattack by Clarke's armored unit to try to save his surrounded troops. But that estimated arrival time was only for the initial convoy elements of the unit to *begin* showing up at St.-Vith; the "closure time" (that is, the estimated time when all elements of the unit would be at their destination) was no earlier than *1900* hours. Whether First Army staff or Middleton or Jones caused the confusion in transmitting these arrival times is unknown. However, given their subsequent actions, it seems more than likely that the root of the problem lay at First Army headquarters. Moreover, First Army staff introduced more delay by proving unable to obtain timely road clearances for the 7th Armored to *begin* the journey south. The earliest that combat elements of 7th Armored Division were permitted to begin the move was 0330 hours on 17 December, even though the unit itself had been alerted to move the previous afternoon. This situation (as well as the fact that it took First Army nearly as long to get road clearance for Bill Hoge's combat command of the 9th Armored—a unit even closer to St.-Vith) supports the charge that First Army simply didn't think the threat was very serious. Had they promptly discerned the real nature of the attack, First Army staff surely must have endeavored to get these critical clearances earlier.[155]

However, even though Middleton was merely passing on to Jones the First Army staff's information that 7th Armored would "arrive at 0700 and close at 1900,"[156] it seems incredible that even the inexperienced 106th Division staff could believe the entire 7th Armored could travel from Holland in so short a time and be prepared to launch an immediate attack. At any rate, there is nothing in all of this that can be attributed directly to Clarke's leadership. He went to St.-Vith when ordered and was told his combat command would be sent after him. When he got to St.-Vith, he quickly radioed for his unit to join him. The fact that it took several more hours to force its way through the fleeing traffic to get to the crossroads would appear more Jones's fault than Clarke's since the 106th Division was responsible for traffic control of the roads in its sector.

The second criticism of Clarke's leadership also deals with the trapped regiments: Why did he not attack to relieve them? Those who make this criticism claim that Clarke missed a great opportunity to save the surrounded units by failing to counterattack quickly toward Schoenberg late on 17 December (or early on 18 December at the latest). Had he done so, they argue, the thin crust of German units bottling up the Americans on the plateau could have been pierced and the units relieved. This could have averted the disastrous surrender and freed about 8,500 troops to join the St.-Vith defense.

Much of this same ground, of course, has been covered earlier while discussing the leadership actions taken by Jones. Jones, after failing to decide to pull the two regiments off of the plateau (and, of course, failing to receive an order by Middleton to do so), was desperately hoping Clarke could quickly attack and break through to them. But Jones not only had no plan to accomplish this, he couldn't even coordinate such an attack with his cutoff troops. He had failed to appoint one overall commander within the pocket and had earlier missed the chance to force a linkup using Bill Hoge's Combat Command B, 9th Armored. Clarke's observations support the view of the 106th's ill preparedness; he said, "The 106th made no advance preparations for maps or gasoline which we [CCB, 7th Armored] had need for, at once, after our 80-mile march."[157]

Apparently, Jones, too, must have begun to realize that an attack to relieve the units was impossible, for Clarke reported, "At no time on 17 December did anyone, including General Jones, speak to me of attacking toward the east after the loss of communications with the troops there."[158]

After Jones gave command of the St.-Vith defense to Clarke, the armored commander had his hands full throwing his units into battle as they arrived and reacting frantically to each of the German attacks. Clarke made what is probably the best summing up of his part of the whole issue concerning the surrounded regiments when he said, "I was too busy from 4:30 P.M. on December 17th to pay too much attention to them."[159] Given the circumstances then existing, it is hard to imagine how even the entire 7th Armored could have rescued those doomed units. The only way they could have been saved was for Jones (or, more properly, Middleton) to have pulled them back earlier.

Clarke's leadership has also been criticized from the position that, since he was junior to Jones, he was automatically under Jones's command from the time he and his unit arrived in St.-Vith, and should, therefore, have reacted to Jones's orders. If he had, these critics claim, he would have launched the counterattack to save the trapped regiments, as Jones ordered. Dupuy's account repeatedly refers to Clarke's unit as being "attached" to the 106th, and treats the combat command as if it were operating under Jones's command and control during most of the fighting.[160] In reality, the command arrangements were confused and convoluted. Middleton contributed to the confusing command arrangements by failing to appoint an overall commander, choosing instead to merely ask Hasbrouck and Jones to cooperate and "carry the ball for me up there."[161]

It has always been Clarke's stated position that he remained under Hasbrouck's command throughout the fighting. He insists that he was never under Jones's command because his combat command was never formally attached to Jones's division. Clarke points out that he and his division were given oral orders simply to report to Middleton at Bastogne, and he, personally, was merely told by the VIII Corps commander to "give Alan Jones some help if he needs it." Clarke claims that he represented his division commander as an "advance party" for the 7th Armored and was never ordered to serve under Jones.[162] Furthermore, because Jones seemed clearly to be overwhelmed by the events and handed over the defense to Clarke, the point seems a moot one. Nevertheless, it cannot be denied that the command situation (throughout the fighting and withdrawal from St.-Vith) remained one of confusion.

Perhaps the best face that can be put on this whole issue is to remember that Clarke, when command of the St.-Vith defense was thrust upon him by an overwhelmed Jones, accepted the challenge without hesitation. Such an interpretation, it seems, compliments both men's battle leadership. Dupuy's assertion that, somehow, Jones and the 106th staff retained command and effective control of that defense (including directing the efforts of Clarke's combat command) is fiction, regardless of who was the ranking officer.

A final criticism of Clarke's battle leadership concerns the defense of the so-called "fortified goose egg." Recall that when Ridgway's command was enlarged to include the 7th Armored Division as well as the other units in the St.-Vith area, he was extremely reluctant to give up any more ground than absolutely necessary. He was firmly against allowing the St.-Vith defenders to withdraw across the Salm River when that question arose on 22 December. Ridgway, used to fighting surrounded, thought that Clarke and the other units to the east of the Salm could defend the goose-egg perimeter while fighting encircled.[163] Neither Clarke nor Hasbrouck thought their armored units could fight long while surrounded. Hasbrouck stressed his reasons for thinking this in a message to Ridgway on 22 December. They seemed solid enough for the tankers. But for Ridgway, such talk was defeatism. He genuinely questioned Clarke's motives for arguing for a withdrawal and suspected the combat commander was losing his nerve. Ridgway, who knew neither Clarke nor Hasbrouck, thought that the tankers' leadership lacked firmness and resolve. Clarke, however, had good reasons for counseling withdrawal in this situation. He recalled his tense meeting with his new corps commander:

> I don't believe that Ridgway had any [hidden] purpose except that he did not know how to use an armored division. He wanted me to dig in and hold ground. He didn't understand the maneuverability of an armored unit. We [Clarke and Hasbrouck] were against it because of the logistics situation. Our division wouldn't last long cut-off, no more than a day. When Ridgway showed the plan to me I said, "I've been fighting day and night for about a week, and I'm nearly out of gasoline, ammunition and rations." He said, "That is a problem for you tankers" and walked away and left me. He [Ridgway] had no knowledge or apparent interest in, an armored division.[164]

The situation was resolved in favor of Clarke and Hasbrouck when Montgomery, now in overall command in the north, overruled Ridgway and ordered the St.-Vith defenders to withdraw "with all honor."[165] Despite the favorable outcome, the incident was probably the closest Clarke came to being relieved of command—an outcome that would have been a tragic injustice.

"TO PREVENT THE CONFUSION FROM BECOMING DISORGANIZED"

It is impossible not to compare the battle leadership of Jones and Clarke. It might seem unfair to compare the inexperienced Jones with the combat-proven Clarke. But war isn't fair, and inexperienced leaders aren't provided with some handicap designed to put them on an equal footing with experienced ones. Despite the numerous disadvantages Jones was forced to confront, he (and Clarke, too) had to attempt to command to the limit of his ability at St.-Vith and provide the best defense he was capable of coaxing out of his staff and troops. One measure to gauge the success of a battle commander's leadership in such a defense can be found in Bruce Clarke's observation: "The job of a commander in a battle when attacked by an overwhelming force is to prevent the confusion from becoming disorganized, and to eliminate command and staff inertia so that the reaction to crises can be swift and effective."[166] Clarke recognizes that, at best, combat is a confusing and chaotic environment, even when things seem to be going right. The challenge to any leader's exercise of command is to bring enough order out of the chaos to force his will on the enemy through the combat power of his unit.

It can never be precisely determined if the 106th Infantry Division would have been destroyed had a more experienced commander been at its head, or if it was already doomed because of the terrible circumstances of its introduction to combat. It can be said that Jones's battle leadership failed to provide the kind of steady, decisive stewardship that would have given his division the fighting chance it desperately needed. His personal state and the condition of his staff by midmorning of 17 December show clearly that Jones was overcome by the stresses and demands of intense combat. The best epitaph on Jones's battle leadership is provided by Charles Whiting in his postmortem on the 106th, *Death of a Division*. Whiting's examination of Jones's situation and his performance reveals not merely a failed commander, but a man who was "a casualty of the battle just as surely as if he had been struck by a bullet."[167]

Clarke, on the other hand, salvaged a great victory from what seemed a lost cause by taking charge at the critical point of the battle and by conducting a mobile defense that succeeded in delaying the German attack for a week. He not only prevented the confusion from becoming disorganized, he turned that confusion against his enemy. Clarke's battle leadership in the defense of St.-Vith was characterized by many positive aspects: Without much guidance he knew what needed to be done; drawing on his combat experience, he knew how to go about doing it; he projected self-confidence and competence which inspired his staff and troops; and, perhaps above all, he saw it through to a successful ending.

Although the full impact and importance of Clarke's successful battle leadership at St.-Vith have not been widely publicized over the past seventy years, usually taking a back seat to the more famous siege at Bastogne, students of the Ardennes fighting are coming to realize more and more the value of the St.-Vith defense and to appreciate its critical relationship to the entire campaign. Historian Russell Weigley, for example, writes:

> The St.-Vith defense . . . epitomized the American's application everywhere in the Ardennes of their army's tactical doctrine for countering just such a breakthrough . . . constrict the avenue of the enemy's advance. But more, perhaps than any other of the many defensive stands in the Ardennes . . . it was the battle of St.-Vith that bought the time required by Allied generalship to recapture control of the battle.[168]

For Clarke, the primary architect of that successful battle, that's not a bad verdict.

AFTERWORD

Leaders of Skill and Character

The situation at the beginning of the Battle of the Bulge was a daunting one for American forces along the thinly manned line in the rugged Ardennes region. Having achieved total surprise at the strategic and tactical levels, the Germans attacked the 80-mile sector with a 2.5:1 initial advantage in assault infantry, a 4:1 edge in tanks, and a 4.7:1 superiority in artillery.[1] That the battered American line bent—or, more appropriately, "bulged"—but did not break is at combat's most basic level a tribute to the courage, tenacity, and sacrifice of the individual GIs who chose to stand and fight against such seemingly overwhelming odds. Yet, the leadership actions of American senior commanders—the "generals of the Bulge"—ultimately determined whether the GIs' sacrifice in the U.S. Army's greatest battle would yield victory or defeat.

The Battle of the Bulge, therefore, put American leaders at all levels to the test in what was, in effect, the greatest "leadership laboratory" of the war in Northwest Europe. Evaluating how American senior leaders met that challenge—their successes as well as their failures—reveals not only their level of skill at battle command but, importantly, their strength of character.

Further, simply pointing out the successes and failures of American battle leadership in this watershed battle begs an overall assessment. Historian Forrest Pogue said, "You never get it absolutely right.

History is always escaping us."[2] Yet, "history" also demands an attempt at a comprehensive accounting and a fair appraisal of the performance of American senior leadership in the Battle of the Bulge.

SUCCESS OR FAILURE?

The shortest and simplest answer to the question of how American senior leaders performed in the Ardennes fighting is perhaps best summed up by a quote from historian Martin Blumenson's reflective essay on Eisenhower and his top lieutenants: "Success on the battlefield speaks for itself."[3] That is, because the ultimate test of the effectiveness of combat leadership is battlefield victory, American commanders in the Ardennes should therefore be judged successful leaders. However, such a simplistic answer not only ignores the failures of senior commanders before and during the battle, it also slights the truly outstanding successes of those individual leaders whose command decisions proved vital in achieving, as Charles B. MacDonald characterized it, "the greatest single victory in U.S. history."[4]

Certainly, failures in American leadership led to a situation that permitted Hitler to organize and launch his great offensive against a sector of the line so weakened that German battlefield success seemed highly probable.[5] This leadership failure and the resulting German strategic surprise were later compounded by the inability of the Allies to launch a timely, coordinated counteroffensive that could have trapped and destroyed the bulk of German troops in the bulge. Both of these leadership failures represented serious lapses in battle command on the Allied, principally American, side of the battle line. To these two failures at the strategic level must be added the biggest leadership failure of the battle at the tactical level—the mass surrender of two regiments of the 106th Infantry Division.[6]

Examining the actual conduct of the battle once the German attack began, however, yields an overwhelmingly positive assessment of how American battle leadership fought that campaign. Although American senior commanders were responsible for the one-sided conditions in the Ardennes through their actions in the months preceding the attack, they nevertheless responded to the assault in a timely fashion with solid, effective, competent leadership that proved successful in gaining control of the battle and winning it. Their actions at the operational and tactical level combined to overcome the strategic blunders and turn a potentially disastrous situation to the Allies' favor.

Eisenhower may have invited the German riposte in the first place with his insistence on a general Allied offensive advancing along multiple axes that left the Ardennes thinly manned, but he largely redeemed the situation by reacting to counter quickly, then defeat, the German attack.[7] Similarly, Bradley's egregious failure to exert aggressive, positive command of his army group from the very beginning of the battle was effectively offset by Eisenhower's unusually active role in the actual conduct of the fighting. For once forsaking his habitual hands-off approach to the exercise of battle command, Ike intervened early and appropriately to create the conditions leading to the defeat of the German offensive.[8] Moreover, Bradley's "intransigence in failing to move his headquarters" to a position from which he could exercise firm and effective control of the fast-moving battle prompted Eisenhower's most morally courageous decision of the war—giving British Field Marshal Bernard Montgomery command of all U.S. forces in the northern half of the bulge.[9] A "team player" throughout his career, Ike again demonstrated this defining characteristic at a critical moment in the battle by placing the good of the Allied coalition ahead of national pride or any personal animosity he felt toward the abrasive British field marshal. By doing so, Eisenhower clearly proved that he was an Allied commander, not merely an American one—even though his action effectively relieved of command his longtime friend and West Point classmate, Bradley.

Although Bradley vehemently decried Ike's decision to give Montgomery command of two-thirds of Bradley's 12th Army Group—calling it Eisenhower's "worst possible mistake"[10]—the chaotic tactical situation and Bradley's (and First Army commander Courtney Hodges's) own failures made the command change the course of action most likely to accomplish Ike's intent of regaining control of the battlefield and then trapping the bulk of German forces in the Ardennes. That Eisenhower's plan—clearly outlined to his senior subordinates at the 19 December 1944 meeting in Verdun—failed to cut off and destroy most enemy troops in the Ardennes was due more to the inherent nature of coalition command than to any egregious leadership failure on Ike's part. Like politics, coalition command is "the art of the possible," relying on building consensus rather than merely issuing orders. Eisenhower did all that seems reasonably possible as a coalition commander to achieve his goal of trapping the Germans: Ike told the British field marshal his commander's intent—and impatiently reminded Montgomery several times over subsequent days; he gave Montgomery command of the forces sufficient to accomplish that objective; and Ike quickly set in motion Patton's counterattack as the southern pincer in his planned envelopment. In short, Eisenhower had given Montgomery all the tools the British field marshal needed to launch a timely attack from the north. However, as leader of an *allied* coalition Ike lacked any practical means of *forcing* Montgomery to promptly obey. Eisenhower could—and did—attempt to motivate Montgomery into launching a timely attack from the north, but he could not compel the British commander to do so as he could his American subordinates.

Yet, even though Ike failed to motivate Montgomery to launch a more timely counterattack on the north of the bulge that in conjunction with Patton's thrust in the south *might* have cut off and annihilated nearly all enemy forces, the 100,000 (or more) precious combat troops, hundreds of panzers, and last major reserves of war materiel the Germans lost in the battle were, nonetheless, unavailable to confront Ike's armies—and Stalin's massive forces in the East—during the subsequent battles for Germany.[11]

And, at the operational level, Patton's aggressive development and execution of the American counterstroke from the south more than made up for Bradley's lack of a firm hand at the helm of 12th Army Group. Patton really didn't need Bradley's help anyway.[12]

It was Patton again, along with his West Point classmate, William H. Simpson, and some outstanding subordinate commanders at the corps, division, and regimental levels who created battlefield success when Hodges's failures and bad decisions threatened to doom First Army. With Simpson rapidly flooding First Army area with reinforcements, Patton striking swiftly to relieve Bastogne, and solid subordinate commanders like Middleton, Gerow, Hasbrouck, Cota, Barton,

Fuller, and Clarke stubbornly frustrating every enemy move, Hodges's army not only survived, it ultimately triumphed, despite the First Army commander's poor leadership.[13]

Mistakes of leadership and command at the tactical level, including the horrendous disaster that befell the 106th Infantry Division, also tended to be redeemed by the successes of American battle leadership in the Ardennes. Even though Middleton and Jones failed to save the 422nd and 423rd Infantry Regiments of Jones's 106th Division from encirclement and surrender on the Schnee Eifel in front of St.-Vith, Clarke's masterful mobile defense of the area with his combat command of the 7th Armored Division and attached units largely compensated for the loss of the infantrymen. Further, despite the Germans' rapid rush through the Losheim Gap, the Americans' stalwart defense of the commanding Elsenborn Ridge stymied the enemy's ability to exploit the rupture. It seems clear that when the leadership successes and failures of this battle are closely examined—when the actions and command decisions of the senior American commanders and their resulting impact on the battle's outcome are weighed and measured on the scales of victory and defeat—American battle leadership was a tremendous success.

The senior leaders like Eisenhower, Simpson, Patton, Middleton, and Clarke actually *won* this greatest land battle in U.S. history; they didn't merely survive it. Their battle leadership in the Ardennes was not that of military incompetents or amateurs who didn't know their jobs. Ike and the other successful American commanders showed they knew exactly what had to be done, and they quickly set about doing it. On balance, American battle leadership in America's greatest land battle proved decisively successful.

KNOWLEDGE AND PROFESSIONAL SKILL

These U.S. Army senior World War II commanders all had to study and learn their trade, then practice it before they could become successful battle leaders, and they had all engaged in the systematic study of warfare, in one form or another, their whole adult lives. With few exceptions, these leaders attended a progressively higher series of schools and professional military education courses, alternating with ever more demanding command and staff officer assignments. Through these alternating line and school duties, they gained a background of knowledge and professional skill leading to positions of ever-increasing responsibilities. Once the war began, they gained combat experience and learned valuable lessons in combat command on the battlefields of North Africa, Sicily, and France.[14]

The meek, the incompetent, and the troublesome were, for the most part, weeded out on those same battlefields, their places taken by others who, having been similarly prepared, were moved up from subordinate commands or were impatiently waiting in the wings for their own chance.[15] They all learned the basics of their trade between the World Wars in service schools like the Command and General Staff School, the War College, and the Army Industrial College.[16] They supplemented the basics with practical knowledge gleaned from a variety of command and staff assignments in troop units spread over the globe in such places as the Philippines, Hawaii, the Canal Zone, and the United States.[17] While still junior officers, they challenged their ingenuity and broadened their perspectives and experience in other varied duties such as organizing and running the Civilian Conservation Corps, teaching ROTC and coaching college football, or managing an engineer district the size of Texas.[18] They served apprenticeships under more senior commanders like George Marshall, Douglas MacArthur, Fox Conner, and Adna R. Chaffee and they continued to learn.[19] And throughout their careers, they interacted with and learned from each other, growing as leaders.[20] When the lucky few were chosen from the pack and given senior command during the war, the competent ones gained valuable combat experience they put to good use and continued to advance. Those found lacking in competence, skill, and higher command ability typically were summarily sent back to the States to serve in training units or to perform administrative duties—often, the humiliation of being removed from overseas combat assignments was made even worse when the failed leaders were, in effect, demoted by being forced to revert to their much lower prewar "peacetime Army" ranks.

CHARACTER COUNTS

The commonality of prewar training, education, and experience of the U. S. Army's senior World War II leaders raises another vital question:

If these officers' preparation and backgrounds were so similar, why did some succeed while others failed? The answer has little to do with their prewar career experiences or even the unpredictable vagaries of luck. The answer lies *within* each man. It's called *character*. The phrase "character counts" is a time-worn, often overused platitude. Yet, it has the single redeeming virtue of being true. The personalities of leaders vary. The specific techniques, procedures, and command styles leaders use to control the ebb and flow of battle typically are unique to the individual. But the key, defining quality that separates leadership success from failure is *character* and it does, indeed, count. Strength of character is the common denominator shared by successful leaders of such disparate personalities and command styles as Eisenhower, Simpson, Patton, Middleton, and Clarke. And it is the quality most often found lacking in those instances of leadership failure displayed notably by Bradley, Hodges, and Jones.

Character is created by the values and beliefs instilled in an individual from an early age by family, trusted friends, and admired role models; then, it becomes deeply embedded and reinforced through defining life experiences; and, finally, it is internalized by faithful adherence to a strong ethical code that places selfless service and duty above purely personal gain. Strength of character not only allows leaders to recognize what "the right thing to do" is in a difficult situation, but also provides them the inner strength and moral courage to actually do it when they otherwise might be tempted to take the easy way out.

The Battle of the Bulge placed incredible stress on commanders at all levels, particularly American senior leaders whose decisions determined the fate of thousands of soldiers reeling under the German onslaught. Under such phenomenal pressure leaders of character showed their mettle. Leaders lacking in this defining quality usually failed, unless they were incredibly lucky or an exceptionally competent subordinate stepped forward to fill the leadership void. Several instances of contrasting character among senior commanders during the U.S. Army's greatest battle stand out.

Eisenhower's morally courageous decision on 20 December 1944 to relieve Bradley of army group command for the duration of the battle demonstrated the strength of Ike's character and revealed a weakness in Bradley's. Ignoring the fact that his command failures to this point in the battle had essentially forced Eisenhower to implement the action while unable to provide valid tactical reasons as to why he should retain his entire command, Bradley's protests seem clearly to be motivated by how Ike's decision would affect his own image and career. As Jonathan Jordan perceptively wrote, although Bradley could not articulate to Ike why giving Monty command of two-thirds of his army group was a bad idea tactically, he clearly realized that "it was certainly a bad move for Omar Bradley" professionally.[21]

At the army level, the command decisions, prompt actions, and coolness under stress of both the steady Simpson and the volatile, brilliant Patton stand in stark contrast to Hodges's egregious lapses in character and judgment. In particular, Simpson's unselfish and key contributions to providing Eisenhower with many of the troops Ike needed to turn the tide of the battle—and his loyal support of Ike's decision to place Ninth Army under Montgomery's command—demonstrated superb strength of character.

VIII Corps commander, Middleton, not only demonstrated character that was calm and cool under fire, but featured Middleton's moral courage in going against accepted tactics, organization, and procedures. When he broke up Roberts's 10th Armored Division Combat Command B into smaller formations and when he used combat engineers as fighting infantrymen, Middleton realized that his actions would inevitably garner criticism. Yet, he knew that in the desperate situation it was "the right thing to do" and had the moral courage to do it.

Perhaps the starkest contrast in character revealed by the Battle of the Bulge was that between Bruce C. Clarke and Alan Jones. Although the precarious situation of Jones's 106th Division at St.-Vith during the first two days of the German onslaught was hardly of his making, Jones nevertheless failed to exhibit the necessary strength of character that *might* have prevented a bad situation from becoming the disaster for his division that it was. Clarke was disturbed at the chaos that Jones's weak leadership allowed to reign in his division headquarters, but he was personally appalled when he witnessed that Jones, in Clarke's words, "deliberately lied" to his corps commander Middleton by intentionally misrepresenting the dire situation as "things are looking up . . . we are going to be all right"—and according to Clarke, continued to lie to cover it up over the next few days.[22] In contrast to Jones, Clarke's character was severely tested during the week-long cauldron of his magnificent defense of St.-Vith—and came through in flying colors.

The best of the U.S. senior commanders had their share of failures, and even the unluckiest ones, those most victimized by the unexpected German offensive, experienced at least some measure of success. Combat is an incredibly confusing and obscure environment, and the waging of war is an imprecise science that, if it follows any law, seems most faithful to the Law written by the mythical Murphy. Sorting out the "good" leaders from the "bad" is no easy task; they are often two manifestations of the same commander's leadership and character. But, in the end, whether they were good leaders or bad, heroes or victims, most of the senior combat leaders of the American Army in northwest Europe found themselves in the Ardennes that terrible December to face what became one of the greatest tests of their battle leadership the war would produce. In this final exam in battle leadership that called on all their knowledge and experience they had gained over the decades leading up to the Battle of the Bulge, it seems clear that the leaders of skill and character passed this test.

Chain of Command,
Allied Expeditionary Force,
February 1944
(Forrest Pogue, *Supreme Command*, 54)

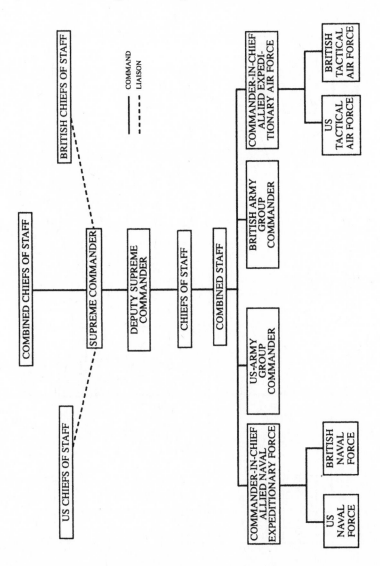

SHAEF Headquarters, 6 June 1944
(Forrest Pogue, *Supreme Command*, 67)

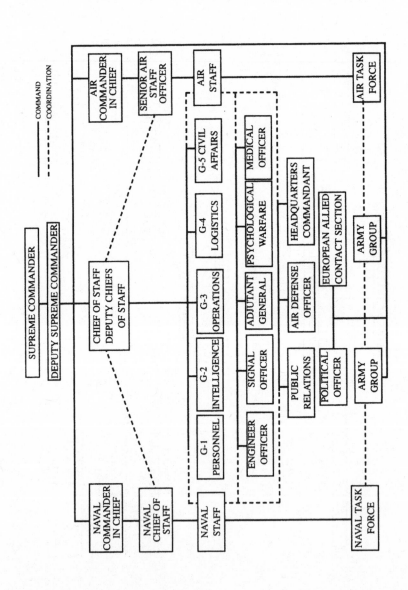

APPENDIX C

Operational Allied Chain of Command, May 1945
(Forrest Pogue, *Supreme Command*, 454)

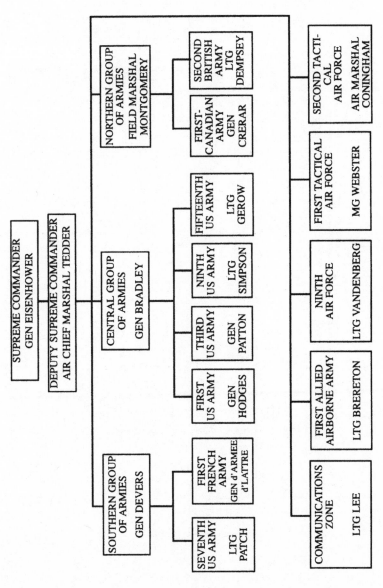

Ardennes Command Arrangement
from 20 December 1944

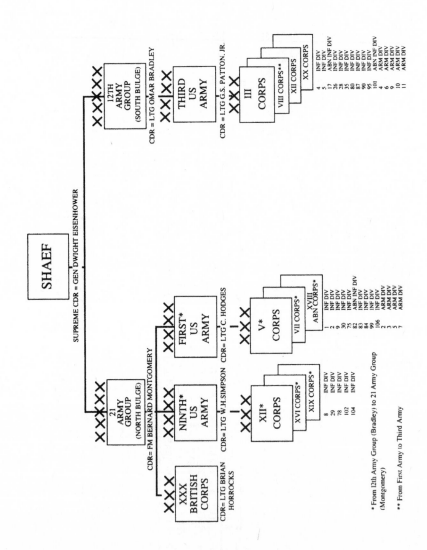

* From 12th Army Group (Bradley) to 21 Army Group (Montgomery)

** From First Army to Third Army

12th Army Group, 16 December 1944

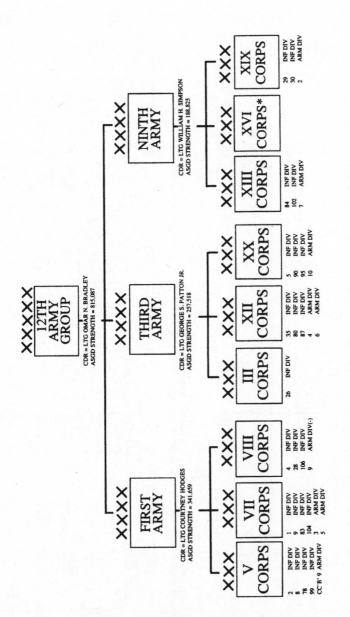

XXXXX
12TH ARMY GROUP
CDR = LTG OMAR N. BRADLEY
ASGD STRENGTH = 815,087

XXXX
FIRST ARMY
CDR = LTG COURTNEY HODGES
ASGD STRENGTH = 341,659

XXX **V CORPS**
2 INF DIV
8 INF DIV
78 INF DIV
99 INF DIV
CC'B' 9 ARM DIV

XXX **VII CORPS**
1 INF DIV
9 INF DIV
83 INF DIV
104 INF DIV
3 ARM DIV
5 ARM DIV

XXX **VIII CORPS**
4 INF DIV
28 INF DIV
106 INF DIV
9 ARM DIV(-)

XXXX
THIRD ARMY
CDR = LTG GEORGE S. PATTON JR.
ASGD STRENGTH = 257,518

XXX **III CORPS**
26 INF DIV

XXX **XII CORPS**
35 INF DIV
80 INF DIV
87 INF DIV
4 ARM DIV
6 ARM DIV

XXX **XX CORPS**
5 INF DIV
90 INF DIV
95 INF DIV
10 ARM DIV

XXXX
NINTH ARMY
CDR = LTG WILLIAM H. SIMPSON
ASGD STRENGTH = 188,825

XXX **XIII CORPS**
84 INF DIV
102 INF DIV
7 ARM DIV

XXX **XVI CORPS***

XXX **XIX CORPS**
29 INF DIV
30 INF DIV
2 ARM DIV

* On 16 December 1944, XVI Corps had no divisions assigned to it. Its strength, 9,549, consisted of headquarters, service, and assorted, non-divisional combat troops.

First Army, 16 December 1944

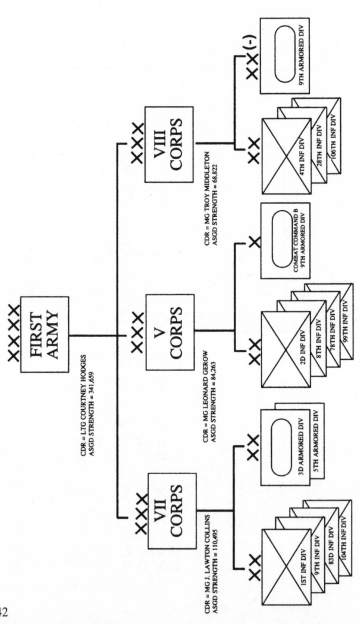

VIII Corps, 16 December 1944

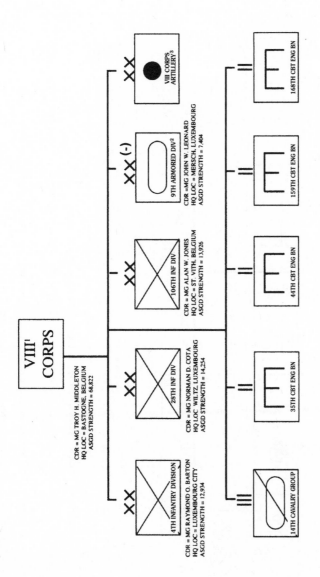

VIII¹ CORPS
CDR = MG TROY H. MIDDLETON
HQ LOC = BASTOGNE, BELGIUM
ASGD STRENGTH = 68,822

4TH INFANTRY DIVISION
CDR = MG RAYMOND O. BARTON
HQ LOC = LUXEMBOURG CITY
ASGD STRENGTH = 12,934

28TH INF DIV
CDR = MG NORMAN D. COTA
HQ LOC WILTZ, LUXEMBOURG
ASGD STRENGTH = 14,254

106TH INF DIV
CDR = MG ALAN W. JONES
HQ LOC = ST. VITH, BELGIUM
ASGD STRENGTH = 13,926

9TH ARMORED DIV²
CDR =MG JOHN W. LEONARD
HQ LOC = MERSCH, LUXEMBOURG
ASGD STRENGTH = 7,404

VIII CORPS ARTILLERY³

14TH CAVALRY GROUP

35TH CBT ENG BN

44TH CBT ENG BN

159TH CBT ENG BN

168TH CBT ENG BN

1. Primarily infantry-heavy VIII Corps had 242 M4 (**Sherman**) medium tanks and 185 tank destroyers available.

2. Combat Command B, 9th Armored Division, was temporarily attached to V Corps in support of that unit's recently begun attack on the Roer River Dams; Combat Command R was held as a corps reserve by MG Middleton; only Combat Command A occupied a portion of the front line.

3. VIII Corps units totaled 394 pieces (105mm and larger).

106th Infantry Division,
16 December 1944

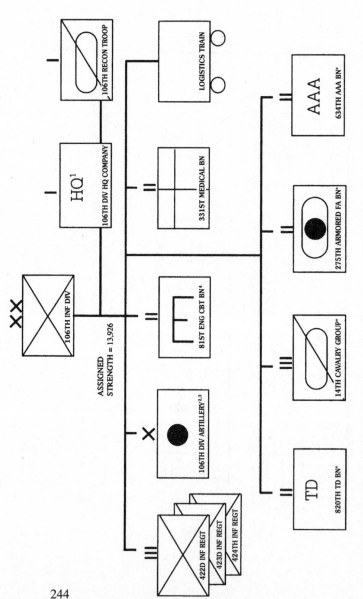

1. 106th INF DIV Special Troops included: 106th Signal Company; 806th Ordance Company; 106th Quartermaster Company; and 106th Military Police Platoon.

2. 106th Divarty included: 3 x 105 Howitzer Battalions (589, 590, 591 FA); 1 x 155 Howitzer Battalion (592 FA).

3. In addition to organic and attached artillery units, VIII Corps had positioned Nine Corps Artillery battalions in the 106th Division Sector (174th, 333rd, and 402nd Field Artillery Groups).

4. On 15 Dec, VIII Corps attached the 168th Engineer Combat Battalion, which answered to Commander, 81st Engineer Combat Battalion.

* Indicates attached units not organic to 106th Infantry Division. Overall strength about 18,000.

Combat Command B, 7th Armored Division, 17–23 December 1944

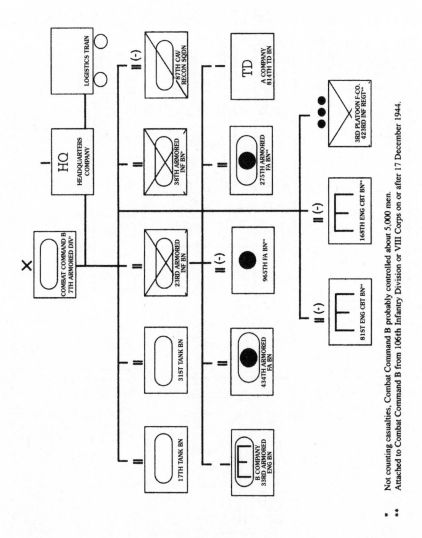

* Not counting casualties, Combat Command B probably controlled about 5,000 men.

** Attached to Combat Command B from 106th Infantry Division or VIII Corps on or after 17 December 1944.

German Order of Battle, 16 December 1944

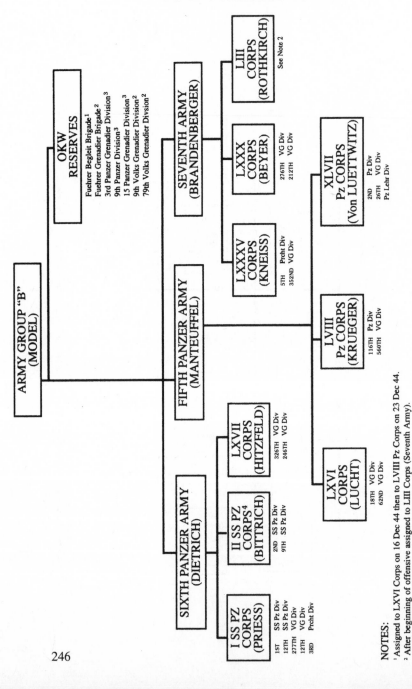

ARMY GROUP "B"
(MODEL)

OKW RESERVES

Fuehrer Begleit Brigade[1]
Fuehrer Grenadier Brigade[2]
3rd Panzer Grenadier Division[3]
9th Panzer Division[3]
15 Panzer Grenadier Division[3]
9th Volks Grenadier Division[2]
79th Volks Grenadier Division[2]

SEVENTH ARMY
(BRANDENBERGER)

LIII CORPS
(ROTHKIRCH)

See Note 2

LXXX CORPS
(BEYER)

276TH VG Div
212TH VG Div

LXXXV CORPS
(KNEISS)

5TH Prcht Div
352ND VG Div

FIFTH PANZER ARMY
(MANTEUFFEL)

XLVII Pz CORPS
(Von LUETTWITZ)

2ND Pz Div
26TH VG Div
Pz Lehr Div

LVIII Pz CORPS
(KRUEGER)

116TH Pz Div
560TH VG Div

LXVI CORPS
(LUCHT)

18TH VG Div
62ND VG Div

SIXTH PANZER ARMY
(DIETRICH)

LXVII CORPS
(HITZFELD)

326TH VG Div
246TH VG Div

II SS PZ CORPS[4]
(BITTRICH)

2ND SS Pz Div
9TH SS Pz Div

I SS PZ CORPS
(PRIESS)

1ST SS Pz Div
12TH SS Pz Div
277TH VG Div
12TH VG Div
3RD Prcht Div

NOTES:

[1] Assigned to LXVI Corps on 16 Dec 44 then to LVIII Pz Corps on 23 Dec 44.
[2] After beginning of offensive assigned to LIII Corps (Seventh Army).
[3] After 24 Dec 44 assigned to XLVII Pz Corps.
[4] Did not participate in the initial attack.

(Source: Dept of Army, US Army Armor School, *The Battle at St.-Vith, Belgium, 17–23 December 1944*)

Principal Personalities

Field Marshal Sir Harold Alexander. (British) Commander of British troops in North Africa during the last phases of the Tunisian campaign. Was Eisenhower's ground commander (Army Group) for Sicily and Italy invasions. Later assumed Supreme Allied Command of the Mediterranean Theater of Operations.

Lieutenant General Kenneth A. N. Anderson. (British) Commander of British First Army during the Allied Tunisian campaign, 1942–43.

General of the Army Henry H. (Hap) Arnold. (American) Beginning in 1938, was head of Army Air Forces; served in this capacity throughout the war. One of the members of the Combined Chiefs of Staff.

Major General Raymond O. Barton. (American) Commander of 4th Infantry Division during the Battle of the Bulge.

General of the Army Omar N. Bradley. (American) Brought to North Africa to assist Eisenhower in overseeing ground war in 1943. II Corps commander in Sicily invasion; First Army commander during Normandy invasion; 12th Army Group commander 1944–45 in Europe; operational commander for largest number of U.S. troops in history (1,300,000).

General der Panzertruppen Erich Brandenberger. (German) Commander of German 7th Army during the Ardennes Offensive. This primarily infantry force was to guard the offensive's left flank.

Lieutenant General Lewis H. Brereton. (American) Commanded several numbered Air Forces in Pacific and in Europe. Later Commander-in-Chief First Allied Airborne Army in Europe, 1944–45.

Field Marshal Sir Alan Brooke. (British) Chairman, British Chiefs of Staff committee. Chief of the Imperial General Staff for most of World War II.

Captain Harry C. Butcher. (American) Naval officer who served as Eisenhower's aide, keeping a detailed diary throughout the European war.

Major General Adna R. Chaffee. (American) Armored Corps champion in the years prior to WWII. Commanded the experimental 7th Mechanized Brigade during the 1940 Maneuvers, helping to validate theories of mechanized warfare and garner support for a separate U.S. armored force. Commanding General of 1st U.S. Armored Corps, 1940–41. Died of cancer August 1941, at age fifty-six, on eve of U.S. entry into the war.

General Mark W. Clark. (American) Commander of Fifth Army during the Italian campaign. Later commanded 15th Army Group in Italy.

Brigadier General Bruce C. Clarke. (American) Commander of Combat Command "A," 4th Armored Division, leading unit of Patton's Third Army during the "race across France," summer 1944. Commander of Combat Command "B," 7th Armored Division at St.-Vith, Belgium, during the Battle of the Bulge.

Lieutenant Colonel Roy U. Clay. (American) Commander of 275th Armored Field Artillery Battalion at St.-Vith, Belgium during the Battle of the Bulge.

Lieutenant General J. Lawton Collins. (American) Aggressive, energetic commander of VII Corps. Led breakout at St.-Lô.

Air Marshal Sir Arthur Coningham. (British) In North Africa commanded First Tactical Air Force; later commanded Second Tactical Air Force in Europe.

Major General Fox Conner. (American) Pershing's Operations Officer in World War I. "Discovered" Eisenhower in 1920, mentored him, and rescued his career in 1920s–30s. Commanded 20th Infantry Brigade in Panama with Eisenhower as Executive Officer, 1922–24.

Major General Norman D. Cota. (American) Commander of 28th Infantry Division during the battle of the Huertgen Forest and the Battle of the Bulge.

General Henry D. G. Crerar. (Canadian) Chief of Canadian General Staff. Later division, corps, then First Canadian Army commander in Europe.

Admiral Sir Andrew Cunningham. (British) Commander of British Naval Forces in Mediterranean; Eisenhower's naval component commander for TORCH landings.

Charles De Gaulle. (French) Commander of Free French forces, 1940–45.

Major General Sir Francis De Guingand. (British) Montgomery's Chief of Staff in the Eighth Army in North Africa and 21st Army Group in Europe.

Lieutenant General Sir Miles Dempsey. (British) Corps commander of British forces in Tunisia and Sicily; British Second Army commander in Europe.

General Jacob L. Devers. (American) Commander-in-Chief of European Theater of Operations in 1943; commanding general of North African Theater in 1943–44; later Deputy Supreme Allied Commander in Mediterranean Theater; commanded 6th Army Group in Europe, August 1944–45.

Colonel Mark Devine. (American) Commander of the 14th Cavalry Group during the first days of the Battle of the Bulge.

Colonel-General (SS) Josef "Sepp" Dietrich. (German) Early Hitler Nazi crony who became commander of Sixth Panzer Army during the Ardennes Offensive.

Major General Lloyd R. Fredendall. (American) Commanded II Corps during TORCH landings and subsequent operations in Tunisia. Relieved of command after Kasserine Pass loss; returned to United States and commanded Second Army (training unit).

Colonel Hurley Fuller. (American) Commander of the 110th Infantry Regiment (28th Infantry Division) during the Battle of the Bulge. Captured when Clervaux was overrun.

Lieutenant General Leonard T. Gerow. (American) Commanded V Corps in Europe, 1944–45. Later commanded Fifteenth Army in Europe, 1945.

Major General Ernest N. Harmon. (American) Eisenhower's special representative to II Corps immediately after the debacle at Kasserine Pass; thereafter, commander of the 1st and 2nd Armored Divisions, 1942–45.

Brigadier General Robert W. Hasbrouck. (American) Commander of the 7th Armored Division during the Battle of the Bulge.

Lieutenant General Courtney H. Hodges. (American) Commander of First Army in Europe, 1944–45.

Brigadier General William M. Hoge. (American) Commander of Combat Command "B," 9th Armored Division during the Battle of the Bulge. Later, as 9th Armored Division commander, his unit captured the bridge over the Rhine at Remagen.

Major General Clarence R. Huebner. (American) Commanded 1st Infantry Division from Sicily through D-Day to end of Battle of the Bulge. Assumed command of V Corps at conclusion of Ardennes campaign.

Major General Alan W. Jones. (American) Commander of the 106th Infantry Division during the Battle of the Bulge. Two-thirds of his division surrendered outside of St.-Vith, marking the largest capitulation of U.S. troops in the European Theater.

Major General William B. Kean Jr. (American) Chief of Staff for First U.S. Army, 1944–45, serving in that position under both Bradley and Hodges.

Fleet Admiral Ernest J. King. (American) Chief of Naval Operations, 1941–45.

General Jean de Lattre de Tassigny. (French) Commander-in-Chief of French First Army, 1944–45.

Lieutenant General John C. H. Lee. (American) Commanded the Communications Zone (Comm "Z") in Europe 1944–45.

Air Chief Marshal Sir Trafford Leigh-Mallory. (British) Commanded Fighter Command, 1942–43; Commander-in-Chief of Allied Expeditionary Air Force, SHAEF, 1943–44.

General of the Army Douglas MacArthur. (American) Army Chief of Staff, 1930–35. Oversaw buildup of Philippine Defense Force, 1935–41. Supreme Allied Commander of South West Pacific Area theater of operations, 1942–45.

General der Panzertruppen Hasso von Manteuffel. (German) Outstanding Panzer commander. Commanded Fifth Panzer Army during the Ardennes Offensive. Achieved greatest success of any German commander during the Battle of the Bulge.

General of the Army George C. Marshall. (American) Chief of Staff of U.S. Army, 1939–45. Known as "Architect of Victory" for his influence on winning World War II. Later Secretary of Defense and Secretary of State.

Brigadier General Anthony C. McAuliffe. (American) Acting commander of the 101st Airborne Division during the Battle of the Bulge. Senior commander of forces in Bastogne during the siege. Famous for "Nuts!" reply to German surrender demand.

General Lesley J. McNair. (American) Commander of Army Ground Forces, 1942–44. Created much of the doctrine, organization, and structure of U.S. Army of World War II. Killed by errant American bomb during the carpet bombings of St.-Lô in July 1944.

Major General Troy H. Middleton. (American) VIII Corps commander in Europe, 1944–45. Commanded units attacked during the Battle of the Bulge and oversaw defense, counterattack.

Feldmarschal Walter Model. (German) Pro-Nazi commander of Army Group B, 1944–45. Ardennes Offensive Panzer Armies under his Army Group's Command.

Field Marshal Sir Bernard Montgomery. (British) Commanded Eighth Army in North Africa. Defeated Rommel at El Alamein. Led attack during Sicily invasion; Allied ground commander during Normandy invasion and commanded 21st Army Group in Europe 1944–45.

Brigadier General James E. Moore. (American) Chief of Staff for Ninth U.S. Army 1944–45, under Simpson.

Lieutenant General Sir Frederick E. Morgan. (British) Deputy Chief of Staff for SHAEF 1944–45.

Admiral Lord Louis Mountbatten. (British) Supreme Allied Commander in Southeast Asia 1944–45.

Lieutenant General Alexander Patch. (American) Seventh Army commander 1944–45.

General George S. Patton Jr. (American) Commanded ground forces during TORCH landings (western area). II Corps commander in Tunisia (after Fredendall relief); Seventh Army commander in Sicily campaign; Third Army commander in Europe 1944–45. Spearheaded Allied breakout from Normandy and pursuit across France.

Ernie Pyle. (American) War correspondent famous for living with troops and reporting the GI story. Killed 18 April 1945 during the Battle of Okinawa.

Major General Elwood R. Quesada. (American) Ninth Tactical Air Force commander 1944–45.

Admiral Sir Bertram Ramsay. (British) Sicily Task Force commander; Commander-in-Chief of Allied Naval Forces.

Lieutenant General Matthew B. Ridgway. (American) 82nd Airborne Division Commander in Sicily and Italy. Later XVIII Airborne Corps commander in Europe 1944–45.

Lieutenant Colonel Thomas J. Riggs Jr. (American) Commander of 81st Engineer Combat Battalion at St.-Vith during the Battle of the Bulge.

Colonel William B. Roberts. (American) Commander of Combat Command "B," 10th Armored Division during the Battle of the Bulge.

Major General Walter Robertson. (American) Commander of 2nd Infantry Division during the Battle of the Bulge.

Feldmarschal Erwin Rommel. (German) Commander of *Afrika Korps* 1941–43. Defeated by Montgomery at El Alamein 1942. Won tactical victory against Americans at Kasserine Pass 1943. Commander of Army Group B in France, 1943–1944. Implicated in plot to kill Hitler and committed suicide October 1944.

Feldmarschal Gerd von Rundstedt. (German) Commander-in-Chief of Army Group West 1942–44.

Lieutenant General William H. Simpson. (American) Commanded the Ninth Army in Europe 1944–45. Part of Montgomery's 21st Army Group, December 1944 to April 1945. First Allied troops to reach Elbe River, April 1945.

Lieutenant General Walter Bedell Smith. (American) Eisenhower's Chief of Staff at AFHQ and SHAEF 1942–45.

General Carl A. Spaatz. (American) Commander of United States Strategic Air Forces in Europe 1944–45.

Henry L. Stimson. (American) Secretary of War 1941–45.

Major General Kenneth W. D. Strong. (British) SHAEF G-2, 1943–45.

Air Chief Marshal Sir Arthur Tedder. (British) Air commander in Middle East Theater, then Mediterranean Theater. Deputy Supreme Allied Commander for SHAEF 1944–45.

Major General Orlando Ward. (American) Commander of 1st Armored Division during the Kasserine Pass debacle, Tunisia, 1943.

Major General J. F. M. Whiteley. (British) Intelligence and operations advisor to Eisenhower in SHAEF 1943–45.

General Sir Henry Maitland Wilson. (British) Supreme Allied Commander in Mediterranean Theater of Operations in 1944.

Major General John S. "P" Wood. (American) Commander of 4th Armored Division 1942 to December 1944. After the Normandy breakout, unit led the "race across France" in the summer of 1944 as Patton's Third Army's lead unit.

NOTES

PREFACE

1. Eugene Garrett, "The Malmedy (Baugnez Crossroads) Massacre." Interview with author, November 1987, Drumwright, OK; Danny S. Parker, *Fatal Crossroads: The Untold Story of the Malmedy Massacre at the Battle of the Bulge* (Boston, MA: Da Capo Press, 2011); James Pontolillo, *Murderous Elite: The Waffen SS and Its Record of War Crimes* (Solna, Sweden: Leandoer and Eckholm, 2009); Peter Judson Richards, *Extraordinary Justice: Military Tribunals in Historical and International Context* (New York: New York University Press, 2007); James J. Weingartner, *A Peculiar Crusade: Willis M. Everett and the Malmedy Massacre* (New York: New York University Press, 2000); Hugh M. Cole, *The United States Army in World War II. European Theater of Operations. The Ardennes: The Battle of the Bulge* (Washington, D.C.: Office of the Chief of Military History/GPO, 1965), 377. The 17 December 1944 Malmedy Massacre was no isolated aberration in the wartime conduct of the *Waffen-SS* soldiers of 1st SS Panzer Division—in fact, it was "business as usual" for the outfit formed originally as *Leibstandarte* Adolf Hitler (LAH), Hitler's personal bodyguard. On 1 July 1934 the LAH had helped the Nazi dictator purge the *Sturm Abteilung* (SA) in the "Night of the Long Knives" killing spree. The unit entered World War II as a combat regiment and began murdering POWs during the war at least as early as 28 May 1940 when it perpetrated the Wormhoudt Massacre in France (eighty captured British soldiers murdered). Increased to division size for Germany's June 1941 invasion of Russia, the 1st SS Panzer Division fought on the East Front alongside regular *Wehrmacht* divisions until mid-July 1943. Although it justifiably earned a reputation as a tough, highly effective combat division in hard-fought actions such as the Third Battle of Kharkov (February–March 1943) and the Battle of Kursk (July 1943), it routinely shot Red Army prisoners and murdered Soviet civilians (including the February 1943 annihilation of the entire village of Yefremovko near Kharkov, Ukraine, in which the unit herded over 900 Russian civilian men, women, and children into the village church and burned all of them to death). Peiper's *Kampfgruppe* of the 1st SS Panzer Division spearheaded the advance of Gen. Sepp Dietrich's Sixth Panzer Army during the Battle of the Bulge (Dietrich, in fact, had commanded 1st SS Panzer from August 1938 to April 1943). From 16 December 1944 through 13 January 1945, Peiper's soldiers murdered a total of at least 400 American POWs and Belgian civilians in Malmedy, Honsfeld, Büllingen, Ligneuville, Stoumont, La Gleize, Cheneux, Petit Thier, Trois Ponts, Stavelot, Wanne, and Lutrebois. During all of its World War II service, the 1st SS Panzer Division is estimated to have murdered over 5,000 POWs and civilians (most on the East Front). Dietrich, Peiper, and over seventy members of the 1st SS Panzer Division were tried and convicted of war crimes in the military tribunals held by the United States at Dachau 16 May–16 July 1946. Forty-three defendants, including Peiper, received death sentences.

However, through the efforts of American sympathizers, led by their war crimes trial U.S. defense attorney, Col. Willis M. Everett Jr. of Atlanta, Georgia—and not incidentally due to the United States then seeking the support of Germany to oppose the USSR as the Cold War began—the death sentences were eventually commuted and within a few years all were released from prison (the last set free was Peiper in December 1956). Peiper eventually moved to France and lived under an assumed name, but on 14 July 1976 he was murdered in his house near Traves, France, apparently by French communists soon after they discovered his true identity.

A tragic footnote to the Malmedy Massacre occurred 23, 24, and 25 December 1944 when, despite the fact that Malmedy remained under control of American troops throughout the Battle of the Bulge, U.S. Army Air Forces planes bombed the town—presumably in retaliation for the widely circulated news of the "Malmedy" massacre. At least 200 Belgian civilians and an unknown number of American soldiers were killed by the aerial bombings (37 GIs died in the 24 December bombing alone).

2. Charles B. MacDonald, *A Time for Trumpets: The Untold Story of the Battle of the Bulge* (New York: William Morrow, 1984), 618; Jacques Nobécourt, *Hitler's Last Gamble* (New York: Schocken Books, 1967); Cole, *Ardennes*, 650. This largest battle on the Western Front in northwest Europe eventually involved over a million men (600,000 Americans) from the opening guns on 16 December 1944 until the "bulge" in the Allied line was straightened out at the end of January 1945. About 20 percent of them became casualties. The critical phase of the battle from the U.S. perspective was the December fighting, which included the defense of St.-Vith, the saving of the "northern shoulder" on the Elsenborn Ridge, the siege of Bastogne, and the defeat of the German Seventh Army's attack. Nobécourt describes the battle as "Hitler's last bluff . . . the final act of a great political adventure both on the German and on the Allied side."

3. Dwight D. Eisenhower, *Crusade in Europe* (Garden City: Doubleday, 1948); Omar N. Bradley, *A Soldier's Story* (New York: Henry Holt and Company, 1951); Basil H. Liddell Hart, *The Other Side of the Hill* (London: Cassell and Company, 1951), 10; Nobécourt, *Last Gamble*, 255. Ike's and Bradley's memoirs of their World War II experiences are probably the best known examples of the postwar publications. Liddell Hart warned readers of such memoirs that "it must be recognized that the writers of autobiographies are usually more concerned with their own interests and the service of their own reputations than with the service of history." DeGaulle commented when Eisenhower's book was published, "However eminent the authors of memoirs may be, each has his own view of the truth."

4. Arthur Bryant, *Triumph in the West* (New York: Doubleday and Company, 1959); Chester Wilmot, *The Struggle for Europe* (New York: Harper and Brothers, 1952); Bernard Law Montgomery, *The Memoirs of Field-Marshal the Viscount Montgomery of Alamein, K. G.* (New York: Signet Books, 1958); Field Marshal Lord Alanbrooke, *War Diaries: 1939–1945*, edited by Alex Danchev and Daniel Todman (Berkeley: University of California Press, 2003); Nigel Hamilton, *Monty: The Battles of Field Marshal Bernard Montgomery* (New York: Random

House, 1994); Martin Blumenson, "Eisenhower Then and Now: Fireside Reflections," *Parameters* 21 (Summer 1991): 27. The Bryant and Wilmot books are
replete with examples of British chief of staff Alanbrooke's and Montgomery's
disdain for all the top American generals. Montgomery's memoirs, of course,
point out how he could have won the war quickly if only he had been given the
necessary resources by Eisenhower (whom Monty belittled as "Nice chap—no
general"). Among the numerous comments damning American senior leadership
in Alanbrooke's wartime diary are: "Eisenhower as a general is hopeless. He
knows little if anything about military matters." and "Ike knows nothing about
strategy and is quite unsuited to the post of Supreme Commander." Blumenson's
article contains a typical quote by British field marshal Harold Alexander regarding American soldiers and their leaders: "They simply do not know their jobs as
soldiers. They are soft, green, and quite untrained. There is no policy and no plan
. . . no firm direction or centralized control from above. . . . [The Americans are]
quite useless."
5. Martin van Creveld, *Fighting Power: German and U.S. Army Performance,
1939–1945* (Westport, CT: Greenwood Press, 1982), 168. Van Creveld bases
much of his argument about effectiveness in battle on a "Combat Effectiveness
Table" of seventy-eight World War II engagements between Americans and Germans developed by writer-historian Trevor Dupuy. An attempt to quantify
effectiveness using a mathematical model, it purports to show Germans as being
significantly more effective fighters (in defense as well as offense) throughout
the war. However, upon close scrutiny, the table is revealed as being not only
incomplete but also heavily stacked in the Germans' favor. The majority of
engagements are taken from the Italian campaign, where the rugged terrain heavily favoring German defenders often negated the World War II U.S. Army's most
significant advantages—mobility and firepower—and was as much an enemy to
the Allies as were the Germans. The battles examined in northwest Europe are
taken, principally, from the miserable, rain-soaked, bloody battles of attrition in
the Lorraine campaign (September–December, 1944). The table ignores, for the
most part, the stunningly successful July–August battles in France (which World
War II Army chief of staff Gen. George C. Marshall deemed "the U.S. Army's
greatest achievement"), and, according to van Creveld, unaccountably *excludes*
prisoners captured from casualty counts (no reason is given for excluding what
is routinely considered an important category of battle casualties and which, had
they been included, would have shown a huge, lopsided advantage in the Americans' favor). The table does not include any battle after 7 December 1944; therefore, the Battle of the Bulge and subsequent fighting in the Rhineland and central
Germany are omitted, thereby making it egregiously incomplete. The value of
such a "systems analysis" approach and using a highly selective table to compare
different units, different commanders, and entirely different tactical and strategic
situations seems dubious. As historian Martin Blumenson once stated, "Each
battle is unique."
6. Martin Blumenson, "America's World War II Leaders in Europe: Some
Thoughts," *Parameters* 19 (December 1989): 3. Blumenson exempts Patton from
the general criticism, referring to him as "a notable exception."

7. Ibid.
8. Liddell Hart, 15.
9. Martin Blumenson and James L. Stokesbury, *Masters of the Art of Command* (Boston: Houghton-Mifflin, 1975).

CHAPTER 1

1. Charles B. MacDonald, *A Time for Trumpets: The Untold Story of the Battle of the Bulge* (New York: William Morrow, 1984), 1, 618; Hugh M. Cole, *The United States Army in World War II. European Theater of Operations. The Ardennes: The Battle of the Bulge* (Washington, D.C.: Office of the Chief of Military History/GPO, 1965), 650; Spencer C. Tucker, *Battles That Changed History: An Encyclopedia of World Conflict* (Santa Barbara, CA: ABC CLIO, 2010). MacDonald, an infantry company commander who fought in the Battle of the Bulge and later became a U.S. Army historian who authored two volumes of the army's official history of World War II in Europe, writes that eventually 600,000 Americans were involved in the Ardennes fighting, "including 29 divisions, 6 mechanized cavalry groups, and the equivalent of 3 separate regiments." British forces involved totaled about 55,000. The attacking Germans probably committed close to 500,000 troops (28 divisions and 3 brigades). American casualties were about 80,000 (the British lost 1,400), and German casualties were at least 100,000 (but probably much more). The number of troops involved by both sides brings this Western Front battle to a level approaching the enormous Russo-German encounters on the vast Eastern Front, including Stalingrad (August 1942–February 1943), in which the Germans lost about 300,000 men, and the giant tank battle at Kursk (July 1943), which cost the Germans 100,000 casualties. Russian casualty figures, as with everything in Stalin's paranoidal empire, were never fully revealed but were undoubtedly enormous. Recently declassified records for the now-defunct Soviet Union indicate 1 million Russians died at Stalingrad, 13,500 of whom were shot by the Soviets for "cowardice." American losses in the Ardennes offensive represented nearly 10 percent of total U.S. losses for all of World War II (294,000 killed and 671,000 wounded in all theaters). U.S. participation of 600,000 in the Ardennes offensive dwarfs the American involvement in most other famous U.S. battles, including: Yorktown, 1781 (8,800 Americans allied with 7,800 French); New Orleans, 1815 (5,000); Chapultepec, 1847 (7,200); Gettysburg, 1863 (150,000 total Union and Confederate); Meuse-Argonne Offensive, 1918 (500,000); Okinawa, 1945 (183,000 Army and Marine invasion troops); Inchon, 1950 (75,000 Marine and Army ground troops); Operation Desert Storm, 1991 (about 500,000); and Operation Iraqi Freedom, 2003 (300,000 American and Coalition troops). Only the six-week-long World War I Meuse-Argonne Offensive of September–November 1918 produced more American casualties (122,000).

2. MacDonald, *A Time for Trumpets*, 1.
3. B. H. Liddell Hart, *The Other Side of the Hill* (London: Cassell, 1951), 108–110, 468–469; Russell F. Weigley, *Eisenhower's Lieutenants: The Campaigns of France and Germany, 1944–1945* (Bloomington: Indiana University Press, 1981), 433, 442–444, 459. Weigley commented on the Allied misconception

about Hitler's involvement in operations, writing, "It is hard to understand why as late as December 1944 any [Allied] G-2 should have imagined [Field Marshal] Rundstedt rather than Hitler to be in effective command." Yet, Allied leaders, notably Omar Bradley, persisted in calling the German Ardennes attack the "Rundstedt Offensive," either out of ignorance of the offensive's true author or, more likely, because they preferred the more comforting conceit that the Allies had been caught flat-footed by the genius of a fellow professional soldier (Rundstedt) renowned for his operational brilliance. Acknowledging that Hitler was the creator and driving force behind the offensive that knocked them back on their heels not only threatened Allied commanders' egos, it risked damaging their professional reputations as well.

4. Liddell Hart, *Other Side*, 108–110. He writes: "It was designed to profit by the way the Allies had committed their strength . . . and were unlikely to expect a German counteroffensive at this time, particularly in the Ardennes."

5. Cole, *Ardennes*, 21–23; Liddell Hart, *Other Side*, 446, 448–449; Weigley, *Eisenhower's Lieutenants*, 458; MacDonald, *Time for Trumpets*, 18–30. Liddell Hart reports that Field Marshal von Manteuffel succinctly summed up Hitler's shortcomings as a "grand tactician" by saying in a postwar interview, "He [Hitler] had a real flair for strategy and tactics, especially for surprise moves, but he lacked a sufficient foundation of technical knowledge to apply it properly. Moreover, he had a tendency to intoxicate himself with figures and quantities."

6. Liddell Hart, *Other Side*, 108; Cole, *Ardennes*, 26. Liddell Hart wrote that "Dietrich was an S. S. leader, formerly a rolling stone in various business jobs, who had caught Hitler's fancy by his aggressive spirit. Rundstedt regarded him as responsible for fumbling the crucial part of the offensive."

7. Liddell Hart, *Other Side*, 446; Cole, *Ardennes*, 34. As Manteuffel makes clear, the German Ardennes offensive main effort was launched by Dietrich's Sixth Panzer Army (redesignated "Sixth SS Panzer Army" after the Battle of the Bulge), and it struck along the Ardennes' classic invasion route—the Losheim Gap running east-west just north of St.-Vith and south of Elsenborn Ridge. Manteuffel's Fifth Panzer Army attacking on Dietrich's left supported Sixth Panzer Army's main attack with a powerful advance in the center of the Ardennes sector.

8. Cole, *Ardennes*, 26; MacDonald, *Time for Trumpets*, 24. Cole explains the German Seventh Army's role in the offensive, "The . . . plan called for a single powerful thrust on a front about forty miles wide, the breakthrough to be achieved between the Huertgen Forest and Leutzkampen with the Fifth and Sixth Panzer Armies leading the attack. On the left wing the Seventh Army would not make an immediate advance . . . but would follow in the track of the Sixth Panzer Army as a second wave."

9. Liddell Hart, *Other Side*, 7–8, 18, 108, 471. Robert M. Citino, *The Wehrmacht Retreats: Fighting a Lost War, 1943* (Lawrence: University Press of Kansas, 2012), 280. Liddell Hart conducted extensive interviews with the surviving German generals after the war and provides interesting insight into their character as well as their relationships to Hitler. He considered them to be "the best-finished product of their profession—anywhere," but limited by the fact that "they were

essentially technicians, interested in their professional job, and with little idea of things outside it." He reports that the Ardennes offensive "was purely Hitler's in respect of aim, timing, and place—though improved by the technical suggestions of Manteuffel." Despite the generals' opposition to Hitler's plan, their sense of duty and loyalty caused them to attempt to carry it out to the fullest. In the end, Liddell Hart thought technical competence and loyalty were not enough, concluding, "But along with [loyalty] often ran a sense of personal interest which undercut their loyalty to their fellows, and their country's best interests, in face of a common threat. The play of individual ambitions and the cleavage of personal interests constituted a fatal weakness in their prolonged struggle to maintain their professional claim in the military field, and to preserve it from outside interference. This struggle went on throughout the twelve years from Hitler's rise to Germany's fall." Likewise, Citino concludes that Hitler's "officer corps did not waver. Despite all their alleged disagreements with their Fuhrer, disputes that formed the basis for an entire body of postwar memoirs, the commanders remained loyal. They served his ends, they fought his war, and they eagerly accepted his assignments when another officer was found wanting."

10. Frank J. Price, *Troy H. Middleton: A Biography* (Baton Rouge: LSU Press, 1974), 215; Stephen E. Ambrose, *Eisenhower: Volume I, Soldier, General of the Army, President-Elect, 1890–1952* (New York: Simon and Schuster, 1983), 365; Carlo D'Este, *Eisenhower: A Soldier's Life* (New York: Henry Holt and Company, 2002), 637–638; Robert E. Merriam, *Dark December* (Chicago: Ziff-Davis, 1947), 75; John Toland, *Battle: The Story of the Bulge* (New York: Random House, 1959), 12.

11. R. Ernest Dupuy, *St. Vith: Lion in the Way—The 106th Infantry Division in World War II* (Washington, D.C.: Infantry Journal Press, 1949), 72; MacDonald, *Time for Trumpets*, 83–84. MacDonald observed, "The Ardennes was at once the nursery and the old folks' home of the American command. New divisions came there for a battlefield shakedown, old ones to rest after heavy fighting and absorb replacements for their losses." The 4th and 28th Infantry Divisions had each been devastated in the Huertgen Forest fighting the previous month, and the 106th Infantry Division had just arrived at the front a few days earlier. None of the three was at the peak of combat efficiency.

12. MacDonald, *Time for Trumpets*, 84; Cole, *Ardennes*, 650. One of the two tactical combat commands of the new 9th Armored Division was on loan to the V Corps to support its upcoming offensive to capture the Roer River dams. The other was filling a gap in Middleton's front between the 28th and 4th Infantry Divisions. Neither, therefore, was available to Middleton to employ as a powerful, mobile, armored reserve force to counterattack against the German offensive. Although 9th Armored Division had a third combat command, Combat Command Reserve (CCR) located at Bastogne, it was not typically employed as a tactical maneuver unit like Combat Command A (CCA) and Combat Command B (CCB) except in an emergency (in fact, Middleton did employ elements of CCR tactically when German units threatened to overrun Bastogne early in the battle). When V Corps units in the path of the German attack are counted, there were about 83,000 U.S. troops total to defend against the surprise assault.

13. Cole, *Ardennes*, 34, 650; Merriam, *Dark December*, 75; Toland, *Battle*, 12; Mac-Donald, *Time for Trumpets*, 84. The 200,000 German assault troops were the vanguard of an Ardennes offensive attack force numbering about 500,000. Although Middleton had only 242 medium tanks available, he could supplement these with 182 tank destroyers. More significant, however, were the nearly 400 artillery pieces capable of firing at the German attackers when the battle began.

14. Weigley, *Eisenhower's Lieutenants*, 568, 574; Cole, *Ardennes*, 56, 330–331.

15. Forrest C. Pogue, *The United States Army in World War II. European Theater of Operations: The Supreme Command* (Washington, D.C.: Office of the Chief of Military History/GPO, 1954), 396; Weigley, *Eisenhower's Lieutenants*, 568, 574; Cole, *Ardennes*, 56, 330–331.

16. Cole, *Ardennes*, 364. Cole notes the "revolting atrocities . . . perpetrated on the defenseless Belgians," singling out the murderous actions of the German *kampf-gruppe* (battle group) of the 1st SS Division *Leibstandarte* Adolf Hitler under the command of SS-*Obersturmbannführer* (Lieutenant Colonel) Joachim Peiper as the worst offender, noting that it perpetrated the 17 December 1944 Malmedy Massacre, killed additional American POWs at other locations, and murdered hundreds of Belgian civilian men, women, and children.

17. Weigley, *Eisenhower's Lieutenants*, 564–566, 575–579. Eisenhower, according to Weigley, "interpreted the Ardennes as confirming the necessity for his broad-front strategy."

18. Liddell Hart, *The Other Side*, 110; Weigley, *Eisenhower's Lieutenants*, 571–574; MacDonald, *Time for Trumpets*, 618; Cole, *Ardennes*, 673–676. Liddell Hart concluded, "The offensive fell far short of its aims, and when it ended it had fatally impoverished Germany's reserves, leaving her no chance of long-continued defense."

19. John S. D. Eisenhower, *The Bitter Woods* (New York: G. P. Putnam's Sons, 1959); Carlo D'Este, *Patton: A Genius for War* (New York: HarperCollins, 1995) and *Eisenhower*; Rick Atkinson, *The Guns at Last Light: The War in Western Europe, 1944–1945* (New York: Henry Holt and Company, 2013); Weigley, *Eisenhower's Lieutenants*; MacDonald, *A Time for Trumpets* and *Company Commander*; Pogue, *The Supreme Command*; Cole, *Ardennes*; Ambrose, *Eisenhower*; David Eisenhower, *Eisenhower at War, 1943–45* (New York: Random House, 1986). These are among the best books written about the Ardennes offensive, the Battle of the Bulge, and the principal American senior commanders who fought it. Anyone wishing to study this battle would do well to consult these first.

20. Robert H. Phillips, *To Save Bastogne* (New York: Stein and Day, 1983); Michael Collins and Martin King, *The Tigers of Bastogne: Voices of the 10th Armored Division in the Battle of the Bulge* (Philadelphia: Casemate, 2013); Cole, *Ardennes*, 422; Weigley, *Eisenhower's Lieutenants*, 490; D'Este, *Patton*, 678–702. Although the 20–26 December 1944 siege of Bastogne is justifiably renowned as one of the most epic combat actions in U.S. Army history, its importance to American victory in the Battle of the Bulge as well as the 101st Airborne Division's role in Bastogne's defense have been inflated by mythmaking, ignorance, misinformation, and war reporters' blatant hyperbole. Bastogne was an

important Ardennes road junction, yet, as Weigley correctly points out, "it was the battle of St. Vith [not Bastogne] that bought the time required by Allied generalship to recapture control of the battle." Battle of the Bulge war correspondents, like today's reporters, sought headline-grabbing sound bites and fixated on McAuliffe's dramatic "Nuts!" reply to the German surrender demand, then promoted the siege of Bastogne out of all reasonable proportion to its importance in winning the overall battle. Moreover, paratroopers of the 101st Airborne Division represented only about *half* of Bastogne's defenders during the week-long siege—the rest included tankers and riflemen of Col. William Roberts's CCB 10th Armored Division and CCR 9th Armored Division, survivors of the 28th Infantry Division's stand east of Bastogne, and various VIII Corps troops. Particularly important to Bastogne's ability to withstand the siege yet typically overlooked by historians were the unheralded and largely ignored VIII Corps artillery outfits providing crucial artillery fire support to defending U.S. infantrymen that proved vital to holding off the incessant German assaults. Significantly, Phillips reveals the key role that the sacrifice of the 28th Infantry Division in the early fighting east of the town played to "save Bastogne," thereby making it possible for the 101st to be safely trucked into the town in an administrative road movement and establish defensive positions. Similarly, Patton's astonishing "90-degree turn" of his Third Army to launch an early counterattack into the southern flank of the German penetration was masterful, but as D'Este points out, it was due more to Patton's foresight, situational awareness, effective staff work, and prudent prior planning than to any singular stroke of individual brilliance on his part. D'Este quite rightly concludes that "neither Patton nor the Third Army won the Battle of the Bulge" despite the prominence later historians have given to Patton's role in the battle.

21. Kent Roberts Greenfield, Robert R. Palmer, and Bell I. Wiley, *The United States Army in World War II. The Army Ground Forces: The Organization of Ground Combat Troops* (Washington, D.C.: Center for Military History/GPO, 1947), 161–226. The Army actually consisted of ninety divisions for a short time, reverting to eighty-nine when the 2nd Cavalry Division was deactivated during the war. The total strength figure includes Army Air Forces personnel.

22. Maurice Matloff, "The 90-Division Gamble," *Command-Decisions*, ed. Kent Roberts Greenfield (Washington, D.C.: Office of the Chief of Military History/GPO, 1960), 365–381; Charles E. Kirkpatrick, *An Unknown Future and a Doubtful Present: Writing the Victory Plan of 1941* (Washington, D.C.: U.S. Government Printing Office, Center of Military History, 1992), 1–2; Jim Lacey, "World War II's Real Victory Program," *The Journal of Military History* 75 (July 2011): 811–834; Weigley, *Eisenhower's Lieutenants*, 13. Initial estimates of American war planners were that an army of over 200 divisions would be necessary to win the war. General Marshall's "bold, calculated risk" to maintain the ground combat strength at ninety divisions has been described as "wise, courageous, foresighted, and successful." Matloff wrote, "The decision was a striking illustration of acceptance by Army war leaders of the fact that there were limits to their slice of the American manpower pie. The 90-division troop basis represented their attempt to provide a realistic meeting ground of three fundamentals of modern warfare—strategy, production, and manpower." Matloff credits the

manpower burden borne by Russia and other Allies as permitting the United States to maintain a worldwide coalition on such a small troop basis and concludes that the heavy investment of manpower in an "effective, heavy-fisted, long air arm" helped make the ground gamble successful. Kirkpatrick supports Maj. (later Gen.) Albert C. Wedemeyer as the influential army staff planner who "foresaw and laid out America's mobilization and production effort during World War II," a view that until recently mainly has been uncritically accepted by historians. Lacey, however, convincingly challenges Wedemeyer's supposed overwhelming influence on America's World War II "victory program," revealing that Wedemeyer's sole input to U.S. Army planning—his September 1941 nineteen-page *Ultimate Requirements Study: Estimate of Army Ground Forces* staff paper—"was wrong in nearly every particular" and that it had no influence on World War II U.S. Army mobilization or on American war production. Lacey claims that Wedemeyer's supposed overwhelming influence "is a myth perpetuated for over fifty years by Wedemeyer himself."

23. Pogue, *Supreme Command*, 540–542.
24. Omar N. Bradley, *A Soldier's Story* (New York: Henry Holt and Company, 1951), 225–226; Omar N. Bradley and Clay Blair, *A General's Life: An Autobiography by General of the Army Omar N. Bradley* (New York: Simon and Schuster, 1983).
25. Pogue, *Supreme Command*, 543. This European Theater casualty total accounted for approximately half of the American losses in World War II—294,000 dead and 671,000 wounded.
26. Greenfield et al., *The US Army*, 2–5.
27. Weigley, *Eisenhower's Lieutenants*, 1–31.
28. Greenfield et al., *The US Army*, 272–278.
29. Russell F. Weigley, *The History of the United States Army* (New York: MacMillan Publishing Company, 1967), 470; Matloff, "90-Division Gamble," 367. Matloff stresses the importance of the United States as the "Arsenal of Democracy" by writing, "The Allies had from the beginning accepted the proposition that the single greatest tangible asset the United States brought to the coalition in World War II was the productive capacity of its industry."
30. Weigley, *History of the US Army*, 461–471. The U.S. Army World War I "square" division got its name from being comprised of four infantry regiments (two large brigades composed of two infantry regiments each) plus a powerful artillery brigade. These U.S. "square" divisions were massive, containing around 28,000 soldiers—over twice the size of a World War I British, French, or German division and nearly the size of a corps in other armies of that era. McNair's "triangular" U.S. Army World War II division organization eliminated one infantry regiment and "pooled" artillery assets at division, corps, and army levels.
31. Greenfield et al., *The US Army*, 273.
32. Weigley, *Eisenhower's Lieutenants*, 21–28. The "pooling" concept fits the very nature of the employment of modern fire support, primarily field artillery. Never held in reserve, artillery is meant to be used continually, its fires shifted to targets, in priority, all across the battlefield. Although some artillery units are more or less in continual support of one maneuver element, its fires remain subject to call when a priority target is engaged.

33. Weigley, *Eisenhower's Lieutenants*, 2, 18–28.
34. Kirkpatrick, *Victory Plan of 1941*, 105. Kirkpatrick noted, "In World War I, the Army had one vehicle for every 37 soldiers. By the end of World War II, the ratio was one vehicle for every 4.3 soldiers."
35. Weigley, *History of the US Army*, 470. Kirkpatrick, *Victory Plan of 1941*, 105. Despite the overwhelming advantages of motorization, Kirkpatrick points out that increasing the number of motor vehicles also required a corresponding increase in the number of soldiers necessary to keep them properly maintained and in running order: "The number of soldiers devoted to vehicle maintenance and repair therefore increased proportionately at a cost to the sharp edge [combat units] of the Army."
36. Weigley, *History of the US Army*, 468–469.
37. Ibid., 470.
38. Ibid. Weigley observed, "The standard triangular infantry division proved a suitable instrument for all theaters in which American ground forces fought."
39. Weigley, *Eisenhower's Lieutenants*, 30.
40. Greenfield et al., *The US Army*, 276–280.
41. John K. Mahon, *History of the Militia and the National Guard* (New York: Macmillan Publishing Company, 1983), 187–188.
42. Greenfield et al., *The US Army*, 274–275.
43. Pogue, *Supreme Command*, 541.
44. Weigley, *History of the US Army*, 464, 468. Weigley wrote, "McNair recognized that the standard division would have to be modified in various theaters to meet various situations, and the theater commanders were the more free to make de facto modifications in the constituents of a division because of the flexibility afforded by pooling the support elements. In practice, the infantry division came to operate usually with a tank battalion and other supporting elements in quasi-permanent attachment." McNair said at the time that "Although the division organically probably will aggregate something like 11,000, you may make it 20,000 if you so desire, simply by adding armored or infantry battalions." The 1st Infantry Division had, by 1 March 1945, twelve company- and battalion-sized combat units attached to it on a more or less permanent basis, as opposed to only nine organic formations of battalion and regimental size.
45. Pogue, *Supreme Command*, 541.
46. Weigley, *History of the US Army*, 467–468.
47. Weigley, *Eisenhower's Lieutenants*, 17–19.
48. Martin Blumenson, *Kasserine Pass* (New York: Jove Books, 1983), 303–320; Weigley, *History of the US Army*, 467–468. Although leadership and organization were primary factors in the American disaster at Kasserine Pass (February 1943), the performance of U.S. armored vehicles highlighted the superiority of the Axis machines and contributed to the defeat.
49. Weigley, *History of the US Army*, 467–468.
50. John Ellis, *Brute Force: Allied Strategy and Tactics in the Second World War* (New York: Viking Books, 1990), xviii, 424–26; Weigley, *Eisenhower's Lieutenants*, 24–31.
51. U.S. Army Center of Military History, *Fact Sheet: World War II* (Washington, D.C.: U.S. Government Printing Office, 1994). During the fiftieth anniversary

years of World War II, the Center published a series of superb, highly useful fact sheets that provide a quick, authoritative reference tool for historians.

52. Kenneth P. Werrell, "The Strategic Bombing of Germany in World War II: Costs and Accomplishments," *Journal of American History* 73 (December 1986), 702–703. Although the 1946 U.S. Strategic Bombing Survey vindicated the Army Air Forces' strategic bombing campaign, it taints its favorable conclusion by conflating "strategic bombing" with the more all-inclusive term "air power." Air Force historian Werrell's critical judgment seems a much more honest assessment: "Strategic bombing did not achieve the goals that some thought. It neither broke German morale nor deprived the German military of needed weapons. Despite tremendous efforts and costs, the war proved the prewar air prophets wrong. The bomber's potential and the airmen's promises exceeded bombing results: World War II strategic bombing of Germany was not a clean, quick, cheap, surgical, or revolutionary force . . . Did strategic bombing win the war? While most hold that air power, as contrasted to strategic bombing, was decisive and vital, none asserts that air power alone won the war."

53. Robert K. Palmer, Bell I. Wiley, and William R. Keast, *The United States Army in World War II. The Army Ground Forces. The Procurement and Training of Ground Combat Troops* (Washington, D.C.: Historical Division, U.S. Army/GPO, 1948), 82; V. R. Cardozier, *The Mobilization of the United States in World War II* (Jefferson, NC: McFarland & Co., 1995), 109; Byron Fairchild and Jonathan Grossman, *The United States Army in World War II. The War Department. The Army and Industrial Manpower* (Washington, D.C.: Office of the Chief of Military History/U.S. Government Printing Office, 1959), 196. Just as the infantry replacement problem in Europe was reaching crisis proportions in the fall of 1944, 100,000 men were diverted from the nation's manpower pool to the Army Air Forces' B29 strategic bomber project. Cardozier points out another major "competitor" with army ground forces for the available personnel—civilian war industries. As the Allies' "Arsenal of Democracy," American war industries were absolutely vital to achieving final victory and required a massive commitment of manpower. Fairchild and Grossman calculate that the civilian workforce averaged 53,750,000 (workers of all ages and gender) during each of the four years of American participation in the war.

54. Weigley, *Eisenhower's Lieutenants*, 27.

55. Palmer, et al., *Procurement and Training of Ground Combat Troops* (Washington, D.C.: Historical Division, U.S. Army/GPO, 1948), 3.

56. Ibid. Although expected to fulfill the most physically demanding tasks at the fighting front, the infantrymen in the sample averaged half an inch shorter and 6 pounds lighter than the army average.

57. Special Services Division, Army Service Forces Survey, *Subject: What the Soldier Thinks*, August 1943.

58. Palmer, et al., *Procurement and Training of Ground Combat Troops*, 50. Col. T. J. Cross, Assistant Chief of Staff, G-3, Second Army, Fort George G. Meade, MD, manuscript, "Notes on Infantry Divisions"; Leonard Lerwill, *The Personnel Replacement System in the United States Army, Department of the Army Pamphlet no. 20-211* (Washington, D.C.: U.S. Government Printing Office, August 1950), 467.

59. Jerry D. Morelock, *A Single Soldier: World War II Mobilization, Manpower and Replacement Policies and Their Influence on the Conduct of US Army Operations in Northwest Europe, 1944–45*, PhD diss., University of Kansas, 2000.

60. Ellis, *Brute Force*, 424–26; Weigley, *Eisenhower's Lieutenants*, 24–31.

61. Ian V. Hogg, *The Encyclopedia of Infantry Weapons of World War II* (New York: Thomas Y. Crowell Co., 1977), 38; Weigley, *Eisenhower's Lieutenants*, 26–30.

62. Hogg, *Infantry Weapons*, 78.

63. Ibid.

64. Ian Hogg, *Artillery 1920–1963* (New York: Arco Publishing, 1980), 181–187. An illustration of the great disparity between the American and German antitank weapons is the tremendous difference in armor penetration ability. The best the U.S. weapons could manage was 70mm of armor plate (the 37mm weapon could only go through 50mm), yet the German weapons could penetrate nearly 200mm (all at ranges from 500 to 1,000 meters).

65. Weigley, *Eisenhower's Lieutenants*, 20–21.

66. Hogg, *Artillery*, 19; Weigley, *Eisenhower's Lieutenants*, 20–21. The German 88mm cannon was a superb weapon and rightly feared by the Allies. Whether used as a towed antitank gun or mounted as the main gun of a PzKpfw VI Tiger tank, it was a devastating weapon. However, its fearsome reputation was such that it often produced an irrational fear among Allied troops, who tended to characterize any incoming fire as "88." Troops terrorized themselves with the fiction that every weapon trained on them was an "88," causing many to panic or proceed overcautiously. Psychologically, it could be intimidating to advancing troops.

67. Christopher R. Gabel, *Seek, Strike and Destroy: U.S. Army Tank Destroyer Doctrine in World War II* (Leavenworth Paper Number 12) (Fort Leavenworth, KS: U.S. Army Command and General Staff College, 1985), 72.

68. Weigley, *Eisenhower's Lieutenants*, 27–28.

69. Weigley, *History of the US Army*, 473.

70. Combat Studies Institute, *Conversations With General J. Lawton Collins* (Fort Leavenworth, KS: U.S. Army Command and General Staff College, 1983), 4–5; Weigley, *Eisenhower's Lieutenants*, 28. General Collins, the outstanding commander of the VII Corps during the campaigns of France and Germany, relates that, "At one time, I massed twenty-two [artillery] battalions on one target." Since a World War II U.S. field artillery battalion typically consisted of three batteries, each containing four or six artillery pieces, Collins's "twenty-two battalions on one target" represented concentrating the devastating fires of 260 to 400 individual cannons on a single German position.

71. Weigley, *Eisenhower's Lieutenants*, 28.

72. Weigley, *History of the US Army*, 479.

73. Ibid., 471.

74. Weigley, *Eisenhower's Lieutenants*, 25–26.

75. Ibid.

76. Weigley, *History of the US Army*, 471.

77. Allen H. Mick, ed., *With the 102nd Infantry Division Through Germany* (Nashville: Battery Press, 1980), 147.

78. Hanson Baldwin, *Tiger Jack* (Fort Collins, CO: Old Army Press, 1979), 25–32, 156.

79. 4th Armored Division Combat interviews. The Lorraine Campaign proved a sharp contrast to the heady days of the "race across France" because bad weather and improved German resistance caused much tougher going.

80. Weigley, *History of the US Army*, 471–472.

81. Weigley, *Eisenhower's Lieutenants*, 26. Weigley relates Bradley's frustration with trying to push the use of "marching fire" among the American troops. Bradley finally resignedly said, "They seem to need something to shoot at."

82. Walter E. Kretchik, *US Army Doctrine: From the American Revolution to the War on Terror* (Lawrence: University Press of Kansas, 2011), 157. Kretchik correctly judges that "By 1945, [U.S. Army] doctrine had become an effective means to organize, train, and fight a service that employed combined arms warfare in three dimensions."

83. Mick, *102nd Infantry Division*, 25.

84. Ibid.

85. Weigley, *History of the US Army*, 464–482.

86. Weigley, *Eisenhower's Lieutenants*, 28.

87. Wesley Frank Craven and James Lea Cate, *The Army Air Forces in World War II. Europe: Argument to V-E Day, January 1944 to May 1945* (Washington, D.C.: Office of Air Force History/GPO, 1983), 228–277.

88. Ibid. Allied air power was so overwhelming by the end of the war, that at least one former German antiaircraft gunner admitted to the author that his crew often sabotaged their own gun so they could seek safety in a bunker rather than face the aerial onslaught.

89. Adolf Galland, *The First and the Last: The Rise and Fall of the German Fighter Forces, 1938–1945* (New York: Ballantine, 1957), 199–280; John Killen, *A History of the Luftwaffe*, (New York: Bantam, 1987), 264–332.

90. Mick, *102nd Infantry Division*, 66.

91. Morris Janowitz, *The Professional Soldier* (New York: Free Press, 1960), 106; Mahon, *Militia and National Guard*, 186–187; Weigley, *History of the US Army*, 425–430. Janowitz illustrates the profound effect that World War II had on the American professional army officer corps when he shows the percentage of U.S. Military Academy graduates in the corps over the years: 1910, 79 percent; 1920, 86 percent; 1935, 81 percent; 1950, 48 percent. The world leadership assumed by the United States and the resulting large peacetime postwar army have fundamentally changed the face of the army officer corps. Mahon gives the breakout of World War II commissioning sources as follows: 100,000 from the National Guard; 180,000 from the Reserve Officer Training Corps; 100,000 received a direct commission; and 300,000, the largest share, from Officer Candidate Schools.

92. Mahon, *Militia and National Guard*, 186–187.

93. Weigley, *History of the US Army*, 477.

94. Martin Blumenson and James L. Stokesbury, *Masters of the Art of Command* (Boston: Houghton Mifflin, 1975), 4; Weigley, *History of the US Army*, 477. Blumenson and Stokesbury remarked on the timing involved in being in the right

place in history, "Ideally, for World War II, a soldier would have graduated from West Point about 1912, had service in France in World War I as a company or battalion officer, taken the right courses and done the appropriate tours during the interwar years, and been a brigadier general or senior colonel in his mid-forties when World War II broke out. With that sequence he could hardly avoid a place in the history books; whether it was a good or a bad place would depend more on personal qualities, but the time sequence itself would be highly desirable."

95. Weigley, *History of the US Army*, 478.
96. Robert H. Berlin, "United States Army World War II Corps Commanders: A Composite Biography," *The Journal of Military History* 53 (April 1989): 149, 162.
97. D. K. R. Crosswell, *The Chief of Staff: The Military Career of General Walter Bedell Smith* (New York: Greenwood Press, 1991), 31–68; Berlin, "Corps Commanders," 156, 166; Weigley, *History of the US Army* and *Eisenhower's Lieutenants*. Berlin, writing of the thirty-four corps commanders, but, nonetheless, speaking of the experiences of all the senior American commanders in the war, records, "Their professional military education, experience in a variety of positions, and operational knowledge combined with combat leadership prepared them to serve the army ably at war." Berlin also refers to this question when he notes the comments of Ernest Harmon, outstanding commander of the 1st and 2nd Armored Divisions in World War II: "A military historian recently asked me how the United States, indifferent and even contemptuous of the military in peacetime, had been able to produce a group of generals proficient enough to lead armies successfully against German might. . . . I am now convinced that the intensive and imaginative training at the Command and General Staff College had a great deal to do with it." It seems obvious that the American senior leaders who commanded the U.S. Army in Europe in World War II were prepared for this task by a combination of professional military education in schools, alternating with command and staff assignments, and supplemented by challenging duties, extensive reading and self-study, professional and personal interaction, and apprenticeships to senior officers. The issue that remains less clear is the manner in which these officers were *selected* to hold the positions they held during the war. Relying on Marshall's "little black book" is not a "system" per se, and, at least in some cases, put the wrong man in a critical position. It certainly discriminated against those who did not come in contact with Marshall and overlooked some otherwise outstanding leaders.
98. Janowitz, *The Professional Soldier*, 296–297; Blumenson, "America's World War II Leaders," 5; Daniel P. Bolger, "Zero Defects: Command Climate in First US Army, 1944–1945," *Military Review* 71 (May 1991): 64–67. Janowitz describes the "Marshall Method": "Just as Marshall's appointment represented a departure from seniority appointment, so he, in turn, was vigorous in recruiting officers for higher command. His personal appointments filled central staff positions in Washington and manned key posts in the military structure for the European Theater. . . . Many of these officers were deeply influenced by Marshall's leadership, and came to reflect his sentiments. For years, Marshall, like other

aspiring officers, had been keeping lists of officers whose talents had impressed him, and whom he intended to select as commanders, if he were appointed Chief of Staff, or in a position to influence the selection of commanders. Being an innovator, he selected for his list men who were energetic and who had demonstrated ability at problem-solving by his standards." Blumenson points out the importance of the "Benning Connection": "Particularly lucky were those, like Omar Bradley, who had been with Marshall at the Infantry School at Fort Benning between 1927 and 1932, when he was Assistant Commandant. Outstanding students and faculty members were especially well-regarded and in his good graces. They had proved their potential for heavy responsibility, and Marshall looked after them during the war. They were generally excellent in discharging their duties, and they flourished and rose in rank and in authority." Bolger puts a darker spin on the "Marshall Connection" by pointing out that the "frosty, reserved Marshall" was a "tester rather than a teacher" or helpful coach, and that a single mistake on the part of even a promising subordinate could "finish" him in Marshall's book. "Once a man failed," Bolger writes, "Marshall rarely granted a second chance." Bolger proposes that this "Marshall legacy" led to his chosen commanders, such as Bradley and his successor in First Army command, Courtney Hodges, creating a hostile and brutal command climate in that Army.

99. Stephen E. Ambrose, *The Supreme Commander: The War Years of General Dwight D. Eisenhower* (Garden City, NY: Doubleday and Co., 1970), 597; Thomas E. Ricks, *The Generals: American Military Command from World War II to Today* (New York: Penguin Books, 2013), 57–58. Once Marshall had selected a commander, it sometimes proved difficult to remove him, even if the commander performed poorly in combat. After Eisenhower relieved the hapless, troublesome, and inept Lloyd Fredendall from command of II Corps after he had bungled the battle of Kasserine Pass in February 1943, Marshall still tried, from time to time, to get Eisenhower to take him back in a combat command assignment. Ike declined. Nevertheless, despite his well-deserved relief from command, Fredendall was promoted to lieutenant general and given command of the Second Army, a stateside training command, for the duration of the war—all at Marshall's insistence. Thomas Ricks's outstanding examination of U.S. Army generalship, *The Generals*, contains the Marshall quote explaining the qualities the chief of staff explained in 1943 that he was looking for in men chosen for senior command.

100. Interview with Lt. Col. (Ret.) John Van Vliet III. Another problem with such a personal sponsorship selection system is that human beings—even Marshall—are not infallible. The most famous example of an egregious case of mistaken identity that Marshall made is when he confused James A. Van Fleet, Eisenhower's West Point class of 1915 classmate, with an officer whose last name was very similar but whom Marshall had once discovered drunk on duty. As a result, Van Fleet remained only a colonel in regimental command until mid-1944 when Ike was finally able to convince Marshall of the mistake. Van Fleet soon rose rapidly, was promoted to general, and finished the war in command of the III Corps. The officer Marshall discovered drunk on duty was Colonel John Van Vliet (pronounced almost identically to "Van Fleet"). Van Vliet was never

promoted or given the chance to serve overseas in World War II, but after drying out in an alcoholic clinic, he continued to serve until his post-World War II retirement. Interestingly, Van Vliet's son, an army lieutenant colonel in World War II captured at Kasserine Pass, was one of the senior Allied prisoners taken by their German captors to witness the exhumation of the remains of approximately 4,000 Polish officers murdered by Stalin's NKVD in 1940 and buried in mass graves in Katyn Forest, Russia. The younger Van Vliet's report verifying that it was Stalin's henchmen, not the Germans, who had murdered the Poles, was suppressed by U.S. government officials, presumably to protect our World War II Soviet ally's reputation.

101. Blumenson, "America's World War II Leaders," 94.
102. Cole C. Kingseed, "Eisenhower's Pre-war Anonymity: Myth or Reality?" *Parameters* 21 (Autumn 1991), 87–98; Blumenson, "America's World War II Leaders," 94. Kingseed exposes as myth the supposed anonymity of Eisenhower in the last years leading up to America's entry into World War II. He writes: "Few if any officers of Eisenhower's generation matched his versatile record of unsurpassed skill in administration, management, command, staff work, and communications. And what is perhaps more important, this record was known to the people who mattered before the United States entered World War II." Blumenson has correctly pointed out that we will never know just how good those officers waiting in the wings were.
103. Bradley and Blair, *A General's Life*, 200.
104. Ambrose, *Supreme Commander*, 341.
105. Ibid., 175–176.
106. Blumenson and Stokesbury, *Masters of the Art of Command*, 244, 305, 307; Pogue, *Supreme Command*, 34, 42.
107. Crosswell, *Chief of Staff*, 298–299.
108. Thomas R. Stone, "He Had the Guts to Say No: A Military Biography of General William Hood Simpson," PhD diss., Rice University, 1974, 2–3.
109. Ibid.
110. Ambrose, *Eisenhower*, 385.
111. Raymond S. McLain, "One of the Greatest: A Study in Leadership," *Military Review* 49 (December 1969): 19.
112. Price, *Middleton*, 268.
113. Weigley, *Eisenhower's Lieutenants*, 2.
114. Weigley, *History of the US Army*, 477–478.
115. Liddell Hart, *Other Side*, 110.
116. Citino, *The Wehrmacht Retreats*, 280; Weigley, *Eisenhower's Lieutenants*, 28–30. Citino attributes much of the battered but still dangerous German army's continued effectiveness to its leadership, concluding that the *Wehrmacht* was led by "men of will and determination who considered retreat a personal insult and were willing to fight to the last German soldier in a hopeless war."
117. Ellis, *Brute Force*, 388–392, 426–428.
118. John Toland, *The Last 100 Days* (New York: Random House, 1965).
119. Ibid.

120. Liddell Hart, *Other Side*, 468–469. Manteuffel provides some interesting insight into the "production numbers" that figured so prominently in the postwar analysis of the effectiveness of the Allied bomber offensive. He related: "When one was discussing a problem with [Hitler], he would repeatedly pick up the telephone, ask to be put through to some departmental chief, and inquire—'How many so and so have we got?' Then he would turn to the man who was arguing with him, quote the number, and say: 'There you are'—as if that settled the problem. He was too ready to accept paper figures, without asking if the numbers stated were available in reality. It was always the same, whatever the subject might be—tanks, aircraft, rifles, shovels. . . . Even if the numbers had actually been produced, a large part of them were still in the factories, and not with the troops."

121. Ellis, *Brute Force*, 421.

122. Weigley, *Eisenhower's Lieutenants*, 30–31; Ellis, *Brute Force*, 425.

123. Weigley, *History of the US Army*, 479.

124. Ibid.

125. Weigley, *Eisenhower's Lieutenants*, 24.

126. Mick, *102nd Infantry Division*, 51–53.

127. Ibid.

128. Charles B. MacDonald, *The United States Army in World War II. European Theater of Operations. The Siegfried Line* (Washington, D.C.: Office of the Chief of Military History/GPO, 1963), 617, 621–622.

129. Mick, *102nd Infantry Division*, 40.

130. *Conquer: The Story of the Ninth Army 1944–1945* (Nashville: Battery Press, 1980), 269–330.

131. Martin Blumenson, "Breakout and Pursuit," S. L. A. Marshall Lecture, Fort Leavenworth, Kansas, 13 March 1984.

132. The most exhaustive, detailed accounts of how the U.S. Army planned and fought World War II in Europe are the seven volumes on the European Theater of Operations in the seventy-nine-volume official history *The United States Army in World War II* written by the skilled historians of the U.S. Army Office of the Chief of Military History (later, Center of Military History). Originally published 1950–1993 by the U.S. Government Printing Office, the seven European Theater volumes (in chronological order by date of the World War II campaigns they cover) are: Gordon A. Harrison, *Cross Channel Attack*; Martin Blumenson, *Breakout and Pursuit*; Hugh M. Cole, *The Lorraine Campaign*; Charles B. MacDonald, *The Siegfried Line Campaign*; Hugh M. Cole, *Ardennes: The Battle of the Bulge*; Jeffrey J. Clarke and Robert Ross Smith, *Riviera to the Rhine*; and Charles B. MacDonald, *The Last Offensive*. Weigley's authoritative *Eisenhower's Lieutenants* relies heavily on these official history volumes. A superbly written, exhaustively researched, three-volume narrative history of the U.S. Army in the European Theater is Rick Atkinson's masterful *Liberation* trilogy—*An Army at Dawn: The War in North Africa, 1942–1943* (New York: Henry Holt and Company, 2002), *Day of Battle: The War in Sicily and Italy, 1943–1944* (New York: Henry Holt and Company, 2007), and *The Guns at Last Light: The*

War in Western Europe, 1944–1945 (New York: Henry Holt and Company, 2013). Excellent single-volume books on the World War II U.S. Army in Europe are Peter R. Mansoor, *The GI Offensive in Europe: The Triumph of American Infantry Divisions, 1941–1945* (Lawrence: University Press of Kansas, 1999) and Michael D. Doubler, *Closing With the Enemy: How GIs Fought the War in Europe, 1944–45* (Lawrence: University Press of Kansas, 1994).

133. Pogue, *Supreme Command*, 175, 189.

134. Ibid., 192.

135. Martin Blumenson, "The Decision to Take Brest," *Army* 10 (March 1960): 51.

136. Jeffrey J. Clarke and Robert Ross Smith, *The United States Army in World War II. European Theater of Operations. Riviera to the Rhine* (Washington, D.C.: U.S. Government Printing Office, 1993); William B. Breuer, *Operation Dragoon: The Allied Invasion of the South of France* (New York: Jove Books, 1988); Pogue, *Supreme Command*, 244.

137. Bernard Law Montgomery, *The Memoirs of Field-Marshal the Viscount Montgomery of Alamein, KG.* (New York: Signet Books, 1958), 242–281. The bitter fighting for control of the Scheldt Estuary—much of the combat borne by Canadian troops—did not succeed in clearing the region of German resistance until early November, and Allied shipping to Antwerp did not begin until after extensive mine-clearing operations of the waterway were concluded on November 29.

138. Ibid., 257–280.

139. W. Denis Whitaker and Shelagh Whitaker, *Rhineland: The Battle to End the War* (New York: St. Martin's Press, 1989), 1–4, 345–348; *Conquer*, 114–198.

140. Pogue, *Supreme Command*, 302.

141. Charles B. MacDonald, *The Battle of the Huertgen Forest* (New York: Jove Books, 1984), 195–208. MacDonald, *Siegfried Line Campaign*. MacDonald judged the Huertgen battle phase of the Siegfried Line Campaign as "a misconceived and basically fruitless battle that should have been avoided." The fighting in the Huertgen cost the Americans 33,000 casualties and chewed up entire V Corps and VII Corps divisions (including the 4th and 28th Infantry Divisions that were in mid-December 1944 still recovering but sitting squarely in the path of the German Ardennes offensive).

CHAPTER 2

1. David Eisenhower, *Eisenhower: At War, 1943–1945* (New York: Random House, 1986), 572. David Eisenhower's book about his famous grandfather's military experience as supreme Allied commander in Europe is a good one-volume reference on the subject and contains very little obvious bias. When it first appeared, criticism of Eisenhower's war leadership, led mainly by Montgomery's biographer, Nigel Hamilton, was prominently featured in popular publications along with their reviews of the book. Hamilton's pro-Monty bias, however, colors his parochial view of Eisenhower's leadership of the Alliance and lessens the value and impact of his criticism. David Eisenhower's assessment of Ike's wartime leadership is a model of objectivity compared to Hamilton's polemic.

2. Ibid., 574. David Eisenhower explains, "The German plan had banked heavily on speed and maneuver to offset the lack of frontline divisions available and the weight of American air and ground mobility, but ninety-six hours after the

attack, it was apparent that what was to have been a quick breakthrough in the Ardennes Forest along prearranged lines to be exploited by armor was evolving into a major battle for control of the Ardennes Forest itself in which the Allied buildup would match the Germans."

3. Field Marshal Lord Alanbrooke, *War Diaries, 1939–1945.* Alex Danchev and Daniel Todman, ed. (Berkeley: University of California Press, 2003); Arthur Bryant, *Triumph in the West: A History of the War Years Based on the Diaries of Field-Marshal Lord Alan Brooke, Chief of the Imperial General Staff* (Garden City, NY: Doubleday and Company, 1959), 273. Often Montgomery's co-conspirator in behind-the-scenes political maneuvering against Eisenhower, Brooke resented Ike's command of the Allied Army and probably jealously coveted the position for himself. Bryant's account is based nearly totally on Brooke's diaries and so reflects the field marshal's undisguised contempt for Ike and the Americans. Brooke used the Ardennes attack to immediately renew his own political offensive to get Monty named overall ground commander. Once again, his efforts failed (as they would until the end of the war).

4. Omar N. Bradley, *A Soldier's Story.* (New York: Henry Holt and Company, 1951), 475; D. Eisenhower, *Eisenhower At War,* 570. Bradley and the 12th Army Group staff accused the entire SHAEF organization of having "an acute case of the shakes," not just the supreme commander. It seems, however, that Bradley's staff was trying to make SHAEF appear unduly nervous and overly concerned about the 12th Army Group situation after the latter was stung by a curt SHAEF reminder to ensure the enemy captured no intact bridges over the Meuse. Bradley's chief of staff complained, "What the devil do they think we're doing, starting back for the beaches?" But SHAEF had discovered that Bradley, despite orders from Ike to the contrary, had allowed large supply dumps to be located in the Ardennes area. SHAEF wanted to make sure there was absolutely no question of its intentions on this critical issue. SHAEF could tolerate no further mistakes from Bradley's army group.

5. Omar N. Bradley and Clay Blair, *A General's Life: An Autobiography of General of the Army Omar N. Bradley* (New York: Simon and Schuster, 1983), 368. Finished after Bradley's death, this book spares no criticism of Bradley's contemporaries. It attempts to justify most of Bradley's mistakes by blaming others. Bradley viewed his loss of command of the First and Ninth Armies during the Battle of the Bulge as the worst period of his life, and he never stopped speaking out against it.

6. Martin Blumenson, *Eisenhower* (New York: Ballantine Books, 1972), 156–159. This book, written by one of the premier scholars of American commanders in the European Theater of Operations in World War II, focuses solely on Eisenhower's World War II coalition leadership. Blumenson considers Ike the most successful leader of an Allied coalition in history. The book includes a short biography of Ike's early career and professional development.

7. Carlo D'Este, *Eisenhower: A Soldier's Life* (New York: Henry Holt and Company, 2002), 5. In his definitive biography of Eisenhower, D'Este noted Ike's "well-concealed but towering ambition" and explained that "Eisenhower's . . . drive to succeed was, like Patton's, one of the best-kept secrets of his extraordinary success."

8. Ibid., 5, 45.
9. Ibid., 92. D'Este notes that for all his outwardly congeniality, Ike could show flashes of temper: "For those who knew Eisenhower or worked for him, his temper was as notorious as his grin was famous."
10. D. K. R. Crosswell, *Beetle: The Life of General Walter Bedell Smith* (Lexington: The University Press of Kentucky, 2010), 1–5, 39. Although in his superb biography of "Beetle" Smith, Crosswell challenges the "received wisdom" of the "'good cop' (Eisenhower)—'bad cop' (Smith) school," concluding that the Ike-Smith, commander-chief of staff relationship was more nuanced and less simplistic, he admits that Smith's "reputation as a one-dimensional SOB" dominates "because that was precisely the persona [Smith] labored so hard to project." Therefore, whether Smith was truly Ike's "attack dog" or merely acted like one seems a moot point. As Crosswell judges, Smith's "assignment was to get results, not to make friends," and to Eisenhower's great benefit that is exactly what "Beetle" did.
11. D'Este, *Eisenhower*, 5. D'Este quotes historian Eric Larrabee's judgment of Eisenhower's intelligence, including Larrabee's observation that Ike's high intelligence "was a quality that Eisenhower himself went to some lengths to conceal from the public."
12. Ibid., 92.
13. Ibid., 229.
14. Cole C. Kingseed, "Eisenhower's Prewar Anonymity: Myth or Reality?" *Parameters* 21 (Autumn 1991), 87–98; D'Este, *Eisenhower*, 270–271. D'Este notes that by the time Ike was a lieutenant colonel, his "reputation as a staff officer" was well-established in pre-World War II senior army circles. "Major General Walter Krueger, one of the army's most highly regarded officers," D'Este relates, began lobbying Washington to assign Eisenhower as Krueger's chief of staff in the autumn of 1940. Krueger finally got Ike as his Third Army chief of staff in June 1941 after he "wrote directly to his friend George Marshall to 'urgently request'" Eisenhower's assignment to Third Army on the eve of the Louisiana Maneuvers.
15. Stephen E. Ambrose, *Eisenhower: Volume I, Soldier, General of the Army, President-Elect, 1890–1952* (New York: Simon and Schuster, 1983), 13, 18, 38–54; D'Este *Eisenhower*, 51–84; Lawrence Van Gelder, *Ike: A Soldier's Crusade* (New York: Universal Publishing, 1969), 3–10. Eisenhower's family was of modest means, and the chance for a college education appeared none too promising for the young man. However, a family friend suggested he try for admission to one of the service academies. He passed the competitive exam and, on 14 June 1911, twenty-one-year-old Ike entered the Military Academy. Eisenhower's cadet career was less than brilliant and he chafed under West Point's harsh discipline and strict rules. By his senior year, Eisenhower stood a lowly 125th of 164 cadets in his class in "discipline." His many demerits were received for such "offenses" as smoking, untidiness, and pulling harmless pranks. He maintained his sense of humor, however, and he was genuinely popular among his classmates. He performed adequately in academics and was a football star until a

knee injury ended his playing days. Eisenhower stood 61st among the 164 members of the Class of 1915 who graduated that June and was commissioned in the Infantry. It seems that Eisenhower chose Infantry branch as a result of his bad knee, combined with a relatively low class standing. At his commissioning physical, the army doctor told him that he could have either Coast Artillery or Infantry, but not Cavalry, since it was considered to be more strenuous than the other branches on his knee. Eisenhower's 1915 USMA class has gone down in West Point lore as "the class the stars fell on," since 59 of its 164 graduates attained general officer rank. These included Bradley, Stratemeyer, Ryder, McNarney, and Van Fleet.

16. D'Este, *Eisenhower*, 85–126; Ambrose, *Eisenhower*, 56, 60. Lieutenant Eisenhower's first assignment took him to Fort Sam Houston, Texas, for duty with the 19th Infantry Regiment. He missed out on chasing Pancho Villa with Gen. John J. Pershing's Mexican Punitive Expedition in 1916. Instead, he stayed in San Antonio and trained Illinois National Guardsmen. Ike was given several different assignments over the next two years, but none got him what he really wanted: overseas combat duty in World War I.

17. Van Gelder, *Ike*, 14–18; Ambrose, *Eisenhower*, 60–63; D'Este, *Eisenhower*, 127. Eisenhower's later difficulties with the leadership of Infantry branch may have begun during the 1915–18 period when he "pestered the War Department with requests for overseas duty." He even tried for a branch transfer in an effort to get to France. Ike was promoted to major in May 1918 and lieutenant colonel that October, only the second member of the class of 1915 to reach that rank.

18. Ambrose, *Eisenhower*, 61–66. Ambrose correctly points out that failing to command soldiers in combat does not necessarily lead to a conclusion that "this fact somehow disqualified him for high command." It certainly helped Ike avoid refighting World War I when he received field command in World War II. Indeed, the best of his chief critic Montgomery's battles, including his famous victory at El Alamein, were more like those of the First World War than those of the Second, and were characterized by an extreme cautiousness, which fit rather uncomfortably in the blitzkrieg era. The third battle of Ypres (Passchendaele), fought from July to November 1917, cost the British 300,000 casualties for a gain of about 5 miles. It came to epitomize the futile trench warfare mentality of World War I, and the cry, "Passchendaele!" became a rallying-call for the pacifist and peace movements on England's university campuses between the wars. Despite missing out on the combat experience, Eisenhower at least avoided the trauma.

19. D. K. R. Crosswell, *The Chief of Staff: The Military Career of General Walter Bedell Smith* (New York: Greenwood Press, 1991), 356; Ambrose, *Eisenhower*, 71–72. Eisenhower's article, "A Tank Discussion," appeared in the November 1920 *Infantry Journal*. Patton, whom Eisenhower met and worked with during World War I, published a similar article on "Tanks in Future War" in the May 1920 *Journal*. The articles summarized the two men's conclusions about the importance of the tank in future warfare. The official view of the tank was that, since its mission was primarily to assist the infantry in crossing "no man's land," it must not be designed to travel faster than a walking infantryman.

20. D'Este, *Eisenhower*, 157; Van Gelder, *Ike*, 20–21; Ambrose, *Eisenhower*, 73–78; Bradley and Blair, *A General's Life*, 72–73. There can be little doubt that Infantry branch had decided Eisenhower's career was not worth their efforts, and that "choice" assignments should not be wasted on someone with no future. They consistently refused to assign him to career-enhancing positions and persistently kept him away from the Infantry School—the place Bradley described as the "nursery school for generals" of World War II. Ike was even denied attendance at the Infantry Officer's Advanced Course since, in those days, it was a stepping stone to the Command and General Staff School.

21. Robert H. Berlin, "Dwight David Eisenhower and the Duties of Generalship," *Military Review* 70 (October 1990): 20; D'Este, *Eisenhower*, 163–170; D. Eisenhower, *Eisenhower At War*, 829; Ambrose, *Eisenhower*, 73–79. Maj. Gen. Fox Conner had been Pershing's operations officer in World War I and was acknowledged as "the brains of the AEF [American Expeditionary Force]." Patton, who had met Conner in France, introduced him to Eisenhower in 1919. It was chiefly through Conner that Ike later became known to Pershing and Marshall. He became Eisenhower's friend and true mentor and "saved" the younger officer from a mediocre career of petty assignments. Eisenhower served as Conner's brigade executive officer in the 20th Infantry Brigade in Panama, 1922–24. D'Este judges that meeting Conner was "one of the most fateful encounters of Eisenhower's military life." David Eisenhower writes that Conner "impressed upon Eisenhower the idea of fighting in cooperation with allies, which he believed the next war would necessitate." Berlin further emphasizes this point by writing, "The man who was reading books about coalition warfare in Panama in 1922 would be organizing and conducting coalition warfare 20 years hence."

22. Mark C. Bender, *Watershed at Leavenworth: Dwight D. Eisenhower and the Command and General Staff College* (Fort Leavenworth, KS: U.S. Army Command and General Staff College, 1990), 37–41; Ambrose, *Eisenhower*, 79–81. Conner arranged for Eisenhower's appointment to the Command and General Staff School by engineering his assignment to recruiting duty in Colorado with the adjutant general's branch. Ike spent the first part of 1925 as a recruiter, biding his time while waiting for his orders to Leavenworth. Infantry Branch continued to refuse to further Ike's career in any way, and the chief of infantry's aide-de-camp wrote Eisenhower to warn him, "You will probably fail" the course at Leavenworth.

23. Ambrose, *Eisenhower*, 93; Russell F. Weigley, *The History of the United States Army* (New York: MacMillan Publishing Company, 1967), 421–422. MacArthur's claim that Eisenhower "is the best officer in the Army" was high praise, but Marshall had received his own share of such superlatives during his career. In 1916, one of Marshall's commanders even went so far as to write on his efficiency report that he "would prefer to serve *under*" Marshall's command—a remarkable statement, even among the inflated rhetoric found in fitness reports!

24. D'Este, *Eisenhower*, 217.

25. Douglas MacArthur, *Reminiscences* (New York: McGraw-Hill, 1964), 315. MacArthur says little about his association with Eisenhower in his autobiography,

but mentions, somewhat condescendingly that "I have always felt for him something akin to the affection of an older man for a younger brother. His amazingly successful career has filled me with pride and admiration."

26. D'Este, *Eisenhower*, 234–249.
27. Blumenson, *Eisenhower*, 16; D'Este, *Eisenhower*, 274–275; Ambrose, *Eisenhower*, 127. Eisenhower's series of chief of staff positions (3rd Infantry Division, IX Corps, and Third Army) were the result of his superiors' recognition of his exceptional ability as an organizer, planner, and coordinator who got the job done. He was requested, by name, for each of these positions. D'Este concluded that "Eisenhower and Krueger made an ideal pair. Eisenhower brought the vast staff experience Krueger needed and was undaunted by the challenge the forthcoming maneuvers presented. Experience and foresight were the traits Krueger sought, and in his new chief of staff he gained both."
28. Richard M. Ketchum, "Warming Up On the Sidelines For World War II," *Smithsonian* 22 (September 1991): 88–103; Christopher R. Gabel, "The 1941 Maneuvers," *Military Review* 71 (August 1991): 88–89; Ambrose, *Eisenhower*, 128–131. The maneuvers run on the eve of World War II were an important proving ground for some of the American Army leaders who would rise to prominence during the war, such as Eisenhower and Patton. However, as Gabel points out, only eleven of the forty-two division, corps, and army commanders who led in the maneuvers subsequently commanded in combat.
29. Forrest C. Pogue, *The United States Army in World War II. European Theater of Operations: The Supreme Command.* (Washington, D.C.: Office of the Chief of Military History/GPO, 1954), 33–34; D'Este, *Eisenhower*, 284–285; Van Gelder, *Ike*, 24; Blumenson, *Eisenhower*, 16; Ambrose, *Eisenhower*, 131–133. Pogue, the supreme command's official historian, relates that Ike's call to the War Plans Division was "in part for his work [Louisiana Maneuvers], but also because of his knowledge of the Philippines," since his position was that of deputy chief for the Pacific and Far East.
30. Pogue, *Supreme Command*, 33–34; D'Este, *Eisenhower*, 284–285; Ambrose, *Eisenhower*, 133–136. Marshall tested the newly arrived Eisenhower on his first afternoon in town (on Sunday, 14 December 1941), when he called him in and requested that Ike provide him with his assessment of a "general line of action" for the Pacific war. D'Este writes that "The Chief of Staff already knew the answer, but Eisenhower's first audience with Marshall was merely the start of a series of appraisals of an officer he believed had great potential." Eisenhower requested "a few hours" to develop his answer and was sent off to work on a reply. At dusk that evening, he presented Marshall with a handtyped sheet of paper outlining a Pacific strategy. Marshall agreed with Eisenhower's proposed strategy and sent him back to work to implement it. Ambrose characterizes this incident as Marshall's test of Eisenhower's ability to function successfully under the pressures of war. Ike passed the test. Today, Ike's original paper, now in a simple frame, hangs in the Pentagon office of the army's director of strategy, plans, and policy.
31. Ambrose, *Eisenhower*, 135–136.

32. Ibid., 146–147. Ike's ability to work closely with British officers seemed remarkable to Marshall for, according to Ambrose, "Many American officers found their British opposite numbers to be insufferable not only in their arrogance but their timidity about striking the enemy." Eisenhower, who shared many of these feelings, was able to keep them hidden and confined to his diary. Outwardly, he always projected a spirit of allied cooperation and partnership.

33. Chester Wilmot, *The Struggle for Europe* (New York: Harper and Brothers, 1952), 116; Ambrose, *Eisenhower*, 151–152; Pogue, *Supreme Command*, 34; Alanbrooke, *War Diaries*. Wilmot praises Eisenhower's "immediate and continuous loyalty to the concept of unity" and claimed "nobody else revealed Eisenhower's remarkable capacity for integrating the efforts of different allies and rival services, and for creating harmony between individuals with varied backgrounds and temperaments." Ambrose points out that the British high command was not unanimous in its high regard for Eisenhower. Most notably, the Chief of the Imperial General Staff, Field Marshal Alan Brooke, maintained a "deepseated prejudice against Americans," and "put Eisenhower down as an affable type with no strategic sense or command ability." Brooke, who obviously coveted the supreme commandership for himself, continued to bash Eisenhower in his diary, even after Ike proved extremely successful in the command. For his part, Eisenhower, who thought it was better not to mention someone if nothing good could be said of them, "seldom mentioned Brooke."

34. Maurice Matloff, *The United States Army in World War II. The War Department: Strategic Planning for Coalition Warfare, 1943–1944* (Washington, D.C.: Office of the Chief of Military History/U.S. Government Printing Office, 1953), 10–17; Blumenson, *Eisenhower*, 19; Ambrose, *Eisenhower*, 180–187; Pogue, *Supreme Command*, 42. Although both Eisenhower and Marshall were disappointed that North Africa (TORCH) was chosen over the cross-channel invasion of France (BOLERO-ROUNDUP), both Roosevelt and Churchill were in agreement in the decision—Roosevelt, because he insisted on getting U.S. troops into combat in 1942; and Churchill, because he considered an early attack on France too risky. There were other practical factors that favored the Mediterranean action, including limited shipping and landing craft, the small number of American troops in theater, and the need to free Mediterranean sea lanes.

35. Dwight D. Eisenhower, "Command in War." Speech, National War College, Fort McNair, Washington, D.C., 30 October 1950; Blumenson, *Eisenhower*, 19–20. In his speech on command to the National War College, General of the Army Eisenhower emphasized that "Allied commands depend on mutual confidence . . . by development of common understanding of the problems, by approaching these things on the widest possible basis with respect for each other's opinions, and above all, through the development of friendships, this confidence is gained . . . in Allied Staffs." Epitomizing the "allied unity" attitude at Ike's headquarters is the oft-repeated story that an American could call a British officer an "S.O.B.," provided he didn't refer to him as a "*British* S.O.B."

36. Forrest C. Pogue, "The Supreme Allied Command in Northwest Europe, 1944–45," *Essays in History and International Relations*, edited by Dwight E. Lee and George McReynolds (Worcester, MA: Clark University Press, 1949),

175; Rick Atkinson, *An Army at Dawn: The War in North Africa, 1942–1943* (New York: Henry Holt and Company, 2002), 170–173, 411–413. In *Army at Dawn*, the first volume of his masterful *Liberation* trilogy, Atkinson reveals how Eisenhower—and the green U.S. troops he led—faced a steep "learning curve" during the North African campaign and how Ike overcame it to evolve as an effective coalition commander: "If the winter [of 1942–1943] campaign in North Africa had revealed Eisenhower's infirmities, just as it revealed those of his army, spring would elicit strengths of character and competence in both the man and the host he commanded. Eisenhower had been naïve, sycophantic, unsure of his judgment, insufficiently vigorous, and more titular than actual commander . . . These traits did not abruptly slough away, molting into brilliances of generalship and élan. But new martial lineaments emerged, and they became the stuff of victory and liberation . . . With his equilibrium restored and his job apparently secure, Eisenhower's leadership ripened with the season."

37. Martin Blumenson, *Kasserine Pass* (New York: Jove Books, 1983), 303–320; D'Este, *Eisenhower*, 393–395, 399–403. The Battle of Kasserine Pass (14–24 February 1943) was actually the culmination of a series of actions centering around critical mountain passes in Tunisia.

38. Thomas Ricks, *The Generals: American Military Command from World War II to Today* (New York: Penguin Books, 2013), 51–58; Martin Blumenson and James L. Stokesbury, *Masters of the Art of Command* (Boston: Houghton Mifflin, 1975), 267–286; Ambrose, *Supreme Commander*, 166–184; Blumenson, *Kasserine Pass*, 83–87, 121–123.

39. D'Este, *Eisenhower*, 403; Ambrose, *Supreme Commander*, 175–178. D'Este reports that Bradley "thought [Eisenhower] would have been sacked after Kasserine" and that "Bradley went on to say that [Ike's] 'African record clearly demonstrates [that] he did not know how to manage a battlefield.'" However, given the fact that Rommel had to withdraw, and since the final victory in North Africa for the Allies seemed inevitable, Eisenhower suffered no permanent damage to his position as commander in chief. He turned the reverses to his own troops' advantage by capitalizing on their newfound realization that victory would have to be won the hard way. Ike directed that training would never stop, even for units in the line, and circulated the lessons of this first combat throughout U.S. forces.

40. Ambrose, *Supreme Commander*, 175–176, 341. Ambrose relates that Eisenhower told Patton upon assuming command of the fired Fredendall's II Corps that "you must not retain for one instant any man in a responsible position where you have become doubtful of his ability to do the job." Ambrose asserts that this attitude of quickly relieving those who can't measure up "was the great lesson of Kasserine Pass."

41. Ibid., 168–169, 174.

42. Alfred D. Chandler et al., editor, *The Papers of Dwight David Eisenhower, The War Years (Volumes I–V)*. (Baltimore: Johns Hopkins Press, 1970), 2:1353; Ambrose, *Supreme Commander*, 167–168. In North Africa, Eisenhower perceived this trait in Bradley, later writing that he "never caused one moment of worry [and has] the respect of all associates, including the British officers."

43. Pogue, *Supreme Command*, 34–35. Pogue makes another perceptive observation of Eisenhower's abilities when he writes, "General Eisenhower's conciliatory attitude was at times misleading. While genial in his approach, he could be extremely stern if the occasion demanded. His temper . . . was sometimes explosive and his reprimands could be blistering. Those traits were balanced by the gift of enormous patience."

44. Ambrose, *Eisenhower*, 237. The British politician to whom Eisenhower made his "our" victory remark was Harold Macmillan, a future prime minister.

45. Dwight D. Eisenhower, *Crusade in Europe* (Garden City, NY: Doubleday, 1948), 206–208; Ambrose, *Eisenhower*, 271.

46. Supreme Headquarters Allied Expeditionary Forces. Office of the Chief of Staff: Secretary, General Staff, *General Correspondence Files, May 1943–August 1945*, Incoming Message 13 February 1944; Pogue, *Supreme Command*, 53–55. The Combined Chiefs of Staff directive, dated 12 February 1944, is an eight-paragraph document also containing general information on command, logistics, coordination, and relationships with other United Nations forces and Allied governments. The directive to Eisenhower begins, "You are designated Supreme Allied Commander of forces for operations for liberation of Europe from Germans" and includes "You are responsible to the Combined Chiefs of Staff."

47. Gordon A. Harrison, *The United States Army in World War II. European Theater of Operations: Cross-Channel Attack* (Washington, D.C.: Office of the Chief of Military History/GPO, 1951), 269–321; Blumenson, *Eisenhower*, 86–90.

48. Pogue, *Supreme Command*, 175.

49. Bernard Law Montgomery, *The Memoirs of Field-Marshal the Viscount Montgomery of Alamein, KG* (New York: Signet Books, 1958), 289–299; John Keegan, *Six Armies in Normandy: From D-Day to the Liberation of Paris* (New York: Penguin Books, 1982), 55–60. Montgomery wrote in his memoirs: "It will be manifest to the reader that from 1st September 1944 onwards I was not satisfied that we had a satisfactory organisation for command or operational control." He harped on this point until forced to drop the subject in the spring of 1945. By then, the end of the war was nearly reached, making the question mostly academic.

50. Eisenhower, *Crusade in Europe*, 305. Ike referred to Monty's plan as a "pencil-like thrust" to emphasize its vulnerability.

51. Martin Van Creveld, *Supplying War: Logistics from Wallenstein to Patton* (New York: Cambridge University Press, 1977), 224–230. Van Creveld calculates that Montgomery's "40 divisions" would, realistically, have been quickly reduced to about 18 when all logistical and operational requirements were considered. He weighs all the many factors in the "Broad Front-Narrow Front" strategy question and concludes, "In the final account, the question as to whether Montgomery's plan presented a real alternative to Eisenhower's strategy must be answered in the negative."

52. Walter Bedell Smith, *Eisenhower's Six Great Decisions (Europe 1944–1945)* (New York: Longmans, Green and Company, 1956), 158–159; Ambrose, *Eisenhower*, 375. Francis de Guingand, Montgomery's chief of staff, was the one who warned his boss that Ike had prepared a cable. De Guingand pleaded with

Eisenhower not to send it until he had talked with Montgomery. Monty quickly realized the impact of such a message, that neither Brooke nor Churchill would step in to save him, and immediately sent Ike a conciliatory note, dropping the ground command question.

53. Joseph E. Persico, *Roosevelt's Centurions: FDR and the Commanders He Led to Victory in World War II* (New York: Random House, 2013), 356; David Rigby, *Allied Master Strategists: The Combined Chiefs of Staff in World War II* (Annapolis, MD: Naval Institute Press, 2012), 145–146, 148, 158–161.

54. Blumenson, *Eisenhower*, 155–156; Ambrose, *Eisenhower*, 149–154, 216–237; Pogue, *Supreme Command*, 34–37. Blumenson calls Eisenhower's "management of the complex establishment that won the war in northwestern Europe" his "superb accomplishment in the Second World War," including, as it did, the full spectrum of military, political, and diplomatic responsibilities. Blumenson concluded that no one else could have done it as well (including Eisenhower's old boss, MacArthur). Churchill remained an unflagging Eisenhower proponent throughout the war and never failed to support the supreme commander's decisions (despite his continual meddling in the military realm). In fact, Churchill was more supportive of the American general than Roosevelt during the North African campaign.

55. Weigley, *Eisenhower's Lieutenants*, 459.

56. Ambrose, *Supreme Commander*, 552; Chandler et al., *Eisenhower Papers*, 4:2350. Ike wrote, "I still have nine days, and while it seems almost certain that you will have an extra five pounds for Christmas, you will not get it until that day."

57. Maurice Matloff, "The 90-Division Gamble." *Command Decisions*. Kent Roberts Greenfield, ed. (Washington, D.C.: Office of the Chief of Military History/GPO, 1960).

58. Weigley, *Eisenhower's Lieutenants*, 461–464. Weigley's book is the best reference on this subject, as the inappropriateness of American strategy is one of his book's theses. His major premise, that the American command's inability to reconcile the U.S. Army's dual, competing legacies—mobility and attrition warfare—cites the ninety-division gamble as one of his central proofs.

59. U.S. Department of the Army, 12th Army Group, *G-1 Section, 12th Army Group Report of Operations*, 1948, 135–136; Jerry D. Morelock, *A Single Soldier: World War II Mobilization, Manpower, and Replacement Policies and Their Influence on the Conduct of U.S. Army Operations in Northwest Europe, 1944–45*, PhD diss., University of Kansas, 2000; Bradley and Blair, *A General's Life*, 354. On the day the German attack began, the 12th Army Group was short 30,000 replacements, nearly 20,000 of them infantrymen. This chronic shortage in units already in the theater was exacerbated by the lack of fresh divisions arriving from the States. There were no more units.

60. Despite the personnel shortages in Great Britain, however, Churchill announced a call-up of an additional 250,000 men during the Ardennes crisis. This controversial action threatened to strip some of Britain's critical war industries of their last pool of trained manpower. By the time any of these men could be inducted, trained, and sent to the battlefront, the war would be over.

61. Weigley, *Eisenhower's Lieutenants*, 464.

62. Ibid., 457.

63. Ambrose, *Supreme Command*, 556; Bradley and Blair, *A General's Life*, 351–356. Referring to the entire question of predicting the German attack and assessing its significance, Bradley wrote that he (and others) "were all wrong, of course—tragically and stupidly wrong."

64. Bradley and Blair, *A General's Life*, 356.

65. Weigley, *Eisenhower's Lieutenants*, 457; Eisenhower, *Crusade in Europe*, 342. Ike wrote: "I was immediately convinced that this was no local attack; it was not logical for the enemy to attempt merely a minor offensive in the Ardennes, unless of course it should be a feint to attract our attention while he launched a major effort elsewhere. This possibility was ruled out . . . other portions of [our] front . . . were so strong that the Germans could not hope to attack successfully . . . Moreover, we knew . . . German troop strength in the Ardennes area had been gradually increasing."

66. Ambrose, *Supreme Commander*, 556.

67. Weigley, *Eisenhower's Lieutenants*, 458; Bradley and Blair, *A General's Life*, 356. Bradley admits that "Ike sensed it [the importance of the attack] before I did," but characterizes the dispatching of the two armored divisions with the words, "urged on by Ike . . . I made telephone calls . . . to order the 10th Armored and the 7th Armored" to move. Bradley places the onus on Patton for "demurring," but other accounts support Bradley's reluctance to confront Patton about the 10th Armored move.

68. Peter Paret and Michael Howard (trans.), Carl von Clausewitz, *On War* (Princeton: University Press, 1976), 119–121; Crosswell, *Chief of Staff*. Crosswell attributes the commonality of the staff and school experiences (especially Leavenworth's Command and Staff School) as ensuring that a common doctrine and response would be understood and applied. Clausewitz cautions, however, that, although everything in war is simple, the simplest things are difficult to accomplish.

69. D. Eisenhower, *Eisenhower At War*, 558; Ambrose, *Supreme Commander*, 555–557.

70. Weigley, *Eisenhower's Lieutenants*, 480–484; Eisenhower, *Eisenhower At War*, 562–565; Eisenhower, *Crusade in Europe*, 344; Ambrose, *Supreme Commander*, 556–558; Bradley and Blair, *A General's Life*, 357. After the defense of Bastogne became iconized as the quintessential American defensive stand during the Battle of the Bulge, everyone who had anything to do with getting the 101st Airborne to the vital crossroads wanted to take the credit for sending it there. In fact, it was only natural that units sent to reinforce the Ardennes should gravitate to the two major road junctions in the area—Bastogne and St.-Vith. Since Bastogne was also the headquarters of Maj. Gen. Middleton's VIII Corps, it required no great amount of military genius or special prescience to determine reinforcing units should be directed there. Somewhat disgusted by the scurry to grab the glory for sending the 101st to Bastogne, Middleton wrote, "One did not have to be a genius to know that St.-Vith and Bastogne were critical points during the Battle of the Bulge." All one had to do, Middleton asserted, was look at a map.

71. Ambrose, *Supreme Commander*, 556.
72. Ibid., 557.
73. Jerry D. Morelock, "General Jacob L. Devers: Commonsense Commander." *Forward Observer* 3 (December 1988–February 1989).
74. Chandler et al., *Eisenhower Papers*, 4:2356.
75. D. Eisenhower, *Eisenhower At War*, 567.
76. Weigley, *Eisenhower's Lieutenants*, 499–501; D. Eisenhower, *Eisenhower At War*, 567; Ambrose, *Supreme Commander*, 367.
77. Chandler et al., *Eisenhower Papers*, 4:2355; Ambrose, *Supreme Commander*, 556.
78. D'Este, *Eisenhower*, 643–644. D'Este writes, "As always during periods of crisis, Eisenhower's chief weapon of motivation to defuse tense situations was optimism."
79. Ambrose, *Supreme Commander*, 558; D'Este, *Eisenhower*, 644.
80. Carlo D'Este, *Patton: A Genius for War* (New York: HarperCollins, 1995), 679–681; D'Este, *Eisenhower*, 644; Blumenson, *Patton*, 247; Ambrose, *Supreme Commander*, 558.
81. D. Eisenhower, *Eisenhower At War*, 567. David Eisenhower, writing about his grandfather's wartime leadership, noted: "This set the tone as the group got down to business."
82. D'Este, *Patton*, 679–681; Blumenson, *Patton*, 247.
83. Hugh Cole, *The United States Army in World War II. European Theater of Operations: Ardennes, The Battle of the Bulge* (Washington, D.C.: Office of the Chief of Military History/GPO, 1965), 486–488; Bradley and Blair, *A General's Life*, 359.
84. Weigley, *Eisenhower's Lieutenants*, 499–501. Weigley explains, "The discrepancy between Patton's and Eisenhower's intentions should also be noted. Eisenhower had asked how soon Patton could attack with six divisions. Patton responded that he could attack within a mere three days with three divisions. Eisenhower doubted that three divisions could strike a hard enough blow and expressed a preference for less speed but greater force: 'I did not want him [Patton] to start until he was in sufficient force so that, once committed, he could continue gradually to crush in the southern flank of the developing salient.'"
85. Nobécourt, *Last Gamble*, 206.
86. Bradley and Blair, *A General's Life*, 357. Bradley insisted the location of his headquarters was not a problem for him, and that he could easily exercise command of his armies in the north. He thought the most important point was to stand fast in his headquarters in Luxembourg City to avoid a panicked response. Yet, with no direct supervision by Bradley or any of his staff forthcoming, panic was very nearly the situation in Hodges's First Army headquarters (which retreated twice during the battle).
87. Ambrose, *Supreme Commander*, 563; Crosswell, *Chief of Staff*, 286; D. Eisenhower, *Eisenhower At War*, 573; Weigley, *Eisenhower's Lieutenants*, 503–506. David Eisenhower points out that "Eisenhower's timely decision removed all command barriers to containing and defeating the German counteroffensive. In a single stroke he eliminated Bradley's dual mission of containing the Germans in

the north and attacking from the south. Montgomery was now able to release Horrock's XXX Corps to man the Meuse between Namur and Dinant, which assured Hodges of British support in Belgium and the British of American support in Holland."

88. Wilmot, *The Struggle for Europe*, 116. Written in the early days of the Cold War, pro-British Australian Chester Wilmot sets out "to explain how the present situation came about; how and why the Western Allies, while gaining military victory, suffered political defeat." In so doing, he fired some of the first salvoes in the postwar transatlantic sniping between the Allied commanders. A Montgomery partisan, he faults American political naiveté for the postwar European situation vis-à-vis the Soviet Union. It is, therefore, a significant compliment when he heaps heavy praise on Eisenhower, an American, as an outstanding Allied commander.

89. D. Eisenhower, *Eisenhower At War*, 570.

90. Weigley, *Eisenhower's Lieutenants*, 504–505; D. Eisenhower, *Eisenhower At War*, 572–573; Ambrose, *Supreme Commander*, 562–563; Crosswell, *Chief of Staff*, 286–287. Smith had also called Bradley about the impending command change, but Bradley failed to provide Smith with strong, valid reasons why the change should not take place. In fact, Bradley said he would not object if Montgomery were an American commander.

91. D'Este, *Eisenhower*, 647–649; Ambrose, *Eisenhower*, 368–369; D. Eisenhower, *Eisenhower At War*, 572.

92. D. Eisenhower, *Eisenhower At War*, 572.

93. Ibid.

94. Montgomery, *Memoirs*, 281–289; Cole, *Ardennes*, 411–413. Despite the much-publicized anger of several of the top American commanders (such as Bradley and Patton) at Montgomery's receiving command in the north, many lower level U.S. commanders were delighted to hear the field marshal was taking charge of the confusing situation in First Army area. Among the latter were Brig. Gen. Robert Hasbrouck, commander of the 7th Armored Division, and Brig. Gen. Bruce C. Clarke, tenaciously defending St.-Vith.

95. Bradley and Blair, *A General's Life*, 357–363. Bradley later insisted, "I had been in closest telephone conversation with Hodges and Simpson. As a precaution, we were already laying auxiliary circuits west of the Meuse."

96. Weigley, *Eisenhower's Lieutenants*, 358; Bradley and Blair, *A General's Life*, 363.

97. D. Eisenhower, *Eisenhower At War*, 572; Weigley, *Eisenhower's Lieutenants*, 500–501.

98. D'Este, *Eisenhower*, 644–646; Ambrose, *Eisenhower*, 367; Weigley, *Eisenhower's Lieutenants*, 499–501; D. Eisenhower, *Eisenhower At War*, 568–569.

99. Cole, *Ardennes*, 445–508.

100. D. Eisenhower, *Eisenhower At War*, 578; Weigley, *Eisenhower's Lieutenants*, 546–547.

101. J. Lawton Collins, *Conversations with General J. Lawton Collins* (Fort Leavenworth, KS: U.S. Army Command and General Staff College, 1983); J. Lawton Collins, *Lightning Joe: An Autobiography* (Baton Rouge: LSU Press, 1979); D. Eisenhower, *Eisenhower At War*, 577.

102. Weigley, *Eisenhower's Lieutenants*, 541.

103. Ibid., 544–546.

104. Ibid., 566. Weigley quotes Patton's words at a 1 January 1945 press conference: "If you get a monkey in a jungle hanging by his tail, it is easier to get him by cutting his tail than kicking him in the face."

105. Rick Atkinson, *The Guns at Last Light: The War in Western Europe, 1944–1945*, Volume Three of the *Liberation* Trilogy (New York: Henry Holt and Company, 2013), 470; Eisenhower, *Crusade in Europe*, 365; Ambrose, *Supreme Commander*, 576.

106. D. Eisenhower, *Eisenhower At War*, 622; Weigley, *Eisenhower's Lieutenants*, 575–577.

107. Crosswell, *Chief of Staff*, 301.

108. Ibid.

109. Pogue, "Supreme Command," 192.

110. Ibid.

111. Weigley, *Eisenhower's Lieutenants*, 201–209. Bradley's aide, Maj. Chet Hansen recorded that the 12th Army Group commander felt that "had he forced the issue [at Falaise] and insisted on the advance of our troops, our bag at Falaise might have been considerably more than it was."

112. Montgomery, *Memoirs*, 285–289; Weigley, *Eisenhower's Lieutenants*, 545.

113. Weigley, *Eisenhower's Lieutenants*, 556–558.

114. Nobécourt, *Last Gamble*, 215.

115. Crosswell, *Chief of Staff*, 286; Weigley, *Eisenhower's Lieutenants*, 504; Ambrose, *Supreme Commander*, 563; Bradley and Blair, *A General's Life*, 363–364.

116. Pogue, "Supreme Command," 188–189.

117. Ibid.

118. Weigley, *Eisenhower's Lieutenants*, 463–464. Weigley points out that despite the (primarily British) criticism that Ike's strategy was only an emulation of the old Lincoln-Grant strategy of the American Civil War, that strategy did, in fact, produce a victory—that is, it worked.

119. Bradley and Blair, *A General's Life*, 356.

120. Weigley, *Eisenhower's Lieutenants*, 461–463.

121. Ambrose, *Eisenhower*, 365–366.

122. Chandler et al., *Eisenhower Papers*, 4:2368; Ambrose, *Eisenhower*, 369.

123. Eisenhower, *Crusade in Europe*, 340–341.

124. Chandler et al., *Eisenhower Papers*, 4:2361.

125. Supreme Headquarters Allied Expeditionary Forces. Office of the Chief of Staff: Secretary, General Staff, *General Correspondence Files, May 1943–August 1945*, Incoming Message 162050A January 1945; Chandler et al., *Eisenhower Papers*, 4:2363–2365. Montgomery refused to acknowledge that his command in the Bulge led to disappointing results. He sent a self-congratulatory "eyes only" message to Eisenhower on 16 January 1945 trumpeting his "tactical victory": "I have the great pleasure in reporting to you that the task you gave me in the Ardennes is now concluded. First and Third Armies have joined hands at Houffalize and are advancing eastwards. It can therefore be said we have now achieved tactical victory within the salient. I am returning First Army to Bradley

tomorrow as ordered by you. I would like to say what a great pleasure it has been to have such a splendid Army under my command and how very well it has done." Montgomery's boasting of his "tactical victory within the salient" instead of achieving the strategic triumph that Eisenhower clearly intended must have infuriated an already exasperated Ike.

126. Chandler et al., *Eisenhower Papers*, 4:2363–2365.
127. Supreme Headquarters Allied Expeditionary Forces. Office of the Chief of Staff: Secretary, General Staff, *General Correspondence Files, May 1943–August 1945*, Incoming Message 180028A January 1945; Weigley, *Eisenhower's Lieutenants*, 544. Pushed to the limit by Monty's badgering for sole command of Allied ground forces during the Ardennes offensive, Ike finally prepared a "him or me" cable to send to the combined chiefs. When De Guingand, Monty's capable and popular chief of staff read the cable, he convinced Ike not to send it until he'd had a chance to get Montgomery to change his ways. The field marshal, finally realizing he'd pushed the genial supreme commander past his breaking point, sent a chastened note to Ike asking him to tear up his previous letter and promising to carry out his orders. It saved Monty's job. The tone of another Montgomery "eyes only" message to Eisenhower on 18 January 1945 clearly reflects Monty's revised attitude toward the supreme commander: "Dear Ike, Brad is, I hope, coming to see me tomorrow. Would this be OK with you? Yours Ever, Monty."
128. Crosswell, *Chief of Staff*, 294–301. Crosswell asserts that, because of the position Ike was in as an Allied commander, he was required to reach compromises, build consensus, and smooth ruffled feathers, but Ike needed someone like Smith to "do the dirty work for him."
129. Weigley, *Eisenhower's Lieutenants*, 543.
130. Jonathan Jordan, *Brothers, Rivals, Victors: Eisenhower, Patton, Bradley, and the Partnership That Drove the Allied Conquest in Europe* (New York: NAL Caliber, 2011), 456.
131. The overriding requirement for maintaining a successful coalition was building consensus, not self-promotion of one's countrymen at the expense of the Allies.
132. D. Eisenhower, *Eisenhower At War*, 595–609.
133. Weigley, *Eisenhower's Lieutenants*, 565.
134. Crosswell, *Chief of Staff*, 294–296.
135. Pogue, *Supreme Command*, 55; Ambrose, *Eisenhower*, 408. Marshall gave Eisenhower these accolades in a congratulatory message at the end of the war in Europe. Ambrose observes that "it was the highest possible praise from the best possible source. It had been earned."
136. Blumenson and Stokesbury, *Masters of Command*, 303.

CHAPTER 3

1. Martin Blumenson, Interview by author, June 1994, Washington, D.C. Professor Blumenson began the interview by asserting: "Bradley was relieved of command by Eisenhower during the Battle of the Bulge." This was the first time that the author had heard Eisenhower's 20 December 1944 action characterized as

Bradley being *relieved* of army group command. Being relieved of command—"relief for cause" in the army's lexicon—is, of course, one of the most damning indictments of a commander's leadership and character that an officer can receive. Yet, Blumenson's impeccable credentials as the most distinguished historian of U.S. Army operations in the European Theater whose first-hand knowledge of the personalities and events during the 1944–1945 campaigns in France and Germany gave him a unique perspective adds overwhelming weight and authority to his judgment. Although none of the principals—Eisenhower, Bradley, and Montgomery—characterized the command change as Bradley having been relieved, a critical examination and evaluation of the reasons for and the practical effect of Ike's decision clearly supports Blumenson's characterization.

2. Carlo D'Este, *Eisenhower: A Soldier's Life* (New York: Henry Holt and Company, 2002), 648–649; Rick Atkinson, *The Guns at Last Light: The War in Western Europe, 1944–1945* (New York: Henry Holt and Company, 2013), 447–450. Atkinson notes that "At 12:52 p.m., a SHAEF log entry confirmed that 'Field Marshal Montgomery has been placed in charge of the northern flank.' He would command the U.S. First and Ninth Armies, as well as his own [21] army group; Twelfth Army Group was left with only Patton's Third Army." Moreover, Bradley's sole remaining U.S. First Army unit—Middleton's VIII Corps—was attached to Third Army on 20 December 1944 and remained in Patton's army until 21 April 1945.

3. Jonathan W. Jordan, *Brothers, Rivals, Victors: Eisenhower, Patton, Bradley, and the Partnership That Drove the Allied Conquest of in Europe* (New York: NAL Caliber, 2011), 456; D'Este, *Eisenhower*, 648–649. Jordan judges that "the Ardennes crisis seemed to bring out the steel in Dwight Eisenhower . . . and in the heat of battle he had pulled rank on his classmate and friend . . . But militarily, Ike knew he had made the right move, and to Ike, an officer's personal feelings were worth little or nothing. It was what you signed up for when you took the oath." D'Este concludes that "In short, despite his complaints, Bradley needed to look no farther than himself to determine the reasons for Eisenhower's decision."

4. Alfred D. Chandler et al., eds., *The Papers of Dwight David Eisenhower, The War Years* (Baltimore: Johns Hopkins Press, 1970), 4:2375. Eisenhower wrote: "I consider Bradley the greatest battle-line commander I have met in this war." This accolade was contained in a cable Eisenhower sent to Marshall on 30 March 1945, primarily complimenting Bradley's overall performance throughout his tenure as army group commander and, perhaps, also drawing some publicity for Bradley's accomplishments (and away from Patton who was, by this time in the war, monopolizing the press coverage).

5. Omar N. Bradley and Clay Blair, *A General's Life: An Autobiography of General of the Army Omar N. Bradley* (New York: Simon and Schuster, 1983), 368, 370. This book, completed two years *after* General Bradley died, caused some controversy because of Blair's insistence that it was an autobiography. He purportedly explained the fact that he, not Bradley, had written much of the book by saying that because he and Bradley had worked so closely together on preparing the book, he had come to think like Bradley, thereby justifying his completion of the

book as a posthumous autobiography. Despite the difficulty in determining exactly what part of the book is Bradley and what part is Blair, this account relies upon *A General's Life* as the best available first-hand information about how Bradley viewed his life and career, as well as his thoughts and opinions about people and events. When possible, information has been verified in other sources; however, in general, Bradley (or Blair writing as Bradley) has been taken at his word. Concerning Eisenhower informing Bradley of his decision to give Montgomery command of Bradley's two northernmost armies, Bradley wrote: "It required every fiber of my strength to restrain myself from an insulting outburst."

6. Chandler, et al., *Eisenhower Papers*, 4:2237. The issue of Bradley's promotion to four-star general had been raised before the Battle of the Bulge began, but it had not been approved or acted upon before the end of the battle. In his 12 January 1945 cable to Marshall urging that Bradley's promotion be approved, Ike prefaced his hope that Marshall would consider Bradley for promotion "at once" with this important caveat: "if [Bradley] can only make some significant penetration from his [south] side of the salient, particularly one that might result in the destruction or capture of considerable enemy forces." Ike also included another reason for Bradley's promotion that, knowing Marshall, he thought would help sway the chief of staff to support it, writing, "I think it would have a fine *general effect*" (emphasis added). The "general effect," of course, meant that Bradley's promotion would serve as a morale booster for the entire army officer corps as well as send an unambiguous signal to the American public that—despite the early setbacks—the Battle of the Bulge was producing a great victory.

7. Joseph R. Fischer, "Omar Nelson Bradley," *Generals of the Army: Marshall, MacArthur, Eisenhower, Arnold, Bradley*, edited by James H. Willbanks (Lexington, KY: University Press of Kentucky, 2013), 223; Thomas E. Ricks, *The Generals: American Military Command from World War II to Today* (New York: Penguin Books, 2013), 116–118. In his insightful examination of the evolution of American generalship from World War II to current operations, Ricks makes this perceptive observation concerning Bradley's longstanding reputation: "Even if he was never quite the beloved 'GI's general' presented by wartime journalist Ernie Pyle, Bradley was an even-tempered man with a reputation for decency in his personal interactions. Yet during the war he had run an unhappy headquarters, one that during 1944–45 had developed a reputation for 'irritable suspiciousness.'"

8. U.S. Department of the Army, Headquarters Department of the Army, *General Orders Number 11*, 27 April 1981. This document is the official announcement of General Bradley's death. It contains an abbreviated military biography. Bradley's promotion to five-star General of the Army rank was on 22 September 1950, over a year after his 19 August 1949 appointment as the first chairman of the Joint Chiefs of Staff and nearly six years after the December 1944 promotions of the other four generals of the army (Marshall, MacArthur, Eisenhower, and Arnold). With his promotion coming just as the conflict between President Harry S. Truman and his field commander in Korea, General of the Army

Douglas MacArthur, was intensifying, Bradley's elevation to five-star rank was obviously engineered by the Truman administration to give Bradley equal rank—and therefore serve as a potential counterweight—to MacArthur. Moreover, just three days before Bradley's promotion, Truman added another five-star general to MacArthur's chain of command—the president fired his civilian secretary of defense, Louis Johnson, and replaced him with General of the Army George Marshall (whose promotion to that rank in December 1944 preceded MacArthur's by two days). For the most comprehensive, exhaustively researched, and balanced examination of the Truman-MacArthur controversy, see Michael D. Pearlman, *Truman and MacArthur: Policy, Politics and the Hunger for Honor and Renown* (Bloomington, IN: Indiana University Press, 2008).

9. Jordan, *Brothers, Rivals, Victors*, 550.
10. Russell F. Weigley, *Eisenhower's Lieutenants: The Campaigns of France and Germany, 1944–1945* (Bloomington, IN: Indiana University Press, 1981), 171.
11. Rick Atkinson, *An Army at Dawn: The War in North Africa, 1942–1943* (New York: Henry Holt and Company, 2002), 485. Atkinson considered that, in being "simple, direct and ruthless," Bradley was "like Patton" in that regard.
12. *The Howitzer* (West Point: The United States Military Academy, 1915); Bradley and Blair, *A General's Life*, 30–35. Bradley's entry in *The Howitzer*, the West Point yearbook (written by his classmate and friend Eisenhower), uses the telling phrase: "[Bradley's] most promising characteristic is 'getting there,' and if he keeps up the clip he's started, some of us will some day be bragging to our grandchildren that, 'Sure, General Bradley was a classmate of mine.'"
13. Bradley and Blair, *A General's Life*, 35–36. Bradley related that engineers and field artillery were sought-after commissions because the army then promoted officers by branch (instead of at large) and promotions in these two branches occurred more quickly. When that policy was changed in 1916, all officers were placed on equal footing, and Bradley then felt better about his promotion opportunities in the Infantry branch.
14. Ibid. Eisenhower described Mexican border duty: "This service was disagreeable. Usually, it separated a man from his family. Living conditions were rough. Anything was better to most officers than the border."
15. Ibid., 44–46. Russell F. Weigley, *History of the United States Army* (New York: Macmillan Publishing Company, 1967), 396. Bradley kept trying desperately to finagle an assignment to an outfit slated to deploy overseas but was unsuccessful. He wrote, "As a professional soldier and a West Pointer . . . I sincerely believed that if I did not get to France I would be professionally ruined." Soon after the November 1918 Armistice, the inevitable "down-sizing" of the army began in earnest. Weigley laments, "The laws authorizing the wartime army entitled nearly all who served in it to prompt discharge, and the soldiers returned to the United States and to their homes in a rush that dwarfed the Civil War demobilization: 2,608,218 enlisted men and 128,436 officers received discharges by June 30, 1919. By January 1, 1920, only 130,000, mainly the Regular Army, stood under arms . . ."

16. James L. Stokesbury, A *Short History of World War I* (New York: William Morrow and Company, 1981), 259, 313; Bradley and Blair, *A General's Life*, 47–48; Weigley, *History of the U.S. Army*, 399–414. The Allied intervention in Russia, including about 13,000 U.S. soldiers located primarily near Archangel in North Russia and Vladivostok in Siberia, eventually involved 15 anti-Soviet nations. Although ostensibly neutral, the American troops nevertheless frequently found themselves in armed combat with Bolshevik forces. Without achieving much, save long-lasting distrust and hard feelings from the Soviets, it ended "after some ineffectual interference." Bradley's assignment to teach ROTC was a relatively common duty for Regular Army officers during the interwar period. Some of Bradley's contemporaries who served in lengthy ROTC assignments and later became notable generals in World War II included Troy H. Middleton, John S. Wood, Bruce C. Clarke, and James A. Van Fleet.

17. Harold R. Winton, *Corps Commanders of the Bulge: Six American Generals and Victory in the Ardennes* (Lawrence: University Press of Kansas, 2007), 372–373; Bradley and Blair, *A General's Life*, 30–35, 46–79; Stephen E. Ambrose, *Eisenhower: Volume I. Soldier, General of the Army, President-Elect, 1890–1952* (New York: Simon and Schuster, 1983), 72, 74, 78–79. Bradley proved a more successful student in army schools than he had been as a cadet at West Point. He graduated ranked 44 in his 1915 West Point class of 164 but finished second in his Infantry Advanced Course class at Fort Benning, just behind Leonard T. "Gee" Gerow (later V Corps, then 15th Army commander in 1944–1945). Gerow was Ike's study-mate at Leavenworth during Command and Staff School, 1925–1926. Gerow graduated near the top of that class of 1925–1926—not second in the class as is sometimes claimed, as Winton has discovered—while Eisenhower was first.

18. Bradley and Blair, *A General's Life*, 59.

19. Ambrose, *Eisenhower*, 85; Bradley and Blair, *A General's Life*, 71, 74–75. In fact, Bradley's friend and fellow faculty member at the Infantry School, Joe Stilwell, advised him not to go to the War College, saying, "Brad, why would you go to a school and prepare yourself for a job you don't want?" Bradley also remembered Marshall's example from World War I, where Marshall's excellent reputation as a staff officer had kept him in Pershing's headquarters and out of a combat troop command throughout that war. However, another close friend, Forrest Harding, pointed out that the school had a good reputation and would be valuable preparation for any later higher level assignment to troop or staff duty. When Harding pointed out that War College attendance was also looked for as a qualification for promotion to general, Bradley followed Harding's advice. Ambrose described the War College of this era: "The college, in theory, was the capstone of an officer's postgraduate education. Its mission was to prepare men for high command. In practice, it was a reward rather than a challenge, a relaxing year [students were neither examined nor ranked], spent mainly listening to lectures on world affairs by government officials and army generals. The idea was to broaden the outlook of officers tapped for future high command; the reality was more a pleasant sabbatical."

20. Bradley and Blair, *A General's Life*, 59. Of the National Guard assignment, Bradley wrote: "In effect, I became liaison officer between the U.S. Army and the Hawaiian National Guard, responsible for training standards and a wide variety of administrative duties, none of them overly taxing or challenging. Duty called; I responded, but not happily."

21. Ibid., 62. There can be little doubt that Bradley's fortuitous association with Marshall at the Infantry School marks the real beginning of his rise to prominence in the Army. Marshall was immediately impressed with the younger officer and added Bradley's name near the top of his list of promising officers to help him mold the World War II army.

22. Forrest C. Pogue, "General of the Army Omar N. Bradley," *The War Lords: Military Commanders of the Twentieth Century*, ed. Field Marshal Sir Michael Carver (Boston: Little, Brown and Company, 1976), 539; Bradley and Blair, *A General's Life*, 63–73. According to Pogue, Marshall said Bradley was "conspicuous for his ability to handle people and his ability to do things carefully and simply."

23. *General Orders Number 11*, 1; Bradley and Blair, *A General's Life*, 80–81, 83–92.

24. Bradley and Blair, *A General's Life*, 94. With this promotion to brigadier general (skipping the rank of colonel completely), Bradley jumped ahead of his (until now) faster-moving classmate, Eisenhower. Ike would catch, then pass him, however, in the next eighteen months.

25. John K. Mahon, *History of the Militia and the National Guard* (New York: Macmillan, 1983), 186–187; Robert R. Palmer, et al., *The United States Army in World War II: The Army Ground Forces. The Procurement and Training of Ground Combat Troops* (Washington, D.C.: Office of the Chief of Military History/GPO, 1948), 91–92, 489–493; James W. Bradin, "28th Infantry Division: The Forgotten Pennsylvanians," *Army* 37 (August 1987): 62–67; Bradley and Blair, *A General's Life*, 97, 102–105, 108–109. It should be noted that at least two other major training projects were occurring at Fort Benning during Bradley's tenure: the formation of the first U.S. airborne combat units and the 2nd Armored Division. Although Bradley became an ardent supporter of both airborne and armored forces during the war, there is no evidence that he was instrumental in their development or fielding. Nevertheless, as commandant of the school, he must have kept abreast of new developments in both formations, a fact which would benefit his battle leadership in the Mediterranean and northern Europe. After leaving Benning for division command, Bradley complained: "The 28th National Guard Division, to which Marshall had consigned me in June 1942, was plagued with all the faults of most Guard divisions. It was based at Camp Livingston, ten miles north of Alexandria, Louisiana, only thirty-eight miles from our own camp, part of Oscar Griswold's IV Corps, to which the 82nd Division was assigned. Griswold and I had often discussed its problems in private."

26. Bradley and Blair, *A General's Life*, 112. The cable informing Bradley of his selection for corps command, received at noon on 12 February 1943, read: "It is only fitting that your birthday should precede by only a few days your transfer to command a corps which comes as a long-delayed acknowledgment of your splendid record with the 28th Division. Congratulations and Best Wishes. Marshall."

27. Stephen E. Ambrose, *The Supreme Commander: The War Years of General of the Army Dwight D. Eisenhower* (Garden City, NY: Doubleday and Company, 1970), 174–176, 185; Bradley and Blair, *A General's Life*, 131; Chandler, et al., *Eisenhower Papers*, 2:816. In an 11 February 1943 cable to Marshall, Eisenhower listed, in this order, the following general officers (major generals) who would be acceptable to act as his "eyes and ears": John H. Hester (CG, 43rd Infantry Division); Terrell (CG, 90th Infantry Division); Bradley; Rapp Brush (CG, 40th Armored Division); "Pinky" Bull (Head of Replacement and School Command, Army Ground Forces); Charles H. Gerhardt (CG, 91st Infantry Division); Matthew B. Ridgway (CG, 82nd Airborne Division); Paul L. Ransom (CG, 98th Infantry Division); Charles H. Corlett (upcoming CG, 7th Infantry Division); John B. Wogan (CG, 14th Armored Division); and William G. Livesay (35th Infantry Division, then CG, 91st Infantry Division). Interestingly, Ike also listed a retired officer, recently recalled to active duty on the War Department Manpower Board, Lorenzo D. Gasser. Eisenhower specified that the job required "brains, tact and imagination more than it does thorough acquaintanceship with the theater, so that any man of ability could begin to operate efficiently after a week of indoctrination." Marshall wired back that Bradley was immediately available and Ike quickly accepted.

28. Martin Blumenson, *Kasserine Pass* (New York: Jove Books, 1983), 1–7; Martin Blumenson and James L. Stokesbury, *Masters of the Art of Command* (New York: Da Capo, 1975), 263–286; Carlo D'Este, *Patton: A Genius for War* (New York: HarperCollins, 1995), 457–460; D'Este, *Eisenhower*, 393–403; Martin Blumenson, *Patton: The Man Behind the Legend, 1885–1945* (New York: Berkley Books, 1987), 182; Bradley and Blair, *A General's Life*, 133, 151, 155; Atkinson, *An Army at Dawn*, 359–392, 396–400. Bradley described his duties: "When I concluded my indoctrination at Ike's headquarters and received my formal orders, I was not overjoyed at my assignment. I was not only to act as Ike's eyes and ears on the Tunisian front, reporting back to him directly, I also had authority to make 'suggestive changes' (as Ike put it) to American commanders at the front. Inevitably, I would be regarded as an odious spy for Ike, carrying tales outside the chain of command. Any suggested corrections from a rank newcomer from an exalted rear-echelon headquarters would be bitterly resented and probably ignored or laughed at behind my back. I decided my best policy was to keep a very low profile, eyes and ears open, mouth shut." Considering what would transpire later during the Battle of the Bulge, it is interesting to note that, even in this early point in Ike's exercise of coalition command in North Africa, Bradley claims that Eisenhower tended to favor the British too much: "If I were to continue to serve as one of [Eisenhower's] battlefield lieutenants, it was clear that I must be much, much firmer in advancing American interests and strategy."

29. D'Este, *Patton*, 533–555; Blumenson, *Patton*, 207–215; Bradley and Blair, *A General's Life*, 201–202; Ambrose, *Eisenhower*, 250–252, 274–275. There were two "slapping" incidents, occurring a week apart, August 3 and 10, 1943. Both soldiers were suffering from combat fatigue but drew Patton's wrath since they showed no outward manifestations or obvious wounds. Bradley soon learned of the second incident: "After leaving the hospital, Patton came to my CP. He

mentioned that he had had to slap a malingering soldier, but the remark was so casual and vague it didn't fully register on me. Two days later I had good reason to recall his remark. Bill Kean [Bradley's chief of staff] handed me an explosive official letter to the II Corps from the hospital commander reporting in damning detail the entire incident. I was horrified. Even for George Patton it was excessive conduct. I realized that if word of this incident got out, we might lose Patton's talents forever. I ordered Kean to lock the letter in my safe and say nothing whatsoever about it. Not aware of the first slapping incident, I naively hoped the matter would be forgotten or go away." Bradley's inaction in this famous incident is disappointing for one who has a reputation as a "soldier's general." His excuse for covering up the incident seems weak. Apparently, he never even confronted Patton with the official report he received, let alone alerted Eisenhower to a potentially disastrous situation. Bradley's cover-up not only let down the soldiers victimized by Patton but also placed Eisenhower in an extremely embarrassing position a short time later when the story, inevitably, got out. If these actions had occurred in today's army, it is highly likely that Bradley would also have been relieved of command. D'Este reveals that despite Bradley initially covering up the incident, the "soldier's general" later claimed that, if Patton had been his subordinate at the time, "I would have relieved him instantly and would have had nothing more to do with him."

30. Bradley and Blair, *A General's Life*, 159, 200. Concerning the Ernie Pyle story, Bradley writes: "Pyle caught up with me in Nicosia (Sicily, August 1943). I was still very leery of publicity, but my aide Chet Hansen convinced me I should cooperate. Pyle was a little leery, too. Up to now, he had written exclusively about GI's and he was not comfortable with the brass. He stuck with me like a shadow for three days. Then he wrote a six-part series (about 5,000 words) that was widely published in the States. The series hardly made me a household name, but it was my first extensive national publicity. Even with all his creative gifts, Pyle had a difficult time making me 'colorful.'"

31. Omar N. Bradley, *A Soldier's Story* (New York: Henry Holt and Company, 1951), 8; Chandler, et al., *Eisenhower Papers*, 2:1205. The choice for the principal U.S. ground commander for OVERLORD was narrowed down to Lt. Gen. Mark Clark, then involved in planning the Italian campaign, and Bradley. Marshall and Eisenhower exchanged several cables discussing the merits of the officers and, in one of these Ike gave his assessment of Bradley's abilities: "Next Bradley. There is little I need to tell you about him because he is running absolutely true to form all the time. He has brains, a fine capacity for leadership and a thorough understanding of the requirements of modern battle . . . He is perfectly capable of commanding an army . . . I am very anxious to keep him . . . as long as we have any major operations to carry out." In his first autobiography, *A Soldier's Story*, published shortly after the end of the war, Bradley described his feelings at being told by Ike on 1 September 1943 that he would have a major command in OVERLORD: "A bare five months before, I had been given command of a corps; now it was to be an Army. After 28 years of snail's-pace, peacetime promotions, I was now finding it difficult to keep stars in stock. As a result of the Tunisian campaign I had become the only U.S. corps commander with

battle experience against the Germans. And in Sicily I had cut my teeth on a large-scale amphibious assault. Both assignments were invaluable experience of me for the invasion of Europe."

32. Chandler, et al., *Eisenhower Papers*, 2:1209–1214.
33. Bradley and Blair, *A General's Life*, 208.
34. Gordon A. Harrison, *United States Army in World War II: The European Theater of Operations. Cross-Channel Attack* (Washington, D.C.: Office of the Chief of Military History, 1951), 183–187; John Keegan, *Six Armies in Normandy: From D-Day to the Liberation of Paris* (New York: Penguin Books, 1983), 21–67; Bradley, *A Soldier's Story*, 233–236; Bradley and Blair, *A General's Life*, 226–227. Bradley reports that British Air Marshal Leigh-Mallory, the most vocal opponent of large-scale airborne landings, estimated that paratroopers would take casualties of up to 50 percent and glider troops up to 70 percent. According to Bradley, Ike had to make the final decision and "after hearing all the pros and cons, ruled in [Bradley's] favor." In the event, Leigh-Mallory's dire prediction of airborne casualties was substantially borne out when the paratroopers and glider troops of the two U.S. airborne divisions (82nd and 101st) suffered nearly 50 percent casualties (killed, wounded, and missing in action).
35. Bradley and Blair, *A General's Life*, 226.
36. Ambrose, *Supreme Commander*, 597.
37. Bradley and Blair, *A General's Life*, 251.
38. Ibid., 252, 259.
39. Martin Blumenson, *United States Army in World War II: European Theater of Operations. Breakout and Pursuit* (Washington, D.C.: Office of the Chief of Military History/GPO, 1961), 36–47. Blumenson summed up the situation facing Bradley and his American troops: ". . . the situation of the U.S. First Army just before it began its July offensive [was] an attack pointed through a flooded pastoral region of 10,000 little fields enclosed by hedgerows. Through this region, made for ambush, where the German defenders had dug into the hedgerow banks and erected strong defense, the Americans were to fight from field to field, from hedgerow to hedgerow, measuring the progress of their advance in yards. Over it all a steady rain was to pour, and the odors of the Normandy soil were to mingle with the smell of decaying flesh and become part of the war."
40. Harold J. Meyer, *Hanging Sam: A Military Biography of General Samuel T. Williams, From Pancho Villa to Vietnam* (Denton: University of North Texas Press, 1990), 72–73; Ricks, *The Generals*, 1–7; Blumenson, *Breakout and Pursuit*, 36–47. Brig. Gen. Jay W. MacKelvie led the 90th Infantry Division in just four days of combat (10–14 June 1944) before being relieved for cause by Bradley. He was replaced by Maj. Gen. Eugene Landrum, whom Bradley also relieved a short time later. Ricks wrote that "The swift reliefs of World War II were not an instrument of precision, and, while often effective in leading to more capable commanders, they were sometimes clearly the wrong move."
41. Bradley and Blair, *A General's Life*, 269.
42. Daniel P. Bolger, "Zero Defects: Command Climate in First US Army, 1944–1945," *Military Review* 71 (May 1991): 61–73.
43. *General Orders Number 11*, 1; Bradley, *A Soldier's Story*, 358; Bradley and Blair, *A General's Life*, 283, 321; Weigley, *Eisenhower's Lieutenants*, 175–286.

Montgomery remained Ike's ground commander (and technically Bradley's immediate superior) until 1 September 1944, when Eisenhower took formal command of all ground forces. Bradley and Montgomery then became co-equal army group commanders.

44. Ambrose, *Eisenhower*, 331–334; Bradley and Blair, *A General's Life*, 299.
45. Bradley, *A Soldier's Story*, 375–377; Bradley and Blair, *A General's Life*, 293–297.
46. Charles B. MacDonald, *The Battle of the Huertgen Forest* (New York: Jove Books, 1984), 2–4. Robert Sterling Rush, *Hell in Hürtgen Forest: The Ordeal and Triumph of an American Infantry Regiment* (Lawrence: University Press of Kansas, 2001). The phrase "Passchendaele with tree bursts" is attributed by MacDonald to Ernest Hemingway. Passchendaele refers to the bloody World War I battle in Flanders (Third Battle of Ypres, July–November 1917) which cost the British 300,000 casualties for a gain of about 5 miles. In the September through December 1944 Huertgen battle, U.S. forces suffered 33,000 casualties against German losses of only 16,000.
47. Combat Studies Institute, *Conversations With General J. Lawton Collins* (Fort Leavenworth, KS: U.S. Army Command and General Staff College, 1983), 9–10. Collins comment that "someone had to cover that sector" begs the question of why an all-out U.S. offensive was thrown into the Huertgen. It was only later that First Army awoke to the key objective of the Roer River dams in the Huertgen area, so it seems likely that Collins's offensive was launched because poorly prepared staff officers and commanders thought the Siegfried Line could be easily breached in this area.
48. MacDonald, *Battle of the Huertgen Forest*, 195–205.
49. U.S. Department of the Army, 12th Army Group, *G-1 Section, 12th Army Group Report of Operations*, 1948, 135–136; Bradley and Blair, *A General's Life*, 354. Bradley signed a memorandum to Eisenhower dated 15 December 1944, the day prior to the Ardennes attack, which complained that 12th Army Group had a total understrength of 19,069 infantrymen (17,581 riflemen) out of a total understrength of 30,327. The situation showed no signs of improving and appeared to Bradley to have reached a crisis stage.
50. Bradley and Blair, *A General's Life*, 355–356.
51. Weigley, *Eisenhower's Lieutenants*, 458.
52. Bradley and Blair, *A General's Life*, 356; Ambrose, *Eisenhower*, 365; Weigley, *Eisenhower's Lieutenants*, 458. Ambrose, referring to the decision to send the two armored divisions to the Ardennes, reports that Ike said, "'I think you had better send Middleton some help,' he told Bradley. Studying the operations map with Strong [Ike's G-2], Eisenhower noted that the 7th Armored Division was out of the line in Ninth Army sector, and that the 10th Armored Division, a part of Third Army, was currently uncommitted. He told Bradley to send the two divisions to Middleton, in the Ardennes. Bradley hesitated; he knew that both Hodges [sic] and Patton would be upset at losing the divisions, Patton especially, as the 10th Armored was one of his favorites. With a touch of impatience, Eisenhower overruled Bradley, and orders went out that night, sending the 10th to the southern flank of the penetration, while the 7th occupied a road junction named St. Vith, on the northern flank."

53. Bradley and Blair, *A General's Life*, 356.

54. Supreme Headquarters Allied Expeditionary Forces. Office of the Chief of Staff: Secretary, General Staff, *General Correspondence Files, May 1943–August 1945*, Outgoing Message 101839A January 1945; Price, *Middleton*, 214; Bradley and Blair, *A General's Life*, 354. In an "eyes only" message to Marshall, Eisenhower referred to the issue of risk in the Ardennes: "I personally discussed this matter with Bradley, but his attitude was that it would be an unprofitable region for the enemy to use and if he made such an attack it would subsequently lead to our advantage. At the worst it was a reasonable sector in which to take a risk and risks have to be taken somewhere." Ike does not mention that Bradley had prepared no contingency plan in case the Germans did in fact attack in the Ardennes, but his message to Marshall was sent at the same time Eisenhower was lobbying the chief of staff for Bradley's promotion to four-star general rank to be approved.

55. Hugh M. Cole, *The United States Army in World War II: European Theater of Operations. Ardennes: Battle of the Bulge* (Washington, D.C.: Office of the Chief of Military History/GPO, 1965), 305–306.

56. Ibid., 269, 289.

57. Weigley, *Eisenhower's Lieutenants*, 465–490.

58. Ibid., p. 465.

59. Bradley and Blair, *A General's Life*, 357.

60. Ibid., 368.

61. Cole, *Ardennes*, 411.

62. Weigley, *Eisenhower's Lieutenants*, 503; Jordan, *Brothers, Rivals, Victors*, 444–445. At the time Eisenhower made his decision to transfer command of U.S. First and Ninth Armies to Montgomery, Jordan emphasizes that "Bradley was still trying to run things from Luxembourg, south of the bulge and out of direct [physical] contact with Hodges," using only "the slender thread of communications"— telephone wire lines vulnerable to being cut as the German advance progressed and VHF radio signals that "needed two relay stations to convey the messages [between Bradley and Hodges] across the weak transmissions."

63. Ambrose, *Eisenhower*, 368. Ambrose reports that Ike had a stormy conversation with Bradley when he notified him of the command change on the morning of 20 December: "He called Bradley on the telephone to inform him. By now, Bradley was set against any such change. Strong [Ike's G-2] could hear him shouting at Eisenhower, 'By God, Ike, I cannot be responsible to the American people if you do this. I resign.' Eisenhower flushed with shock and anger, drew a deep breath, then said, 'Brad, I—not you—am responsible to the American people. Your resignation therefore means absolutely nothing.' There was a pause, then another protest from Bradley, but this time without any threats. Eisenhower declared, 'Well, Brad, those are my orders.' He then turned the conversation to Patton's counterattack, which he declared he wanted mounted in the greatest possible strength."

64. Bradley and Blair, *A General's Life*, 368.

65. Ibid., 364.

66. D'Este, *Patton*, 672–699; Blumenson, *Patton*, 246–250; Weigley, *Eisenhower's Lieutenants*, 498–501; Cole, *Ardennes*, 331–334.

67. Blumenson, *Patton*, 246–247; D'Este, *Patton*, 676; Bradley and Blair, *A General's Life*, 358; Weigley, *Eisenhower's Lieutenants*, 498. Weigley, quoting Ladislas Farago, one of Patton's biographers, writes that even prior to the German attack, Patton had surmised that there was something brewing across the front from Middleton's VIII Corps: "Patton sniffed danger, ' . . . the First Army is making a terrible mistake,' he confided to his diary on November 25, 'in leaving the VIII Corps static, as it is highly probable the Germans are building up east of them.' By December 12, Patton's hunch about an enemy assault against VIII Corps was strong enough that he instructed General [Hobart] Gay, his chief of staff, and Colonel Halley G. Maddox, his G-3, to study 'what the Third Army would do if called upon to counterattack through . . . a breakthrough' in VIII Corps front." He had his staff prepare contingency counterattack plans for three axes, one of which turned out to be the Bastogne "corridor." Patton was prepared, therefore, on the morning of 19 December when asked what he could bring to bear against the bulge.

68. D'Este, *Patton*, 680, 682–683. D'Este judges that "Patton proved to be Omar Bradley's savior on this occasion."

69. Weigley, *Eisenhower's Lieutenants*, 499; D'Este, *Patton*, 680; Blumenson, *Patton Papers II*, 599–600; Blumenson, *Patton*, 252; Weigley, *Eisenhower's Lieutenants*, 500. Weigley, while admiring Patton's "masterfully executed" plan, notes perceptively, "the operation should also be kept in appropriate perspective; it was not a unique stroke of genius. Other competent military commanders have accomplished similarly rapid disengagements, turns of direction, and recommitments." Patton, rather immodestly, bragged to his wife, "The relief of Bastogne . . . is the most brilliant operation we have thus far performed and is in my opinion the outstanding achievement of this war." At a press conference on New Year's Day 1945, he praised his troops' "marvelous feat," claiming, "I know of no equal to it in military history." Like the 101st Airborne Division's defense of Bastogne, Patton's maneuver has become a military icon, the brilliance of which is accepted on faith. Anyone having the temerity to challenge either of these actions is at risk of being branded a heretic and dismissed out of hand.

70. Bradley and Blair, *A General's Life*, 369.

71. Weigley, *Eisenhower's Lieutenants*, 520–521.

72. Atkinson, *Guns at Last Light*, 470.

73. Bradley and Blair, *A General's Life*, 371.

74. Ibid., 370.

75. Atkinson, *Guns at Last Light*, 470. Atkinson explains that Bradley favored a link-up at Houffalize "not least because Eisenhower had promised to return First Army to his command when the town fell."

76. Martin Van Creveld, *Fighting Power: German and U.S. Army Performance 1939–1945* (Westport, CT: Greenwood Press, 1982), 65–66; Bradley and Blair, *A General's Life*, 385. Bradley wrote: "Our forces met at Houffalize on January 16, cutting the German salient at the waist, exactly one month after von

Rundstedt launched the Bulge offensive. But we were too late to trap the mass of Germans. They had withdrawn toward the Westwall, maneuvering skillfully under difficult circumstances." Throughout the campaigns of France and Germany, the German Army demonstrated a remarkable ability to reconstitute forces that continued to fight effectively right up to the end of the war.

77. Bernard L. Montgomery, *The Memoirs of Field Marshal the Viscount Montgomery of Alamein, K. G.* (New York: Signet Books, 1958), 28.

78. Weigley, *Eisenhower's Lieutenants*, 540–547.

79. Ibid., 545.

80. Bradley and Blair, *A General's Life*, 387.

81. Chandler, et al., *Eisenhower Papers*, 4:2375; Blumenson, *Patton* 228, 306; Blumenson, *Patton Papers II*.

82. Bradley and Blair, *A General's Life*, 156.

83. Meyer, *Hanging Sam*, 88–89; Bradley and Blair, *A General's Life*, 269. The relieved officer was Maj. Gen. Eugene Landrum, 90th Infantry Division. Meyer quotes Bradley's war diary: "Everytime I went to see [Landrum], he was in his command post, which was usually in the basement of some building. He never got outside of it."

84. Montgomery, *Memoirs*, 283.

85. Weigley, *Eisenhower's Lieutenants*, 505.

86. Bradley and Blair, *A General's Life*, 358.

87. Weigley, *Eisenhower's Lieutenants*, 501–504.

88. Weigley, *Eisenhower's Lieutenants*, 465; Cole, *Ardennes*, 53–54.

89. Bradley and Blair, *A General's Life*, 155–156; Pogue, "General Bradley," 547–548, 551–553.

90. Bradley and Blair, *A General's Life*, 364–365.

91. Bruce C. Clarke, "Defense of St. Vith," Interview, 10 November 1987; Robert W. Hasbrouck to Bruce C. Clarke, undated (probably circa 1983–84). Hasbrouck goes so far as to say that Montgomery "saved the 7th Armored Division."

92. Hasbrouck to Clarke, undated. General Hasbrouck wrote: "I am sure you remember how First Army HQ fled from Spa leaving food cooking on the stoves, officers' Xmas presents from home on their beds and, worst of all, top secret maps still on the walls . . . First Army HQ never contacted us with their new location and I had to send an officer to find them. He did and they knew nothing about us. That's when Montgomery got into the picture. He was at First Army HQ when my officer arrived. A liaison officer from Montgomery arrived in my HQ within 24 hrs. His report to Montgomery is what saved us. . . ."

93. Harrison, *Cross-Channel Attack*, 183–187; Keegan, *Six Armies in Normandy*, 21–67; Bradley and Blair, *A General's Life*, 226–227.

94. Bradley and Blair, *A General's Life*, 295.

95. Weigley, *Eisenhower's Lieutenants*, 626–633.

96. Blumenson, *Breakout and Pursuit*, 655–656.

97. Bradley and Blair, *A General's Life*, 302–305. In retrospect, Bradley referred to his action as "imprudent" and a "mistake."

98. Weigley, *Eisenhower's Lieutenants*, 460–463. Weigley remarks, "Bradley did not imagine a [German] stroke so unorthodox as a beaten enemy's rising up for an

armored counteroffensive through some of the worst tank country on the Western front."

99. Ibid., 491–501.
100. Bradley and Blair, *A General's Life*, 46.
101. Ibid., 47.
102. Ibid., 60, 71.
103. Chandler, et al., *Eisenhower Papers*, 4:2237.
104. Bradley and Blair, *A General's Life*, 368.
105. Chandler, et al., *Eisenhower Papers*, 4:2375. Eisenhower's true motivation in sending this glowing evaluation of Bradley to Marshall is revealed by putting his comments within the context of the entire message. Indeed, in that same message Ike lavished effusive praise on Hodges as "the spearhead and scintillating star" of the ongoing final advance into central Germany and implored the chief of staff that "I should like very much to see Hodges get credit in the United States for his great work." Eisenhower then goes on to write: "Equally with Hodges, the part that Bradley has played in this campaign should be painted in more brilliant colors." Ike laments that the two generals have "been seemingly overlooked by the headline writers and others have received credit for things for which Hodges and Bradley were primarily responsible." The chief "other" whom Ike is referring to—but not mentioning by name—is George Patton, who was dominating all of the European Theater war news headlines. Eisenhower's bottom line in the cable exposed his true purpose: "I hope that [General] Surles [War Department director of public relations] will put his imagination to work to figure out some way of giving Hodges his proper credit and showing that Bradley's handling of 12th Army Group has been masterful."
106. Ricks, *The Generals*, 116.
107. Ibid., 116–117.
108. Victor Davis Hanson, *The Soul of Battle: From Ancient Times to the Present Day, How Three Great Liberators Vanquished Tyranny* (New York: The Free Press, 1999), 270, 333–334. Hanson also notes that "A half century after World War Two no American veterans would brag 'I rolled with Bradley,' even though the latter was Ernie Pyle's ideal GI general, who purportedly best understood the mind of the average soldier." However, the veterans who had served under Patton "always replied: 'I was with the Third Army.'"
109. Jordan, *Brothers, Rivals, Victors*, 550.
110. Ibid., 551.
111. Four of the authors who already have critically examined Bradley's leadership and command and have concluded that Bradley's reputation overrates his actual accomplishments are D'Este (*Eisenhower*), Atkinson (*Liberation* trilogy), Ricks (*The Generals*), and Hanson (*The Soul of Battle*).

CHAPTER 4

1. U.S. Department of Army, 12th Army Group, *G-1 Section, 12th Army Group Report of Operations*, 1948, 81–83. Forrest C. Pogue, *The United States Army in World War II: European Theater of Operations. The Supreme Command* (Washington, D.C.: Office of the Chief of Military History, 1954), Map IV; Rick

Atkinson, *The Guns at Last Light: The War in Western Europe, 1944–1945* (New York: Henry Holt and Company, 2013), 411. Strengths of the three armies as of 2400 hours on 15 December 1944 were: First Army—341,569; Third Army—257,518; Ninth Army—188,285. Shortages (mostly combat infantrymen) for all of 12th Army Group on that day totaled 32,000.

2. Omar N. Bradley, *A Soldier's Story* (New York: Henry Holt and Company, 1951), 225–226, 422. Bradley used these adjectives to characterize Hodges's command in his first autobiography, written shortly after the war: "Without the flair of Patton's Third Army and the breeziness of Simpson's Ninth, First Army trudged across Europe with a serious and grim intensity."

3. Omar N. Bradley and Clay Blair, *A General's Life: An Autobiography of General of the Army Omar N. Bradley* (New York: Simon and Schuster, 1983), 94–95. Bradley writes of Hodges: "For countless years [prior to Bradley taking over from Hodges as commandant of the Infantry school at Fort Benning in 1941] Hodges had been to me an august figure like Marshall and a man I admired almost equally . . . he was on a par with George Patton [as an army commander], but owing to his modesty and low profile, has been all but forgotten." Hodges, born 5 January 1887 in Perry, Georgia, had entered West Point with the class of 1908 but flunked out in mathematics his first year there. He enlisted in the army and received a commission from the ranks in 1909. On the battlefield in France in World War I, Hodges won a Distinguished Service Cross, a Silver Star, and a Bronze Star for bravery. He rose to temporary lieutenant colonel and commanded a battalion in combat for several months. A crack shot, Hodges was on the army rifle team in national rifle matches for many years. He served on the Infantry Board at Fort Benning while Marshall was there at the Infantry School. Upon handing over duties as commandant of the Infantry School to Bradley in 1941, Hodges became the chief of infantry in Washington, D.C..

4. Russell F. Weigley, *Eisenhower's Lieutenants: The Campaigns of France and Germany 1944–1945* (Bloomington: Indiana University Press, 1981), 84–85.

5. Carlo D'Este, *Patton: A Genius for War* (New York: HarperCollins, 1995), 615–616; Bradley and Blair, *A General's Life*, 98–99; Weigley, *Eisenhower's Lieutenants*, 170–171, 177. Weigley notes the deteriorating good feelings between Patton and his Army Group commander, Bradley, by July 1944: "Close friends in North Africa, Bradley and Patton since Sicily had come more and more to regard each other warily under an outward show of continued camaraderie. Bradley feared the activation of Patton's army as the inauguration of a generalship reckless to the point of utter irresponsibility. Patton in turn disdained Bradley's generalship as "unsufferably orthodox, predictable, and cautious . . . Bradley's . . . devoted followers . . . developed a strong dislike of the bombastic, egotistical 'gorgeous George' with his tailored green jackets, bright buttons, fancy leather belt and boots, and initialed pistols . . . When George came visiting at Bradley's headquarters, the staff made no effort to be more than lukewarm, and when possible . . . 'quickly turned him to a movie' to be rid of him." Patton, on the other hand, looked down on Bradley with the cavalryman's disdain for the foot soldier, writing, "I am also nauseated by the fact that Hodges and Bradley state that all human virtue depends on knowing infantry tactics."

6. Weigley, *Eisenhower's Lieutenants*, 180–181.
7. Bradley, *A Soldier's Story*, 422; Weigley, *Eisenhower's Lieutenants*, 180;
8. Martin Blumenson, *Patton: The Man Behind the Myth 1885–1945* (New York: Berkley Books, 1987), 233; Weigley, *Eisenhower's Lieutenants*, 238; D'Este, *Patton*, 574. D'Este writes: "As units arrived and were indoctrinated into the Third Army way of doing business, everyone knew who their new army commander was . . . Patton inspired great loyalty in the troops of the Third Army. They came to identify with and to have confidence in him; they understood that a professional soldier and genuine fighting man was commanding them."
9. Thomas Ricks, *The Generals: American Military Command from World War II to Today* (New York: Penguin Books, 2013), 107; Bradley and Blair, *A General's Life*, 395. Ricks describes Simpson as "a man of quiet optimism, the very model of the modern American general" who was "smart, adaptive, and aggressive . . . a team player, plain-spoken and self-effacing." Bradley wrote: "[Ike and I] were immensely impressed with Simpson and his staff and the planning they had done. Simpson's Chief of Staff, [Brig. Gen.] James E. Moore, was one of the least known yet ablest officers in the [European Theater of Operations] . . . Moore 'minded the store' while Simpson toured his corps and division headquarters. Owing to Moore's intelligence and talent for administration, Ninth Army's staff, although least experienced in battle, was in some respects superior to any in my command. Moreover, both Simpson and Moore get along remarkably well with Monty and the British staffs . . ."
10. Bradley and Blair, *A General's Life*, 395.
11. Dwight D. Eisenhower, *Crusade in Europe* (New York: Doubleday and Company, 1948), 376. Ike recorded a short assessment of Simpson's abilities as well: "Alert, intelligent, and professionally capable, he was the type of leader that American soldiers deserve."
12. Bradley, *A Soldier's Story*, 422.
13. Thomas R. Stone, "He Had the Guts to Say No: A Military Biography of General William Hood Simpson" (PhD diss., Rice University, 1974), 3; T. M. Dunleavy, ed., "Lieutenant General William H. Simpson," *Generals of the Army and the Air Force* 2 (June 1954): 19–21; Ricks, *The Generals*, 107. Much of the information in this chapter on the life, career, and impact of General Simpson is based on Colonel Stone's excellent dissertation, as well as the two articles he has written about him (including his award-winning article in *Military Review*). Colonel Stone's works are the primary start points for anyone wishing to study the life of this outstanding soldier. The "Simpson" listing in *Generals of the Army* contains much factual data concerning his career, including promotions, assignments, awards, and decorations.
14. *Generals of the Army*, 19; Stone, "Simpson," 3.
15. Weigley, *Eisenhower's Lieutenants*, 84; Blumenson, *Patton*, 52–52; Bradley and Blair, *A General's Life*, 95, 340–341; Stone, "Simpson," 3.
16. *The Howitzer* (West Point: The United States Military Academy, 1909), 77.
17. Ibid.
18. *Generals of the Army*, 19; Stone, "Simpson," 3. Often, when discussing the merits of famous West Point graduates, much is made of their relative class rankings

at graduation, the presumption being that a high class standing ensures a brilliant career (and vice-versa). In fact, one can find successful and outstanding military leaders who represent the top, middle, and bottom of their respective classes at the Military Academy. For example, while MacArthur and Lee were at the top of their classes, Eisenhower and Bradley were closer to the middle. Patton actually flunked out of the class of 1908, requiring an extra year to graduate. Grant was an indifferent student, excelling only in horsemanship. Additionally, it can be considered something of a feat merely to graduate from an institution in which fully one-third of each entering class fails to complete the four years (and that is one-third of a carefully screened, highly competitive group). Therefore, it appears that no special significance should be attached to Simpson's place at the bottom of his class. His outstanding military career certainly makes his class ranking irrelevant. Further, because he lacked a high school diploma when he entered West Point, the simple fact that he managed to graduate at all seems remarkable.

19. Stone, "Simpson," 3.
20. *Generals of the Army*, 19.
21. Bradley and Blair, *A General's Life*, 340; *Generals of the Army*, 19.
22. Stone, "Simpson," 3; *Generals of the Army*, 19; Bradley and Blair, *A General's Life*, 340.
23. Stephen E. Ambrose, *Eisenhower: Volume One, Soldier, General of the Army, President-Elect 1890–1952* (New York: Simon and Schuster, 1983), 64–65; Bradley and Blair, *A General's Life*, 44–45; Stone, "Simpson," 3; *Generals of the Army*, 19. Eisenhower and Bradley complained so much about missing out on overseas combat duty during World War I that Simpson's good luck in getting to France and into action seems even more fortuitous. Ike and Bradley feared their careers were ruined; they must have assumed, therefore, that the "lucky ones" like Simpson had had their future careers made.
24. Private Louie Hummel to Kathryn Hoffert, 4 March 1918. It is interesting to note that, at least in some parts of the World War I army, the terms "draftee" and "enlisted man" were not synonymous. In this letter, written by a recently drafted Iowa soldier training at Camp Cody, New Mexico, to his sister in Colfax, Iowa, the term "enlisted men" is used to distinguish those who had volunteered from those like himself who had been drafted. Later, of course, the term has been applied to any soldier who is not a commissioned or warrant officer.
25. *Generals of the Army*, 19.
26. Center for Military History, *American Armies and Battlefields in Europe* (Washington, D.C.: GPO, 1992) (reprint of 1938 edition prepared by the American Battle Monuments Commission), 515–518; Stone, "Simpson," 3; *Generals of the Army*, 19. The "Prairie Division" (33rd Infantry Division, Illinois National Guard) trained at Camp Logan, Texas, and sailed for France in May 1918. It served with the Australians in the Amiens sector and had units at Verdun and the Meuse-Argonne. The 33rd spent 27 days in active sectors, capturing 3,987 prisoners—a record for a National Guard Division—and advanced 36 kilometers. The price was 989 dead Americans and over 6,000 wounded.
27. *Generals of the Army*, 19; Stone, "Simpson," 3.

28. *Generals of the Army*, 19–20.
29. Ibid. Camp Grant, located west of Chicago, served as one of the demobilization centers for the rapidly disappearing army.
30. Stone, "Simpson," 3; Ambrose, *Eisenhower*, 72. Considering the problems Eisenhower's career suffered after his run-in with the powerful chief of infantry at about this same time, Simpson's future must have been brighter after successful service in the chief's own office.
31. *Generals of the Army*, 19; Stone, "Simpson," 3.
32. Bradley and Blair, *A General's Life*, 54. Bradley writes that it was customary for two groups of officers to begin classes at the Infantry School each fall—an Advanced Course (senior captains, majors, and lieutenant colonels), and a lower level Company Officers' Course. About seventy officers were in the senior class. As a major, Simpson was in the Advanced Course.
33. Stone, "Simpson," 3; *Generals of the Army*, 19.
34. Mark C. Bender, *Watershed at Leavenworth: Dwight D. Eisenhower and the Command and General Staff College* (Fort Leavenworth, KS: U.S. Army Command and General Staff College, 1990), 28–34; Timothy K. Nenninger, "Casualties at Leavenworth: A Research Problem," *The Journal of Military History* 76 (April 2012): 497–506. Prior to the reorganization of the Command and General Staff School in 1923, Bender notes, officers first attended the year-long School of the Line, which focused on "military operations up to division level." A second year, focusing on the corps and army level, was the General Staff School course. Since the second year's General Staff School was reserved for only the top 40 to 60 percent of graduates of the School of the Line, "competition became quite keen for admission to the second year course"—a competition not always seen as healthy. The school commandant at the time of the consolidation, Brig. Gen. Robert H. Allen, noted: "The consolidation into one class will do away with the disappointment which heretofore existed in the minds of those who had not made the General Staff class." Bender records, however, that the real "purpose of the consolidation was to accommodate a large group of over 1,000 officers who had entered service during World War I and who had no schooling in general staff or higher command duties. In order to consolidate the two courses into a single course (now renamed the Command and General Staff School), some of the instruction in the separate arms was transferred to the various branch schools. Subjects pertaining to army and theater levels of operation were transferred to the Army War College." Although the school, for a time, returned to two-year courses in 1928, Simpson's class was one of the standard one-year courses. Nenninger's meticulously researched article exposes as a myth the long-held belief that the Staff College placed such pressure on students to excel that each class experienced at least one student suicide. Officer deaths at Leavenworth—both students and permanent faculty—were exceedingly rare and not related to the Staff College course.
35. Ibid., 34–35. According to Bender, "The major subjects emphasized the tactics and techniques of the various branches, including their individual capabilities and their potency when incorporated with other branches. The command, staff, and logistics subject area required officers to compare administrative and field

orders, to develop the details of moving a division by truck and rail, and to determine the logistics of supply during attack, pursuit, and defense. Perhaps the most important course, Tactical Principles and Decisions, took up the full spectrum of tactical considerations and principles and was reinforced by the students' application in staff rides, map maneuvers, and problem solving."

36. Ibid., 3, 31–35. Bender notes: "The mission of the new Command and General Staff School was to provide instruction on (1) the combined use of all arms in the division and in the army corps; (2) the proper functions of commanders of divisions and of army corps; and (3) the proper functions of general staff officers of divisions and of army corps." During Simpson's attendance, "the bulk of the . . . curriculum consisted of three main subjects: tactics and techniques; tactical principles; and command, staff, and logistics. Other subjects taught included history, training, leadership, military organization, combat order, field engineering, military intelligence, strategy, and legal principles."

37. *Generals of the Army*, 19; Stone, "Simpson," 3.

38. Stone, "Simpson," 3; *Generals of the Army*, 19.

39. Ambrose, *Eisenhower*, 85; Stone, "Simpson," 3; *Generals of the Army*, 19.

40. Bradley and Blair, *A General's Life*, 74. Bradley writes: "There was very little pressure. We were not graded on our work; there was no class standing to be achieved, no one of importance to impress."

41. Ambrose, *Eisenhower*, 85.

42. Stone, "Simpson," 3.

43. *Generals of the Army*, 19–20; Stone, "Simpson," 3.

44. *Generals of the Army*, 20.

45. Ibid.

46. Stone, "Simpson," 3–4.

47. *Generals of the Army*, 19–20.

48. Robert R. Palmer, et al., *The United States Army in World War II: The Army Ground Forces. The Procurement and Training of Ground Combat Troops* (Washington, D.C.: Office of the Chief of Military History, 1948), 102; *Generals of the Army*, 20. While commanding general of XII Corps, Simpson made an observation tour of the North African Theater of Operations. He was fortunate to be allowed to do so, since the powerful, influential commander of Army Ground Forces, Gen. Lesley J. McNair, felt that a commander's place during training was always with his unit. Palmer wrote: "By supervising the training of his unit . . . a commander trained himself for his role in combat. General McNair insisted that the principle of keeping officers with troops applied to generals as well as to others . . . as a rule General McNair frowned upon higher commanders taking trips which diverted them from their essential duties. The opening of operations in North Africa gave training commanders an inviting opportunity to make tours of observation [but] . . . when General Marshall asked whether it might be wise for division commanders, halfway through their training periods, to see some combat operations in North Africa, General McNair replied that division commanders were needed with their divisions; he suggested that a few corps commanders go instead." Simpson was one of only four corps commanders allowed to tour North Africa.

49. *Generals of the Army*, 19.
50. *Conquer: The Story of the Ninth Army 1944–1945* (Nashville: Battery Press, 1980), 15–17; Stone, "Simpson," 4. *Conquer* is the "official" history of the Ninth Army, written shortly after the war by the Ninth Army staff under the direction of its chief of staff, Brigadier General Moore. It is an excellent operational history of the unit, well organized, straightforward, and lacking the usual "how great we were" flavor of the typical postwar unit histories.
51. Alfred D. Chandler, et al., ed., *The Papers of Dwight D. Eisenhower, The War Years (Volumes I–V)* (Baltimore: Johns Hopkins Press, 1970), 3:1795. There was no question that Eisenhower preferred Simpson to Fredendall, since Ike had fired the former II Corps commander the previous year for Fredendall's terrible leadership performance at the American defeat at Kasserine Pass. Marshall, however, who had gotten the relieved Fredendall promoted to lieutenant general with command of a training army in the States (Second U.S. Army), continued to try to get Ike to take him back in a combat command capacity. Eisenhower would have none of it. Ike would prefer one of his combat-seasoned corps commanders as his next army commander, but realized that circumstances made that impractical.
52. Weigley, *Eisenhower's Lieutenants*, 431. Weigley points out that Marshall's use of Simpson as an example to the other training commanders who were conscientiously building combat units in the States, was, in principle, "similar to the elevation of General [Raymond] McLain with his National Guard background to a corps" command (XIX) later in the war. Both would serve as examples to their different classes of officer.
53. Ibid.
54. Thomas R. Stone, "General William Hood Simpson: Unsung Commander of US Ninth Army," *Parameters* 11 (February 1980): 46.
55. Ibid.
56. Ibid.
57. Charles B. MacDonald, *The United States Army in World War II: European Theater of Operations. The Siegfried Line* (Washington, D.C.: Office of the Chief of Military History, 1963), 379–380; *Conquer*, 15.
58. U.S. Department of the Army, *Army Service Forces Report No. 169, Command and Staff Procedures*, 31 July 1945; U.S. Department of the Army, *Ninth United States Army Administrative Instructions*, 30 November 1944; Stone, "Unsung Commander," p. 44. The agreed-upon staff procedures of the general staff sections were basically those as taught in the army's service schools. Unlike those of the First and Third Armies, the special staff sections did not function under any general staff section, although they coordinated closely. Furthermore, unlike First and Third Armies, Simpson's deputy chief of staff did not directly supervise any of the special staff sections, whose heads reported directly to the chief of staff. A review of Simpson's Administrative Instructions confirms the "normalcy" of the army's organizational arrangements, showing a standard G1/G4 standing operating procedures. Stone notes that "headquarters functions were conducted according to well established principles . . . and the lessons learned at Leavenworth were followed in practice."
59. *Conquer*, 16.

60. Stone, "Simpson," 27–28.
61. *Conquer*, 17.
62. Ibid., 37. Ninth Army's relatively late introduction to combat allowed Simpson's staff the opportunity to reap the benefits of the early mistakes of First and Third Armies. Before deploying to combat in France, First and Third Army permitted some staff visits by Ninth Army officers.
63. Stone, "Simpson," 28.
64. Ibid., 13–14.
65. *Conquer*, 17–18; Stone, "Simpson," 1–2. A new Ninth Army patch was adopted after the change in designation. The new patch was a white heraldic rosette placed on a red nonagon. Based on its Fourth Army heritage, this new patch strongly resembles the Fourth Army's old one—a white clover on a red diamond background.
66. U.S. Department of the Army, *Ninth United States Army After Action Report, January 1945*, 3; Stone, "Simpson," 87.
67. *Conquer*, 366.
68. Martin Blumenson, "The Decision to Take Brest," *Army* 10 (March 1960): 44–47; *Conquer*, 47, 366–367. Instead of a quick siege of six days as the high command expected, Middleton's VIII Corps was tied up for a month and had 10,000 casualties. In addition to attacking the port city, Ninth Army units had to guard an exposed flank of some 250 miles; receive and process all incoming personnel replacements of the theater (regardless of ultimate unit of assignment); and provide trucks, personnel, and "housekeeping detachments" to run the famed "Red Ball Highway." This simultaneous accomplishment of these important but very diverse tasks was a truly monumental endeavor for the brand-new Ninth Army.
69. *Conquer*, 47–48.
70. Blumenson, "Brest," 47; *Conquer*, p. 366.
71. Martin Blumenson, *The United States Army in World War II. European Theater of Operations. Breakout and Pursuit* (Washington, D.C.: Office of the Chief of Military History, 1961), 637, 644; *Conquer*, 38–39.
72. Ricks, *The Generals*, 107; Stone, "Simpson," 81.
73. *Conquer*, 55, 366.
74. Ibid., 54.
75. Bradley and Blair, *A General's Life*, 340; Stone, "Simpson," 103. Bradley wrote: "In preparation for [the November] offensive, I shifted Simpson's Ninth Army from the southern Belgium-Luxembourg area to the area north of Aachen formerly held by Hodges' XIX Corps. This, in effect, inserted the Ninth Army between Monty's forces and Hodges' forces. I did this for two principal reasons. First, I felt there was a good likelihood that at some future date Monty would again attempt to incorporate a U.S. army into his command. The U.S. First Army staffers—those mule-headed, swaggering veterans of North Africa and Sicily— were so bitterly anti-Monty that I feared they might mutiny if they were again compelled to serve under him. Simpson and his staff had not yet been subjected to Monty's megalomania and were, on the whole, more diplomatic and adaptable. Secondly, the Ninth Army was far less experienced than the First Army. If I

were again forced to lend Monty an army, I preferred to give him my green troops rather than trusted lieutenants such as Collins, Gerow . . . Middleton and others."

76. Stone, "Simpson," 101.

77. *Conquer*, 72, 366–367.

78. Allen H. Mick, ed., *With the 102nd Infantry Division Through Germany* (Nashville: Battery Press, 1980), 41. Another "official" unit history written shortly after the end of the war, this one is truly impressive in its ability to capture the flavor and feel of the battlefield and the common soldiers' reactions to it.

79. Mick, *102nd Division*, 40.

80. Harold P. Leinbaugh and John D. Campbell, *The Men of Company K: The Autobiography of a World War II Rifle Company* (New York: Bantam Books, 1987), 16, 39. This book, co-authored by two former commanders of Company K, 333rd Infantry Regiment, is one of the best, most realistic accounts of combat to be written about the European Theater. It follows the unit from its call-up and training, through combat, to the end of the war.

81. Weigley, *Eisenhower's Lieutenants*, 430–431. Weigley writes: "In twenty-three days of campaigning, the [Ninth] army had advanced only nine to twenty kilometers. It had lost 1,133 killed, 6,864 wounded and 2,059 missing. How many German casualties the Ninth Army had inflicted was and is unknown, though the bag of prisoners was 8,321, and the army buried 1,264 enemy dead."

82. Ibid., 431.

83. Combat Studies Institute, *Conversations With General J. Lawton Collins* (Fort Leavenworth, KS: U.S. Army Command and General Staff College, 1983), 10; Weigley, *Eisenhower's Lieutenants*, 320–321, 434, 603. Weigley describes the importance of the Roer River dams: "Just ahead [of the advance of the 12th Army Group] lay the Schwammenauel and a series of other dams on the Roer River and its tributaries, which if opportunely ruptured by the Germans could flood [the armies'] invasion path and effectively close it for several weeks . . . The Roer dams were soon [fall of 1944] to cast their shadows over almost every movement of [the American armies]"; years after the war, Gen. J. Lawton Collins, wartime commander of First Army's VII Corps, explained why the dams were initially overlooked: "They [intelligence people] didn't [see the dams as an important objective] and they didn't recognize the threat they posed. We all knew there were some dams. We had not studied that particular part of the zone. They came as a surprise to most of the intelligence people in the army. There were two or three of them [dams]. It was sometime before First Army realized their capacity to flood the southern [sic; actually northern] part of the army zone of action. That was an intelligence failure, a real combat intelligence failure, on the part of the top intelligence people." As it happened, by the time the dams were finally captured by First Army troops (February 1945), the enemy had sabotaged the discharge valves, delaying Simpson's assault crossings of the Roer for about two weeks.

84. Hugh M. Cole, *The United States Army in World War II: European Theater of Operations. The Ardennes. Battle of the Bulge* (Washington, D.C.: Office of the Chief of Military History, 1965), 22, 75–92.

85. Ibid., 78, 80.
86. Charles B. MacDonald, *A Time For Trumpets: The Untold Story of the Battle of the Bulge* (New York: Bantam Books, 1985), 101–123; Cole, *Ardennes*, 80–95.
87. Cole, *Ardennes*, 39–47, 110.
88. Alex Kershaw, *The Longest Winter: The Battle of the Bulge and the Epic Story of World War II's Most Decorated Platoon* (Boston: Da Capo Press, 2004); Charles B. MacDonald, *The Mighty Endeavor: The American War in Europe* (New York: Quill/William Morrow, 1986), 400–403. Kershaw's book is a masterful account of the brutal combat endured by 99th Infantry Division soldiers facing the German onslaught. MacDonald, a participant in this phase of the battle, writes: "In a brutal four-day fight [2nd and 99th Infantry Divisions] had jammed the north shoulder of what would become known as the 'bulge.' They had denied the vital road network in the north. Together with the 99th, the 2nd Division had incurred heavy casualties—probably a total of six thousand . . . Yet in the process the two units had dealt heavy losses to three German divisions and . . . 'knocked a part of Hitler's personal operations plan into a cocked hat.'"
89. MacDonald, *A Mighty Endeavor*, 427.
90. John S. D. Eisenhower, *The Bitter Woods* (New York: G. P. Putnam's Sons, 1969), 221; Weigley, *Eisenhower's Lieutenants*, 465, 471; MacDonald, *A Time for Trumpets*, 188.
91. MacDonald, *Mighty Endeavor*, 427; Weigley, *Eisenhower's Lieutenants*, 471; Cole, *Ardennes*, 103–104.
92. Weigley, *Eisenhower's Lieutenants*, 471.
93. Ambrose, *Eisenhower*, 144; Weigley, *Eisenhower's Lieutenants*, 471. Leonard "Gee" Gerow had been Eisenhower's study-mate during their year at the Command and General Staff School at Fort Leavenworth. Gerow was also an Honor Graduate of their class (top 10 percent). In early 1942, Gerow had initially been Eisenhower's boss as the head of the War Plans Division on the army staff, but Ike replaced him in that position in February 1942 when Gerow left to take command of a division.
94. Weigley, *Eisenhower's Lieutenants*, 471, 520; MacDonald, *Mighty Endeavor*, 427.
95. Cole, *Ardennes*, 102, 109–110, 656–660.
96. Ibid., 659.
97. Weigley, *Eisenhower's Lieutenants*, 473; Cole, *Ardennes*, 656–660.
98. Eisenhower, *Bitter Woods*, 220–222; MacDonald, *A Time for Trumpets*, 188–189. In fairness to Hodges and Kean, it should be noted that, on the afternoon of 16 December and during the night of 16–17 December, First Army headquarters approved the movement, or alert of movement, of several units to the threatened sector. One of these was Brig. Gen. William Hoge's Combat Command B, 9th Armored Division, on loan from VIII Corps to Gerow's V Corps. This unit, released back to Middleton at his request, significantly assisted in the defense of the area surrounding St.-Vith. Other units alerted for movement included the 1st Infantry Division and a combat command of the 3rd Armored Division. But MacDonald notes that, despite these actions, "When Gee Gerow telephoned [late on 16 December] to ask authority to call off the 2d Division's attack for the Roer

River dams, Hodges said no. If the Germans were trying to divert that attack, why give them what they were after."

99. Frank J. Price, *Troy H. Middleton: A Biography* (Baton Rouge: LSU Press, 1974), 215.

100. Weigley, *Eisenhower's Lieutenants*, 480; Cole, *Ardennes*, 311.

101. MacDonald, *A Time for Trumpets*, 188–189; Weigley, *Eisenhower's Lieutenants*, 486; Cole, *Ardennes*, 157–158.

102. Weigley, *Eisenhower's Lieutenants*, 458.

103. Bradley and Blair, *A General's Life*, 356; Weigley, *Eisenhower's Lieutenants*, 458.

104. Bradley and Blair, *A General's Life*, 356–357.

105. Ibid., 356.

106. Robert H. Berlin, "United States Army World War II Corps Commanders: A Composite Biography," *Journal of Military History* 53 (April 1989): 166; Eisenhower, *Bitter Woods*, 221; Cole, *Ardennes*, 103–104; Weigley, *Eisenhower's Lieutenants*, 491, 493, 562, 668, 678. Gerow weathered the incident successfully and, in January 1945, was promoted to command the newly formed Fifteenth Army. This unit was intended to relieve the other armies of mopping-up and occupation duties west of the Rhine. Gerow continued to retain Ike's confidence and was highly rated by the supreme commander (Ike placed him eighth overall on a list of general officers in the European Theater of Operations near the close of the war).

107. Bradley and Blair, *A General's Life*, 356.

108. D'Este, *Patton*, 676; Blumenson, *Patton*, 245–247; Weigley, *Eisenhower's Lieutenants*, 497–500. Weigley observed: "Patton's military intuition was as acute as any in the American army. He was so intent on attacking that it made him nervous not only to stand idle himself, but to observe idleness in any friendly troops on his flank . . . Thus, during the weeks when Middleton's VIII Corps on his left flank had not done these things, Patton sniffed danger." D'Este notes that "Third Army made plans to deal with what no one else believed would occur."

109. Weigley, *Eisenhower's Lieutenants*, 500–501; Blumenson, *Patton*, 250–253.

110. Chester Wilmot, *The Struggle for Europe* (New York: Harper and Brothers, 1952), 588–589. An Australian journalist, Wilmot spent much time at Montgomery's headquarters during the war. His obvious admiration for the field marshal is nearly unbounded and lacks objectivity.

111. Ibid.

112. Eisenhower, *Bitter Woods*, 215; Bradley and Blair, *A General's Life*, 356; Weigley, *Eisenhower's Lieutenants*, 458.

113. U.S. Department of the Army, *Ninth United States Army G-3 After Action Report, 16–31 December 1944*, 1; *Conquer*, 115–118.

114. Eisenhower, *Bitter Woods*, 215.

115. Bruce C. Clarke, "The Defense of St. Vith," interview by author, 10 November 1987; U.S. Department of the Army, U.S. Armor School, *The Battle of St.-Vith, Belgium, 17–23 December 1944*, 1949, 4.

116. Clarke interview; *Battle of St.-Vith*, 6–9.

117. Cole, *Ardennes*, 274–275. The issue of road clearances, seemingly a rather mundane subject, is directly related to the arrival time of 7th Armored Division

combat elements at St.-Vith. First Army staff's delays in getting road clearances for 7th Armored's move south is further evidence that Hodges and his staff were slow in realizing the size and scope of the German offensive.

118. Weigley, *Eisenhower's Lieutenants*, 490.

119. *Conquer*, 117; Cole, *Ardennes*, 333.

120. Raymond S. McLain, "One of the Greatest: A Study in Leadership," *Military Review* 44 (December 1969): 26. McLain commanded the XIX Corps under Simpson during the majority of the unit's time in combat and was the only National Guard officer to command a corps in World War II.

121. *Ninth Army After Action Report*, 2–3.

122. Cole, *Ardennes*, 333.

123. *Ninth Army After Action Report*, 2–3; Weigley, *Eisenhower's Lieutenants*, 520–521.

124. *Conquer*, 116.

125. Ibid., 117.

126. Ibid., 119.

127. Weigley, *Eisenhower's Lieutenants*, 520–521.

128. Bradley and Blair, *A General's Life*, 368.

129. D'Este, *Patton*, 683; Blumenson, *Patton*, 251–252; Bradley and Blair, *A General's Life*, 364.

130. Weigley, *Eisenhower's Lieutenants*, 493, 505; Bradley and Blair, *A General's Life*, 367. Bradley records that, upon hearing of Montgomery's dissatisfaction with Hodges, Ike wrote Monty, saying, "I know you realize that Hodges is the quiet, reticent type and does not appear as aggressive as he really is. Unless he becomes exhausted he will always wage a good fight." Bradley lobbied vigorously to keep Hodges in command.

131. Chandler, et al., *Eisenhower Papers*, 4:2369. Ike sent identical messages to Hodges and Simpson on 22 December 1944. They read, in part: "Now that you have been placed under the Field Marshal's operational command I know that you will respond cheerfully and efficiently to every instruction he gives. The slogan is 'Chins Up.' Please make sure that all your subordinate commanders exert the maximum of leadership and example in sustaining morale and convincing every man that he is in better condition than the enemy. Good luck and let us seek real victory." Ike also sent a message to Monty the same day explaining his directives to Hodges and Simpson.

132. Weigley, *Eisenhower's Lieutenants*, 615. The conspicuous use of "cheerfully" is obviously in response to Ike's use of it.

133. Chandler, et al., *Eisenhower Papers*, 4:2545. Ike's reference to "British seniors" can only mean Montgomery.

134. Ambrose, *Eisenhower*, 380.

135. *Conquer*, 115–160.

136. D'Este, *Patton*, 684–691; Weigley, *Eisenhower's Lieutenants*, 520–521; Bradley and Blair, *A General's Life*, 367–368.

137. Bradley, *A Soldier's Story*, 225–226, 422.

138. Weigley, *Eisenhower's Lieutenants*, 505.

139. Supreme Headquarters Allied Expeditionary Forces. Office of the Chief of Staff: Secretary, General Staff, *General Correspondence Files, May 1943–August*

1945, Incoming Message, 230115 December 1944; Bradley and Blair, *A General's Life*, 367.

140. Bradley and Blair, *A General's Life*, 367.
141. Robert W. Hasbrouck to Bruce C. Clarke, undated (probably circa 1983–1984).
142. Ibid.
143. Weigley, *Eisenhower's Lieutenants*, 465.
144. Ibid., 84.
145. Bradley and Blair, *A General's Life*, 354–356; Weigley, *Eisenhower's Lieutenants*, 457–458; MacDonald, *Mighty Endeavor*, 427.
146. Weigley, *Eisenhower's Lieutenants*, 505.
147. Wilmot, *Struggle for Europe*, 592. Another factor that would make it difficult for Montgomery to understand the lack of direction Hodges had received was the different degrees of control of subordinates in the British and American command systems. While it was common in the British system for higher commanders to be very specific in their instructions to subordinate commanders, dictating the "how" as well as the "what" in most cases, the American system was quite different. Americans were taught to give only broad mission statements to subordinates, allowing the subordinate commander nearly a free hand in determining the "how" of the mission. As a result, many American commanders were reluctant to intervene in a subordinate's conduct of a battle, even if he appeared to be doing badly. Senior British commanders, such as Montgomery, felt no such compunctions, intervening when they felt it necessary.
148. Jacques Nobécourt, *Hitler's Last Gamble: The Battle of the Bulge* (New York: Schocken Books, 1967), 218–219. To Montgomery's suggestion, Hodges replied, "No. American troops will not withdraw."
149. Clarke, interview.
150. Hasbrouck to Clarke.
151. Cole, *Ardennes*, 330–331.
152. Weigley, *Eisenhower's Lieutenants*, 84.
153. Ibid., 180–181.
154. Ibid., 519–520.
155. Blumenson, *Patton*, 245.
156. D'Este, *Patton*, 702; Blumenson, *Patton*, 245. D'Este explains: "What the Battle of the Bulge demonstrated is that, while possessed of tremendous vision—the ability to anticipate and react with impeccable foresight to an enemy move or countermove—Patton's greatest strength was not so much as a tactician but as an organizer, a mover and shaker."
157. Blumenson, *Patton*, 246.
158. Weigley, *Eisenhower's Lieutenants*, 501.
159. Ibid., 521.
160. Ibid., 520. The 4th Armored Division task force that entered Bastogne on 20 December was desperately needed by the hard-pressed defenders. Task Force Ezell consisted of a company each of tanks, infantry, and artillery—a significant addition to the defenders' forces. But the 4th Armored's commander, Maj. Gen. Hugh Gaffey, fearful lest his unit be used piecemeal (as other units were—and to good effect) withdrew the unit later in the day. The question seems to remain that, if Task Force Ezell could drive unopposed into Bastogne that day, why

couldn't Gaffey have pushed the rest of the unit in behind it? Granted, the 4th Armored's main body was strung out to the south, struggling along icy roads, but a better explanation may lie in the fact that the 4th Armored's brilliant former commander, Maj. Gen. John S. Wood, was no longer at the head of what had become, during the previous summer's lightning warfare, "Patton's Best."

161. Cole, *Ardennes*, 515–555.

162. Weigley, *Eisenhower's Lieutenants*, 520–521.

163. Ibid.

164. Ibid., 519.

165. Ibid., 520.

166. Stone, "Unsung Commander," 49–50.

167. *Conquer*, 115–119; Eisenhower, *Bitter Woods*, 215.

168. Weigley, *Eisenhower's Lieutenants*, 520–521; *Conquer*, 115–119; *Ninth Army After Action Report*, 1–2.

169. Chandler, et al., *Eisenhower Papers*, 4:2564–2565. Ike cabled Marshall on 30 March 1945, attempting to enlist Marshall's aid in helping to publicize the exploits of Bradley and the army commanders (other than Patton). Ike felt the others' achievements had been overlooked in favor of the flashy Patton. Chandler noted, however, "Eisenhower was fighting a hopeless cause, at least insofar as the *New York Times* was concerned. Every European headline . . . prominently mentioned Patton by name; Hodges', Simpson's and Patch's (7th Army) forces were identified only by number."

170. Weigley, *Eisenhower's Lieutenants*, 384.

171. Ibid.

172. Ibid., 520.

173. Stone, "Unsung Commander," 47.

174. Alvan C. Gillem Jr., "William H. Simpson,"*Leadership at Higher Levels of Command as Viewed by Senior and Experienced Combat Commanders*, Edmund B. Sebree, ed. (Monterey: USALRU, 1961), 26.

175. Ricks, *The Generals*, 109. Ricks attributes the "most forgotten" quote that he includes in his book to historian John English.

176. The finest combat exploits of Simpson's Ninth Army came after the close of the Battle of the Bulge. Operation GRENADE, the Roer River crossings, took place in February–March 1945, and the Rhineland Campaign followed on its heels. The Ninth Army performed magnificently during these battles, earning praise from American as well as British commands. Simpson's army participated in Montgomery's set-piece crossings of the northern Rhine near Wesel, and, once across the Rhine, the Ninth raced across Germany. Simpson was returned to American control on 3 April 1945, then was the first Allied commander to reach the Elbe. Simpson pushed a bridgehead across the Elbe at Magdeburg and was prepared to fling his army at Berlin when Eisenhower ordered him to stop. General Simpson retired from active service for health reasons shortly after the end of the war and was promoted to four-star rank on the retired list in 1954. He died in 1980 at age ninety-two.

CHAPTER 5

1. Frank J. Price, *Troy H. Middleton: A Biography* (Baton Rouge: LSU Press, 1974), 215. Price had been a student of Middleton's at LSU and worked extensively with him on the preparation of this biography, the only major book on Middleton's life and career. A large portion of the book deals with Middleton's experiences during the Ardennes offensive of December 1944 to February 1945. While the book provides many outstanding examples of Middleton's character and personality, it appears that Price may have too readily accepted some of Middleton's reminiscences of events of thirty years previous without independent verification.

2. Services Cinema Corporation, prod. *The Ardennes Offensive, 1944* (London: United Kingdom Ministry of Defence, 1979). Gen. (Ret.) Julian Ewell, a battalion commander in the 101st Airborne Division at Bastogne, gives this graphic description of Middleton's composure in an on-camera interview in this film prepared for the British Army. He went on to say that the VIII Corps staff appeared "physically beaten" and "psychologically spent," but that Middleton, in addition to his calmness, appeared to be in complete control of the situation, exerting a steadying influence. A discussion of Eisenhower's selection of Middleton for command of the VIII Corps is presented in Stephen E. Ambrose, *Eisenhower: Volume I, Soldier, General of the Army, President-Elect, 1890–1952* (New York: Simon and Schuster, 1983), 296; and Carlo D'Este, *Eisenhower: A Soldier's Life* (New York: Henry Holt and Company, 2002), 487.

3. Harold R. Winton, *Corps Commanders of the Bulge: Six American Generals and Victory in the Ardennes* (Lawrence: University Press of Kansas, 2007), 36; Price, *Middleton*, 135. On the eve of the U.S. entry into World War II, Middleton, in retirement at LSU, petitioned the War Department to return to active duty. Army Chief of Staff Gen. George C. Marshall wrote across the top of the file copy of Middleton's request, "This man was the outstanding infantry regimental commander on the battlefield in France."

4. Hugh M. Cole, *The United States Army in World War II. European Theater of Operations. The Ardennes: The Battle of the Bulge* (Washington, D.C.: GPO. 1965), 55. Russell F. Weigley, *Eisenhower's Lieutenants: The Campaigns of France and Germany 1944–1945* (Bloomington: Indiana University Press, 1981), 157–158. Price, *Middleton*, 206–207, relates that "When he was faced with the necessity of relieving a commander, Middleton did not hesitate."

5. Price, *Middleton*, 4–141. The details of Middleton's life and early years of service are adequately covered in Price's biography, which serves as the primary reference for this section.

6. Winton, *Corps Commanders*, 36; Price, *Middleton*, 67–68. Middleton was promoted to lieutenant colonel on 17 September 1918 and to colonel on 14 October 1918, three days after assuming command of the 39th Infantry Regiment. At the time of his promotion to colonel, he was the youngest officer in the U.S. Army to hold that rank, having passed his twenty-ninth birthday two days earlier.

7. U.S. Department of the Army, *Annual Reports of the Commandant, the General Service Schools, 1923–1928* (Fort Leavenworth, KS); Price, *Middleton*, 89–91; Winton, *Corps Commanders*, 37. Officers attending during Middleton's tenure

as an instructor who later attained higher command in the European Theater of Operations (ETO) were: Devers, Patch, Simpson, Haislip, and Hodges (1924–25); Eisenhower, Gerow, Millikin, Terry Allen, Collins, and Walton Walker (1925–26); George Kenny (1926–27); and Lewis Brereton (1927–28). Price makes much of Middleton's tenure as an instructor, claiming, "Through the four classes Middleton taught from 1924–1928 came almost all the men who were to command divisions in Europe in World War II. At one time in World War II, every corps commander in Europe had been a student under Middleton at the Command and General Staff School." Price's claim may be somewhat exaggerated. Inspection of the General Staff School records shows that, while this was true very early in the campaigns following D-Day, as the number of corps rose, the number of corps commanders who attended the Staff School during Middleton's tenure dropped. However, of the officers who completed Staff School while Middleton was there, a large number were highly placed leaders.

8. Ambrose, *Eisenhower*, 114; Price, *Middleton*, 113–122; Winton, *Corps Commanders*, 37. Middleton had formed a close association with LSU during his service there as an ROTC instructor and commandant of cadets. When the lucrative offer came to join the staff of the university as a civilian, he had completed twenty-seven years of active duty and his outlook for further promotion and advancement in the army was not promising. At the time of his retirement, his promotion to full colonel, a rank he had previously held in 1918, appeared to be several years away. Nevertheless, Eisenhower apparently held Middleton's retirement against him, at one point late in the war recommending that Marshall not promote Middleton to permanent Regular Army two-star rank. Ambrose writes that Eisenhower growled, "He left us when the going was tough." In fairness to Eisenhower, it was obvious that Middleton would return to retirement at the close of the war. Since promotion is not a reward for "services rendered" but a recognition of *potential* value to the service, Eisenhower wanted to promote those officers who would lead the postwar army.

9. Rick Atkinson, *The Day of Battle: The War in Sicily and Italy, 1943–1944* (New York: Henry Holt and Company, 2007), 38; Price, *Middleton*, 137, 140–141. Marshall thought very highly of Middleton's abilities and quickly accepted his offer to return to active duty. He remained a Middleton supporter throughout the war despite Eisenhower's occasional slights. After leading the 45th Division to the Mediterranean Theater, Atkinson writes, Middleton said, "I know I have a fighting outfit . . . I can tell that from the provost marshal's report."

10. Omar N. Bradley and Clay Blair, *A General's Life: An Autobiography of General of the Army Omar N. Bradley* (New York: Simon and Schuster, 1983), 171; Price, *Middleton*, 143–147.

11. Weigley, *Eisenhower's Lieutenants*, 121–122; Price, *Middleton*, 170–171; D'Este, *Eisenhower*, 487. However, one D-Day corps commander, Maj. Gen. Leonard T. Gerow, an Eisenhower intimate and longtime friend, did not have the extensive combat experience of Middleton or Collins. Throughout his combat service in World War II, Middleton was plagued by an arthritic knee, which prevented him from being in top physical condition at all times. Hospitalized in November 1943, he was forced to give up command of the 45th Division in Italy

and seek treatment at Walter Reed Hospital. It was during this treatment that Eisenhower selected him, despite his physical disability, to lead a corps in Europe. Ambrose, *Eisenhower*, 296, repeats the following anecdote about Middleton's selection: "For the first follow-on corps, Eisenhower picked . . . Middleton, but only after an exchange of views with Marshall. An objection had been raised to Middleton on physical grounds, which—according to Bradley—led Marshall to remark, 'I would rather have a man with arthritis in the knee than one with arthritis in the head.' Eisenhower's version was different; he recalled that he had asked Marshall for Middleton, but Marshall replied, 'Fine. I agree with you in his values. But he's in Walter Reed Hospital with his knees.' To which Eisenhower replied, 'I don't give a damn about his knees; I want his head and his heart and I'll take him into battle on a litter if we have to.'"

12. John S. D. Eisenhower, *The Bitter Woods* (New York: G. P. Putnam's Sons, 1969), 39.

13. Martin Blumenson, *The United States Army in World War II. European Theater of Operations. Breakout and Pursuit* (Washington, D.C.: GPO, 1961) is the best reference for the costly Normandy campaign and the subsequent race across France; Weigley, *Eisenhower's Lieutenants*, 174.

14. Martin Blumenson, "The Decision to Take Brest," *Army*, 10 (March 1960): 44, contains a good explanation of why a significant share of the Allied forces turned westward, away from the main German force; Blumenson, *Breakout and Pursuit*, 367; Weigley, *Eisenhower's Lieutenants*, 179–180; Winton, *Corps Commanders*, 39.

15. Robert W. Grow, "Mobility Unused," *Military Review* 32 (February 1953): 22–24. Grow, commander of the 6th Armored Division, bitterly attacked Middleton and other Allied commanders for what he felt was a tragically missed opportunity to swiftly capture the fortress city of Brest, and thereby free his division for the fight against the large German formations to the east. Grow termed the whole operation "totally without value." Blumenson, "Decision to Take Brest," 46; Blumenson, *Breakout and Pursuit*, 635–636. Expected by the higher command echelons to take six days and to be completed by 1 September, Brest's capture on 19 September came after twenty-seven days of grueling, bloody fighting; Middleton's headquarters documented the effort as well as "lessons learned" in U.S. Department of the Army, *VIII Corps, Attack of a Fortified Zone*, 9 October 1944.

16. Bradley and Blair, *A General's Life*, 352–353; Price, *Middleton*, 211–215.

17. U.S. Department of the Army, *VIII Corps After Action Report, June to December 1944*, records that VIII Corps assumed responsibility for the Ardennes sector at noon on 4 October 1944. When VIII Corps initially occupied the Ardennes sector, the front was manned by only the 2nd and 8th Infantry Divisions. Later (11 October 1944), the 83rd Infantry Division joined the other two, and then the new 9th Armored Division arrived on 20 October. When units began to be badly chewed up in the disastrous Huertgen Forest offensive, VIII Corps' divisions were used to replace them, with the shattered units taking their place in the Ardennes. By 16 December 1944, the VIII Corps consisted of the 4th, 28th, and 106th Infantry Divisions and most of the 9th Armored. Price, *Middleton*, 210–212; Bradley and Blair, *A General's Life*, 352–353; Cole, *Ardennes*, 56.

18. Charles B. MacDonald, *The Battle of the Huertgen Forest* (New York: Jove, 1984), 120. James W. Bradin, "28th Infantry Division: The Forgotten Pennsylvanians," *Army*, 37 (August 1987): 62–67; Robert Sterling Rush, *Hell in Hürtgen Forest: The Ordeal and Triumph of an American Infantry Regiment* (Lawrence: University Press of Kansas, 2001). In Bradin's article, he gives an alternate story of how the 28th got its "Bloody Bucket" nickname. In Bradin's version, enemy soldiers first began referring to the unit as *"Blutig Eimer"*; U.S. soldiers adopted the English translation later. Both MacDonald's and Rush's books are excellent sources on the nightmarish combat in the Huertgen Forest and the extreme punishment the attacking American units suffered.

19. MacDonald, *Huertgen Forest*, 180; Eisenhower, *Bitter Woods*, 205.

20. U.S. Department of the Army, *VIII Corps Letter of Instruction, 7 December 1944*, which directed the handover reads, in part, "b. Relieve 2d Inf Div, in place, on or about 11 December 44. c. Responsibility for defense of 2d Inf Div Z, protection N (L) flank of VIII Corps and maintenance of contact with V Corps will pass to CG, 106th Inf Div at a time to be mutually agreed upon by CG's concerned. CG 106th Inf Div will notify this headquarters when change of responsibility has been accomplished."; Price, *Middleton*, 211; Weigley, *Eisenhower's Lieutenants*, 448; Robert E. Merriam, *Dark December* (Chicago: Ziff-Davis, 1947), 79; R. Ernest Dupuy, *St. Vith: Lion in the Way—The 106th Infantry Division in World War II* (Washington, D.C.: Infantry Journal Press, 1949); Charles Whiting, *Death of a Division* (New York: Stein and Day, 1981); L. Martin Jones, "Destruction of 106th Infantry Division, Capture and POW Experiences." Interview by author, June 2005, Lawrence, Kansas.

21. *VIII Corps After Action Report*, 145, describes the "Siegfried Line" positions as follows: "In the two areas of the Siegfried Line in which V Corps had made penetrations, the construction and arrangement of the fortifications . . . consisted [first] of dragon's teeth arranged in rows and usually six rows deep. In a few cases, a concrete wall 31 in high and 21 in thick was built in front of the dragon's teeth. Roadways through these tank barriers were blocked by heavy steel gates, concrete plates or removable I beams. The dragon's teeth were not continuous . . . in . . . places no artificial barrier was present, as the rugged country and thick forest were sufficient to bar the progress of tanks. Behind the tank barriers were the main defenses, consisting of a double row of concrete forts. These varied in size and design, but could be classified into three general categories; viz., machine gun forts, anti-tank forts and command posts. The forts contained from 3 to 6 rooms and accommodated from 12 to 25 men. The embrasures were small and were covered with 4 in. armor plate. They permitted a limited field of fire, usually to the flanks. The entrances to the forts were protected by steel doors and these were covered by the fire from an adjacent fort. No tunnels nor connecting trenches between forts were found, but the forts were connected by power and communications cables. Apparently the Germans did not improve or maintain the installations . . . after the fall of France. Four years of natural growth of trees and brush obstructed many of the fields of fire and the anti-tank pillboxes, designed to accommodate the 37mm weapon, had never been modified to house the modern . . . calibers. Nevertheless, the system of fortifications still furnished

an excellent defensive line on which to place the mobile elements of defense."
Price, *Middleton*, 211; Cole, *Ardennes*, 55.

22. Cole, *Ardennes*, 55; Weigley, *Eisenhower's Lieutenants*, 480; Gen. Bruce C.
Clarke explained to the author that, although the combat command armored division was formed on a triumvirate of tank, infantry, and artillery battalions, only
Combat Command A and Combat Command B were intended to be regularly
used as maneuver units. Combat Command R was used essentially to control
movement of the reserve and seldom for combat. This became a source of confusion and friction between senior infantry and armor commanders from time to
time when the senior infantry commander assumed all three combat commands
were equally capable of operating as maneuver units. Bruce C. Clarke, interview
by author, McLean, Virginia, April 1985. See also U.S. Department of the Army,
4th Armored Division Tactics and Administration, Armored Division, War
Department Observer's Board Draft Report, June 1945, 1–2.

23. Cole, *Ardennes*, 56; Weigley, *Eisenhower's Lieutenants*, 480, 574; Ambrose,
Eisenhower, 365. On the first day of the German assault, sixteen divisions struck
the four-division equivalents in the VIII Corps zone. Eventually, as the attack
proceeded, twenty-four German divisions were involved. Cole, *Ardennes*, 650,
has documented the balance sheet (including the V Corps units also struck) and
writes: "On the morning of 16 December the American forces in the path of the
German counteroffensive comprised four and two-third divisions with an effective strength of about 83,000 men [includes V Corps' 99th Infantry Division].
The heavy weapons then available numbered 242 Sherman tanks, 182 tank
destroyers, and 394 pieces of corps and divisional artillery. The troops and
weapons were deployed on a meandering front of 104 miles [includes part of V
Corps' sector]. The enemy assault divisions poised to the east had concentrated
behind some ninety miles of front manned by Army Group B, and during the
night of 15 December over 200,000 combat troops gathered in the forward
assembly area, about three miles in depth. The German attack . . . was made on an
assault front of sixty miles and included 5 armored divisions, 12 $2/3$ infantry divisions, and about 500 medium tanks, the whole supported by the fires of 1,900
guns and werfers [rocket launchers]."

24. Cole, *Ardennes*, 310–311; Weigley, *Eisenhower's Lieutenants*, 480; Ambrose,
Eisenhower, 366–367. The progress of the German main attack in the northern
area rapidly cut off Middleton's northernmost units—106th Infantry Division
and 14th Cavalry Group—from the remainder of VIII Corps. Although Middleton maintained communications with the defenders of St.-Vith, the fighting was
controlled by the commanders on the ground at that location. The 7th Armored
Division, the unit providing the bulk of the defenders for St.-Vith beginning 17
December, received only eight messages from VIII Corps headquarters during
the days prior to Eisenhower's 20 December reorganization of the command
lines. Of these messages, one was simply a retransmission of a "hold at all costs"
order previously issued by Middleton (and of only historical interest by the time
it was received), one was Middleton's exhortation to VIII Corps troops to "take
apart" the enemy's "final and desperate" attack, two were unit boundary confir-
mations, two were to establish supply procedures, and one was a false report that

the Germans had captured Malmedy. Most of the messages appear to be of little practical use to the St.-Vith defenders. U.S. Department of the Army, *7th Armored Division After Action Report*, 84–85.

25. Price, *Middleton*, 215.

26. Jacques Nobécourt, *Hitler's Last Gamble* (New York: Schocken Books, 1967), 146–147; Cole, *Ardennes*, p 306; Bradley and Blair, *A General's Life*, 354. Bradley claims to have "discussed the possibility [of a German Ardennes attack] in detail with Middleton and . . . made plans to defend against it. If the Germans hit his sector Middleton was to make a fighting withdrawal—all the way back to the Meuse River if necessary . . . he would slow the enemy as much as possible, and I would order reserve armored divisions . . . and other units to close pincers at the base of the German salient and cut him off." Bradley even identifies the 7th and 10th Armored Divisions as specific units he had planned to use, although these units weren't even selected until Eisenhower picked them and directed Bradley to send them to VIII Corps' assistance on 16 December. Also making Bradley's postwar assertions suspect is his claim that on 8 November he "toured part of the long, desolate front and inspected several of [Middleton's] divisions, including the . . . badly mangled 28th, which had been assigned to VIII Corps for rest and rebuilding." The 28th didn't even arrive in the Ardennes until 29 November (Cole, *Ardennes*, 179). It's possible that Bradley is confusing this inspection of the Ardennes with an actual meeting he attended with Eisenhower, Hodges, and Gerow at Cota's 28th Division headquarters in the Huertgen Forest on 8 November (MacDonald, *Huertgen Forest*, 119).

27. John Toland, *Battle: The Story of the Bulge* (New York: Random House, 1959), 53; Cole, *Ardennes*, 170, 274–275, 331; Merriam, *Dark December*, 111–112, 150; Dupuy, *Lion in the Way*, 23; Price, *Middleton*, 216; Weigley, *Eisenhower's Lieutenants*, 451; Jones, interview by author.

28. Cole, *Ardennes*, 240–245.

29. Franklin Institute, *Art and Requirements of Command, Volume 2, Generalship Study* (Philadelphia: Systems Science Department of the Franklin Institute, 1967), "Middleton Questionnaire," 15. The question that elicited Middleton's observation of the obviousness of the criticality of St.-Vith and Bastogne concerned command follow-up and monitoring of execution. It asked respondents how to be at the critical place at the critical time.

30. U.S. Department of the Army, *4th Armored Division, Armor at Bastogne*, May 1949, 6.

31. Price, *Middleton*, 269.

32. Cole, *Ardennes*, 513.

33. Ibid., 311.

34. Bruce C. Clarke, "The Battle for St.-Vith: Armor in the Defense and Delay," *Armor* 83 (November–December 1974): 40. Clarke found Middleton reading in his headquarters van at 0400 hours, 17 December, and received the simple instructions from the VIII Corps commander; Clarke, interview.

35. Franklin Institute, *Generalship Study*, 10; Weigley, *Eisenhower's Lieutenants*, 451, writes that "Jones later telephoned Middleton, suggested that the Schnee Eifel would have to be abandoned, and predictably found the Corps commander passing the buck back to him as the man on the spot."

36. Merriam, *Dark December*, 111–112; Dupuy, *Lion in the Way*, 23; Weigley, *Eisenhower's Lieutenants*, 448.

37. Cole, *Ardennes*, 275; Weigley, *Eisenhower's Lieutenants*, p. 451; Dupuy, *Lion in the Way*, 23–24; Price, *Middleton*, 216; Whiting, *Death of a Division*, 51–53. Another manifestation of Jones's inexperience was his reluctance to order a "retreat" that, if proven premature, would not reflect positively on his unit or himself. The foul-up at the switchboard, which helped result in the misunderstanding on the 16 December call, was not generally known until 1986 when the operator, a military government soldier helping out at the switchboard that night, began circulating letters about the incident to some surviving participants. The individual's motivation in waiting over forty years to publicize his role in the incident is not completely known, but the thrust of the communications appeared to be an attempt to place the majority of blame on General Clarke and the "late" arrival of Combat Command B, 7th Armored. Bruce C. Clarke and J. C. Triplett, interview by author, Carlisle Barracks, PA, February 1986. The announced arrival time of the 7th Armored Division at St.-Vith (0700 hours, 17 December) was an unreasonably early expectation. The unit had to road march from Holland on icy roads, clogged with fleeing units, across the path of the German offensive. Cole's book provides one source of the confusion. Apparently, First Army headquarters had notified Middleton on the evening of 16 December that "the west column [of 7th Armored] would arrive at 0700 and close [all units present] at 1900 on the 17th . . . It was on this estimate that . . . their plans for a counterattack [were based]."

38. Cole, *Ardennes*, 513.

39. Ibid., 224–226.

40. Price, *Middleton*, 224.

41. Cole, *Ardennes*, 294–295.

42. Ibid., 296, relates, "The early winter night gave the Americans a chance. Captain Rose broke out cross-country with five tanks and his assault gun platoon, rolling fast without lights through little villages toward Houffalize, near which the detachment was ambushed. A few vehicles and crews broke free and reached Bastogne."

43. Michael Collins and Martin King, *The Tigers of Bastogne: Voices of the 10th Armored Division in the Battle of the Bulge* (Havertown, PA: Casemate Publishers, 2013); Weigley, *Eisenhower's Lieutenants*, 458.

44. Eisenhower, *Bitter Woods*, 308; *Armor at Bastogne*, 181, severely criticized Middleton's decision which caused "Portions of CC'B', 10th Armored [to be] drawn into separate isolated actions instead of being employed decisively as a unit."

45. Price, *Middleton*, 270.

46. Cole, *Ardennes*, 311, reports that the 1128th Engineer Group, a First Army unit of three engineer combat battalions, was working in the VIII Corps sector in direct support of the "normal operations" of the corps. These, along with the four VIII Corps engineer combat battalions, gave Middleton an additional seven "infantry" units with which to continue his delaying tactics.

47. Ibid., 312–313.

48. Weigley, *Eisenhower's Lieutenants*, 480; Nobécourt, *Last Gamble*, 171; Price, *Middleton*, 228; Cole, *Ardennes*, 450.

49. Cole, *Ardennes*, Chapter XIV, provides an excellent and detailed account of the engineers and other VIII Corps troops who created, manned, and fought the "Barrier Line" battle.

50. Ibid., 329. Cole goes on to point out, however, that "the story of the Ardennes barrier line does make clear that the use of engineers in their capacity as trained technicians often paid greater dividends than their use as infantry, and that a squad equipped with sufficient TNT could, in the right spot, do more to slow the enemy advance than a company armed with rifles and machine guns." This assessment is certainly a correct one, provided the engineers had time to prepare properly the defensive positions—exactly the point in question.

51. Ralph M. Mitchell, *The 101st Airborne Division's Defense of Bastogne* (Fort Leavenworth, KS: Combat Studies Institute, 1986), 8–10; Weigley, *Eisenhower's Lieutenants*, 484; Cole, *Ardennes*, 460; Eisenhower, *Bitter Woods*, 321.

52. John C. McManus, *Alamo in the Ardennes: The Untold Story of the American Soldiers Who Made the Defense of Bastogne Possible* (New York: NAL Caliber, 2008); Robert H. Phillips, *To Save Bastogne* (New York: Stein and Day, 1983). Both books are fine overall accounts of the fighting by small units of the 28th Infantry Division to buy time for reinforcements, such as the 101st Airborne, to occupy Bastogne. Phillips correctly points out: "Overshadowed by accounts of the 101st Airborne Division's gallant defense of Bastogne in December 1944, the story of the desperate delaying actions east of Bastogne which bought time for the occupation and defense of that city by American troops has so far been a closed book to most of the world." Phillips, 11; Cole, *Ardennes*, 307–308, 323; Price, *Middleton*, 269.

53. Mitchell, *The 101st Airborne*, 8–10; Weigley, *Eisenhower's Lieutenants*, 484; Cole, *Ardennes*, 460; Eisenhower, *Bitter Woods*, 321; Winton, *Corps Commanders*, 169.

54. Eisenhower, *Bitter Woods*, 311, 320; Merriam, *Dark December*, 177; Cole, *Ardennes*, 309; Nobécourt, *Last Gamble*, 230.

55. Franklin Institute, *Generalship Study*, 24–25. Middleton answers a question concerning what "inadequate techniques" of command were used during the Battle of the Bulge by writing, "Failure of Allied troops on the north side of the Bulge to launch an earlier counter attack. To me this was one of the great mistakes of the war." Cole, *Ardennes*, Chapter XXIV; Price, *Middleton*, 264–273.

56. Chester Wilmot, *The Struggle for Europe* (New York: Harper and Brothers, 1952), 583; Price, *Middleton*, 292–293.

57. Lt. Col. Boyd M. Harris, Leadership and Ethics Committee, Department of Command, U.S. Army Command and General Staff College, Fort Leavenworth, Kansas, interview with author, 9 September 1983.

58. Virtually every visitor to VIII Corps headquarters during this time made it a point to remark upon Middleton's calm outward appearance and coolness under pressure. These included Ridgway, Clarke, McAuliffe, and Ewell; "The Ardennes Offensive"; Eisenhower, *Bitter Woods*, 244, 311; Cole, *Ardennes*, 55; Nobécourt, *Last Gamble*, 168, attributed this characteristic to self-control when he wrote that "General Middleton was . . . expert at concealing any fears he may have had. . . ."

59. Franklin Institute, *Generalship Study*, 18–19, 26.
60. Eisenhower, *Bitter Woods*, 311, quotes Ewell, who elaborates on his earlier-noted personal assessment of Middleton's nature under fire.
61. Ibid., 244. These are Ridgway's words describing Middleton's demeanor.
62. Alfred D. Chandler Jr., et al., eds., *The Papers of Dwight David Eisenhower, The War Years* (Baltimore: Johns Hopkins Press, 1970) 3:1971.
63. Matthew B. Ridgway, *Soldier: The Memoirs of Matthew B. Ridgway (As Told to Harold H. Martin)* (New York: Harper and Brothers, 1956); Price, *Middleton*, 228.
64. Price, *Middleton*, 228, relates that the Germans helped VIII Corps gain a better understanding of the overall situation when, on 16 December, "American troops had captured a young German officer carrying complete plans for the lightning stroke at the VIII Corps area." Middleton rapidly forwarded the captured documents up through the chain of command.
65. Cole, *Ardennes*, 311–312, 513.
66. Franklin Institute, *Generalship Study*, 26. Middleton wrote that there was "no place for the showman in command of others . . . the bluffer would not last long in command of troops."
67. *Armor at Bastogne*, 19; Price, *Middleton*, 230; Eisenhower, *Bitter Woods*, 308. It was only after Middleton explained the advantages of continuing to physically occupy the crucial transportation center that Patton later referred to Middleton's action as "a stroke of genius."
68. Price, *Middleton*, 217–218; Eisenhower, *Bitter Woods*, 205; Weigley, *Eisenhower's Lieutenants*, 454.
69. Cole, *Ardennes*, 310.
70. Price, *Middleton*, 85, 270.
71. Harold J. Meyer, *Hanging Sam: A Military Biography of General Samuel T. Williams* (Denton: University of North Texas Press, 1990), 59–100, presents the story of one of Middleton's "victims" in the reliefs for cause during the post-invasion, hedgerow fighting. General Williams, at the time of his relief, was the assistant division commander of the 90th Infantry Division until 16 July 1944. Williams, who was also reduced from brigadier general to colonel at the time of his relief, felt strongly that he had been unfairly treated by Middleton, who "barely knew him." Williams may be right, but from Middleton's perspective, it seems a reasonable action given the 90th's poor record of combat achievement up to that time. In addition to the fact that Williams's division commander at the time, Maj. Gen. Eugene Landrum, had formally requested that Middleton relieve Williams, the fiery assistant was the only "common denominator" remaining in the division's hierarchy (he had already seen three division commanders reassigned or relieved). It doesn't seem unreasonable that the senior remaining officer who had any personal responsibility for the unit's pre-combat training (and, at least by implication, for the unit's poor performance in combat up to that time) should be removed, too. At any rate, Williams had engaged in loud, public remonstrances with both Landrum and his predecessor, MacKelvie, on more than one occasion. It seems no great mystery, then, that Landrum sought his relief. Landrum, of course, was also relieved of command of the division by

Bradley at about the same time. To Williams's credit, he served on, regained his lost rank, and retired as a lieutenant general in 1960. Eisenhower, *Bitter Woods*, 39; Blumenson, *Breakout and Pursuit*, 63.

72. Blumenson, *Breakout and Pursuit*, 350–351.

73. Ibid.

74. Weigley, *Eisenhower's Lieutenants*, 480; Cole, *Ardennes*, 311.

75. With the obvious exception of Patton (cavalry, armor), as well as the not-so-obvious exception of Gen. Jacob L. Devers (field artillery), commander of the 6th Army Group, all of the men in senior command under Eisenhower were infantrymen. This can undoubtedly be traced directly to Marshall and the "Ft. Benning connection." Sometimes it caused resentment when an outstanding officer who was not an infantryman perceived himself as being "passed over" in favor of someone wearing crossed rifles on his collar. For example, this may explain some of the problems that the 4th Armored Division's outstanding commander, Maj. Gen. John S. Wood (field artillery), began experiencing when command of the XII Corps was given to Maj. Gen. Manton S. Eddy (infantry). Bruce C. Clarke, serving under Wood's command in the 4th Armored at the time, related that Wood thought the corps command was rightfully his, and subsequently resented Eddy's appointment. Clarke told the author that during a conversation with Patton in the fall of 1944, while Clarke was still a colonel, the Third Army commander said, "Hell, Clarke, if you had been an infantryman instead of an engineer and had served at Fort Benning you would be a major general by now."

76. Raymond S. McLain, "One of the Greatest: A Study in Leadership," *Military Review*, 49 (December 1969): 24; Bradley, *Soldier's Story*, 453–454; Bradley and Blair, *A General's Life*, 354.

77. Dwight D. Eisenhower, *Crusade in Europe* (Garden City: Doubleday and Company, 1948), 347–350; Weigley, *Eisenhower's Lieutenants*, Chapter 26; Cole, *Ardennes*, 56, 305–306.

78. Price, *Middleton*, 178.

79. Franklin Institute, *Generalship Study*, 2–5.

80. Peter Paret and Michael Howard (trans.), Carl von Clausewitz, *On War* (Princeton: University Press, 1976), 119–121. This translation continues with, "Countless minor incidents—the kind you can never really foresee—combine to lower the general level of performance, so that one always falls short of the intended goal . . . The military machine . . . is basically very simple and very easy to manage. But we should bear in mind that none of its components is of one piece: each part is composed of individuals, every one of whom retains his potential of friction."

81. Eisenhower, *Bitter Woods*, 235, 286; Dupuy, *Lion in the Way*, 160–161.

82. Clarke, "Battle for St.-Vith," 40; Clarke, interview.

83. Clarke, interview. Whenever the subject of command at St.-Vith was raised after the war, Clarke always maintained that, at all times during the fighting, he remained under command of Hasbrouck, his parent division commander. He insists that he was never under Jones's command at any time prior to Hasbrouck's actual arrival in the area. Clarke's position was that, since Combat

Command B, 7th Armored, never formally received orders placing it under Jones's 106th Infantry, he answered to Hasbrouck regardless of Jones's rank. Since Jones was clearly overwhelmed by the events and turned over command to Clarke on 17 December, the point seems moot.

84. Eisenhower, *Bitter Woods*, 286.
85. Price, *Middleton*, 223, 226; Bradley and Blair, *A General's Life*, 363.
86. It should be noted that his Third Army was newly engaged in an offensive while Simpson's Ninth Army had not yet begun its Rhineland campaign. This fact was strongly emphasized in a letter to the author from historian Hugh M. Cole, 4 September 1990.
87. Eisenhower, *Bitter Woods*, 235.
88. Ibid., 311.
89. Ibid., 320.
90. Cole, *Ardennes*, 136, 170; Dupuy, *Lion in the Way*, 18, 160–161; Merriam, *Dark December*, 150.
91. Franklin Institute, *Generalship Study*, 10.
92. Weigley, *Eisenhower's Lieutenants*, 451; Dupuy, *Lion in the Way*, 23; Merriam, *Dark December*, 111–112, 150; Price, *Middleton*, 216.
93. Merriam, *Dark December*, 74. Apparently, Middleton even went so far as to withdraw some of his most exposed units without authority and blew up about twenty-five pillboxes on his own initiative. It's clear, therefore, that he was extremely concerned about the vulnerability of the Schnee Eifel positions.
94. Price, *Middleton*, 268. Middleton's remarks were: "It sometimes gives me the creeps when some of our latter day tacticians ask why Middleton didn't hold the Germans at the Our River. If the Germans had launched their attack against the divisions originally on that line, they'd never have broken through."
95. Price, *Middleton*, 176.
96. McLain, "One of the Greatest," 25; Winton, *Corps Commanders*, 350–351. General McLain served under Middleton as commander of the 90th Infantry Division in the last stages of the Cotentin fighting. After his successful handling of this troubled division, he was promoted to command of a corps in Simpson's Ninth Army. McLain finished the war as the highest ranking National Guard officer in Europe. In his final assessment of Middleton's leadership, Winton raises an intriguing "what if?" Winton makes a reasonable case that, had Middleton not left the army in 1937, he might well have "been a leading candidate, if not *the* leading candidate, to command First Army in the Normandy invasion," noting that Middleton "had far better credentials than Bradley and far more balance than Patton." If that had happened, Winton surmises, Middleton "would almost assuredly have risen to command of 12th Army Group, with Bradley perhaps stepping up to command First Army." Winton judges that "a command triumvirate under Eisenhower of Middleton as army group commander with Patton and Bradley as his principal lieutenants inspires much more confidence than the trio of Bradley, Patton and Hodges." General Middleton returned to retirement after the war, was promoted on the retired list to lieutenant general, and became, eventually, President Emeritus of LSU. He spent the remaining years of his life at the university. Price, *Middleton*.

CHAPTER 6

1. William D. Ellis and Thomas J. Cunningham Jr., *Clarke of St. Vith: The Sergeant's General* (Cleveland: Dillon-Liederbach, 1974), 13. This is the only full-length book about Gen. Bruce C. Clarke and his long, distinguished career. It was written with General Clarke's cooperation and assistance. The book is somewhat episodic, containing mainly Clarke's reminiscences of what took place. Although it is an adequate portrayal of Clarke's career, it doesn't contain much independent verification of the general's recounting of events, and is never critical of Clarke's actions. Alan Jones's quote about losing his division was made to Clarke about 2 P.M. on 17 December 1944, while the two men waited in Jones's office at St.-Vith for Clarke's troops to arrive.

2. Hugh Cole, *The United States Army in World War II. European Theater of Operations. The Ardennes: The Battle of the Bulge* (Washington, D.C.: GPO, 1965), 170. According to Cole in his official history, "The number of officers and men taken prisoner on the capitulation of the two regiments and their attached troops cannot be accurately ascertained. At least 7,000 were lost here and the figure is probably closer to 8,000 or 9,000. The amount lost in arms and equipment, of course, was very substantial. The Schnee Eifel battle, therefore, represents the most serious reverse suffered by American arms during the operations of 1944–45 in the European Theater."

3. U.S. War Department, *Army List and Directory, 1891–1943* (Washington, D.C.: GPO, 1891–1943). Information concerning Alan Jones's background and early career (prior to 1944) was taken primarily from this multivolume source, an official listing of assignments, unit addresses, promotions, and schooling for all officers serving in the U.S. Army between 1891 and 1943. There are no other published references available for Jones's early career. Unless otherwise cited, all information regarding Jones's background was derived from this source. Charles Whiting, *Death of a Division* (New York: Stein and Day, 1981), 29–30, 143–144. Whiting's chronicle of the destruction, in its first combat, of Jones's inexperienced division contains some brief references, neither extensive nor detailed, to the 106th Infantry Division's commander's early career.

4. Russell F. Weigley, *Eisenhower's Lieutenants: The Campaigns of France and Germany 1944–1945* (Bloomington: Indiana University Press, 1981), 2. Professor Weigley's excellent history of the development, organization, and European operations of the U.S. Army in World War II aptly points out that "Historically, the American army was not an army in the European fashion, but a border constabulary for policing unruly Indians and Mexicans." The rapid demobilization that has historically (until recently) characterized the American approach to war operated in full swing after the end of World War I. The army was slashed from a high of 3.6 million men in 1918 to 137,000 by 1922. Omar N. Bradley and Clay Blair, *A General's Life: An Autobiography by General of the Army Omar N. Bradley* (New York: Simon and Schuster, 1983), 46–48.

5. Martin Blumenson, *Patton: The Man Behind the Legend 1885–1945* (New York: Berkley Books, 1987) 69, 145. Patton was one of the few officers who enjoyed a comfortable lifestyle, independent of his amy pay. Blumenson points out that

"During the Depression, [Patton's] horses and polo ponies had provoked resentment among some officers whose families were barely getting by on reduced pay scales. . . ." Perhaps Patton's normally high standard of living caused him to be less than enthusiastic about his own prospects of serving in the Philippines when he wrote that he "would probably have to serve a tour of duty in the Philippines, an obligation for every officer. With the insurrection there at an end and the islands quiet, he considered possible assignments better suited to his aims."

6. Bradley and Blair, *A General's Life*, 69–70.
7. Jerry D. Morelock, "General Jacob L. Devers: Commonsense Commander," *Forward Observer* 3 (December 1988): 10. Much of the curricula of the Field Artillery School at Fort Sill had been recently updated and revitalized by its director of gunnery, then Maj. Jacob L. Devers, by the time Jones attended classes there. Devers, who became the 6th Army Group commander in Europe in World War II, was a forward-thinking, extremely capable commander who had a major impact on the army during and after the war. A favorite of Marshall, Devers finished Gen. Adna Chaffee's work by fielding our World War II Armored Force between 1941 and 1943. He ended the war as senior in rank to Bradley and his equal as army group commander. This overlooked and underrated soldier has never received the credit he deserves for his many significant contributions.
8. Bruce C. Clarke, "The Revolution in Army Organization, Tactics and Equipment in the Period 1940–1945," unpublished lecture notes, 15 March 1982. In a lecture given to the Corps of Cadets at West Point, Clarke pointed out many of the "great things" directed by Gen. George C. Marshall to change the army and prepare it to fight World War II. One of these was to "do away" with the powerful position of the chiefs of branches (except for the Corps of Engineers) in 1940. The branch chiefs were very influential in the army between the wars and substantially controlled the careers of the officers in their branches.
9. U.S. War Department, *Army List and Directory*.
10. Clarke, "Revolution in Army Organization." Clarke points out several of the significant changes Marshall introduced into the army as chief of staff immediately prior to America's entry into the war. These included: creation of the modern Armored Force; reorganization of army divisions; nearly complete motorization, with all horse-drawn equipment eliminated; overall rapid expansion of army manpower; elimination of outdated branches and concepts; and staffing the War Department and Army Staff with bright, promising, capable officers he had earlier identified.
11. U.S. War Department, *Army List and Directory*.
12. Weigley, *Eisenhower's Lieutenants*, 10–11. Weigley describes McNair as "The most influential single architect of the American ground forces in preparation for the European war . . . [He was] from March 1942 commander of the Army Ground Forces . . . [and] . . . a bantam, efficient, decisive, even-opinionated artilleryman whose career as a staff officer and instructor and lack of field and combat experience did not temper his assurance that he knew what was good for troops in combat. McNair's passion was to keep the American army lean and mobile."
13. U.S. War Department, *Army List and Directory*.

14. Stephen E. Ambrose, *Eisenhower: Volume I, Soldier, General of the Army, President-Elect, 1890–1952* (New York: Simon and Schuster, 1983), 43–153; Bradley and Blair, *A General's Life*, 36–113. The career patterns of Eisenhower, Bradley, and Jones show striking similarities, but the most important element the three have in common is their becoming known to George Marshall. That alone was sufficient to propel their rapid rise, provided they had favorably impressed Marshall. Had they not so impressed him, Marshall surely would have relegated them to history's dustbin.

15. U.S. War Department, *Army List and Directory*; R. Ernest Dupuy, *St. Vith: Lion in the Way—The 106th Infantry Division in World War II* (Washington, D.C.: Infantry Journal Press, 1949), 5–6.

16. Dupuy, *Lion in the Way*, 5.

17. Ibid., 7.

18. Jerry D. Morelock, *A Single Soldier: World War II Mobilization, Manpower, and Replacement Policies and Their Influence on the Conduct of U.S. Army Operations in Northwest Europe, 1944–45*. PhD diss., University of Kansas, 2000; Dupuy, *Lion in the Way*, 5–7. The author's PhD dissertation examines the background, development, and implementation of U.S. Army policies, and the final chapter is a case study of the unit that, arguably, suffered most from the army's policy failures—the 106th Infantry Division. Dupuy explains: "It was a sound theory [division training concept]. Unfortunately its preceptors did not take into account the abnormally large casualty lists which would call for replacements, nor did they realize that Army Service Forces would amount to an empire within and without the United States; an empire of sound, able-bodied men, fit for combat but placed in non-combatant positions and hence unavailable for conflict. Nor did they see the unwarranted but prevalent impression which rose during the early summer of 1944 that the war would soon be over." Dupuy may be too hard on the Army Service forces in his polemic attack. Modern armies require huge "tails" to permit the armies' "teeth" to strike the enemy. Eisenhower, in fact, felt that too much teeth and not enough tail hampered his campaign in North Africa, contributing to the Kasserine Pass debacle. Ike saw his austere logistic support network in North Africa as "strained" and doubted it could support more troops on the critical Tunisian front than were already there, although many more were needed. Martin Blumenson, *Kasserine Pass* (New York: Jove Books, 1983), 1–80. Dupuy's inference that the dregs and castoffs of an army are sufficient to run the complete logistical support systems for sophisticated, modern war machines is a parochial prejudice that modern armies can no longer afford. Good people are required in all branches.

19. Cole, *Ardennes*, 140; Dupuy, *Lion in the Way*, 6–7.

20. L. Martin Jones, "Destruction of 106th Infantry Division, Capture and POW Experiences." Interview by author, June 2005, Lawrence, Kansas; Whiting, *Death of a Division*, 26–27; Dupuy, *Lion in the Way*, 7–9, Cole, *Ardennes*, 140.

21. Dupuy; *Lion in the Way*, 9.

22. U.S. Department of the Army, *VIII Corps Letter of Instruction, 7 December 1944*; Charles B. MacDonald, *Company Commander* (New York: Bantam, 1982), 104–105. MacDonald, an historian as well as participant in the Battle of

the Bulge, was assigned to the 2nd Infantry Division, east of St.-Vith, when it was relieved by the 106th Division on 11 December 1944. MacDonald reports, "They [106th Division soldiers] were overjoyed at the prospect of seeing their first combat in such ideal defensive positions, and they showed little fear of the thinly spread lines." Cole, *Ardennes*, 140.

23. Bruce C. Clarke, "The Creating of an Outstanding Battalion in 1941–1942," unpublished manuscript, nine pages, undated. Clarke describes his background in this paper and relates many incidents that formed his early experiences. The paper culminates in a description of how he organized and trained his engineer battalion in the 4th Armored Division in 1941 and 1942; Ellis and Cunningham, *Clarke of St.-Vith*, 285.

24. Ellis and Cunningham, *Clarke of St.-Vith*, 286; Clarke, "Creating an Outstanding Battalion," 2.

25. Clarke, "Creating an Outstanding Battalion," 2.

26. Ambrose, *Eisenhower*, 43–52; Bradley and Blair, *A General's Life*, 30–35. Clarke seems to have done better than both Eisenhower and Bradley during his four years at West Point. While Clarke was a cadet captain and company commander, Bradley was only a cadet lieutenant, and Ike had demerit problems for most of his cadetship. Clarke's class rank (33/248) was higher than both Bradley's (44/164) and Ike's (61/164). Clarke was the only one of the three to receive his first choice of commissioning branch (Engineers). Ike, who wanted Cavalry, and Bradley, who preferred Engineers or Field Artillery, settled for Infantry; Clarke, "Creating an Outstanding Battalion," 2.

27. Clarke, "Creating an Outstanding Battalion," 2.

28. Ibid., 4.

29. Ibid., 2.

30. Bruce C. Clarke, "How to Motivate Soldiers," unpublished manuscript, two pages, undated. This incident had a lasting impact on Clarke, and he frequently repeated it to emphasize the improper way to motivate soldiers. His company commander in this incident, however, was more motivated to win the Regimental Commander's Trophy than to encourage good marksmanship among his troops; Clarke, "Creating an Outstanding Battalion," 2.

31. Clarke, "Creating an Outstanding Battalion," 2–3.

32. Bruce C. Clarke, "The Violation of Regulations and Channels of Communications Can Be Justified," unpublished manuscript, two pages, 14 March 1987. During the ROTC assignment, Clarke was confronted with a situation which he called "a great crisis to me." Apparently, "an ambitious [senior] officer without ethics" wished Clarke out of the way and convinced the university athletic council to request that Clarke ask for a transfer. Clarke refused and, after much soul-searching, reported the incident to his branch chief in Washington. The incident was resolved in Clarke's favor, and the senior officer resigned. Nonetheless, Clarke received a written reprimand from his ROTC Corps Area commander for "bypassing official channels." Clarke, "Creating an Outstanding Battalion," 2.

33. Clarke, "Creating an Outstanding Battalion," 3.

34. Bruce C. Clarke to J. D. Morelock, 12 June 1985. Clarke was unimpressed with the course of instruction at Fort Leavenworth (although he had high regard for

the school commandant, General McNair). Clarke wrote, "In 1939–1940 [CGSC] was so far behind the times that General Marshall closed it on 1 February 1940. I hope it is better." Clarke demonstrates Leavenworth's backwardness by relating a story he titles, "How an Early Bird Got an 'F.'" It explains how Clarke exasperated his instructors by using tanks in an unorthodox (for then) and imaginative attack in a map exercise. He was awarded a failing grade but delights in recalling that he used the exact same tactics with phenomenal success in his dash across France in 1944. "Patton gave me an 'A,'" he used to say; Clarke, "Creating an Outstanding Battalion," 3; Timothy K. Nenninger, "Leavenworth and Its Critics: The U.S. Army Command and General Staff School, 1920–1940," *The Journal of Military History* 58 (April 1994): 199–231.

35. Bruce C. Clarke, "The Corps of Engineers in the Armored Force, 1940–45," unpublished manuscript, five pages, 1986; Clarke, "Creating an Outstanding Battalion," 3.

36. Bruce C. Clarke, "Carrying Out Orders," *EurArmy* 23 (August 1984). Clarke appears to have been extremely valuable and instrumental in Chaffee's victory over the 1st Infantry Tank Brigade in these maneuvers. He relates that, when Chaffee realized how Clarke's engineers had prepared the way to victory for his armored force, "He [Chaffee] broke down and shed a few tears. He said, 'Clarke, we are going to win!'" Chaffee's victory and the overwhelming success of Hitler's panzers against France and Britain persuaded Marshall to create the U.S. Armored Force, separate from Infantry branch; Chaffee was its first chief. Clarke, "Armored Force," 1–2.

37. Clarke, "Armored Force," 2–3.

38. Clarke, "Carrying Out Orders"; Clarke, "Armored Force," 3.

39. Clarke, "Creating an Outstanding Battalion," 3.

40. Hanson W. Baldwin, *Tiger Jack* (Fort Collins, CO: Old Army Press, 1979), 187. Also known as "Patton's Best," the 4th Armored Division has been called the finest unit in Europe in World War II. It spearheaded Patton's Third Army across France, led the relief of Bastogne on 26 December 1944, and fought its way across Germany. Clarke commanded Combat Command A from 1 November 1943 to 31 October 1944 during its most successful combat.

41. Baldwin, *Tiger Jack*, 113–118.

42. Kenneth Koyen, *The Fourth Armored Division: From the Beach to Bavaria* (Watertown, NY: Hungerford-Holbrook, 1949), 19; Nat Frankel and Larry Smith, *Patton's Best: An Informal History of the 4th Armored Division* (New York: Jove, 1984), 14–15; Weigley, *Eisenhower's Lieutenants*, 438, asserts that the 4th had "probably been the best of the armored divisions" and that its commander, General Wood, "was so evidently one of the best of the division commanders—perhaps the very best."

43. Koyen, *Fourth Armored Division*, 19.

44. Martin Blumenson, *The United States Army in World War II. European Theater of Operations. Breakout and Pursuit* (Washington, D.C.: U.S. Government Printing Office, 1961), 359, 365–367; Weigley, *Eisenhower's Lieutenants*, 179–180.

45. U.S. Department of the Army, *4th Armored Division, Armor in the Exploitation. The 4th Armored Division Across France to the Moselle River*, May 1949, 6; Dr.

Christopher R. Gabel, *The 4th Armored Division in the Encirclement of Nancy* (Fort Leavenworth: Combat Studies Institute, 1986), 8–10, characterizes the 4th Armored's drive across France as a 700-mile-long pursuit.

46. Hugh Cole, *The United States Army in World War II. European Theater of Operations. The Lorraine Campaign* (Washington, D.C.: U.S. Government Printing Office, 1950), 16, 84. Although the sweep across France had been spectacularly successful, the offensive sputtered to a halt all along the broad front as the fragile, overextended supply system broke down at the end of August 1944. The lull gave the Allied forces a chance to rest tired men and repair worn equipment, but it also allowed the Germans to once more demonstrate their remarkable capacity to regenerate forces and rejuvenate worn-out units.

47. Gabel, *Encirclement of Nancy*, 12–14; Cole, *Lorraine Campaign*, 84; Interview with Bruce C. Clarke, 13 April 1985. Clarke used the phrase "my greatest victory" in this interview to describe the conduct of operations during the Arracourt tank battles and the battles' successful conclusion.

48. U.S. Department of the Army, U.S. Army Command and General Staff College, *Battle Analysis Student Resource Packet. The Arracourt Tank Battles (The Lorraine Campaign 5 September–19 December 1944)* (Fort Leavenworth, KS, 1983). These tank battles have been studied as part of the overall Lorraine Campaign during the Battle Analysis phase of the USACGSC core instruction. This packet is from the 1983–84 academic year.

49. Gabel, *Encirclement of Nancy*, 19–21.

50. Harry Balish, "The Battle of Nancy: A Double Envelopment," *Military Review* 29 (January 1950): 17, calls the Nancy-Arracourt fighting "one of the finest armored actions of the war."; Gabel, *Encirclement of Nancy*, 21–23, characterizes the whole Nancy-Arracourt campaign as "a brilliant episode in the annals of the 4th Armored Division."

51. Baldwin, *Tiger Jack*, 188–189; Bruce C. Clarke, "Rehabilitation of Troops in Battle," unpublished manuscript, one page, 15 June 1986; Bruce C. Clarke, "Clarke's Transfer," unpublished manuscript, five pages, undated, describes Clarke's transfer from the 4th to the 7th Armored Division: "General Patton's recommendation for Colonel Clarke's promotion to Brigadier General was approved in late October 1944 and a position . . . opened up in the 7th Armored Division, Ninth U.S. Army . . . Brigadier General Robert Hasbrouck and Colonel Clarke were both ordered to the 7th Armored in Holland on 1 November 1944 to replace . . . two [relieved] general officers . . . General Wood drove Colonel Clarke to Nancy in his jeep and saw him off for Holland in an L-4 Liaison plane . . . It was a sorrowful parting; they were a team."

52. Bruce C. Clarke to J. D. Morelock, 12 August 1986.

53. Clarke, "Clarke's Transfer," 5.

54. Ibid. Clarke also points out that "these same men and units [7th Armored Division] won a Presidential Unit Citation in battle only a few weeks later."

55. Dupuy, *Lion in the Way*, 5–7. Officers who did have combat experience, such as the Assistant Division Commander, Gen. Herbert Perrin, and the 423rd Regimental Commander, Col. Charles Cavender, had gotten it during World War I, over twenty years earlier. Cole, *Ardennes*, 140.

56. Cole, *Ardennes*, 140–142; Dupuy, *Lion in the Way*, 9–11.

57. U.S. War Department, *106th Infantry Division After Action Report, December 1944*, 27 January 1945; *VIII Corps Letter of Instruction*, 7 December 1944; Dupuy, *Lion in the Way*, 9–11; Cole, *Ardennes*, 140–145.

58. *106th Division After Action Report*; Dupuy, *Lion in the Way*, 12.

59. Cole, *Ardennes*, 148, 272.

60. Dupuy, *Lion in the Way*, 9–11; Cole, *Ardennes*, 272–273, makes an interesting point about the importance of the St.-Vith road network. Cole says that although the hub at St.-Vith was important, it was not initially on the planned axis of any of the enemy's main armored thrusts. However, soon the Germans came to realize that St.-Vith "had to be taken early in the game" to ensure isolation of the Schnee Eifel plateau, to cover the extensive German supply lines behind each thrust, and to feed reinforcements laterally into the main attacks.

61. Dupuy, *Lion in the Way*, 16; Cole, *Ardennes*, 140–142; Weigley, *Eisenhower's Lieutenants*, 448–449.

62. Cole, *Ardennes*, 140.

63. *106th Division After Action Report*.

64. Charles Whiting, *Ardennes: The Secret War* (New York: Stein and Day, 1984), described the intensity of the opening barrage: "Suddenly the complete length of the Ghost Front erupted in fire and flame. The whole weight of the artillery of three Armies, ranging from 16-inch [sic] railway guns to 3-inch mortars, descended upon the startled Americans . . . holding the line . . . The great attack had started at last! For one solid hour [sic] the great barrage continued, cutting telephone links, destroying front-line pillboxes, smashing foxholes, turning the American first-line positions into a smoking, churned-up lunar landscape. Then abruptly it ceased. For a few minutes there was a stunned silence as the men in the line, the survivors, attempted to collect themselves, faces ashen, unspoken questions in their wide, wild eyes." Although this description seems melodramatic, the barrage truly was powerful and severed most landline communications.

65. *106th Division After Action Report*; Dupuy, *Lion in the Way*, 21–25; Cole, *Ardennes*, 151–158.

66. Cole, *Ardennes*, 272.

67. *106th Division After Action Report*; Dupuy, *Lion in the Way*, 21–23; Cole, *Ardennes*, 150–160.

68. Dupuy, *Lion in the Way*, 23.

69. *106th Division After Action Report*; Cole, *Ardennes*, 273.

70. Cole, *Ardennes*, 272–275; Dupuy, *Lion in the Way*, 22.

71. Frank J. Price, *Troy H. Middleton: A Biography* (Baton Rouge: LSU Press, 1974), 216, lets Middleton off the hook too easily by allowing Jones to take all the blame. Despite the foul-up on the switchboard and the other confusion reigning during that critical time, it was Middleton's responsibility as Jones's experienced senior to order the regiments withdrawn; Dupuy, *Lion in the Way*, 23–24; Whiting, *Death of a Division*, 51–53; Cole, *Ardennes*, 275; Weigley, *Eisenhower's Lieutenants*, 451.

72. Cole, *Ardennes*, 275; Dupuy, *Lion in the Way*, 22–25; Weigley, *Eisenhower's Lieutenants*, 451.

73. Thomas J. Riggs Jr. to Bruce C. Clarke, 28 January 1986, 2.

74. Riggs to Clarke, 28 January 1986; John Hanlon, "Tom Riggs' Remarkable World War II Odyssey," *Providence Sunday Journal*, 29 December 1985. Riggs's story is a fascinating one and reads like a Hollywood adventure script. Knocked unconscious by German mortar fire on 22 December, Riggs was captured and sent to a POW camp in Germany. About ten days later he was transferred to a camp in occupied Poland. One month later, Riggs escaped and headed east toward the advancing Russians. He finally met Polish partisans who led him to a Soviet tank unit. Riggs remained with the tankers for ten days, observing their fighting and steady push toward Berlin. His Soviet tank commander finally sent him east to Warsaw in preparation for eventual repatriation. For ten days in Warsaw, Riggs helped construct a displaced persons camp, but then hopped a ride on a Russian train to Odessa, 750 miles away on the Black Sea. He talked his way onto a British tanker bound for Istanbul, then hitched another ride on a freighter to Port Said, Egypt. There he managed to talk his way onto one more ship and eventually made it to Naples, Italy. Riggs turned himself over to U.S. military authorities, but had to force his way through red tape to get back to his old outfit, the 81st Engineer Battalion, which was refitting in France. He finished the war building POW cages in the Ruhr area of Germany, where he processed over a million German POWs. Cole, *Ardennes*, 273. Although Cole credits the bulk of the engineer defensive effort east of St.-Vith to the 168th Combat Engineer Battalion (an VIII Corps unit), Riggs claims his 81st Engineer Battalion bore the brunt of the fighting. Riggs says, "The CO of the 168 Engrs. reported at the defense line east of St.-Vith [and] described his battalion as being at 50% strength . . . he further stated that he was not an enthusiastic supporter of the secondary infantry responsibility for combat engineers. Thus it did not surprise me to receive less than a company from this battalion."

75. U.S. Department of the Army, U.S. Armor School, *The Battle at St.-Vith, Belgium, 17–23 December 1944*, 1949, 4; Bruce C. Clarke, "Move to Saint Vith, 16–18 December 1944," unpublished manuscript, four pages, undated.

76. Ellis and Cunningham, *Clarke of St.-Vith*, 7–8; Armor School, *Battle at St.-Vith*, 4; Clarke, "Move to Saint Vith," 1.

77. Bruce C. Clarke, "The Battle for St.-Vith: Armor in the Defense and Delay," *Armor* 83 (November–December 1974): 40; Clarke interview, 13 April 1985.

78. Bruce C. Clarke, "Defense of St.-Vith," interview by the author, 10 November 1987, tape recording. Clarke said, "My detailed description of [Jones] on the 17th and 18th of December [1944] would be unbelievable . . . Jones was constantly concerned about his son [a lieutenant in one of the 106th's regiments]. It was a mistake to have him in his division."

79. Owen E. Woodruff Jr. to Bruce C. Clarke, 27 January 1987.

80. U.S. War Department, *Army List and Directory*. Jones's son, Alan W. Jones Jr., graduated from the U.S. Military Academy in 1943. Commissioned in the infantry, he was assigned to the staff of the 423rd Infantry Regiment in his father's 106th Infantry Division. When the German attack surrounded that unit on the Schnee Eifel plateau on 17 December 1944, 1st Lt. Alan Jones was with his unit. He was captured on 20 December and spent the duration of the war in a prisoner-of-war camp in Hammelburg, Germany.

81. Clarke, interview, 10 November 1987; Armor School, *Battle at St.-Vith*, 4; Clarke, "Move to Saint Vith," 2.
82. Woodruff to Clarke, 27 January 1987; Armor School, *Battle at St.-Vith*, 7–9; Ellis and Cunningham, *Clarke of St.-Vith*, 13.
83. Dupuy, *Lion in the Way*, 16–17; Clarke, interview, 10 November 1987.
84. Cole, *Ardennes*, 272–275; Dupuy, *Lion in the Way*, 23.
85. Ellis and Cunningham, *Clarke of St.-Vith*, 13; Clarke, interview, 10 November 1987. About noon on 17 December Clarke witnessed a bizarre scene when the 14th Cavalry Group commander, Col. Mark Devine, burst into Jones's office claiming to have been "chased into the building by a Tiger tank!" When Jones hesitated, Clarke suggested the distraught cavalryman go to Bastogne and report the situation to his corps commander, Middleton. Devine stared at Clarke and Jones, then rushed out of the room. Neither man saw him again during the battle.
86. Clarke, "Move to Saint Vith," 2; Clarke, interview, 10 November 1987; Alfred D. Chandler Jr., et al., eds. *The Papers of Dwight David Eisenhower, The War Years*, vol. 4 (Baltimore: Johns Hopkins Press, 1970), 2335. Eisenhower recognized the "abnormal strains" placed upon a division commander in active combat and sent several "home for a rest." Ike wrote to Marshall (5 December 1944) that these strains "are really more than any one man should be called upon to bear . . . Corps, Army and Army Group commanders stand up well. They are in the more fortunate middle area where their problems involve tactics and local maintenance, without on the one hand having to burden themselves with politics, priorities, shipping and maquis, while they are spared the more direct battle strains of a Division commander." He also fully appreciated the additional "shock and stress" of division commanders like Maj. Gen. Donald A. Stroh (8th Infantry Division) and Maj. Gen. John W. O'Daniel (3rd Infantry Division), who had both lost only sons in the war.
87. Clarke, interview, 10 November 1987; Clarke, "Move to Saint Vith," 2. Later Clarke wrote that Jones had "deliberately lied" to Middleton and charged he continued to lie over the next few days to cover it up. Despite Jones's misrepresentation to his corps commander, it seems that it could have little impact on the fighting at St.-Vith. By then, Middleton had no control over the events occurring at the beleaguered crossroads and was unable to influence the action there in any case. It did, of course, cause Clarke to lose much respect for the harassed Jones.
88. Clarke, "Move to Saint Vith," 2.
89. Ibid.
90. Ellis and Cunningham, *Clarke of St.-Vith*, 13; Clarke, "Move to Saint Vith," 2; Clarke, interview, 10 November 1987.
91. Woodruff to Clarke, 27 January 1987; Armor School, *Battle at St.-Vith*, 9.
92. Armor School, *Battle at St.-Vith*, 6–9; Jones, "Destruction of 106th Infantry Division," interview; Cole, *Ardennes*, 275–278. Lt. L. Martin Jones (no relation to 106th Division commander Maj. Gen. Alan Jones) was a platoon leader in Company G, 423rd Infantry Regiment in the 106th Division, manning positions on the Schnee Eifel plateau east of St.-Vith. When the German attack began in the early morning hours of 16 December 1944, the enemy vanguard quickly cut off and surrounded Jones's regiment and its sister unit, the 422nd Infantry Regiment. On the afternoon of 19 December, with very little rations and almost no

ammunition left, Jones's regimental commander surrendered the unit, as did the 422nd's commander. Jones got the word of the surrender from his company commander, who added that since the regimental commander had authorized individual break-out attempts, he was going to try. The captain promptly abandoned his company to its fate and disappeared into the dense woods. The next day, as Jones trudged along drearily as part of a long line of POWs, some of his soldiers came up to him and thanked him for staying with them and not "running away like the Captain did." Jones was a POW at Hammelburg during the failed 27–28 March 1945 raid by Task Force Baum, dispatched far behind German lines by Patton to liberate the American POWs there (including his son-in-law, Lt. Col. John K. Waters). After the failed Hammelburg raid, Jones and other POWs were force-marched by their captors for several weeks, covering over 200 miles. Finally, on 2 May 1945 Jones and his group of POWs were liberated by American troops near the Austrian border.

93. Robert F. Phillips, *To Save Bastogne* (New York: Stein and Day, 1983), 150; Dupuy, *Lion in the Way*, 105.
94. Woodruff to Clarke, 27 January 1987; Clarke, "Move to St.-Vith," 3.
95. Roy Udell Clay, interview by author, 12 March 1986; Clarke interview, 13 April 1985; Armor School, *Battle at St.-Vith*, 9; Ellis and Cunningham, *Clarke of St.-Vith*, 97–98. Clay and his men fought hard to stay in the battle when they could easily have joined in the general retreat. Indeed, later that day a staff officer suggested to Clay that the unit retire westward because "Everybody else is retreating." Clay refused, saying, "We came here to fight the enemy and the way I see it, from this position we can fire in just about any direction and kill Germans."
96. Roy U. Clay, *Curbstone: The History of the 275th Armored Field Artillery Battalion in World War II* (Jackson, TN: Richerson, 1978), 10–18. Clay reports that his forward observer parties stuck by their posts during the assaults, and many were surrounded. Under the cover of darkness, however, most were able to avoid the German units and slip back through enemy lines, rejoining their battalion; Roy U. Clay, interviews by author, 23 and 26 February 1986; Cole, *Ardennes*, 149; Clay, interview, 12 March 1986.
97. John S. D. Eisenhower, *The Bitter Woods* (New York: G. P. Putnam's Sons, 1969), 198; Price, *Middleton*, 215; Clay, interviews, 23 and 26 February 1986. MacMahon, the 106th Division Artillery commander, could do little else but wish Clay and his gunners "good luck." The entire overextended front was exploding and MacMahon had all he could handle just trying to piece together some support for his own hard-pressed regiments.
98. Clay, interviews, 23 February and 12 March 1986. The cavalry troopers retired behind the artillerymen without notice twice during that first terrible day. Clay's gunners were able to occupy new firing positions with little trouble, however, each time this happened. Splitting the battalion into two columns, each using a different route, and moving at staggered intervals reduced the risks and facilitated the retrograde operation. At one point, each column had to cross a bridge over the Our River, which was being interdicted by German artillery. After observing the air bursts for some minutes, however, battalion officers discovered that the rounds were arriving with such regularity that both units were able to cross untouched simply by anticipating the unvarying intervals.

99. Clay, *Curbstone*, 10–18; Clay, interviews, 26 February and 12 March 1986. Clay reports that this was the most frustrating part of the entire battle. The roads in front of them were choked with German troops and vehicles, but Clay's gunners were prohibited from firing for several crucial hours that day. To make matters worse, Colonel Devine, the panicky commander of the 14th Cavalry Group, ordered Clay to emplace his M7 105mm self-propelled howitzers along likely avenues of approach for German armor, intending, apparently, to forsake completely the howitzer's primary role and use Clay's guns as nothing more than tank destroyers. Finally, Clay could take no more and set off to locate Brigadier General MacMahon to resolve the matter. Circumstances overcame events, however, for by the time Clay arrived at the command post in St.-Vith, Clarke's troops were on the way into town. With the cavalry group virtually destroyed as an effective fighting force, Clay's next assignment was obvious to him—support Clarke.

100. Clay, interview, 12 March 1986.

101. Armor School, *Battle at St.-Vith*, 9; Cole, *Ardennes*, 279.

102. Riggs to Clarke, 28 January 1986; Armor School, *Battle at St.-Vith*, 9–10.

103. Clarke, "Move to Saint Vith," 3.

104. Ibid.

105. Armor School, *Battle at St.-Vith*, 10–12; Cole, *Ardennes*, 275–280.

106. Clarke, interviews, 13 April 1985 and 10 November 1987.

107. Clarke, interview, 10 November 1987, described some of his actions during that time by relating, "I had no defensive *lines* but had strong defensive *areas*. The defense was very flexible . . . I constantly imagined where the next crisis or crises would take place, and decided ahead of time what to do if they did." Regarding his personal supervision of events, "I never had my clothes off until 23 December. I visited units [in my jeep and] my driver tied me to my seat with rope so I could sleep and not fall out."

108. Armor School, *Battle at St.-Vith*, 12.

109. Ellis and Cunningham, *Clarke of St.-Vith*, 329.

110. Cole, *Ardennes*, 393.

111. Ibid.

112. Armor School, *Battle at St.-Vith*, 21.

113. Cole, *Ardennes*, 411.

114. Ibid., 412.

115. Clarke, interview, 10 November 1987; Cole, *Ardennes*, 412; Armor School, *Battle at St.-Vith*, 22–25.

116. *7th Armored Division After Action Report*, 95–96.

117. Cole, *Ardennes*, 410–413.

118. Cole, *Ardennes*, 412–413; *7th Armored Division After Action Report*.

119. Whiting, *Death of a Division*, 138.

120. Clarke, interview, 10 November 1987.

121. Robert W. Hasbrouck to Bruce C. Clarke, undated. Hasbrouck wrote of the "fortified goose-egg" idea that "Montgomery . . . saved us from Ridgway's crazy idea of leaving us in the woods east of Vielsalm as an 'island of resistance' to fight back to back . . . Both Ridgway and Bradley thought any withdrawal was disgraceful. Fortunately, Montgomery appreciated the value of a withdrawal on

occasion. That saved the 7th Armored Division."; Whiting, *Death of a Division*, 140–141.

122. Cole, *Ardennes*, 411–413; Armor School, *Battle at St.-Vith*, 25–26.

123. Whiting, *Death of a Division*, 142.

124. U.S. War Department, *Army List and Directory*, shows that Alan W. Jones was medically retired from active duty on 31 October 1945, in the retired rank of major general; Whiting, *Death of a Division*, 143.

125. Ellis and Cunningham, *Clarke of St.-Vith*, 133.

126. Cole, *Ardennes*, 415; Armor School, *Battle at St.-Vith*, 25.

127. Cole, *Ardennes*, 415–422; Armor School, *Battle at St.-Vith*, 25–26; Clarke, interview, 10 November 1987; Clay, interview, 12 March 1986.

128. Armor School, *Battle at St.-Vith*, 26; Clarke, interview, 13 April 1985.

129. Dupuy, *Lion in the Way*, 7, reports: "The worst of this damage was the fact that key men were being seized. These drafts of strength were accomplished under rigorous screening which insisted on taking the best, only the best . . . In their place came groups from Army Specialized Training Program, from the Army Air Forces, the Army Ground Forces Replacement Depots, and volunteers for infantry . . . from anti-aircraft and coast artillery units . . . with a sizeable complement from military police and Army Service Forces units."

130. U.S. War Department, *12th Army Group Report of Operations, G-1 Section*, 1948. It appears the replacement problem was never really solved in time to influence the conduct of the European fighting. Reports contained in the G-1 files for Bradley's 12th Army Group show correspondence concerning ways to try to eliminate the problem throughout the final months of the war.

131. Weigley, *Eisenhower's Lieutenants*, 458.

132. *VIII Corps Letter of Instruction, 7 December 1944*.

133. Bradley and Blair, *A General's Life*, 354.

134. Jerry D. Morelock, "Senior Leadership: The Crucial Element of Combat Power" (Master of Military Art and Science thesis, 1984), 15–19.

135. Ibid., 16.

136. Riggs to Clarke, 28 January 1986; Whiting, *Death of a Division*, 80.

137. Clarke, "Move to Saint Vith," 2.

138. Clarke, interview, 10 November 1987.

139. Morelock, "Senior Leadership," 5.

140. Clarke, "Move to Saint Vith," 3.

141. Whiting, *Death of a Division*, 142.

142. Cole, *Ardennes*, 140; Price, *Middleton*, 268.

143. Riggs to Clarke, 28 January 1986.

144. Clarke, interview, 10 November 1987; Dupuy, in *Lion in the Way*, predictably, is silent on this entire command handover issue, apparently satisfied to pretend it never occurred.

145. Weigley, *Eisenhower's Lieutenants*, 458.

146. Clarke, "Battle for St.-Vith," 40; Clarke, interview, 13 April 1985.

147. Armor School, *Battle at St.-Vith*, 9; Clarke, "Move to Saint Vith," 2.

148. Franklin Institute, *Art and Requirements of Command, Generalship Study* 2 (Philadelphia: Systems Sciences Department, Franklin Institute, 1967), 15.

149. Clarke, interview, 10 November 1987. Clarke did not need Hasbrouck to reiterate the fact that denying the important St.-Vith crossroads to the Germans was key to slowing the attack in their sector. In fact, the armored division commander's orders to Clarke were only "to stop or slow down the German advance and he [Hasbrouck] would support me with the rest of the division."

150. Ibid.

151. Clarke, "Move to Saint Vith," 2.

152. Dupuy, *Lion in the Way*, 65.

153. Cole, *Ardennes*, 274–275.

154. Dupuy, *Lion in the Way*, 100.

155. First U.S. Army, *Road Net Used for Regrouping Army Moves*, 17–26 December 1944 (sixteen maps); Weigley, *Eisenhower's Lieutenants*, 451; Cole, *Ardennes*, 274–275.

156. Cole, *Ardennes*, 274–275.

157. Clarke, interview, 10 November 1987.

158. Woodruff to Clarke, 27 January 1987; Clarke, interview, 10 November 1987.

159. Clarke, interview, 10 November 1987.

160. Dupuy, *Lion in the Way*, 76.

161. Eisenhower, *Bitter Woods*, 286.

162. Clarke, interview, 10 November 1987; Clarke, "Move to Saint Vith," 2.

163. Matthew B. Ridgway, *Soldier: The Memoirs of Matthew B. Ridgway (As Told to Harold H. Martin)* (New York: Harper and Brothers, 1956); Cole, *Ardennes*, 411–413.

164. Clarke, interview, 10 November 1987.

165. Cole, *Ardennes*, 413; Armor School, *Battle at St.-Vith*, 25.

166. Clarke, interview, 10 November 1987. Clarke's "confusion," of course, is simply Clausewitz's "friction" put another way. It's merely a different way of stating Clausewitz's dictum that in war, even the simplest things are difficult to accomplish.

167. Whiting, *Death of a Division*, 144. It's undoubtedly also true that untrained generals and untrained units tend not to perform very well in their first combat.

168. Weigley, *Eisenhower's Lieutenants*, 490. Bruce C. Clarke continued to rise in rank through the postwar years, becoming one of the army's most celebrated combat commanders and trainers. At the close of World War II, he was assigned to Gen. Jacob Devers's Army Ground Forces command, where he was instrumental in creating the postwar army professional military education system. During the last year of the Korean War, the then-lieutenant general commanded the I Corps (whose units included the 7th Infantry Division fighting for Pork Chop Hill). Promoted to full general in 1958, Clarke commanded U.S. Army Europe and Seventh Army during the Berlin crisis in the early 1960s. He retired from active service in 1963 but continued to write about and advise senior army leaders on leadership and command the remainder of his life. Dwight Eisenhower once paid tribute to Clarke by remarking, "The U.S. Army has had two great trainers—Baron von Steuben and Bruce Clarke." General Clarke died in March 1988.

AFTERWORD

1. Hugh M. Cole, *The United States Army in World War II. European Theater of Operations: The Ardennes: The Battle of the Bulge* (Washington, D.C.: Office of the Chief of Military History/GPO, 1965), 650.

2. Forrest C. Pogue, "Over the Beaches: D-Day," S. L. A. Marshall Lecture, Fort Leavenworth, Kansas, 17 January 1984.

3. Martin Blumenson, "Eisenhower Then and Now: Fireside Reflections," *Parameters* 21 (Summer 1991): 29.

4. Charles B. MacDonald, *A Time for Trumpets: The Untold Story of the Battle of the Bulge* (New York: William Morrow, 1984), 1, 618.

5. Forrest C. Pogue, "The Supreme Allied Command in Northwest Europe, 1944–1945," *Essays in History and International Relations*, ed. Dwight E. Lee and George McReynolds (Worcester, MA: Clarke University Press, 1949), 172–173; Jacques Nobécourt, *Hitler's Last Gamble* (New York: Schocken Books, 1967), 84, 130, 284; Russell F. Weigley, *Eisenhower's Lieutenants: The Campaign of France and Germany, 1944–1945* (Bloomington: Indiana University Press, 1981), 463–464; David Eisenhower, *Eisenhower: At War, 1943–1945* (New York: Random House, 1986), 555.

6. John Toland, *Battle: The Story of the Bulge* (New York: Random House, 1959), 53; Cole, *Ardennes*, 170, 274–275, 331; Weigley, *Eisenhower's Lieutenants*, 451; Frank J. Price, *Troy H. Middleton: A Biography* (Baton Rouge: LSU Press, 1974), 216.

7. Pogue, "Supreme Command," 175, 178, 192; Nobécourt, *Last Gamble*, 77–78; Weigley, *Eisenhower's Lieutenants*, 458.

8. D. K. R. Crosswell, *The Chief of Staff: The Military Career of General Walter Bedell Smith* (New York: Greenwood Press, 1991), 294–296.

9. Carlo D'Este, *Eisenhower: A Soldier's Life* (New York: Henry Holt and Company, 2002), 649. D'Este rightly concludes that it was "Bradley's uncharacteristic unwillingness to exercise leadership when it was most needed" that forced Ike's hand.

10. Omar N. Bradley and Clay Blair, *A General's Life: An Autobiography of General of the Army Omar N. Bradley* (New York: Simon and Schuster, 1983), 368.

11. Basil H. Liddell Hart, *The Other Side of the Hill* (London: Cassell, 1951), 465; Weigley, *Eisenhower's Lieutenants*, 574. Liddell Hart condemns the German offensive by writing, "The Ardennes offensive carried to the extreme of absurdity the military belief that 'attack is the best defense.' It proved the 'worst defense'—wrecking Germany's chances for further serious resistance." There were tough battles yet to come, including the bitter Rhineland Campaign, but Hitler had used up his last major mobile reserves in the Ardennes.

12. Martin Blumenson, *Patton: The Man Behind the Legend, 1885–1945* (New York: Berkeley Books, 1987), 246–252; Bradley and Blair, *A General's Life*, 367–368; Carlo D'Este *Patton: A Genius for War* (HarperCollins, 1995), 674–702; Weigley, *Eisenhower's Lieutenants*, 498–506, 519–527. D'Este's account of the 19 December 1944 Bulge strategy meeting of Eisenhower and his key commanders in Verdun includes this revealing observation: "Even he [Bradley] realized that

the only principal players were Eisenhower and Patton." D'Este concludes that "Bradley's role was largely reduced to that of an observer; the battle was Patton's to mastermind and control."

13. The listed commanders are Maj. Gen. Troy Middleton, VIII Corps; Maj. Gen. Leonard Gerow, V Corps; Maj. Gen. Robert Hasbrouck, 7th Armored Division; Maj. Gen. Norman Cota, 28th Infantry Division; Maj. Gen. Raymond Barton, 4th Infantry Division; Col. Hurley Fuller, 110th Infantry Regiment (28th Infantry Division); and Bruce C. Clarke, CCB, 7th Armored Division.

14. Robert H. Berlin, "United States Army World War II Corps Commanders: A Composite Biography," *The Journal of Military History* 53 (April 1989): 149, 162; Martin Blumenson, "America's World War II Leaders in Europe: Some Thoughts," *Parameters* 19 (December 1989): 4; J. Lawton Collins, *Conversations With General J. Lawton Collins* (Ft. Leavenworth, KS: U.S. Army Command and General Staff College, 1983), 5–6.

15. Blumenson, "America's World War II Leaders," 4. Blumenson writes that, once the war began, the "early battles . . . proved out the real leaders and shook out the duds."

16. Robert H. Berlin, "Dwight David Eisenhower and the Duties of Generalship," *Military Review* 70 (October 1990): 17; E. M. Flanagan Jr., "A Force of Professionals," *Army* 42 (March 1992): 57; Berlin, "Corps Commanders," 155; Collins, *Conversations*, 3–4; Blumenson, "America's World War II Leaders," 8. Blumenson describes the professional military education of the era: "Successful officers usually proceeded through a progression of educational institutions. First came the Military Academy at West Point or college work with the ROTC, both leading to a commission. Then arrived the advance branch schooling at Fort Benning for Infantry, Fort Sill for Artillery, Fort Belvoir for the Engineers, and the like. Next came the course variously titled but eventually called the Command and General Staff College at Fort Leavenworth, which was regarded generally as the most important school assignment for all officers, the prerequisite, it was said, for promotion to high rank and major responsibility. Finally, the top of the educational pile was the Army War College." Collins, like many of the top World War II leaders, was a student and instructor in this system and related, "I am a great believer in the Army school system. The thing that saved the American Army—no question about it in my judgment—was this school system, the entire school system. . . . The school system made an army for us. I've said I'd give up a division before I'd give up one of our schools." Flanagan, reporting on the results of a questionnaire he circulated to "between the wars"–era retired generals, wrote that one response summed up the consensus. It said, "The answer to your question can be summed up in three words: Schools, schools, and schools."

17. D'Este, *Eisenhower* and *Patton*; Bradley and Blair, *A General's Life*; Blumenson, *Patton*; Price, *Middleton*; Thomas R. Stone, "General William Hood Simpson: Unsung Commander of US Ninth Army," *Parameters* 11 (February 1980); Weigley, *Eisenhower's Lieutenants* and *History of the United States Army*; Crosswell, *Chief of Staff*; Cole C. Kingseed, "Eisenhower's Prewar Anonymity: Myth or Reality?" *Parameters* 21 (Autumn 1991); Berlin, "Corps Commanders." Virtually all of the interwar regular officers alternated line, staff, and school

assignments to one degree or another. Some, like Bradley and Middleton, spent more time in schools (both as student and instructor) than did others, but they all held a wide variety of troop and staff duties in field units and headquarters throughout the period between the two World Wars. Troop units were spread over the entire United States, from large posts like Forts Benning and Sill to small ones like Camp Dodge (Iowa) and Fort Screven (Georgia). Overseas troop and staff duty was often highlighted by tours in the Philippines, Hawaii, or Panama—all usually sought after because, despite the isolation from the States, a high standard of living was possible, even on an army officer's meager pay. Berlin, examining the interwar careers of the thirty-four officers who commanded corps during the war, wrote: "Command of troop units was a desirable assignment for officers during the interwar period because it could result in highly beneficial officer efficiency reports . . . [and, thus] twenty-two of the thirty-four officers gained extensive command experience during the interwar period. As their experience grew, they usually led successively larger units, moving from company to battalion to regiment." Berlin continues that "staff assignments during the interwar period var[ied] from regimental staff duty to service on the General Staff in Washington where twenty of the future corps commanders served. . . . Often these staff assignments were long tours of duty lasting from three to five years."

18. Bruce C. Clarke, "Creating an Outstanding Battalion in 1941–1942," unpublished; Bradley and Blair, *A General's Life*, 71–72; Kingseed, "Eisenhower's Prewar Anonymity," 88–96.

19. Richard M. Ketchum, "Warming Up on the Sidelines for World War II," *Smithsonian* 22 (September 1991): 102; Kingseed, "Eisenhower's Prewar Anonymity," 90–96; D'Este, *Eisenhower* and *Patton*; Bradley and Blair, *A General's Life*; Blumenson, *Patton*; Weigley, *Eisenhower's Lieutenants*; Berlin, "Duties of Generalship," 16–17. Bradley's service under Marshall and Eisenhower's assignment as an assistant to MacArthur in the Philippines are well-known examples of apprenticeships to famous or to-be-famous leaders. Ike's mentorship by Gen. Fox Conner or Bruce Clarke's close service under Gen. Adna Chaffee are less well known, but were extremely influential in forming these officers' interwar experiences. Ketchum points out the role played by the famous 1941 maneuvers in helping Marshall shape the face of American Army leadership at the beginning of the war. He writes, "Many officers' careers were made, others' broken" by the war games. "Of 42 army, corps and division commanders who participated in the Louisiana maneuvers, only 11 got significant combat assignments during World War II." Ketchum records that Marshall's collaborator in creating the American Army of World War II, Gen. Lesley J. McNair, said in the wake of the maneuvers, "A lot of these Generals who want to fire their Chief of Staff ought to fire themselves. . . . We're going to start at the top and work down. We've got some bum Generals . . . but we're going to weed them out. Have we the bright young Majors and Captains to replace them? Yes."

20. Roger H. Nye, "Whence Patton's Genius?" *Parameters* 22 (Winter 1991–1992): 60–73; Kingseed, "Eisenhower's Prewar Anonymity," 89–90; Berlin, "Duties of Generalship," 16; Blumenson, "America's World War II Leaders," 9; Collins,

Conversations, 3. Many of the World War II leaders interacted personally and professionally throughout the period, to each other's mutual benefit. Indeed, one salutary benefit of bringing officers together in a school environment is so that they may interact and learn from each other. The contacts made while attending the army's schools are often the most important lasting effects of the experience. Eisenhower's and Patton's collaboration and publishing of articles on the future of mechanized warfare in the early 1920s is a well-known example of personal and professional interaction and mutual intellectual stimulation. Nye highlights the importance of a "lifetime program of professional reading," which should not be overlooked as an influence on the future careers and professional development of the World War II leaders. He identifies Patton's extensive library and lifetime habit of reading as one manifestation and source of his military genius. Blumenson supports this conclusion by writing, "George Patton grew professionally through his reading, a 'monumental self-study he charted for himself.'" Blumenson, however, expands this beyond Patton by continuing, "He was hardly alone. Quite a few officers strove for knowledge and [their] development gained professional competence by more or less systematic reading. They also interacted with like-minded officers of their generation, all 'intelligent, stimulating men . . . studying their profession' individually and in small groups, off duty and at the service schools." When Collins was asked how he prepared himself for war, he answered, "To some considerable extent, by reading military history. I told my own son, 'If you really want to learn your trade, you couldn't do any better than studying Freeman's book on Robert E. Lee'. . . . I read military history, and I got a good deal out of the good ones." While he was forming and training the Ninth Army staff, Simpson re-read *Lee's Lieutenants* as a refresher course in the timeless elements of command and leadership, and recommended that his staff do the same. Eisenhower read all aspects of military history in earnest while serving under Fox Conner in the Canal Zone, and "Conner," writes Berlin, "guided Eisenhower in his reading of military literature from Civil War officer memoirs to Carl von Clausewitz's *On War*." Berlin relates that "Eisenhower recalled that 'life with General Conner was a sort of graduate school in military affairs and the humanities.'"

21. Jonathan W. Jordan, *Brothers, Rivals, Victors: Eisenhower, Patton, Bradley, and the Partnership That Drove the Allied Conquest in Europe* (New York: NAL Caliber, 2011), 446. Jordan points out that when Bradley was first approached about the possible command change on the evening of 19 December by Ike's Chief of Staff Walter Bedell Smith, Bradley was unable to provide Smith (and later Eisenhower as well) with any valid tactical and command reasons why two-thirds of his army group should not be placed under Montgomery's command. Jordan writes that Bradley's "instincts told him this was . . . a bad move."

22. Bruce C. Clarke, "The Defense of St. Vith," Interview by author, 10 November 1987.

SELECT BIBLIOGRAPHY

BOOKS

Alanbrooke, Field Marshal Lord. *War Diaries, 1939–1945*. Alex Danchev and Daniel Todman, ed. Berkeley: University of California Press, 2003.

Ambrose, Stephen E. *Eisenhower: Volume I. Soldier, General of the Army, President-Elect, 1890–1952*. New York: Simon and Schuster, 1983.

———. *The Supreme Commander: The War Years of General Dwight David Eisenhower*. Garden City: Doubleday and Company, 1969.

Atkinson, Rick. *An Army at Dawn: The War in North Africa, 1942–1943*. Volume 1 of the *Liberation* Trilogy. New York: Henry Holt and Company, 2002.

———. *Day of Battle: The War in Sicily and Italy, 1943–1944*. Volume 2 of the *Liberation* Trilogy. New York: Henry Holt and Company, 2007.

———. *The Guns at Last Light: The War in Western Europe, 1944–1945*. Volume 3 of the *Liberation* Trilogy. New York: Henry Holt and Company, 2013.

Baldwin, Hanson W. *Tiger Jack*. Fort Collins: Old Army Press, 1979.

Barnett, Correlli, ed. *Hitler's Generals*. New York: Grove Weidenfeld, 1989.

Barron, Leo, and Don Cygan. *No Silent Night: The Christmas Battle for Bastogne*. New York: NAL Caliber, 2013.

Bender, Mark C. *Watershed at Leavenworth: Dwight D. Eisenhower and the Command and General Staff College*. Fort Leavenworth, KS: U.S. Army Command and General Staff College, 1990.

Berlin, Robert H. *US Army World War II Corps Commanders: A Composite Biography*. Fort Leavenworth, KS: Combat Studies Institute, 1989.

Blumenson, Martin. *The United States Army in World War II. European Theater of Operations: Breakout and Pursuit*. Washington, D.C.: Office of the Chief of Military History/GPO, 1961.

———. *The Duel for France, 1944: The Men and Battles That Changed the Fate of Europe*. Boston: Da Capo Press, 1963.

———. *Eisenhower*. New York: Ballantine Books, Inc., 1972.

———. *The Patton Papers II: 1940–1945*. Boston: Houghton Mifflin, 1974.

———. *Kasserine Pass*. New York: Jove Books, 1983.

———. *Patton: The Man Behind the Legend, 1885–1945*. New York: Berkley Books, 1987.

———. *Heroes Never Die: Warriors and Warfare in World War II*. New York: Cooper Square Press, 2001.

——— and James L. Stokesbury. *Masters of the Art of Command*. Boston: Houghton Mifflin, 1975.

Bradley, Omar N., and Clay Blair. *A General's Life: An Autobiography by General of the Army Omar N. Bradley*. New York: Simon and Schuster, 1983.

Bradley, Omar N. *A Soldier's Story*. New York: Henry Holt, 1951.

Breuer, William B. *Operation Dragoon: The Allied Invasion of the South of France*. New York: Jove Books, 1987.

Bryant, Arthur. *Triumph in the West*. Garden City: Doubleday, 1959.

Butcher, Harry C. *My Three Years with Eisenhower: The Personal Diary of Captain Harry C. Butcher, USNR*. New York: Simon and Schuster, 1946.

Cardozier, V. R. *The Mobilization of the United States in World War II*. Jefferson, NC: McFarland & Company, 1995.

Carver, Sir Michael, ed. *The War Lords: Military Commanders of the Twentieth Century*. Boston: Little, Brown and Company, 1976.

Chandler, Alfred D., ed. *The Papers of Dwight David Eisenhower, The War Years*. Vols. I–V. Baltimore: Johns Hopkins Press, 1970.

Citino, Robert M. *The Wehrmacht Retreats: Fighting a Lost War, 1943*. Lawrence: University Press of Kansas, 2012.

Clarke, Jeffrey J. and Robert Ross Smith. *The United States Army in World War II. European Theater of Operations. Riviera to the Rhine*. Washington, D.C.: U.S. Government Printing Office, 1993.

Clausewitz, Carl von. *On War*. Edited and translated by Michael Howard and Peter Paret. Princeton: Princeton University Press, 1976.

Clay, Roy U. *Curbstone: The History of the 275th Armored Field Artillery Battalion in World War II*. Jackson: Richerson, 1978.

Cole, Hugh M. *The United States Army in World War II. European Theater of Operations: The Ardennes: The Battle of the Bulge*. Washington, D.C.: Office of the Chief of Military History/GPO, 1965.

———. *The United States Army in World War II. European Theater of Operations: The Lorraine Campaign*. Washington, D.C.: Office of the Chief of Military History/GPO, 1950.

Collins, J. Lawton. *Lightning Joe: An Autobiography*. Baton Rouge: LSU Press, 1979.

———. *Conversations with General J. Lawton Collins*. Fort Leavenworth, KS: U.S. Army Command and General Staff College, 1983.

Collins, Michael and Martin King. *Voices of the Bulge: Untold Stories from Veterans of the Battle of the Bulge*. Minneapolis: Zenith Press, 2011.

———. *The Tigers of Bastogne: Voices of the 10th Armored Division in the Battle of the Bulge*. Havertown, PA: Casemate Publishers, 2013.

Conquer: The Story of the Ninth Army, 1944–1945. Nashville: Battery Press, 1980.

Craven, Wesley Frank, and James Lea Cate. *The Army Air Forces in World War II. Europe: Argument to V-E Day, January 1944–1945*. Washington, D.C.: Office of Air Force History/GPO, 1983.

Crookenden, Napier. *Battle of the Bulge 1944*. New York: Scribner's, 1980.

Crosswell, D. K. R. *The Chief of Staff: The Military Career of General Walter Bedell Smith*. New York: Greenwood Press, 1991.

———. *Beetle: The Life of Walter Bedell Smith*. Lexington: University Press of Kentucky, 2010.

D'Este, Carlo. *Patton: A Genius for War*. New York: HarperCollins, 1995.

———. *Eisenhower: A Soldier's Life*. New York: Holt and Company, 2002.

———. *Warlord: A Life of Winston Churchill at War, 1874–1945*. New York: HarperCollins, 2008.

Doubler, Michael D. *Closing With the Enemy: How GIs Fought the War in Europe, 1944–45*. Lawrence: University Press of Kansas, 1994.

Dunleavy, T. M., ed. *Generals of the Army and the Air Force.* 1954.

Dupuy, R. Ernest. *St. Vith: Lion in the Way—The 106th Infantry Division in World War II.* Washington, D.C.: Infantry Journal Press, 1949.

Eisenhower, David. *Eisenhower: At War, 1943–1945.* New York: Random House, 1986.

Eisenhower, Dwight D. *Crusade in Europe.* Garden City: Doubleday and Company, 1948.

Eisenhower, John S. D. *The Bitter Woods.* New York: G. P. Putnam's Sons, 1969.

Ellis, John. *The Sharp End: The Fighting Man in World War II.* New York: Charles Scribner's Sons, 1980.

———. *Brute Force: Allied Strategy and Tactics in the Second World War.* New York: Viking Books, 1990.

Ellis, William D., and Thomas J. Cunningham. *Clarke of St. Vith: The Sergeant's General.* Cleveland: Dillon-Liederbach, 1974.

Fairchild, Byron and Jonathan Grossman. *The United States Army in World War II. The War Department. The Army and Industrial Manpower.* Washington, D.C.: Office of the Chief of Military History/U.S. Government Printing Office, 1959.

Fest, Joachim C. *The Face of the Third Reich.* New York: Penguin, 1979.

Frankel, Nat, and Larry Smith. *Patton's Best: An Informal History of the 4th Armored Division.* New York: Jove Books, 1984.

Franklin Institute. *Art and Requirements of Command.* Vol. 1, *Summary Report*; Vol. 2, *Generalship Study.* Philadelphia: Systems Science Department of the Franklin Institute, 1967.

Gabel, Christopher R. *Seek, Strike, and Destroy: US Army Tank Destroyer Doctrine in World War II.* Fort Leavenworth, KS: U.S. Army Command and General Staff College, 1985.

———. *The 4th Armored Division in the Encirclement of Nancy.* Fort Leavenworth, KS: U.S. Army Command and General Staff College, 1986.

———. *The US Army GHQ Maneuvers of 1941.* Washington, D.C.: Center of Military History/GPO, 1991.

Galland, Adolf. *The First and the Last: The Rise and Fall of the German Fighter Forces, 1938–1945.* New York: Ballantine Books, 1957.

Goldstein, Donald M., Katherine V. Dillon, and J. Michael Wenger. *Nuts! The Battle of the Bulge. The Story and Photographs.* Washington, D.C.: Brassey's, 1994.

Greenfield, Kent R., ed. *Command Decisions.* Washington, D.C.: Office of the Chief of Military History/GPO, 1960.

Greenfield, Kent R. *The United States Army in World War II. The Army Ground Forces: The Organization of Ground Combat Troops.* Washington, D.C.: Historical Division, GPO, 1947.

———. *American Strategy in World War II: A Reconsideration.* Malabar, FL: Robert Kreiger Publishing, 1982.

Hamilton, Nigel. *Monty: The Battles of Field Marshal Bernard Montgomery.* New York: Random House, 1994.

Hanson, Victor Davis. *The Soul of Battle: From Ancient Times to the Present Day, How Three Great Liberators Vanquished Tyranny.* New York: The Free Press, 1999.

Harrison, Gordon A. *The United States Army in World War II. European Theater of Operations: Cross-Channel Attack*. Washington, D.C.: Office of the Chief of Military History/GPO, 1951.

Higgins, David R. *The Roer River Battles: Germany's Last Stand at the Westwall, 1944–45*. Havertown, PA: Casemate, 2010.

Hogg, Ian V. *Artillery 1920–1963*. New York: Arco Publishing, 1980.

———. *The Encyclopedia of Infantry Weapons of World War II*. New York: Thomas Y. Crowell Company, 1977.

Howard, Michael, ed. *The Theory and Practice of War*. Bloomington: Indiana University Press, 1965.

Howe, George F. *The United States Army in World War II. Mediterranean Theater of Operations: Northwest Africa: Seizing the Initiative*. Washington, D.C.: Office of the Chief of Military History/GPO, 1957.

Howitzer, The. 1909 ed. West Point, NY: U.S. Military Academy, 1909.

———. 1912 ed. West Point, NY: U.S. Military Academy, 1912.

———. 1915 ed. West Point, NY: U.S. Military Academy, 1915.

Humphrey, Robert E. *Once Upon A Time In War: The 99th Division in World War II*. Norman: University of Oklahoma Press, 2008.

Janowitz, Morris. *The Professional Soldier*. New York: Free Press-Macmillan, 1960.

Jeffers, H. Paul. *Taking Command: General J. Lawton Collins from Guadalcanal to Utah Beach and Victory in Europe*. New York: NAL Caliber, 2009.

Jessup, John E. Jr., and Robert W. Coakley. *A Guide to the Study and Use of Military History*. Washington, D.C.: GPO, 1979.

Jordan, Jonathan W. *Brothers, Rivals, Victors: Eisenhower, Patton, Bradley, and the Partnership That Drove the Allied Conquest in Europe*. New York: NAL Caliber, 2011.

Keegan, John, ed. *Churchill's Generals*. New York: Grove Weidenfeld, 1991.

Keegan, John. *Six Armies in Normandy: From D-Day to the Liberation of Paris*. New York: Penguin Books, 1982.

Kennett, Lee. *G. I.: The American Soldier in World War II*. New York: Warner Books, 1987.

Kershaw, Alex. *The Longest Winter: The Battle of the Bulge and the Epic Story of World War II's Most Decorated Platoon*. Boston: Da Capo Press, 2004.

Killen, John. *A History of the Luftwaffe*. New York: Bantam Books, 1987.

Kirkpatrick, Charles E. *An Unknown Future and a Doubtful Present: Writing the Victory Plan of 1941*. Washington, D.C.: U.S. Government Printing Office, Center of Military History, 1992.

Koyen, Kenneth. *The Fourth Armored Division: From the Beach to Bavaria*. Watertown, NY: Hungerford-Holbrook Company, 1949.

Kretchik, Walter E. *U.S. Army Doctrine: From the American Revolution to the War on Terror*. Lawrence: University Press of Kansas, 2011.

Lamb, Richard. *Montgomery in Europe 1943–1945*. London: Buchan and Enright, 1983.

Lee, Dwight E., and George McReynolds, eds. *Essays in History and International Relations*. Worcester: Clark University Publishing, 1949.

Leinbaugh, Harold P., and John D. Campbell. *The Men of Company K: The Autobiography of a World War II Rifle Company.* New York: Bantam Books, 1987.

Lewin, Ronald. *Churchill as Warlord.* New York: Stein and Day, 1973.

Liddell Hart, Basil H. *The Other Side of the Hill.* London: Cassell and Company, 1951.

———. *The Memoirs of Captain Liddell Hart.* London: Cassell and Company, 1965.

MacArthur, Douglas. *Reminiscences.* New York: McGraw-Hill, 1964.

MacDonald, Charles B. *The United States Army in World War II. European Theater of Operations: The Last Offensive.* Washington, D.C.: Office of the Chief of Military History/GPO, 1973.

———. *The United States Army in World War II. European Theater of Operations: The Siegfried Line Campaign.* Washington, D.C.: Office of the Chief of Military History/GPO, 1973.

———. *Company Commander.* New York: Bantam, 1982.

———. *The Battle of the Huertgen Forest.* New York: Jove Publications, 1984.

———. *A Time for Trumpets: The Untold Story of the Battle of the Bulge.* New York: Bantam, 1985.

———. *The Mighty Endeavor: The American War in Europe.* New York: Quill-William Morrow, 1986.

Mahon, John K. *History of the Militia and the National Guard.* New York: Macmillan Publishing Co., 1983.

Mansoor, Peter R. *The GI Offensive in Europe: The Triumph of American Infantry Divisions, 1941–1945.* Lawrence: University Press of Kansas, 1999.

Marshall, S. L. A. *Bastogne: The First Eight Days.* Washington, D.C.: The Infantry Journal Press, 1946.

———. *Men Against Fire: The Problem of Battle Command in Future War.* Gloucester, MA: Peter Smith, 1947.

Matloff, Maurice. *The United States Army in World War II. The War Department: Strategic Planning for Coalition Warfare, 1943–1944.* Washington, D.C.: Office of the Chief of Military History/GPO, 1953.

———. "The 90-Division Gamble." *Command Decisions.* Greenfield, Kent Roberts, ed. Washington, D.C.: Office of the Chief of Military History/GPO, 1960.

Matthews, Lloyd J., and Dale E. Brown, eds. *The Challenge of Military Leadership.* Washington, D.C.: Pergammon Brassey's, 1989.

McManus, John C. *Alamo in the Ardennes: The Untold Story of the American Soldiers Who Made the Defense of Bastogne Possible.* New York: NAL Caliber, 2008.

———. *Grunts. Inside the American Combat Experience, World War II Through Iraq.* New York: NAL Caliber, 2010.

Merriam, Robert E. *Dark December.* Chicago/New York: Ziff-Davis, 1947.

Meyer, Harold J. *Hanging Sam: A Military Biography of General Samuel T. Williams.* Denton: University of North Texas Press, 1990.

Mick, Allen H., ed. *With the 102nd Infantry Division Through Germany.* Nashville: Battery Press, 1980.

Military History and Publications Section, The Infantry School. *Infantry in Battle.* Washington, D.C.: Infantry Journal, Inc., 1959.

Millett, Allan R., Peter Maslowski, and William B. Feis. *For the Common Defense: A Military History of the United States from 1607–2012.* New York: Free Press, 2012.

Mitchell, Ralph M. *The 101st Airborne Division's Defense of Bastogne.* Fort Leavenworth, KS: Combat Studies Institute, 1986.

Montgomery, Bernard Law. *The Memoirs of Field-Marshal the Viscount Montgomery of Alamein, K. G..* New York: Signet Books, 1958.

Nobécourt, Jacques. *Hitler's Last Gamble.* New York: Schocken Books, 1967.

Palmer, Robert R., Bell I. Wiley, and William R. Keast. *The United States Army in World War II: The Army Ground Forces. The Procurement and Training of Ground Combat Troops.* Washington, D.C.: Office of the Chief of Military History/GPO, 1948.

Paret, Peter, ed. *Makers of Modern Strategy: From Machiavelli to the Nuclear Age.* Princeton: Princeton University Press, 1986.

Parker, Danny S. *Fatal Crossroads: The Untold Story of the Malmedy Massacre at the Battle of the Bulge.* Boston: Da Capo Press, 2011.

Perrett, Geoffrey. *There's A War To Be Won: The United States Army in World War II.* New York: Random House, 1991.

Persico, Joseph E. *Roosevelt's Centurions: FDR and the Commanders He Led to Victory in World War II.* New York: Random House, 2014.

Phillips, Robert H. *To Save Bastogne.* New York: Stein and Day, 1983.

Pogue, Forrest C. *The United States Army in World War II. European Theater of Operations: The Supreme Command.* Washington, D.C.: Office of the Chief of Military History/GPO, 1954.

Pontolillo, James. *Murderous Elite: The Waffen SS and Its Record of War Crimes.* Solna, Sweden: Leandoer and Eckholm, 2009.

Price, Frank J. *Troy H. Middleton: A Biography.* Baton Rouge: LSU Press, 1974.

Reed, Prentiss B. Jr. *Personal Leadership for Combat Officers.* New York: McGraw-Hill, 1943.

Richards, Peter Judson. *Extraordinary Justice: Military Tribunals in Historical and International Context.* New York: New York University Press, 2007.

Ricks, Thomas E. *The Generals: American Military Command from World War II to Today.* New York: Penguin, 2013.

Ridgway, Matthew B. *Soldier: The Memoirs of Matthew B. Ridgway (As Told to Harold H. Martin).* New York: Harper and Brothers, 1956.

Rigby, David. *Allied Master Strategists: The Combined Chiefs of Staff in World War II.* Annapolis: Naval Institute Press, 2012.

Rush, Robert Sterling. *Hell in Hürtgen Forest: The Ordeal and Triumph of an American Infantry Regiment.* Lawrence: University Press of Kansas, 2001.

Saied, Kemal. *Thunderbolt Odyssey: P-47 War in Europe.* Tulsa: Stonewood Press, 1989.

Sebree, Edmund B., ed. *Leadership at Higher Levels of Command as Viewed by Senior and Experienced Combat Commanders.* Monterey: U.S. Army Leadership Research Unit, 1961, "William H. Simpson," by Alvan C. Gillem Jr.

Showalter, Dennis. *Hitler's Panzers: The Lightning Attacks That Revolutionized Warfare*. New York: Berkley Caliber, 2010.

Smith, Jean Edward. *Eisenhower in War and Peace*. New York: Random House, 2013.

Smith, Walter Bedell. *Eisenhower's Six Great Decisions (Europe 1944–1945)*. New York: Longmans, Green and Company, 1956.

Steward, Hal D. *Thunderbolt: The History of the Eleventh Armored Division*. Nashville: Battery Press, 1981.

Stokesbury, James L. *A Short History of World War I*. New York: William Morrow, 1981.

Toland, John. *Battle: The Story of the Bulge*. New York: Random House, 1959.

———. *The Last 100 Days*. New York: Random House, 1965.

Tucker, Spencer C. *Battles That Changed History: An Encyclopedia of World Conflict*. Santa Barbara: ABC-CLIO, 2010.

United States Command and General Staff College. *Dwight D. Eisenhower: The Professional Soldier and the Study of History*. Fort Leavenworth, KS: U.S. Army Command and General Staff College, 1990.

Van Creveld, Martin. *Fighting Power: German and U.S. Army Performance 1939–1945*. Westport, CT: Greenwood Press, 1982.

———. *Supplying War: Logistics from Wallenstein to Patton*. New York: Cambridge University Press, 1977.

Van Gelder, Lawrence. *Ike: A Soldier's Crusade*. New York: Universal Publishing, 1969.

Weigley, Russell F. *History of the United States Army*. New York: Macmillan, 1967.

———. *The American Way of War: A History of U.S. Military Strategy and Policy*. New York: Macmillan, 1973.

———. *Eisenhower's Lieutenants: The Campaign of France and Germany 1944–1945*. Bloomington: Indiana University, 1981.

Weinberg, Gerhard, L. *A World at Arms: A Global History of World War II*. New York: Cambridge University Press, 2005.

Weingartner, James J. *A Peculiar Crusade: Willis M. Everett and the Malmedy Massacre*. New York: New York University Press, 2000.

Whitaker, W. Denis, and Shelagh Whitaker. *Rhineland: The Battle to End the War*. New York: St. Martin's Press, 1989.

Whiting, Charles. *Death of a Division*. New York: Stein and Day, 1981.

———. *Ardennes: The Secret War*. London: Century Publishing, 1984.

Willbanks, James H., ed. *Generals of the Army: Marshall, MacArthur, Eisenhower, Arnold, Bradley*. Lexington: University Press of Kentucky, 2013.

Wilmot, Chester. *The Struggle for Europe*. New York: Harper and Brothers, 1952.

Winton, Harold R. *Corps Commanders of the Bulge: Six American Generals and Victory in the Ardennes*. Lawrence: University Press of Kansas, 2007.

Yeide, Harry. *The Longest Battle: September 1944 to February 1945—From Aachen to the Roer and Across*. St. Paul: Zenith Press, 2005.

Young, Desmond. *Rommel: The Desert Fox*. New York: Quill, William Morrow, 1950.

GOVERNMENT DOCUMENTS

U.S. Department of the Army. *Annual Reports of the Commandant. The General Service Schools, 1923–24 to 1927–28*. Fort Leavenworth, KS: General Service School Press, 1924 to 1928.

————. Clarke, Gen. Bruce C. *St. Vith: Counter offensive*. Industrial College of the Armed Forces, April 1975.

————. Cross, Col. T. J. *Notes on Infantry Divisions*. Report of the Assistant Chief of Staff, G-3, Second Army, Fort George G. Meade, MD, 1946.

————. Fontenot, Maj. Gregory. *The Lucky Seventh in the Bulge: A Case Study for the Airland Battle*. MMAS thesis, Command and General Staff College, 1985.

————. Lerwill, Leonard. *The Personnel Replacement System in the U.S. Army. Department of the Army Pamphlet no. 20-211*. Washington, D.C.: U.S. Government Printing Office, August 1950.

————. Morelock, Maj. Jerry D. *Senior Leadership: The Crucial Element of Combat Power*. MMAS thesis, Command and General Staff College, 1984.

————. Nelson, Maj. Dale. *The Ardennes, 1944—The Defensive Battles*. MMAS thesis, Command and General Staff College, 1981.

————. Armor School. *The Battle at St- Vith, Belgium*. 1949.

————. Armor School. *Campaigns and Battles—Germany 1944, Armor in the Defense, Armor on a Corps Boundary, Ardennes*. 1944.

————. Army Ground Forces. AGF Extracts, *106th Division Artillery Lessons Learned*. 1945.

————. Army Ground Forces. AGF Board Report—Engineer Notes.

————. Army Service Forces. Special Services Division Survey. *What the Soldier Thinks*. August 1943.

————. Command and General Staff College. *Battle of the Bulge Bibliography*. 20 November 1973.

————. Center of Military History. *American Armies and Battlefields in Europe*. Washington, D.C.: GPO, 1992. (Reprint of 1938 edition prepared by the American Battle Monuments Commission.)

————. Center of Military History, German Army Operations in the Ardennes (five documents translated from the German), Dietrich, Wagner, Manteuffel.

————. Center of Military History. *Main Reasons for Failure of the Ardennes Offensive*. Seventeen pages translated from the German.

————. Center of Military History, *Mobilization in World War II*. 1995.

————. Center of Military History, *Fact Sheet: African Americans in World War II*. 1991.

————. Center of Military History, *Fact Sheet: World War II*. 1994.

————. Center of Military History, *Fact Sheet: Women in World War II*. 1991.

————. General Orders No. 11. 27 April 1981.

————. Supreme Headquarters Allied Expeditionary Forces. Office of the Chief of Staff: Secretary, General Staff, *General Correspondence Files. May 1943–August 1945*.

————. Supreme Headquarters Allied Expeditionary Forces. Office of the Chief of Staff: Secretary, General Staff, *Geographic Correspondence Files. 1943–July 1945*.

————. Supreme Headquarters Allied Expeditionary Forces. Office of the Chief of Staff: Secretary, General Staff, *Minutes of SHAEF Conferences and Briefings and Reports of Discussions of Operational Plans. 1942–1944.*

————. Supreme Headquarters Allied Expeditionary Forces. G-2 Section, *Intelligence Reports. 1943–1944.*

————. Supreme Headquarters Allied Expeditionary Forces. G-3 Section, *Records Relating to Planning for Allied Operations. 1943–July 1945.*

————. Supreme Headquarters Allied Expeditionary Forces. G-3 Section, *Incoming and Outgoing Messages. September 21, 1944–November 30, 1945.*

————. Supreme Headquarters Allied Expeditionary Forces. G-3 Section, *Top Secret Incoming and Outgoing Messages. May 1944–May 1946.*

————. 12th Army Group, Report of Operations (Final After-Action Report). Multiple Volumes. Washington, D.C.: Superintendent of Documents, 1948.

————. 12th Army Group. G-1 Section, *Daily Summaries. 1944.*

————. 12th Army Group. G-1 Section, *Documents Relating to War Crimes and Violations of the Geneva Convention. 1944–1945.*

————. 12th Army Group. G-2 Section, *Weekly Intelligence Summaries. January 1944–June 1945.*

————. 12th Army Group. Adjutant General's Section, *Journals. October 1943–July 1945.*

————. 12th Army Group. Adjutant General's Section. *Reports of Operations. October 1943–July 1945.*

————. 12th Army Group. Adjutant General's Section, *After-Action Reports. August 1944–June 1945.*

————. First U.S. Army, *Road Net Used for Regrouping Army Moves.* 17–26 December 1944 (sixteen maps).

————. Seventh U.S. Army, Commanding General Seventh Army Thru Commanding General NATOUSA to Adjutant General, War Department, Letter, *Subject: [Lt. Gen. Omar N. Bradley] Efficiency Report.* 12 September 1943.

————. Ninth U.S. Army. *Corps and Divisions Under Ninth U.S. Army in European Theater of Operations.* 1 September 1944–15 June 1945.

————. Ninth U.S. Army. Army Service Forces, Report No. 169, *Command and Staff Procedures*, 31 July 1945.

————. Ninth U.S. Army, Administrative Instructions, 30 November 1944.

————. Ninth U.S. Army, After Action Report, 1–15 May 1945.

————. Ninth U.S. Army, After Action Report, December 1944, January–May 1945.

————. Ninth U.S. Army, G-3 Journals and File, December 1944–May 1945.

————. Ninth U.S. Army, *Ninth Army Engineer Operations in Rhine River Crossings*, 30 June 1945.

————. V Corps, After Action Report, December 1944.

————. VIII Corps, *Report on the Artillery with the VIII Corps in the Reduction of Brest, 22 August–19 September 1944.* Command and General Staff School.

————. VIII Corps, *American Intelligence on German Counteroffensive*, December 1944.

————. VIII Corps, After Action Report, 1 July 1944–May 1945.

————. VIII Corps, Field Order No. 9, 1 August 1944.

————. VIII Corps, Field Order No. 10, 2 August 1944.

————. VIII Corps, Field Order No. 12, 29 December 1944.

————. VIII Corps, Field Order No. 1, 2 January 1945.

————. VIII Corps, G-3 Journals and File, 16–24 December 1944.

————. VIII Corps, Operations Instructions, 19 August–29 December 1944.

————. VIII Corps, Operations Memorandum No. 3, *Operations in the Ardennes.*

————. VIII Corps, Operations Memoranda No. 20–25, 3 February–25 February 1945.

————. VIII Corps, Letters of Instruction, August 1944–1 January 1945.

————. VIII Corps, *Attack of a Fortified Zone*, 9 October 1944, European Theater of Operations.

————. 4th Armored Division, *Armor at Bastogne*, Armored School, Student Research Report, May 1949.

————. 4th Armored Division, *Armor in the Exploitation, 4th Armored Division Across France to the Moselle River*, Armored School, Student Research Report, May 1949.

————. 4th Armored Division, *Armor versus Mud and Mines, 4th Armored Division in the Sarre-Moselle Area*, Armored School, Student Research Report, 1950.

————. 4th Armored Division, Army Ground Forces, *Tactics and Administration, Armored Division*, War Department Observers Board Draft Report, ETOUSA, June 1945.

————. 4th Armored Division, *Operation of CC'A', 4th Armored Division, Normandy Beachhead to the Meuse River, 28 July–31 August 1944*, Lt. Col. H. C. Pattison, Command and Staff College, 1946–47.

————. 4th Armored Division, *Establishment and Defense of the Nancy Bridgehead*, September 1944.

————. 4th Armored Division, Armor in the Exploitation, Armored School, Student Research Report, May 1950.

————. 4th Armored Division, After Action Report, September–October 1944, European Theater of Operations.

————. 4th Armored Division, After Action Report, 17 July–31 August 1944, European Theater of Operations.

————. 4th Armored Division, After Action Report, 1–30 November 1944, European Theater of Operations.

————. 4th Armored Division, *Relief of Bastogne, 20 December 1944–1 January 1945.*

————. 4th Armored Division, *Lorraine Campaign Combat Interviews*, 9 November–10 December 1944.

————. 4th Armored Division, Memorandum for Commander, Third U.S. Army, 2 October 1944.

————. 4th Armored Division; Training Memorandum to Unit Commanders, 23 September 1944.

————. 7th Armored Division, *Battle Honors, Distinguished Unit Citation—7th Armored Division*, 27 June 1947.

————. 7th Armored Division, After Action Report, September 1944 to May 1945, Summary of Operations, Administrative and Statistical Summary.

————. 7th Armored Division, After Action Report, December 1944, *Battle of St. Vith, Belgium, 17–23 December 1944*.

————. 7th Armored Division, After Action Report, September 1944 to May 1945, Report of Division Artillery.

————. 7th Armored Division, Combat Command B, *History*, 1944.

————. 7th Armored Division, Combat Command B, After Action Reports, 12 August 1944–August 1945.

————. 28th Infantry Division, Unit Report, July 1944–April 1945.

————. 28th Infantry Division, After Action Report, July 1944–May 1945, Division Artillery.

————. 28th Infantry Division, *Operations of 1st Battalion, 110th Infantry Regiment, 16–18 December 1944*.

————. 28th Infantry Division, *Operations of 112th Infantry Regiment, 1944*.

————. 28th Infantry Division, *History of 3rd Battalion, 112th Infantry Regiment, July 1944–April 1945*.

————. 106th Infantry Division, Report of Action Against the Enemy, 7 December 1944–9 May 1945.

————. 106th Infantry Division, After Action Report, December 1944.

————. 106th Infantry Division, *The Story of the 106th Division, 15 March 1943–8 May 1945*.

————. 106th Infantry Division, After Battle Report, 424th Infantry Regiment, ending 31 December 1944.

————. 106th Infantry Division, After Action Report, December 1944, January–May 1945, Report of the DivArty.

————. 32nd Armored Cavalry Reconnaissance Squadron, Action Against the Enemy, 1 January 1945.

————. 275th Armored Field Artillery Battalion, Unit Report, 30 November–31 December 1944.

————. Field Manual (FM) 22-100, *Military Leadership*. Washington, D.C.: Department of the Army, 1983.

————. Field Manual (FM) 100-5, *Operations*. Washington, D.C.: Department of the Army, 1982.

————. Field Manual (FM) 100-5, *Field Service Regulations: Operations*. Washington, D.C.: War Department, 22 May 1941. (Reprint by U.S. Army Command and General Staff College Press, 1992.)

PERIODICALS AND ARTICLES

Albright, John. "Introducing 'P' Wood—4th Armored Division." *Armor* 81 (January–February 1972): 24–29.

Ambrose, Stephen E. "Eisenhower's Legacy." *Military Review* 70 (October 1990): 4–14.

Baldwin, Hanson W. "'P' Wood of the 4th Armored." *Army* 18 (January 1968): 45–54.

Balish, Harry. "The Battle of Nancy: A Double Envelopment." *Military Review* 29 (January 1950): 16–23.

352 GENERALS OF THE BULGE

Berlin, Robert H. "United States Army World War II Corps Commanders: A Composite Biography." *The Journal of Military History* 53 (April 1989): 147–167.
———. "Dwight David Eisenhower and the Duties of Generalship." *Military Review* 70 (October 1990): 15–25.
Blumenson, Martin. "The Decision to Take Brest." *Army* 10 (March 1960): 44–48.
———. "America's World War II Leaders in Europe: Some Thoughts." *Parameters* 19 (December 1989): 2–13.
———. "Eisenhower Then and Now: Fireside Reflections." *Parameters* 21 (Summer 1991).
Bolger, Daniel P. "Zero Defects: Command Climate in First U.S. Army, 1944–1945." *Military Review* 71 (May 1991): 61–73.
Bradin, James W. "28th Infantry Division: The Forgotten Pennsylvanians." *Army* 37 (August 1987): 62–67.
Catagnus, Earl J. Jr. "Infantry Field Manual 7–5. Organization and Tactics of Infantry: The Rifle Battalion (October 1940). *The Journal of Military History* 77 (April 2013): 657–666.
Clarke, Bruce C. "The Battle for St. Vith: Armor in the Defense and Delay." *Armor* 83 (November–December 1974): 39–40.
———. "Carrying Out Orders." *EurArmy* 23 (August 1984): 1–2.
Dupuy, R. Ernest. "'Beat Monty' Spirit Helped U.S. Forces Crush Germany." *Army-Navy Journal* 99 (7 April 1962): 18–19.
Flanagan, E. M. Jr. "A Force of Professionals." *Army* 42 (March 1992): 56–57.
Gabel, Christopher R. "The 1941 Maneuvers." *Military Review* 71 (August 1991): 88–89.
Grow, Robert W. "Mobility Unused." *Military Review* 32 (February 1953): 18–24.
Hanlon, John. "Tom Riggs' Remarkable World War II Odyssey." *Providence Sunday Journal* (29 December 1985).
Harris, Boyd M. "A Perspective on Leadership, Management and Command." *Military Review* 64 (February 1984): 48–57.
Ketchum, Richard M. "Warming Up on the Sidelines for World War II." *Smithsonian* 22 (September 1991): 88–103.
Kingseed, Cole C. "Eisenhower's Prewar Anonymity: Myth or Reality?" *Parameters* 21 (Autumn 1991): 87–98.
Lacey, Jim. "World War II's Real Victory Program." *The Journal of Military History* 75 (July 2011): 811–834.
Lattimer, Philip W. "When the Black Panthers Prowled." *Army* 42 (January 1992): 44–46.
McLain, Raymond S. Edited by Albert N. Garland. "One of the Greatest: A Study in Leadership." *Military Review* 49 (December 1969): 18–27.
Morelock, J. D. "General Jacob L. Devers: Commonsense Commander." *Forward Observer* 3 (December 1988–February 1989).
———. "Death in the Forest: Close Support during the Battle of the Bulge." *Field Artillery Journal* (September–October 1986): 8–14.
Nenninger, Timothy K. "'Casualties' at Leavenworth: A Research Problem." *The Journal of Military History* 76 (April 2012): 497–506.

———. "Leavenworth and Its Critics: The U.S. Army Command and General Staff School, 1920–1940." *The Journal of Military History* 58 (April 1994): 199–231.

Nye, Roger H. "Whence Patton's Genius?" *Parameters* 22 (Winter 1991–1992): 60–73.

Raymond, Allen D., III. "The Battle of St. Vith." *Armor* 73 (November–December 1964): 5–11.

Stone, Thomas R. "General William Hood Simpson: Unsung Commander of the U.S. Ninth Army." *Parameters* 11 (February 1981): 44–52.

———. "1630 Comes Early on the Roer." *Military Review* 53 (October 1973): 3–21.

Werrell, Kenneth P. "The Strategic Bombing of Germany in World War II: Costs and Accomplishments." *Journal of American History* 73 (December 1986): 702–713.

UNPUBLISHED MATERIAL

Clarke, Bruce C. "The Revolution in Army Organization, Tactics, and Equipment in the Period 1940–1945." Lecture notes, 15 March 1982.

———. "Clarke's Transfer."

———. "The Corps of Engineers in the Armored Force, 1940–1945." 1986, Ms.

———. "The Creating of an Outstanding Battalion in 1941–1942."

———. "How to Motivate Soldiers."

———. "The Move to St. Vith, Belgium, 16–18 December 1944."

———. "The Rehabilitation of Troops in Battle." 15 June 1986.

———. "The Violations of Regulations and Channels of Communications Can Be Justified." 14 March 1987.

———, to J. D. Morelock, 12 June 1985.

———, to J. D. Morelock, 12 August 1986.

Clay, Roy U., to J. D. Morelock, 23 February 1986.

———, to J. D. Morelock, 26 February 1986.

Cole, Hugh M., to J. D. Morelock, 4 September 1990.

Eddy, Manton S. "Diary—Activities of General Eddy, 24 March 1944 and 3 June 1944 to 23 May 1945." Fort Benning, GA: U.S. Army Infantry Museum.

Hasbrouck, Robert W., to Bruce C. Clarke.

Hummel, Louie, to Kathryn Hoffert, 4 March 1918.

Morelock, Jerry D. *A Single Soldier: World War II Mobilization, Manpower, and Replacement Policies and Their Influence on the Conduct of U.S. Army Operations in Northwest Europe, 1944–45.* PhD diss., University of Kansas, 2000.

Riggs, Thomas J., to Bruce C. Clarke, 28 January 1986.

Stone, Thomas R. "He Had the Guts to Say No: A Military Biography of General William Hood Simpson." PhD diss., Rice University, 1974.

Woodruff, Owen E. Jr., to Bruce C. Clarke, 27 January 1987.

OTHER SOURCES

Blumenson, Martin. "Breakout and Pursuit." S. L. A. Marshall Lecture, U.S. Army Command and General Staff College, Fort Leavenworth, KS, 13 March 1984.

———. Interview by author, June 1994, Washington, D.C.

Clarke, Bruce C. Interview by author, 13 April 1985, McLean, VA.
————. Interview by author, February 1986, Carlisle Barracks, PA.
————. "The Defense of St. Vith." Interview by author, 10 November 1987.
Clay, Roy U. Interview by author, February 1986, Carlisle Barracks, PA.
————. Interview by author, 12 March 1986, Carlisle Barracks, PA.
Eisenhower, Dwight D. "Command in War." Lecture, National War College, Fort McNair, Washington, D.C., 30 October 1950.
Garrett, Eugene. "The Malmédy (Baugnez Crossroads) Massacre." Interview by author, November 1987, Drumwright, OK.
Harris, Boyd M. Interview by author, 9 September 1983, Fort Leavenworth, KS.
Jones, L. Martin. "Destruction of 106th Infantry Division, Capture and POW Experiences." Interview by author, June 2005, Lawrence, KS.
Pogue, Forrest C. "Over the Beaches: D-Day." S. L. A. Marshall Lecture, U.S. Army Command and General Staff College, Fort Leavenworth, KS, 17 January 1984.
————. Interview by author, 18 January 1984, Fort Leavenworth, KS.
Services Cinema Corporation, Producer. *The Ardennes Offensive 1944.* United Kingdom, London: Ministry of Defence, 1979. Film.

ACKNOWLEDGMENTS

Generals of the Bulge: Leadership in the U.S. Army's Greatest Battle is a significantly revised and updated edition of my 1994 book, *Generals of the Ardennes: American Leadership in the Battle of the Bulge*. It has been exceptionally satisfying over the years to note the number of writers and historians who have found the original version of this book to be useful, citing it in their own works. However, over the two decades since it was first published, countless books and articles on the Battle of the Bulge have appeared. Clearly, for it to remain a useful resource, this book must be revised and updated to incorporate the best and most relevant of these works, so that the examination and analysis of the subject generals is informed by new research conducted by myself and others since 1994. Therefore, I must give a collective thank you to all of my friends, colleagues, and mentors who strongly encouraged me to write this revised edition and who have unstintingly supported me in this effort.

The genesis of the original book was an idea by Lt. Col. Boyd M. "Mac" Harris while he was assigned to the Center for Army Leadership at Fort Leavenworth, Kansas, in 1983. Mac had just completed writing the army's principal field manual on military leadership, FM 22-100, which was directed at junior leaders, the battalion level, and below. It was Mac's inspired creation to use illustrative case studies of historical examples in that manual to help teach and drive home the lessons of combat leadership. He was then just beginning to write a new field manual, this time aimed at army senior leadership, the brigade level, and higher, and approached me to support that effort by investigating, researching, and writing illustrative case studies of some of our World War II senior leaders. The research for those cases studies encompassed examining the military careers and wartime battle leadership demonstrated by Dwight D. Eisenhower, Omar N. Bradley, William H. Simpson, Troy H. Middleton, Bruce C. Clarke, and other outstanding American commanders. Sadly, Mac's untimely death in

October 1983 cut short his efforts on the senior leadership manual and robbed the army of an original and innovative thinker on leadership and command. Without Mac's inspiration, this book would not have been possible.

While researching the initial version of this book, I met three veterans of the Battle of the Bulge whose generous assistance proved invaluable in its completion. Gen. Bruce C. Clarke spent countless hours sharing his experiences of that battle and willingly opened his personal files and correspondence to me. Clarke's lifelong study of command and leadership produced a wealth of material that provided a rich source of personal and professional experiences. Col. Roy U. Clay unselfishly provided much detailed information about the 275th Armored Field Artillery Battalion's key role in the defense of St.-Vith, including his candid observations on the situation leading to the surrender of the 422nd and 423rd Infantry Regiments on the Schnee Eifel, the greatest U.S. capitulation of the European war. Colonel Clay's inspirational example stands as a model of what a battle leader ought to be. Mr. Eugene Garrett, who served in Battery B, 285th Field Artillery Observation Battalion, survived the Battle of the Bulge's most horrifying and infamous incident—the Malmedy Massacre. Silenced for many years by having endured the grief and horror of this war crime, Mr. Garrett nonetheless recounted the details of his terrible experience to me and thereby contributed his unique knowledge and insight about what that terrible combat in the U.S. Army's greatest battle was actually like for the soldiers who fought it.

In 2005, I had the honor of meeting another veteran of the Battle of the Bulge, L. Martin Jones. As an infantry lieutenant in the 106th Division, Jones was captured when his surrounded regiment on the Schnee Eifel was surrendered by its commander; he spent the remainder of the war as a POW. Lieutenant Jones graciously agreed to a several-hour interview, during which he provided his compelling, first-hand, eyewitness account of the fighting and ultimate surrender of the 106th's regiments trapped east of St.-Vith and related his remarkable odyssey as a POW. It was a singular privilege to have known these four outstanding soldiers.

During the research and writing of the original version of this book, *Generals of the Ardennes*, and later when working on this revised edition, I was especially fortunate to receive the guidance, encouragement, assistance, and support of several outstanding historians and colleagues: Dr. Robert H. Berlin; Lt. Col. Roger Cirillo; Col. Peter Mansoor; Brig. Gen. Jack Mountcastle; Brig. Gen. Hal Nelson; Dr. Timothy K. Nenninger; Dr. W. Glenn Robertson; Dr. Roger J. Spiller; Brig. Gen. Bill Stofft; and Professor Ted Wilson. A special thanks is due Carlo D'Este, a longtime dear friend and valued colleague whose superb biographies of Eisenhower and Patton (published after the original version of this book came out) have provided priceless additional insight into the experiences, character, and leadership of these two key Battle of the Bulge commanders and their World War II contemporaries that has proven essential in the preparation of this revised book. I am greatly honored that Carlo has written the new foreword to this edition. And I remain extremely grateful to the late Professor Martin Blumenson, who graciously agreed to write the introduction to the original edition of this book. Martin was a Patton scholar and author of two volumes of the army's official history of the war. As a U.S. Army historian in Europe during the campaigns of 1944–1945, Martin had personal, first-hand knowledge of many of the leaders in this book, and he very willingly shared his vast insight, ideas, opinions, and observations about World War II command and leadership with the author. Sadly, Martin passed away in 2005, and those of us who knew him lost a great friend and generous mentor.

The 1994 publication of the original version of this book, *Generals of the Ardennes*, would not have been possible without the unwavering commitment of National Defense University's Dr. Fred Kiley, Lt. Col. John Clements, Mr. Thomas C. Gill, and editor Mary Sommerville. This revised edition, *Generals of the Bulge*, owes its publication to the unwavering support of M. David Detweiler, CEO of Stackpole Books, who enthusiastically encouraged the effort to update and revise the original version. David's meticulously prepared, well-informed, and extensively-detailed suggestions for changes and additions have proven essential in creating this new edition. I also express my deep gratitude to editor David Reisch and assistant editor Brittany Stoner at Stackpole Books, and to cartographer Jason Petho and images researcher Zachary Bathon, whose superb efforts have resulted in greatly improved maps and photographs in this new edition.

Any errors of fact or judgment in this book, however, are the author's alone.

—Jerry D. Morelock

INDEX

[Page numbers in italics indicates illustrations.]